C Projects

Yashavant Kanetkar

BPB PUBLICATIONS
B-14, CONNAUGHT PLACE, NEW DELHI-110001

FIRST INDIAN EDITION 1995

REPRINTED 2013

Distributors:

MICRO BOOK CENTRE
2, City Centre, CG Road,
Near Swastic Char Rasta,
AHMEDABAD-380009 Phone: 26421611

COMPUTER BOOK CENTRE
12, Shrungar Shopping Centre, M.G. Road,
BANGALORE-560001 Phone: 5587923, 5584641

MICRO BOOKS
Shanti Niketan Building, 8, Camac Street,
KOLKATTA-700017 Phone: 22826518, 22826519

BUSINESS PROMOTION BUREAU
8/1, Ritchie Street, Mount Road,
CHENNAI-600002 Phone: 28410796, 28550491

DECCAN AGENCIES
4-3-329, Bank Street,
HYDERABAD-500195 Phone: 24756400, 24756967

MICRO MEDIA
Shop No. 5, Mahendra Chambers, 150 D.N. Road,
Next to Capital Cinema V.T. (C.S.T.) Station,
MUMBAI-400001 Ph.: 22078296, 22078297

BPB PUBLICATIONS
B-14, Connaught Place, **NEW DELHI-110001**
Phone: 23325760, 23723393, 23737742

INFO TECH
G-2, Sidhartha Building, 96 Nehru Place,
NEW DELHI-110019
Phone: 26438245, 26415092, 26234208

INFO TECH
Shop No. 2, F-38, South Extension Part-1
NEW DELHI-110049
Phone: 24691288, 24641941

BPB BOOK CENTRE
376, Old Lajpat Rai Market,
DELHI-110006 PHONE: 23861747

NOTE: THE CD-ROM INCLUDED WITH THE BOOK HAS NO COMMERCIAL VALUE AND CANNOT BE SOLD SEPARATELY.

ISBN 81-7029-256-5

Published by Manish Jain for BPB Publications, B-14, Connaught Place, New Delhi-110 001 and Printed by him at Akash Press, New Delhi.

Dedicated to
Prabhakar Kanetkar

About the Author

 Yashavant Prabhakar Kanetkar obtained his M. Tech. from IIT Kanpur in 1987 and since then has been the Director of ICIT, a Training and Software development firm which he set up at Nagpur. Already an author of the books 'Let Us C', 'Exploring C' and 'Programming Expertise in Basic', these days he is writing a few more books on C and Unix with his team at ICIT. Mr. Kanetkar conducts'a number of courses including those on C, C++, Unix Internals, Writing Vaccines & removing Viruses and Discrete Data Structures. Mr. Kanetkar writes 'The C Column' in Express Computer every week and is also the creator of COMPGARD anti-viral software.

Contents

Acknowledgments

It took me almost an year to conceive, develop, program and explain the various projects contained in this book. And throughout this year I was lucky to have many people who made invaluable suggestions to improve its quality. Successful completion of this edition is largely due to the suggestions and comments of these eagle eyed reviewers.

Kirthiga Venkataraman, Niranjan Bakre and Sangeeta Karandikar have done so much for this book that I can't thank them enough.

Kirthiga is one C programmer who can get computers through the most unusual kinds of hoops. When she is not writing C programs she is rewriting them. And when she is not rewriting C programs she is rewriting the rewrites. She soon plans to join Syracuse University for her Masters in Computer Science.

Writing a huge program which compiles and runs successfully is only a part of the story. The other part is completed only when the program is put to ardous tests under all conceivable circumstances. And what better person than a Mathematics student can do this. Niranjan gets all the credit for testing the programs in this book.

Sangeeta has been a great help all along. Be it in laying out the final touches, improving the style, correcting the grammar, manning the DTP post, or what have you!

Such book projects require support and understanding in no small measure. And Dada, Ammi, Seema were never short of it. Without their cheerful support and Aditya's smile this book would have remained only a dream.

Introduction

Learning C is one thing. Integrating all that one has learnt into a professional level software is a totally different cup of tea. There are many good books that teach you different concepts in C in their various garbs. Reading them, however may leave you incomplete. This is perhaps because these books time and again tell you that C can be used to develop bestselling softwares like Lotus 1-2-3, dBASE, Wordstar and what not. But rarely does any one of them tell you how. It is this lacuna that this book attempts to fill. I have tried to develop and explain full-fledged softwares, sandpapered with error checks wherever they were relevant. I have tried to cover as wide a cross-section of softwares as possible. And I wish to humbly state that there are many more which remain to be covered. You can pick up any chapter - from the beginning, the middle or the end. Each chapter is independent, unserialised and distinct. But you would be better off if you read the first chapter before the rest, because here we build a set of functions which would help you to perhaps see the rest of the chapters in a slightly different light. This book doesn't attempt to teach you C. It expects that you know C and then proceeds to use it to develop real-world software.

This book is packed with more than 16000 lines of C source code. All the programs on the two disks have been checked umpteen times. However, it's only human that a comma here or a semicolon there may have gone awry. Any mistakes that you may locate are all mine.

Chapter Organisation

The chapters have been organised such that to begin with there are softwares which work in text modes followed by the ones which need graphics capabilities.

Chapter 1: Helpmate It's a multiutility software similar to the popular PC Tools package. It discusses in detail the concept of popup menus and context sensitive help. Moreover, you would learn to build a tool box of various useful functions which you would need throughout this book.

Chapter 2: Easyedit A screen editor which has almost all the features of any professional level editor. One of the most exhaustive chapters in this book, it integrates nearly all the features of C. While reading it exercise enough patience, go through the painstaking details and I am sure you would have a broad smile at the end of it.

Chapter 3: Chart Master A utility which lets you draw graphs like xy, line, bar, stack bar and pie. In addition to learning how these graphs are constructed you would also learn how to write foolproof data entry functions, print graphics images and combine text mode and graphics mode activities in a single software.

Chapter 4: Mycad Though basically a drafting software, interaction with the user while drawing is the focus in this chapter. You will learn to draw irregular shapes like freehand or regular ones like circle, line, ellipse etc., all interactively. It would give you a fair idea about what really goes into the development of bestselling drafting softwares like AutoCad and RoboCad. Text fonts, their point sizes, orientation and justification is another fascinating area covered in this chapter.

Chapter 5: Graphical User Interface (GUI) is the rage of the nineties. It has taken the computer world by storm. Icon and the mouse are the issues here. You would learn how to draw and edit Icons using the Icon Editor program and how to place these Icons in menus and select them using a mouse through the GUI program. The end result is a software which shows the power of GUI and acts as an incentive for you to build further.

Chapter 6: Video games The thing which every computer buff tinkers around with but seldom probes to find out is how the cars and the helicopters and the balls and the bugs are really controlled through a computer program. This chapter examines with a thick lens the idea of images and animation and how to manoeuvre and navigate the objects on the screen. Three full-fledged video games - Bricks, Eater and Paratrooper have been developed here.

Chapter 7: Assorted Utilities This chapter discusses seven interesting utilities which establish the power of C beyond any doubt. You would learn how to write programs to view/edit a sector, diskcopy a disk, change Internal DOS commands, delete files by dates etc.

Chapter 8: Indentor A dream program. One can write a C program in any way one wishes and Indentor would lay it out systematically - comments in the proper place, all **if-else**'s neatly aligned, spaces and blank lines inserted at appropriate places and so on. However, unlike other chapters I haven't given the program readymade. Instead, I have given the EXE file on the disk. It's for you to make the dream come true.

A word of caution

Chapters 3 through 6 make use of graphics capabilties of your PC. Naturally, these programs would not work with PCs which do not have the graphics capabilities. Furthermore, all these programs have been written either for CGA high resolution or for CGA medium resolution graphics mode. Though minimal, the user would have to make some alterations in the program if he wishes to run them in any other graphics modes. All the programs in the afore-mentioned chapters use Borland Graphics Interface (BGI) files and assume that they are present in C:\TC\BGI directory. If your BGI files are present in other directories you will have to set up the appropriate search path in these programs.

What do you need to use this book

You have it in your head to develop real-life, professional level software through C. To that effect you have this book in your hand. In addition what you would need is:

- A PC or PC/XT or PC/AT or higher
- Turbo C compiler, version 2.0 or above
- MS-DOS version 3.2 or above

Disk Contents

Disk No.	File	Related Chapter
1	HELPMATE.C	Chapter 1
1	UTIL.C	Chapter 2
1	CURSOR.C	Chapter 2
1	EDITOR.C	Chapter 2
1	CHARTHDR.C	Chapter 3
1	CHART.C	Chapter 3
1	MYCAD.C	Chapter 4
1	SCREEN.DWG	Chapter 4
2	ICON.C	Chapter 5
2	GUI.C	Chapter 5
2	*.ICN	Chapter 5
2	BRICKS.C	Chapter 6
2	EATER.C	Chapter 6
2	PARATRUP.C	Chapter 6
2	ASSORT?.C	Chapter 7
2	INDENT.EXE	Chapter 8

Lastly, by the time you have turned the last page, if you are able to imagine and develop a commercially viable software on your own then this book has achieved its goal and I would thank you for having added another gloss to the C shine.

1

Helpmate

G ood old DOS offered to do everything for us; create files, copy them, delete them, make directories, list them - in fact it made available all the basic amenities that a computer user may need. But the Homo sapiens have never been satisfied with mere basics. All the softwares that provide the whole bunch of regular utilities and a lot more are a result of this pursuit of better and still better ways of doing things. And the good news is that you - yes, you can create your own package of such services. So, with no more preamble, here we go...

Menu Organisation

What is the similarity between a hotel and a computer? Both survive on menus. We choose dishes from a menu in a hotel; similarly, we can pick items from the menu displayed on the screen. But the similarity ends there because, being an unusual gourmet, the computer finds 'Open file' or 'Save file' menu items more relishing than 'Spring Rolls' or 'Hakka Noodles'. Most software packages today eloquently boast of 'menu driven' capability, meaning thereby that they offer the user a list of options which allow him to move through the entire system at will. Our aim is to unveil the logic behind these menus. So let's get into the kitchen with a light step.

Menus in a computer are as confusing as those you get in hotels. There are too many varieties. You have pop up menus, pull down menus, highlighted bar menus, Lotus like menus, etc. Of these the pop up and pull down menus are the ones which most programmers relish. In Helpmate we have used pop up menus. A pop up menu is superimposed on the matter which is already present on the screen. You make a selection from the menu and off goes the menu, bringing back to life the original matter. Thus, this menu pops up and pops off the screen, and hence the name.

In Helpmate we have grouped the menu items under three major categories: file related services, directory related services and miscellaneous services. The following figure shows these categories along with individual services.

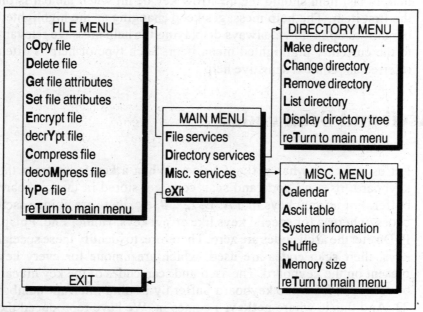

Figure 1.1 Menus in Helpmate

When the menu is displayed on the screen, a menu item can be selected either by hitting the Enter key when the highlighted bar has been positioned on the item to be selected, or by hitting the hot key corresponding to the item to be selected. The hot key for each menu item appears in a different color on the screen. Hot key serves to eliminate the movement of the highlighted bar and hitting of Enter key to select a particular menu item.

The selection of a menu item has been managed by the function **getresponse( )**, which relies on another function **getkey( )** for determining which key was hit by the user. In **getresponse( )**, provision has been made for the movement of highlighted bar and selection of the menu item through either Enter key or hot key. What if the down arrow key is hit when the highlighted bar is on the last item? In such an event **getresponse( )** acts intelligently and moves the highlighted bar from last item to first item. Similarly, the bar moves from first item to last item should the up arrow key be hit when the bar is on the first item. The help messages keep changing as the highlighted bar moves up or down, always displaying the help message relevant to the currently highlighted menu item. Such type of help is often referred as 'context sensitive help'.

Ascii and Scan codes

Let us now see what **getkey( )** does. When a key is hit from the keyboard, its ascii code and scan code get stored in the keyboard buffer. For normal keys like A, B, Z, !, #, etc. there are unique ascii codes, whereas for special keys like arrow keys, Home, End, PgUp, PgDn etc. the ascii codes are zero. Therefore, to identify these special keys, their scan codes are used, which are unique for every key present on the keyboard. The ascii and scan codes of the key hit can be retrieved from the keyboard buffer by issuing interrupt number 22. And this is where **getkey( )** comes in. We have reproduced the function here for your ready reference.

```
getkey()
{
```

```
        union REGS ii, oo ;

        while ( ! kbhit( ) )
            ;

        ii.h.ah = 0 ;  /* Service no. to fetch ascii and scan codes */
        int86 ( 22, &ii, &oo ) ;

        ascii = oo.h.al ;
        scan = oo.h.ah ;
    }
```

Here a standard library function, **kbhit( )** has been used. So long as a key is not hit, **kbhit( )** keeps returning 0. Since **!0** is 1, the condition in **while** keeps getting satisfied, hence the null statement continues to get executed. As soon as a key is hit from the keyboard, **kbhit( )** returns a truth value. **!true** becomes falsity, and hence the **while** loop is terminated. Once outside the **while** loop, interrupt number 22 is issued using the **int86( )** function, and then the variables **ascii** and **scan** are setup with the ascii value and scan code of the key that has been hit. Since **ascii** and **scan** have been declared as global variables, once set, these variables are accessible to other functions as well.

Context Sensitive Help

That's the in thing today. It is provided by almost all professional softwares. As the name suggests, the help provided would be as per the context in which it is requested. In Helpmate this has been done using a help box. Depending upon the menu item which has been highlighted, the appropriate help message is displayed. As the highlighted bar moves from one item to another, the help message in the help box also changes. The exact position of the help box in relation with the main menu is shown in the following figure.

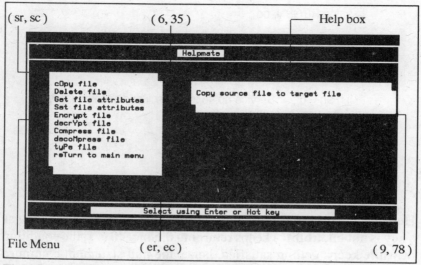

(sr, sc)   (6, 35)   Help box

Helpmate

cOpy file
Delete file
Get file attributes
Set file attributes
Encrypt file
decrYpt file
Compress file
decoMpress file
tyPe file
reTurn to main menu

Copy source file to target file

Select using Enter or Hot key

File Menu   (er, ec)   (9, 78)

Figure 1.2 Position of menu and help box

Accessing the VDU Memory

Throughout Helpmate, the various menus and the help messages have
been placed directly into VDU memory, instead of displaying them
using **printf( )** or **puts( )**. The video system of a computer consists
of a display screen and a display adapter. The microprocessor doesn't
have the ability to produce images - text or graphics on the screen. It
writes the information to be displayed into VDU memory (present in
display adapter), and then the display adapter circuitry transfers this
information from VDU memory to the screen. Therefore, we can
describe the image displayed on the screen as 'memory mapped
display'. Each address in VDU memory corresponds to a specific
location on the screen. The base address of VDU memory changes
from adapter to adapter. For CGA adapter this address is
0XB8000000 (hex), whereas for MA it is 0XB0000000 (hex). In
Helpmate, using a macro it is checked whether the program is being
run on a CGA or an MA, and then that the base address is appropriate-

ly set up in the variable **char far *scr**. To access VDU memory we use a 32 bit pointer, hence **scr** has been declared as a **far** pointer.

Each character present on the screen needs 2 bytes in VDU memory. The first byte contains the ascii value of the character being displayed, whereas the second byte contains the color (attribute) in which it is displayed. Thus, if we are working in CGA text mode, and the character present in row 0, column 0 on the screen is 'A', then its ascii value 65 would be stored at the address 0XB8000000 and its attribute at the address (0XB8000000 + 1). Similarly, the character in row 0, column 1 would have its ascii value and attribute at the addresses (0XB8000000 + 2) and (0XB8000000 + 3) respectively.

The attribute byte controls the foreground and background colors of the character being displayed, as well as whether it should blink or not. The following table shows the breakup of the attribute byte:

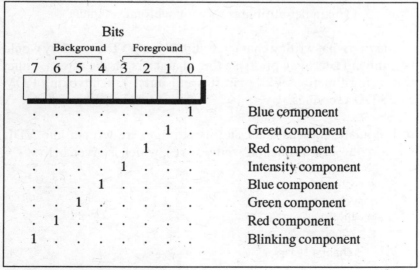

Figure 1.3 The attribute byte break-up

Thus, if the attribute of a character is made to be 10010100, the character will be displayed in red color on a blue background, and would blink.

On a monochrome adapter, though we can't have colors, we can use combinations of foreground and background to achieve the following effects:

Character type	Setting
Normal	Background - Black, Foreground - White
Reverse video	Background - White, Foreground - Black
Invisible	Background - Black, Foreground - Black
Underlined	Background - Black, Foreground - Blue

Figure 1.4 Character attributes for monochrome adapter

It is obvious that writing characters directly into VDU memory would be a much faster way of displaying characters on the screen, rather than using functions like **printf( )** and **puts( )**, or invoking ROM BIOS/DOS services.

In Helpmate, the character and its attribute are written into VDU memory through a function **writechar( )**, which is given below.

```
writechar ( r, c, ch, attb )
char ch ;
int attb, r, c ;
{
    char far *v ;

    v = vid_mem + r * 160 + c * 2 ;  /* calculate address */
    *v = ch ;  /* store character */
    v++ ;
```

```
        *v = attb ;  /* store attribute */
    }
```

This function writes a single character into VDU memory. Using this, another function called **writestring( )** is built, which writes an entire string into VDU memory. **writesting( )** in turn is used in the function **displaymenu( )**, which writes the entire menu into VDU memory.

savevideo( ) and restorevideo( )

If we can write a character directly into VDU memory, can we not read it back from VDU memory? We can, certainly. And that is what the function **savevideo( )** is all about. It reads characters and their attributes from a rectangular portion of the screen and stores them at a place in RAM which has been reserved using the **malloc( )** function. **restorevideo( )** is the other side of the coin. It reads the characters and attributes stored in RAM and puts them back into VDU memory. Once the characters have been restored, the block of memory (in RAM) where they are initially stored is usually freed using the function **free( )**.

Issuing Interrupts

For various utilities dealing with operations on files and directories, we need to access the services of the operating system. This is done by calling ROM BIOS/DOS routines. These routines are called by issuing an interrupt. The micoprocessor is usually busy when these routines get called. Since it is capable of performing only one task at a time, the microprocessor's current activity must be interrupted before the control can be passed to the ROM BIOS/DOS routine. The process of temporarily stopping the microprocessor's current activity is called 'Issuing of Interrupt'. When the interrupt is issued, the microprocessor stops whatever it had been doing, passes control to the appropriate ROM BIOS/DOS routine, and once this routine has been executed, resumes its original interrupted activity.

The interrupt can be generated by hardware or software. For example, the functions **int86( )** and **intdos( )** generate the software interrupt, whereas on hitting a key from the keyboard, a hardware interrupt gets generated. When a ROM BIOS routine is to be called, **int86( )** should be used, whereas for calling a DOS routine, **intdos( )** should be used. While calling **int86( )**, the number of the interrupt to be issued should be passed to it. As against this, the interrupt number is not to be passed to **intdos( )**, since all DOS routines have been grouped together under interrupt number 33.

In Helpmate, for services like deleting file, renaming file, creating directory, renaming directory etc. software interrupts have been issued to call the DOS routines. The arguments which are to be passed to the ROM BIOS/DOS routine being called must be setup in CPU registers. The look alikes of these CPU registers have been created and stored in the file "dos.h" as a datatype **union REGS**. The variables of this datatype must be set up with appropriate values (as required by the ROM BIOS/DOS routine being called) before calling **int86( )** or **intdos( )**. When **int86( )** and **intdos( )** get called, the contents of these variables are placed by these functions into actual CPU registers and then the control is handed over to the ROM BIOS/DOS routine.

The following function shows how to delete a file "PR1.C" by calling the **intdos( )** function.

```
deletefile( )
{
    union REGS ii, oo ;

    ii.h.ah = 65 ;  /* DOS service number to delete file */
    ii.x.dx = "PR1.C"
    intdos ( &ii, &oo ) ;
}
```

File Attributes

In the directory entry of any file, 32 bytes are used for storing information about it, like its name, extension, date, time, etc. Of these, one byte stores the attribute of the file. Bit numbers 0 through 5 of the attribute byte are used to indicate the status of this file, while the 6th and 7th bits are unused. Figure 1.5 shows the 8 bits of this attribute byte and what each bit signifies. The function **setfileattb**( ) in Helpmate allows you to alter any of these bits, so that the attribute of any file can be changed. For instance, if the zeroth bit is made 1, the file would become a read only file. This means this file cannot be modified unless it is made a read/write file, by setting its zeroth bit to zero.

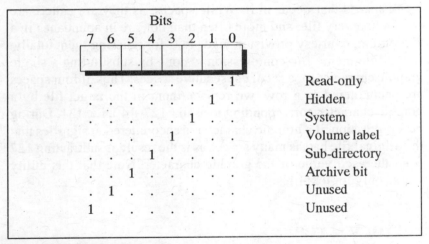

Figure 1.5 File attributes

File Encryption

Another utility on the File Services menu is that of encrypting a file. For this, the function **encryptfile**( ) is used. This function makes use of an offset cipher for coding the file into an unrecognisable form. While encrypting, 127 is added to the ascii value of each character read from the source file, and then the character corresponding to this new value is stored in the target file. Thus, the target file is assigned what seems to be gibberish, as the ascii values 128 onwards correspond to graphic characters. The function **decryptfile( )** restores the file to its original version by removing the offset of 127 that was introduced while encrypting. Make sure that you use this utility for text files only, which do not contain any graphic characters.

File Compression

An effective way of reducing the size of any file is by eliminating the blank spaces that occur in it. White spaces, as they are called, are present in every file, and more often than not, are in abundance in a C program, courtesy provision made in C for ignoring them totally. In the File menu, file compression is done by substituting a single graphic character for a set of consecutive spaces. Thus, if four spaces are encountered in a row, we replace them in the target file by a graphic character corresponding to ascii (127 + 4), i.e. 131. During decompression, if a graphic character is encountered, it signifies that the original file had as many spaces as is the result of subtracting 127 from the ascii value of the graphic character. Note that this utility works only for text files.

Directory Tree

This utility displays all the directories and sub-directories present in the default drive. For this purpose, the function **tree( )** has been written, which calls two standard library functions, **findfirst( )** and **findnext( )**. These functions find the first and consecutive occurrences respectively of directory entries which match the skeleton "*.*". Once a matching entry is found, we check whether it is a sub-directory or not. All sub-directories are displayed in a tree form so that the parent-child relationship between various sub-directories becomes immediately evident.

Miscellaneous services

This menu supplies commonly needed information like the ascii table, the equipment list, etc. And just to let yourself unwind, a video game - Shuffle has been thrown in too. Let's begin with the calendar.

Calendar

This utility displays the calendar for the month and year specified by the user. Due consideration has been given to the leap years and the calendar is framed accordingly. Try out this utility for September 1752 and I am sure you would be taken aback. No, there is nothing wrong with the program. It just so happened that the King of England decreed that 11 days (3rd to 13th) be knocked off from this month. This he did to adjust the number of days while switching over from Julian to Gregorian calendar. As a result, many people missed their Birthday celebrations and many more got paid for the days they didn't work on. This was a boon for the salaried class, since it was in this month that the concept of 'paid leave' was born!

System Information

On booting a computer, the ROM startup routines check and initialise the standard equipment, i.e. VDU, Floppy Disk Drive, Keyboard etc., and store this equipment list at a fixed location (hex 410) in memory. This information can be retrieved by issuing interrupt number hex 11. On doing so this information gets stored in the 2-byte AX register. The bit settings for AX are as shown in Figure 1.6. In the function **systeminfo( )**, we segregate this information by checking which bits are on and which off. Be sure that you are thorough with the Bitwise operators to be able to comprehend this function.

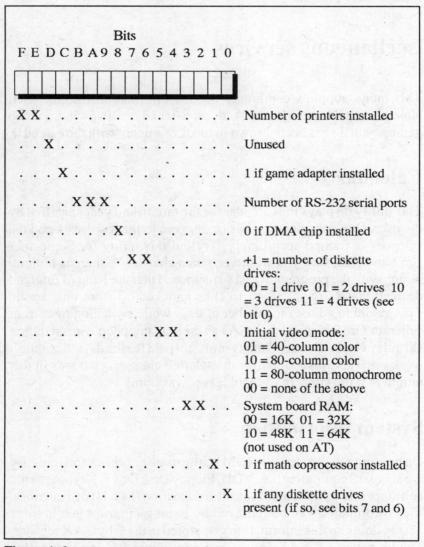

Figure 1.6

Shuffle

Another item in the Miscellaneous Services menu is the game called Shuffle. The player is presented with a grid (as shown in Figure 1.7) having numbers 1 to 15 arranged in a random manner, and a blank space in the lower right corner. The numbers can be moved about in the grid using the arrow keys. The objective is to arrange the numbers in increasing order from 1 to 15, with the blank space back in the lower right corner. The only valid keys are the arrow keys, and the moves are monitored in the function **shuffle( )**. The blank space in the grid corresponds with the position of 0 in the two-dimensional array **num[ ][ ]**. The scan code of the key hit is used to determine the new position of the blank space, and it swaps positions with the appropriate number in the grid. The functions **shufflebox( )** and **display( )** together create the display screen, and **check( )** is called after every move to compare the current order of the numbers in the grid with the aimed one.

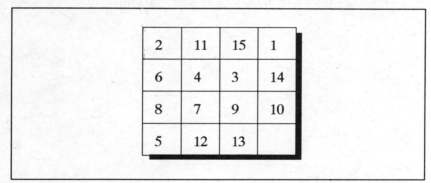

Figure 1.7

Expanding Helpmate

Though most of the commonly needed file and directory services have been provided in Helpmate, there is still scope for improvement.

For example, you can add a full set of disk utilities, which would include services to display and edit the disk sector by sector, format a disk, a diskcopy service, a checkdisk service, etc. The edit/display sector and the diskcopy services have been discussed in Chapter 7 of this book. All that you have to do is to adapt them appropriately for Helpmate. Likewise, you can add the 'undelete file' service in the File Services menu. This service, however, is quite complicated. To be able to incorporate this you must first understand what really happens when a file is deleted. On deletion, the filename's first character is made hex E5 and the clusters belonging to this file are marked as unused. All other directory information about the file is retained. So for undeleting a file, you must first replace the character hex E5 by a valid filename character and then trace the FAT chain for the file and keep adding the clusters belonging to this file as you procced. The file can be undeleted provided the directory entry has not been reused for another file. Be forewarned that whenever a new entry is needed, DOS uses the first available entry, quickly recycling an erased file's old entries, making undeletion impossible.

Program

```c
# include "stdio.h"
# include "process.h"
# include "string.h"
# include "stdlib.h"
# include "ctype.h"
# include "conio.h"
# include "fcntl.h"
# include "types.h"
# include "stat.h"
# include "dir.h"
# include "dos.h"

/* various menu definitions */
/* character following ^ symbol is the hot key */
char *menu[ ] =    {
                        "^File services",
                        "^Directory services",
                        "^Misc. services",
                        "e^Xit"
                   } ;

char *fileservices[ ] =  {
                            "c^Opy file",
                            "^Delete file",
                            "^Get file attributes",
                            "^Set file attributes",
                            "^Encrypt file",
                            "decr^Ypt file",
                            "^Compress file",
                            "deco^Mpress file",
                            "ty^Pe file",
                            "re^Turn to main menu",
                        } ;
```

```c
char *directoryservices[ ] = {
                                "^Make directory",
                                "^Change directory",
                                "^Remove directory",
                                "^List directory",
                                "^Display directory tree",
                                "re^Turn to main menu"
                    } ;

char *miscservices[ ] ={
                        "^Calendar",
                        "^Ascii table",
                        "^System information",
                        "s^Huffle",
                        "^Memory size" ,
                        "re^Turn to main menu"
                    } ;

/* help messages for different menu items and other frequently required
   messages */
char *messages[ ] =   {
                        " Helpmate ",
                        "        Select using Enter or Hot key           ",
                        "Performs various file services",
                        "Performs various directory services",
                        "Performs various miscellaneous services",
                        "Return to DOS",
                        "Copy source file to target file",
                        "Delete a file",
                        "Display current file attributes",
                        "Change existing file attributes",
                        "Code a file using offset cypher",
                        "Decode a coded file",
                        "Compress text file",
                        "Decompress a compressed file",
                        "Display contents of file",
```

```
                              "Return to main menu",
                              "Create a new directory ",
                              "Change default directory",
                              "Remove an existing directory",
                              "List existing directory contents",
                              "Display directory tree",
                              "Return to main menu",
                              "Display calendar of any month & year",
                              "Display Ascii values & characters",
                              "Display equipment list",
                              "A video game",
                              "Display base memory size",
                              "Return to main menu ",
                              "       Press any key to continue...
                              "     Insufficient space! Press any key...
                    } ;

char far *vid_mem ;
int ascii, scan ;

main( )
{
    int mm_choice ;

    /* store base address of VDU memory and set appropriate video mode */
    #ifdef MA

        /* store base address for MA */
        vid_mem = ( char far * ) 0xb0000000L ;
        setmode ( 7 ) ;

    #else

        /* store base address for other display adapters */
        vid_mem = ( char far * ) 0xb8000000L ;
        setmode ( 3 ) ;
```

```
#endif

size ( 32, 0 ) ;  /* hide cursor */

/* create opening screen display */
menubox ( 0, 0, 24, 79, 7, 7 ) ;
drawbox ( 1, 0, 21, 79, 7 ) ;
drawbox ( 1, 0, 23, 79, 7 ) ;
logo( ) ;

/* create screen on which menus are to be popped up */
mainscreen( ) ;

while ( 1 )
{
    /* pop up main menu and collect choice */
    mm_choice = popupmenu ( menu, 4, 5, 5, "FDMX", 2 ) ;

    /* test choice received */
    switch ( mm_choice )
    {
        case 1 :
            fserver( ) ;
            break ;

        case 2 :
            dserver( ) ;
            break ;

        case 3 :
            mserver( ) ;
            break ;

        case 4 :
        case 27 :
            size ( 6, 7 ) ;
            clrscr( ) ;
```

```
                    exit ( 1 ) ;
            }
        }
}

/* sets video mode */
setmode ( mode )
int mode ;
{
    union REGS i, o ;

    i.h.ah = 0 ;  /* service no. */
    i.h.al = mode ;  /* video mode */
    int86 ( 16, &i, &o ) ;  /* issue interrupt */
}


/* prepares the screen for popping up a menu */
mainscreen( )
{
    int i, j ;

    drawbox ( 1, 0, 23, 79, 7 ) ;
    drawbox ( 3, 0, 21, 79, 7 ) ;

    writechar ( 3, 0, 204, 7 ) ;
    writechar ( 3, 79, 185, 7 ) ;
    writechar ( 21, 0, 204, 7 ) ;
    writechar ( 21, 79, 185, 7 ) ;

    for ( i = 4 ; i <= 20 ; i++ )
    {
        for ( j = 1 ; j <= 78 ; j += 2 )
        {
            writechar ( i, j, 177, 7 ) ;
            writechar ( i, j + 1, 177, 7 ) ;
        }
    }
```

```
        writestring ( messages[0], 2, 32, 112 ) ;
        writestring ( messages[1], 22, 14, 112 ) ;
}


/* writes a character and its attribute in VDU memory */
writechar ( r, c, ch, attb )
int r, c, attb ;
char ch ;
{
        char far *v ;

        v = vid_mem + r * 160 + c * 2 ;  /* calculate address in VDU memory
                                    corresponding to row r and column c */

        *v = ch ;  /* store ascii value of character */
        v++ ;
        *v = attb ;  /* store attribute of character */
}

/* writes a string into VDU memory in the desired attribute */
writestring ( s, r, c, attb )
int r, c, attb ;
char *s ;
{
        while ( *s != '\0' )
        {
                /* if next character is hot key, write it in different attribute, otherwise
                   in normal attribute */

                if ( *s == '^' )
                {
                        s++ ;
                        writechar ( r, c, *s, 126 ) ;
                }
                else
                        writechar ( r, c, *s, attb ) ;
```

```
            s++ ;
            c++ ;
        }
}

/* pops up a menu on the existing screen contents */
popupmenu ( menu, count, sr, sc, hotkeys, helpnumber )
int count, sr, sc, helpnumber ;
char **menu, *hotkeys ;
{
    int er, ec, i, l = 0, areareqd, areaforhelp, choice ;
    char *p, *h ;

    /* calculate ending row for menu */
    er = sr + count + 2 ;

    /* find longest menu item */
    for ( i = 0 ; i < count ; i++ )
    {
        if ( strlen ( menu[i] ) > l )
            l = strlen ( menu[i] ) ;
    }

    /* calculate ending column for menu */
    ec = sc + l + 3 ;

    /* calculate area required to save screen contents where menu is to be
       popped up */
    areareqd = ( er - sr + 1 ) * ( ec - sc + 1 ) * 2 ;

    p = malloc ( areareqd ) ;  /* allocate memory */

    /* check if allocation is successful */
    if ( p == NULL )
    {
        writestring ( messages[29], 22, 14, 112 ) ,
```

```
            getch( ) ;
            exit ( 2 ) ;
      }

      /* save screen contents into allocated memory */
      savevideo ( sr, sc, er, ec, p ) ;

      /* draw filled box with shadow */
      menubox ( sr, sc, er, ec, 112, 66 ) ;

      /* display the menu in the filled box */
      displaymenu ( menu, count, sr + 1, sc + 1 ) ;

      /* calculate area required for help box */
      areaforhelp = ( 9 - 6 + 1 ) * ( 78 - 35 + 1 ) * 2 ;

      h = malloc ( areaforhelp ) ;
      if ( h == NULL )
      {
            writestring ( messages[29], 22, 14, 112 ) ;
            getch( ) ;
            exit ( 3 ) ;
      }
      savevideo ( 6, 35, 9, 78, h ) ;
      menubox ( 6, 35, 9, 78, 112, 66 ) ;

      /* display help message */
      writestring ( messages[helpnumber], 7, 36, 112 ) ;

      /* receive user's choice */
      choice = getresponse ( menu, hotkeys, sr, sc, count, helpnumber ) ;

      /* restore original screen contents */
      restorevideo ( sr, sc, er, ec, p ) ;
      restorevideo ( 6, 35, 9, 78, h ) ;

      /* free allocated memory */
```

```
            free ( p ) ;
            free ( h ) ;

            return ( choice ) ;
}

/* displays or hides the cursor */
size ( ssl, esl )
int ssl, esl ;
{
            union REGS i, o ;

            i.h.ah = 1 ;  /* service number */
            i.h.ch = ssl ;  /* starting scan line */
            i.h.cl = esl ;  /* ending scan line */
            i.h.bh = 0 ;  /* video page number */

            /* issue interrupt for changing the size of the cursor */
            int86 ( 16, &i, &o ) ;
}

/* gets the ascii and scan codes of the key pressed */
getkey( )
{
            union REGS ii, oo ;

            /* wait till a key is hit */
            while ( ! kbhit( ) )
                   ;

            ii.h.ah = 0 ;  /* service number */

            /* issue interrupt */
            int86 ( 22, &ii, &oo ) ;

            scan = oo.h.ah ;
            ascii = oo.h.al ;
```

```
}

/* saves screen contents into allocated memory in RAM */
savevideo ( sr, sc, er, ec, buffer )
int sr, sc, er, ec ;
char *buffer ;
{
    char far *v ;
    int i, j ;

    for ( i = sr ; i <= er ; i++ )
    {
        for ( j = sc ; j <= ec ; j++ )
        {
            v = vid_mem + i * 160 + j * 2 ;  /* calculate address */
            *buffer = *v ;  /* store character */
            v++ ;
            buffer++ ;
            *buffer = *v ;  /* store attribute */
            buffer++ ;
        }
    }
}

/* restores screen contents from allocated memory in RAM */
restorevideo ( sr, sc, er, ec, buffer )
int sr, sc, er, ec ;
char *buffer ;
{
    char far *v ;
    int i, j ;

    for ( i = sr ; i <= er ; i++ )
    {
        for ( j = sc ; j <= ec ; j++ )
        {
            v = vid_mem + i * 160 + j * 2 ;  /* calculate address */
```

```
              *v = *buffer ;  /* restore character */
              v++ ;
              buffer++ ;
              *v = *buffer ;  /* restore attribute */
              buffer++ ;
          }
      }
}

/* draws filled box with or without shadow */
menubox ( sr, sc, er, ec, fil, shad )
int sr, sc, er, ec ;
char fil, shad ;
{
      int i, j ;

      /* draw filled box */
      for ( i = sr ; i < er ; i++ )
      {
          for ( j = sc ; j < ( ec - 1 ) ; j++ )
              writechar ( i, j, ' ', fil ) ;
      }

      /* if no shadow is required for the filled box */
      if ( shad == 0 )
      {
          for ( i = sr ; i <= er ; i++ )
          {
              writechar ( i, ec, ' ', fil ) ;
              writechar ( i, ( ec - 1 ), ' ', fil ) ;
          }

          for ( j = sc ; j <= ec ; j++ )
              writechar ( er, j, ' ', fil ) ;
      }
      else
      {
```

```
        /* draw vertical and horizontal shadow */
        for ( i = sr + 1 ; i <= er ; i++ )
        {
                writechar ( i, ec, ' ', shad ) ;
                writechar ( i, ( ec - 1 ), ' ', shad ) ;
        }

        for ( j = sc + 2 ; j <= ec ; j++ )
                writechar ( er, j, ' ', shad ) ;
    }
}

/* displays the menu in box drawn by menubox( ) */
displaymenu ( menu, count, sr, sc )
int count, sr, sc ;
char **menu ;
{
    int i ;

    for ( i = 0 ; i < count ; i++ )
    {
        /* write menu item in VDU memory */
        writestring ( menu[i], sr, sc, 112 ) ;
        sr++ ;
    }
}

/* draws double-lined box */
drawbox ( sr, sc, er, ec, attr )
int sr, sc, er, ec, attr ;
{
    int i ;

    /* draw horizontal lines */
    for ( i = sc + 1 ; i < ec ; i++ )
    {
        writechar ( sr, i, 205, attr ) ;
```

```
            writechar ( er, i, 205, attr ) ;
      }

      /* draw vertical lines */
      for ( i = sr + 1 ; i < er ; i++ )
      {
            writechar ( i, sc, 186, attr ) ;
            writechar ( i, ec, 186, attr ) ;
      }

      /* draw four corners */
      writechar ( sr, sc, 201, attr ) ;
      writechar ( sr, ec, 187, attr ) ;
      writechar ( er, sc, 200, attr ) ;
      writechar ( er, ec, 188, attr ) ;
}

/* receives user's response for the menu displayed */
getresponse ( menu, hotkeys, sr, sc, count, helpnumber )
char **menu, *hotkeys ;
int sr, sc, count, helpnumber ;
{
      int choice = 1, len, hotkeychoice ;

      /* calculate number of hot keys for the menu */
      len = strlen ( hotkeys ) ;

      /* highlight first menu item */
      writestring ( menu[choice - 1], sr + choice, sc + 1, 111 ) ;

      while ( 1 )
      {
            getkey( ) ;  /* receive key */

            /* if special key is hit */
            if ( ascii == 0 )
            {
```

```
switch ( scan )
{
      case 80 :  /* down arrow key */

            /* make highlighted item normal */
            writestring ( menu[choice - 1], sr + choice, sc + 1, 112 ) ;

            choice++ ;
            helpnumber++ ;
            break ;

      case 72 :  /* up arrow key */

            /* make highlighted item normal */
            writestring ( menu[choice - 1], sr + choice, sc + 1, 112 ) ;

            choice-- ;
            helpnumber-- ;
            break ;
}

/* if highlighted bar is on first item and up arrow key is hit */
if ( choice == 0 )
{
      choice = count ;
      helpnumber = helpnumber + count ;
}

/* if highlighted bar is on last item and down arrow key is hit */
if ( choice > count )
{
      choice = 1 ;
      helpnumber = helpnumber - count ;
}

/* highlight the appropriate menu item */
writestring ( menu[choice - 1], sr + choice, sc + 1, 111 ) ;
```

```
            menubox ( 6, 35, 9, 78, 112, 66 ) ;

            /* write the corresponding help message */
            writestring ( messages[helpnumber], 7, 36, 112 ) ;
      }
      else
      {

            if ( ascii == 13 )  /* Enter key */
                 return ( choice ) ;

            if ( ascii == 27 )  /* Esc key */
                 return ( 27 ) ;

            ascii = toupper ( ascii ) ;
            hotkeychoice = 1 ;

            /* check whether hot key has been pressed */
            while ( *hotkeys != '\0' )
            {
                  if ( *hotkeys == ascii )
                        return ( hotkeychoice ) ;
                  else
                  {
                        hotkeys++ ;
                        hotkeychoice++ ;
                  }
            }

            /* reset hotkeys to point to the first character in the string */
            hotkeys = hotkeys - len ;
      }
   }
}

/* pops up File Services menu, receives choice and branches to appropriate
   function */
fserver( )
```

```
{
    int fs_choice ;

    while ( 2 )
    {
        fs_choice = popupmenu ( fileservices, 10, 5, 5, "ODGSEYCMPT", 6 ) ;

        switch ( fs_choice )
        {
            case 1 :
                copyfile( ) ;
                break ;

            case 2:
                deletefile( ) ;
                break ;

            case 3:
                getfileattb( ) ;
                break ;

            case 4:
                setfileattb( ) ;
                break ;

            case 5 :
                encryptfile( ) ;
                break ;

            case 6:
                decryptfile( ) ;
                break ;

            case 7 :
                compressfile( ) ;
                break ;
```

```
            case 8 :
                decompressfile( ) ;
                break ;

            case 9 :
                displayfile( ) ;
                break ;

            case 10 :
                return ;
        }
    }
}

/* pops up Directory Services menu, receives choice and branches to
   appropriate function */
dserver( )
{
    int ds_choice ;

    while ( 2 )
    {
        ds_choice = popupmenu ( directoryservices, 6, 5, 5, "MCRLDT", 16 ) ;

        switch ( ds_choice )
        {
            case 1 :
                makedir( ) ;
                break ;

            case 2 :
                changedir( ) ;
                break ;

            case 3 :
                removedir( ) ;
                break ;
```

```
            case 4 :
                  listdir( ) ;
                  break ;

            case 5 :
                  dirtree( ) ;
                  break ;

            case 6 :
                  return ;
         }
      }
}

/* pops up Miscellaneous Services menu, receives choice and branches to
   appropriate function */
mserver( )
{
      int ms_choice ;

      while ( 2 )
      {
            ms_choice = popupmenu ( miscservices, 6, 5, 5, "CASHMT", 22 ) ;

            switch ( ms_choice )
            {
                  case 1 :
                        calendar( ) ;
                        break ;

                  case 2 :
                        asciitable( ) ;
                        break ;

                  case 3 :
                        systeminfo( ) ;
```

```
                    break ;

            case 4 :
                shuffle( ) ;
                break ;

            case 5 :
                memsize( ) ;
                break ;

            case 6 :
                return ;
        }
    }
}

copyfile( )
{
    char sfile[20], tfile[20], buffer[512], *p ;
    int areareqd, inhandle, outhandle, bytes, flag ;

    areareqd = ( 20 - 5 + 1 ) * ( 70 - 5 + 1 ) * 2 ;
    p = malloc ( areareqd ) ;
    if ( p == NULL )
    {
        writestring ( messages[29], 22, 14, 112 ) ;
        getch( ) ;

        writestring ( messages[1], 22, 14, 112 ) ;
        return ;
    }

    savevideo ( 5, 5, 20, 70, p ) ;
    menubox ( 6, 5, 13, 60, 112, 66 ) ;

    writestring ( "            File copy service              ", 22, 14, 112 ) ;
```

```
writestring ( "Enter source file name:", 7, 8, 112 ) ;
size ( 6, 7 ) ;  /* display cursor */
gotoxy ( 33, 8 ) ;
gets ( sfile ) ;
size ( 32, 0 ) ;  /* hide cursor */

/* open source file in low level binary mode for reading */
inhandle = open ( sfile, O_RDONLY | O_BINARY ) ;

/* if unable to open file */
if ( inhandle < 0 )
{
     writestring ( "Unable to open source file!", 9, 8, 112 ) ;
     writestring ( messages[28], 22, 14, 112 ) ;
     getch( ) ;

     writestring ( messages[1], 22, 14, 112 ) ;
     restorevideo ( 5, 5, 20, 70, p ) ;
     free ( p ) ;
     return ;
}

writestring ( "Enter target file name:", 9, 8, 112 ) ;
size ( 6, 7 ) ;
gotoxy ( 33, 10 ) ;
gets ( tfile ) ;
size ( 32, 0 ) ;

/* open target file in low level binary mode for writing */
outhandle = open ( tfile, O_CREAT | O_WRONLY | O_BINARY, S_IWRITE ) ;

/* if unable to open file */
if ( outhandle < 0 )
{
     writestring ( "Unable to open target file!", 11, 8, 112 ) ;
     writestring ( messages[28], 22, 14, 112 ) ;
     getch( ) ;
```

```
            close ( inhandle ) ;
            writestring ( messages[1], 22, 14, 112 ) ;
            restorevideo ( 5, 5, 20, 70, p ) ;
            free ( p ) ;
            return ;
      }

      /* read chunks of 512 bytes from source file and write to target file till there
         are bytes to read */
      while ( ( bytes = read ( inhandle, buffer, 512 ) ) > 0 )
      {
               flag = write ( outhandle, buffer, bytes ) ;
               if ( flag == -1 )
                     break ;
      }

      if ( flag == -1 )
            writestring ( "Unable to copy file!", 11, 8, 112 ) ;
      else
            writestring ( "File has been successfully copied!", 11, 8, 112 ) ;

      writestring ( messages[28], 22, 14, 112 ) ;
      getch( ) ;

      /* close files and restore original screen contents */
      close ( inhandle ) ;
      close ( outhandle ) ;
      writestring ( messages[1], 22, 14, 112 ) ;
      restorevideo ( 5, 5, 20, 70, p ) ;
      free ( p ) ;
}

deletefile( )
{
      union REGS ii, oo ;
      int areareqd ;
```

```
char filename[20], *p ;

areareqd = ( 20 - 5 + 1 ) * ( 70 - 5 + 1 ) * 2 ;
p = malloc ( areareqd ) ;
if ( p == NULL )
{
    writestring ( messages[29], 22, 14, 112 ) ;
    getch( ) ;

    writestring ( messages[1], 22, 14, 112 ) ;
    return ;
}

savevideo ( 5, 5, 20, 70, p ) ;
menubox ( 6, 5, 11, 60, 112, 66 ) ;

writestring ( "          File delete service          ", 22, 14, 112 ) ;

writestring ( "Enter name of file to be deleted:", 7, 8, 112 ) ;
size ( 6, 7 ) ;
gotoxy ( 43, 8 ) ;
gets ( filename ) ;
size ( 32, 0 ) ;

/* issue interrupt for deleting file */
ii.h.ah = 65 ;  /* dos service number */
ii.x.dx = ( unsigned int ) filename ;  /* store base address */
intdos ( &ii, &oo ) ;

/* check if successful in deleting file */
if ( oo.x.cflag == 0 )
    writestring ( "File was successfully deleted!", 9, 8, 112 ) ;
else
{
    switch ( oo.x.ax )
    {
        case 2 :
```

```
                    writestring ( "File not found!", 9, 8, 112 ) ;
                    break ;

            case 3 :
                    writestring ( "Invalid path!", 9, 8, 112 ) ;
                    break ;

            case 5 :
                    writestring ( "Access denied!", 9, 8, 112 ) ;
                    break ;

            case 0x11 :
                    writestring ( "Invalid drive name!", 9, 8, 112 ) ;
                    break ;

            default :
                    writestring ( "Improper request!", 9, 8, 112 ) ;
            }
    }

    writestring ( messages[28], 22, 14, 112 ) ;
    getch( ) ;

    writestring ( messages[1], 22, 14, 112 ) ;
    restorevideo ( 5, 5, 20, 70, p ) ;
    free ( p ) ;
}

/* displays the current attributes of a file */
getfileattb( )
{
    union REGS ii, oo ;
    int a, areareqd ;
    char filename[20], *p ;

    areareqd = ( 20 - 5 + 1 ) * ( 70 - 5 + 1 ) * 2 ;
    p = malloc ( areareqd ) ;
```

```
if ( p == NULL )
{
    writestring ( messages[29], 22, 14, 112 ) ;
    getch() ;

    writestring ( messages[1], 22, 14, 112 ) ;
    return ;
}

savevideo ( 5, 5, 20, 70, p ) ;
menubox ( 6, 5, 16, 60, 112, 66 ) ;

writestring ( "          Get file attribute service          ", 22, 14, 112 ) ;

writestring ( "Enter name of file:", 7, 8, 112 ) ;
size ( 6, 7 ) ;
gotoxy ( 29, 8 ) ;
gets ( filename ) ;
size ( 32, 0 ) ;

ii.h.ah = 67 ;  /* dos service number */
ii.h.al = 0 ;  /* 0 - get attributes, 1 - set attributes */
ii.x.dx = ( unsigned int ) filename ;  /* store base address */
intdos ( &ii, &oo ) ;  /* issue interrupt */

/* if successful display attributes, else display error message */
if ( oo.x.cflag == 0 )
{
    writestring ( "ATTRIBUTES", 9, 27, 112 ) ;
    writestring ( "----------", 10, 27, 112 ) ;
    a = oo.x.cx ;
    writeattr ( a, 24 ) ;
}
else
{
    switch ( oo.x.ax )
    {
```

```
            case 2 :
                writestring ( "File not found!", 9, 8, 112 ) ;
                break ;

            case 3 :
                writestring ( "Invalid path!", 9, 8, 112 ) ;
                break ;

            case 5 :
                writestring ( "Access denied!", 9, 8, 112 ) ;
                break ;

            case 0x11 :
                writestring ( "Invalid drive name!", 15, 8, 112 ) ;
                break ;

            default :
                writestring ( "Improper request!", 9, 8, 112 ) ;
        }
    }

    writestring ( messages[28], 22, 14, 112 ) ;
    getch( ) ;

    writestring ( messages[1], 22, 14, 112 ) ;
    restorevideo ( 5, 5, 20, 70, p ) ;
    free ( p ) ;
}

/* displays attributes passed to variable a */
writeattr ( a, col )
int a, col ;
{
    writestring ( "Read only :", 11, col, 112 ) ;
    if ( ( a & 1 ) == 0 )
        writestring ( "OFF", 11, ( col + 12 ), 112 ) ;
    else
```

```
            writestring ( "ON", 11, ( col + 12 ), 112 ) ;

        writestring ( "Hidden    :", 12, col, 112 ) ;
        if ( ( a & 2 ) == 0 )
            writestring ( "OFF", 12, ( col + 12 ), 112 ) ;
        else
            writestring ( "ON", 12, ( col + 12 ), 112 ) ;

        writestring ( "System    :", 13, col, 112 ) ;
        if ( ( a & 4 ) == 0 )
            writestring ( "OFF", 13, ( col + 12 ), 112 ) ;
        else
            writestring ( "ON", 13, ( col + 12 ), 112 ) ;

        writestring ( "Archive   :", 14, col, 112 ) ;
        if ( ( a & 32 ) == 0 )
            writestring ( "OFF", 14, ( col + 12 ), 112 ) ;
        else
            writestring ( "ON", 14, ( col + 12 ), 112 ) ;
}

/* sets new attributes for a file */
setfileattb( )
{
        union REGS ii, oo ;
        int old, new, areareqd ;
        char filename[20], *p, ch ;

        areareqd = ( 20 - 5 + 1 ) * ( 70 - 5 + 1 ) * 2 ;
        p = malloc ( areareqd ) ;
        if ( p == NULL )
        {
            writestring ( messages[29], 22, 14, 112 ) ;
            getch( ) ;

            writestring ( messages[1], 22, 14, 112 ) ;
            return ;
```

```
}

savevideo ( 5, 5, 20, 70, p ) ;
menubox ( 6, 5, 17, 60, 112, 66 ) ;

writestring ( "          Set file attribute service                ", 22, 14, 112 ) ;

writestring ( "Enter name of file:", 7, 8, 112 ) ;
size ( 6, 7 ) ;
gotoxy ( 29, 8 ) ;
gets ( filename ) ;
size ( 32, 0 ) ;

ii.h.ah = 67 ;  /* dos service number */
ii.h.al = 0 ;  /* 0 - get attributes, 1 - set attributes */
ii.x.dx = ( unsigned int ) filename ;  /* base address of filename */
intdos ( &ii, &oo ) ;  /* issue interrupt */

/* if successful display attributes, else display error message */
if ( oo.x.cflag == 0 )
{
    old = new = oo.x.cx ;
    writestring ( "Existing Attributes", 9, 8, 112 ) ;
    writestring ( "-------------------", 10, 8, 112 ) ;
    writeattr ( old, 8 ) ;  /* display existing attributes */
}
else
{
    switch ( oo.x.ax )
    {
        case 2 :
            writestring ( "File not found!", 9, 8, 112 ) ;
            break ;

        case 3 :
            writestring ( "Invalid path!", 9, 8, 112 ) ;
            break ;
```

```
            case 5 :
                writestring ( "Access denied!", 9, 8, 112 ) ;
                break ;

            case 0x11 :
                writestring ( "Invalid drive name!", 9, 8, 112 ) ;
                break ;

            default :
                writestring ( "Improper request!", 9, 8, 112 ) ;
        }

        writestring ( messages[28], 22, 14, 112 ) ;
        getch( ) ;

        restorevideo ( 5, 5, 20, 70, p ) ;
        free ( p ) ;
        return ;
    }


    /* collect new attributes or keep old attributes */
    writestring ( "Change (Y/N):", 11, 30, 112 ) ;
    size ( 6, 7 ) ;
    gotoxy ( 45, 12 ) ;
    fflush ( stdin ) ;  /* flush keyboard buffer */
    ch = toupper ( getch( ) ) ;
    writechar ( 11, 44, ch, 112 ) ;


    if ( ch == 'Y' )
        new = ( new ^ 1 ) ;


    writestring ( "Change (Y/N):", 12, 30, 112 ) ;
    gotoxy ( 45, 13 ) ;
    fflush ( stdin ) ;
    ch = toupper ( getch( ) ) ;
    writechar ( 12, 44, ch, 112 ) ;
```

```
if ( ch == 'Y' )
    new = ( new ^ 2 ) ;

writestring ( "Change (Y/N):", 13, 30, 112 ) ;
gotoxy ( 45, 14 ) ;
fflush ( stdin ) ;
ch = toupper ( getch( ) ) ;
writechar ( 13, 44, ch, 112 ) ;

if ( ch == 'Y' )
    new = ( new ^ 4 ) ;

writestring ( "Change (Y/N):", 14, 30, 112 ) ;
gotoxy ( 45, 15 ) ;
fflush ( stdin ) ;
ch = toupper ( getch( ) ) ;
writechar ( 14, 44, ch, 112 ) ;

size ( 32, 0 ) ;

if ( ch == 'Y' )
    new = ( new ^ 32 ) ;

/* issue interrupt to set new file attributes */
ii.h.ah = 67 ;
ii.h.al = 1 ;
ii.x.cx = new ;
ii.x.dx = ( unsigned int ) filename ;
intdos ( &ii, &oo ) ;

menubox ( 6, 5, 17, 60, 112, 66 ) ;
writestring ( "File name:", 7, 8, 112 ) ;
writestring ( filename, 7, 19, 112 ) ;

/* if successful display old and new attributes, else display error message */
if ( oo.x.cflag == 0 )
```

```
        {
                writestring ( "Old Attributes", 9, 8, 112 ) ;
                writestring ( "--------------", 10, 8, 112 ) ;
                writeattr ( old, 8 ) ;
                writestring ( "New Attributes", 9, 40, 112 ) ;
                writestring ( "--------------", 10, 40, 112 ) ;
                writeattr ( new, 40 ) ;
        }
        else
                writestring ( "Error - New attributes not set!", 12, 8, 112 ) ;

        writestring ( messages[28], 22, 14, 112 ) ;
        getch( ) ;

        writestring ( messages[1], 22, 14, 112 ) ;
        restorevideo ( 5, 5, 20, 70, p ) ;
        free ( p ) ;
}

encryptfile( )
{
        char sfile[20], tfile[20], *p, ch ;
        FILE *fps , *fpt ;
        int areareqd, flag ;

        areareqd = ( 20 - 5 + 1 ) * ( 70 - 5 + 1 ) * 2 ;
        p = malloc ( areareqd ) ;
        if ( p == NULL )
        {
                writestring ( messages[29], 22, 14, 112 ) ;
                getch( ) ;

                writestring ( messages[1], 22, 14, 112 ) ;
                return ;
        }

        savevideo ( 5, 5, 20, 70, p ) ;
```

```
menubox ( 6, 5, 13, 60, 112, 66 ) ;

writestring ( "            File coding service            ", 22, 14, 112 ) ;

writestring ( "Enter source file name:", 7, 8, 112 ) ;
size ( 6, 7 ) ;
gotoxy ( 33, 8 ) ;
fflush ( stdin ) ;
gets ( sfile ) ;
size ( 32, 0 ) ;

/* open source file */
fps = fopen ( sfile, "r" ) ;
if ( fps == NULL )
{
    writestring ( "Unable to open source file!", 9, 8, 112 ) ;
    writestring ( messages[28], 22, 14, 112 ) ;
    getch( ) ;

    writestring ( messages[1], 22, 14, 112 ) ;
    restorevideo ( 5, 5, 20, 70, p ) ;
    free ( p ) ;
    return ;
}

writestring ( "Enter target file name:", 9, 8, 112 ) ;
size ( 6, 7 ) ;
gotoxy ( 33, 10 ) ;
gets ( tfile ) ;
size ( 32, 0 ) ;

/* open target file */
fpt = fopen ( tfile, "w" ) ;
if ( fpt == NULL )
{
    writestring ( "Unable to open target file!", 11, 8, 112 ) ;
    writestring ( messages[28], 22, 14, 112 ) ;
```

```
            getch( ) ;

            fclose ( fps ) ;
            writestring ( messages[1], 22, 14, 112 ) ;
            restorevideo ( 5, 5, 20, 70, p ) ;
            free ( p ) ;
            return ;
    }

    /* read each character, offset it by 127, write to target file */
    while ( ( ch = getc ( fps ) ) != EOF )
    {
        if ( ch == '\n' )
            flag = putc ( '\n', fpt ) ;
        else
            flag = putc ( ( ch + 127 ), fpt ) ;

        /* if error in writing */
        if ( flag == EOF )
            break ;
    }

    if ( flag == EOF )
        writestring ( "Unable to encrypt file!", 11, 8, 112 ) ;
    else
        writestring ( "File is successfully encrypted!", 11, 8, 112 ) ;

    writestring ( messages[28], 22, 14, 112 ) ;
    getch( ) ;

    fclose ( fps ) ;
    fclose ( fpt ) ;
    writestring ( messages[1], 22, 14, 112 ) ;
    restorevideo ( 5, 5, 20, 70, p ) ;
    free ( p ) ;
}
```

```
decryptfile( )
{
    char sfile[20], tfile[20], *p, ch ;
    FILE *fps, *fpt ;
    int areareqd, flag ;

    areareqd = ( 20 - 5 + 1 ) * ( 70 - 5 + 1 ) * 2 ;
    p = malloc ( areareqd ) ;
    if ( p == NULL )
    {
        writestring ( messages[29], 22, 14, 112 ) ;
        getch( ) ;

        writestring ( messages[1], 22, 14, 112 ) ;
        return ;
    }

    savevideo ( 5, 5, 20, 70, p ) ;
    menubox ( 6, 5, 13, 60, 112, 66 ) ;

    writestring ( "          File decode service          ", 22, 14, 112 ) ;

    writestring ( "Enter source file name:", 7, 8, 112 ) ;
    size ( 6, 7 ) ;
    gotoxy ( 33, 8 ) ;
    gets ( sfile ) ;
    size ( 32, 0 ) ;

    /* open source file */
    fps = fopen ( sfile, "r" ) ;
    if ( fps == NULL )
    {
        writestring ( "Unable to open source file!", 9, 8, 112 ) ;
        writestring ( messages[28], 22, 14, 112 ) ;
        getch( ) ;

        writestring ( messages[1], 22, 14, 112 ) ;
```

```
        restorevideo ( 5, 5, 20, 70, p ) ;
        free ( p ) ;
        return ;
}


writestring ( "Enter target file name:", 9, 8, 112 ) ;
size ( 6, 7 ) ;
gotoxy ( 33, 10 ) ;
gets ( tfile ) ;
size ( 32, 0 ) ;

/* open target file */
fpt = fopen ( tfile, "w" ) ;
if ( fpt == NULL )
{
    writestring ( "Unable to open target file!", 11, 8, 112 ) ;
    writestring ( messages[28], 22, 14, 112 ) ;
    getch() ;

    fclose ( fps ) ;
    writestring ( messages[1], 22, 14, 112 ) ;
    restorevideo ( 5, 5, 20, 70, p ) ;
    free ( p ) ;
    return ;
}

/* read each character, reduce by offset, write to target file */
while ( ( ch = getc ( fps ) ) != EOF )
{
    if ( ch == '\n' )
        flag = putc ( '\n', fpt ) ;
    else
        flag = putc ( ( ch - 127 ), fpt ) ;

    /* if error in writing */
    if ( flag == EOF )
        break ;
```

```c
        }

        if ( flag == EOF )
            writestring ( "Unable to decrypt file!", 11, 8, 112 ) ;
        else
            writestring ( "File successfully decrypted!", 11, 8, 112 ) ;

        writestring ( messages[28], 22, 14, 112 ) ;
        getch( ) ;

        fclose ( fps ) ;
        fclose ( fpt ) ;
        writestring ( messages[1], 22, 14, 112 ) ;
        restorevideo ( 5, 5, 20, 70, p ) ;
        free ( p ) ;
}

compressfile( )
{
        char *p, sfile[20], tfile[20] ;
        FILE *fps, *fpt ;
        int area, count, ch, flag ;

        area = ( 12 - 5 + 1 ) * ( 60 - 5 + 1 ) * 2 ;
        p = malloc ( area ) ;
        if ( p == NULL )
        {
            writestring ( messages[29], 22, 14, 112 ) ;
            getch( ) ;

            writestring ( messages[1], 22, 14, 112 ) ;
            return ;
        }

        savevideo ( 5, 5, 12, 60, p ) ;
        menubox ( 5, 5, 12, 60, 112, 66 ) ;
```

```
writestring ( "           File compress service           ", 22, 14, 112 ) ;

writestring ( "Enter source file name:", 6, 8, 112 ) ;
size ( 6, 7 ) ;
gotoxy ( 33, 7 ) ;
gets ( sfile ) ;
size ( 32, 0 ) ;

/* open source file */
fps = fopen ( sfile, "r" ) ;
if ( fps == NULL )
{
    writestring ( "Unable to open source file!", 8, 8, 112 ) ;
    writestring ( messages[28], 22, 14, 112 ) ;
    getch() ;

    writestring ( messages[1], 22, 14, 112 ) ;
    restorevideo ( 5, 5, 12, 60, p ) ;
    free ( p ) ;
    return ;
}

writestring ( "Enter target file name:", 8, 8, 112 ) ;
size ( 6, 7 ) ;
gotoxy ( 33, 9 ) ;
gets ( tfile ) ;
size ( 32, 0 ) ;

/* open target file */
fpt = fopen ( tfile, "w") ;
if ( fpt == NULL )
{
    writestring ( "Unable to open target file!", 10, 8, 112 ) ;
    writestring ( messages[28], 22, 14, 112 ) ;
    getch() ;

    fclose ( fps ) ;
```

```
            writestring ( messages[1], 22, 14, 112 ) ;
            restorevideo ( 5, 5, 12, 60, p ) ;
            free ( p ) ;
            return ;
}

/* read each character till end of file is reached */
while ( ( ch = getc ( fps ) ) != EOF )
{
        /* check for space */
        if ( ch == ' ' )
        {
                count = 1 ;

                /* count number of consecutive spaces */
                while ( ( ch = getc ( fps ) ) == ' ' )
                        count++ ;

                flag = putc ( count + 127, fpt ) ;
                flag = putc ( ch, fpt ) ;
        }
        else
                flag = putc ( ch, fpt ) ;

        if ( flag == EOF )
                break ;
}

if ( flag == EOF )
        writestring ( "Unable to compress file!", 10, 8, 112 ) ;
else
        writestring ( "File successfully compressed!", 10, 8, 112 ) ;

writestring ( messages[28], 22, 14, 112 ) ;
getch( ) ;

fclose ( fps ) ;
```

```
        fclose ( fpt ) ;
        writestring ( messages[1], 22, 14, 112 ) ;
        restorevideo ( 5, 5, 12, 60, p ) ;
        free ( p ) ;
}

decompressfile( )
{
        char *p, sfile[20], tfile[20] ;
        FILE *fps, *fpt ;
        int ch, count, area, flag ;

        area = ( 12 - 5 + 1 ) * ( 60 - 5 + 1 ) * 2 ;
        p = malloc ( area ) ;
        if ( p == NULL )
        {
            writestring ( messages[29], 22, 14, 112 ) ;
            getch( ) ;

            writestring ( messages[1], 22, 14, 112 ) ;
            return ;
        }

        savevideo ( 5, 5, 12, 60, p ) ;
        menubox ( 5, 5, 12, 60, 112, 66 ) ;

        writestring ( "          File decompress service          ", 22, 14, 112 ) ;
        writestring ( "Enter source file name:", 6, 8, 112 ) ;
        size ( 6, 7 ) ;
        gotoxy ( 33, 7 ) ;
        gets ( sfile ) ;
        size ( 32, 0 ) ;

        /* open source file */
        fps = fopen ( sfile, "r" ) ;
        if ( fps == NULL )
        {
```

```
        writestring ( "Unable to open source file!", 8 , 8, 112 ) ;
        writestring ( messages[28], 22, 14, 112 ) ;
        getch( ) ;

        writestring ( messages[1], 22, 14, 112 ) ;
        restorevideo ( 5, 5, 12, 60, p ) ;
        free ( p ) ;
        return ;
    }

    writestring ( "Enter target file name:", 8, 8, 112 ) ;
    size ( 6, 7 );
    gotoxy ( 33, 9 ) ;
    gets ( tfile ) ;
    size ( 32, 0 ) ;

    /* open target file */
    fpt = fopen ( tfile, "w" ) ;
    if ( fpt == NULL )
    {
        writestring ( "Unable to open target file!", 10, 8, 112 ) ;
        writestring ( messages[28], 22, 14, 112 ) ;
        getch( ) ;

        fclose ( fps ) ;
        writestring ( messages[1], 22, 14, 112 ) ;
        restorevideo ( 5, 5, 12, 60, p ) ;
        free ( p ) ;
        return ;
    }

    /* read each character till end of file is reached */
    while ( ( ch = getc ( fps ) ) != EOF )
    {
        /* if ascii value of character read exceeds 127 */
        if ( ch > 127 )
        {
```

```
                    ch = ch - 127 ;

                    /* write back original spaces */
                    for ( count = 1 ; count <= ch ; count++ )
                        flag = putc ( ' ', fpt ) ;
            }
            else
                flag = putc ( ch, fpt ) ;

            /* if error in writing */
            if ( flag == EOF )
                break ;
        }

        if ( flag == EOF )
            writestring ( "Unable to decompress file!", 10, 8, 112 ) ;
        else
            writestring ( "File successfully decompressed!", 10, 8, 112 ) ;

        writestring ( messages[28], 22, 14, 112 ) ;
        getch( ) ;

        fclose ( fps ) ;
        fclose ( fpt ) ;
        writestring ( messages[1], 22, 14, 112 ) ;
        restorevideo ( 5, 5, 12, 60, p ) ;
        free ( p ) ;
    }

    displayfile( )
    {
        char *p, filename[20], ch, str[5] ;
        int pg = 1, row = 2, col = 1, area ;
        FILE *fp ;

        area = ( 25 - 0 + 1 ) * ( 80 - 0 + 1 ) * 2 ;
        p = malloc ( area ) ;
```

```
if ( p == NULL )
{
    writestring ( messages[29], 22, 14, 112 ) ;
    getch( ) ;

    writestring ( messages[1], 22, 14, 112 ) ;
    return ;
}

savevideo ( 0, 0, 24, 79, p ) ;
menubox ( 5, 5, 10, 60, 112, 66 ) ;

writestring ( "          File display service          ", 22, 14, 112 ) ;

writestring ( "Enter name of file:", 6, 8, 112 ) ;
size ( 6, 7 ) ;
gotoxy ( 29, 7 ) ;
gets ( filename ) ;
size ( 32, 0 ) ;

/* open file to be displayed */
fp = fopen ( filename, "r" ) ;
if ( fp == NULL )
{
    writestring ( "Unable to open source file!", 8, 8, 112 ) ;
    writestring ( messages[28], 22, 14, 112 ) ;
    getch( ) ;

    writestring ( messages[1], 22, 14, 112 ) ;
    restorevideo ( 0, 0, 24, 79, p ) ;
    free ( p ) ;
    return ;
}

menubox ( 0, 0, 1, 79, 7, 7 ) ;
menubox ( 1, 0, 24, 79, 112, 32 ) ;
drawbox ( 1. 0, 23, 78, 112 ) ;
```

```
drawbox ( 1, 0, 21, 78, 112 ) ;
writechar ( 21, 0, 204, 112 ) ;
writechar ( 21, 78, 185, 112 ) ;

/* display file name and current page number */
writestring ( "File :-", 0, 0, 7 ) ;
writestring ( filename, 0, 8, 7 ) ;
writestring ( "Page No :- ", 0, 54, 7 ) ;
itoa ( pg, str, 10 ) ;
writestring ( str, 0, 65, 7 ) ;

/* read each character till end of file is reached */
while ( ( ch = getc ( fp ) ) != EOF )
{
    /* if character read is not a newline, carriage return or tab */
    if ( ( ch != '\n' ) && ( ch != '\r' ) && ( ch != '\t' ) )
        writechar ( row, col, ch, 112 ) ;

    /* if tab, increment column by 4 otherwise by 1 */
    if ( ch == '\t' )
        col += 4 ;
    else
        col++ ;

    /* if column exceeds 77 or end of line is met */
    if ( col > 77 || ch == '\n' )
    {
        col = 1 ;
        row++ ;

        /* if screen is full */
        if ( row > 20 )
        {
            writestring ( messages[28], 22, 17, 112 ) ;
            getch() ;

            row = 2 ;
```

```
                pg++ ;

                menubox ( 2, 1, 20, 77, 112, 0 ) ;

                writestring ( "File :-", 0, 0, 7 ) ;
                writestring ( filename, 0, 8, 7 ) ;
                writestring ( "Page No :- ", 0, 54, 7 ) ;
                itoa ( pg, str, 10 ) ;
                writestring ( str, 0, 65, 7 ) ;
            }
        }
    }

    writestring ( "        Press any key to return...        ", 22, 14, 112 ) ;
    getch( ) ;

    fclose ( fp ) ;
    writestring ( messages[1], 22, 14, 112 ) ;
    restorevideo ( 0, 0, 24, 79, p ) ;
    free ( p ) ;
}

makedir( )
{
    union REGS ii, oo ;
    int areareqd ;
    char dirname[20], *p ;

    areareqd = ( 20 - 5 + 1 ) * ( 70 - 5 + 1 ) * 2 ;
    p = malloc ( areareqd ) ;
    if ( p == NULL )
    {
        writestring ( messages[29], 22, 14, 112 ) ;
        getch( ) ;

        writestring ( messages[1], 22, 14, 112 ) ;
        return ;
```

```
        }

    savevideo ( 5, 5, 20, 70, p ) ;
    menubox ( 6, 5, 11, 60, 112, 66 ) ;

    writestring ( "        Create directory service        ", 22, 15, 112 ) ;

    writestring ( "Enter name of directory:", 7, 8, 112 ) ;
    size ( 6, 7 ) ;
    gotoxy ( 34, 8 ) ;
    gets ( dirname ) ;
    size ( 32, 0 ) ;

    ii.h.ah = 57 ;  /* dos service number */
    ii.x.dx = ( unsigned int ) dirname ;  /* base address of directory name */
    intdos ( &ii, &oo ) ;  /* issue interrupt */

    /* check if successful in creating directory */
    if ( oo.x.cflag == 0 )
        writestring ( "Directory was successfully created!", 9, 8, 112 ) ;
    else
    {
        if ( oo.x.ax == 5 )
            writestring ( "Improper access!", 9, 8, 112 ) ;
        if ( oo.x.ax == 3 )
            writestring ( "Invalid path!", 9, 8, 112 ) ;
    }

    writestring ( messages[28], 22, 14, 112 ) ;
    getch( ) ;

    writestring ( messages[1], 22, 14, 112 ) ;
    restorevideo ( 5, 5, 20, 70, p ) ;
    free ( p ) ;
}

changedir( )
```

```
{
    union REGS ii, oo ;
    int areareqd ;
    char dirname[20], *p ;

    areareqd = ( 20 - 5 + 1 ) * ( 70 - 5 + 1 ) * 2 ;
    p = malloc ( areareqd ) ;
    if ( p == NULL )
    {
        writestring ( messages[29], 22, 14, 112 ) ;
        getch( ) ;

        writestring ( messages[1], 22, 14, 112 ) ;
        return ;
    }

    savevideo ( 5, 5, 20, 70, p ) ;
    menubox ( 6, 5, 11, 60, 112, 66 ) ;

    writestring ( "           Change directory service           ", 22, 14, 112 ) ;

    writestring ( "Enter name of directory:", 7, 8, 112 ) ;
    size ( 6, 7 ) ;
    gotoxy ( 34, 8 ) ;
    gets ( dirname ) ;
    size ( 32, 0 ) ;

    /* issue interrupt for changing directory */
    ii.h.ah = 59 ;
    ii.x.dx = ( unsigned int ) dirname ;
    intdos ( &ii, &oo ) ;

    /* check if successful in changing directory */
    if ( oo.x.cflag == 0 )
        writestring ( "Directory is successfully changed!", 9, 8, 112 ) ;
    else
    {
```

```
        if ( oo.x.ax == 3 )
            writestring ( "Invalid path!", 9, 8, 112 ) ;

        if ( oo.x.ax == 5 )
            writestring ( "Improper access!", 9, 8, 112 ) ;
    }

    writestring ( messages[28], 22, 14, 112 ) ;
    getch( ) ;

    writestring ( messages[1], 22, 14, 112 ) ;
    restorevideo ( 5, 5, 20, 70, p ) ;
    free ( p ) ;
}

removedir( )
{
    union REGS ii, oo ;
    int areareqd ;
    char dirname[20], *p ;

    areareqd = ( 20 - 5 + 1 ) * ( 76 - 5 + 1 ) * 2 ;
    p = malloc ( areareqd ) ;
    if ( p == NULL )
    {
        writestring ( messages[29], 22, 14, 112 ) ;
        getch( ) ;

        writestring ( messages[1], 22, 14, 112 ) ;
        return ;
    }

    savevideo ( 5, 5, 20, 76, p ) ;
    menubox ( 6, 5, 12, 75 ,112, 66 ) ;

    writestring ( "         Delete directory service          ", 22, 15, 112 ) ;
```

```
writestring ( "Directory name:", 7, 8, 112 ) ;
writestring ( "( entire path )", 8, 8, 112 ) ;
size ( 6, 7 ) ;
gotoxy ( 25, 8 ) ;
gets ( dirname ) ;
size ( 32, 0 ) ;

/* issue interrupt for removing directory */
ii.h.ah = 58 ;
ii.x.dx = ( unsigned int ) dirname ;
intdos ( &ii, &oo ) ;

/* check if successful in removing directory */
if ( oo.x.cflag == 0 )
    writestring ( "Directory was successfully removed!", 10, 8, 112 ) ;
else
{
    switch ( oo.x.ax )
    {
        case 3 :
            writestring ( "Invalid path!", 10, 8, 112 ) ;
            break ;

        case 5 :
            writestring ( "Improper access!",10, 8, 112 ) ;
            break ;

        case 2 :
            writestring ( "Directory does not exist!", 10, 8, 112 ) ;
            break ;

        case 0x10 :
            writestring ( "Cannot remove current directory!", 10, 8, 112 ) ;
    }
}

writestring ( messages[28], 22, 14, 112 ) ;
```

```
        getch( ) ;

        writestring ( messages[1], 22, 14, 112 ) ;
        restorevideo ( 5, 5, 20, 76, p ) ;
        free ( p ) ;
}

listdir( )
{
        int areareqd ;
        char *p, filetosearch[20] ;
        char sz[10], dd[10], mm[10], yy[10], hr[10], m[10], temp[3] = "0" ;
        struct ffblk file ;
        unsigned int done, row, col, a, year, month, day, hour, min ;

        areareqd = ( 20 - 3 + 1 ) * ( 70 - 3 + 1 ) * 2 ;
        p = malloc ( areareqd ) ;
        if ( p == NULL )
        {
            writestring ( messages[29], 22, 14, 112 ) ;
            getch( ) ;

            writestring ( messages[1], 22, 14, 112 ) ;
            return ;
        }

        savevideo ( 5, 5, 20, 70, p ) ;
        menubox ( 6, 5, 11, 60, 112, 66 ) ;

        writestring ( "         List directory service         ", 22, 15, 112 ) ;

        writestring ( "Enter skeleton for searching:", 7, 8, 112 ) :
        size ( 6, 7 ) ;
        gotoxy ( 39, 8 ) ;
        gets ( filetosearch ) ;
        size ( 32, 0 ) ;
```

```
/* find first file which matches the skeleton */
done = findfirst ( filetosearch, &file, FA_DIREC ) ;

/* if successful in finding the first file */
if ( done == 0 )
{
    menubox ( 5, 5, 20, 70, 112, 66 ) ;
    row = 8;
    col = 8 ;

    writestring ( "Directory listing", 6, 28, 112 ) ;
    writestring ( "----------------", 7, 28, 112 ) ;

    /* carry out search for rest of the files matching the skeleton */
    while ( done == 0 )
    {
        row++ ;
        writestring ( file.ff_name, row, col, 112 ) ;

        /* if not a sub-directory entry */
        if ( ( file.ff_attrib & 16 ) == 0 )
        {
            ltoa ( file.ff_fsize, sz, 10 ) ;
            writestring ( sz, row, col + 19, 112 ) ;

            /* calculate and print date and time */
            a = file.ff_fdate ;
            year = 80 + ( a >> 9 ) ;
            month = ( a << 7 ) >> 12 ;
            day = ( a << 11 ) >> 11 ;

            itoa ( day, dd, 10 ) ;

            /* if a single digit day, concatenate it to 0 */
            if ( strlen ( dd ) == 1 )
                strcat ( temp, dd ) ;
            else
```

```
        strcpy ( temp, dd ) ;

writestring ( temp, row, col + 30, 112 ) ;
writechar ( row, col + 32, '/', 112 ) ;

/* reinitialise temp */
strcpy ( temp, "0" ) ;

itoa ( month, mm, 10 ) ;

/* if a single digit month, concatenate it to 0 */
if ( strlen ( mm ) == 1 )
    strcat ( temp, mm ) ;
else
    strcpy ( temp, mm ) ;

writestring ( temp, row, col + 33, 112 ) ;
writechar ( row, col + 35, '/', 112 ) ;

strcpy ( temp, "0" ) ;

itoa ( year, yy, 10 ) ;
if ( strlen ( yy ) == 1 )
    strcat ( temp, yy ) ;
else
    strcpy ( temp, yy ) ;

writestring ( temp, row, col + 36, 112 ) ;

strcpy ( temp, "0" ) ;

a = file.ff_ftime ;
hour = ( a >> 11 ) ;
min = ( a << 5 ) >> 10 ;

if ( hour == 0 )
    hour = 12 ;
```

```
            strcpy ( temp, "0" ) ;

            itoa ( hour, hr, 10 ) ;
            if ( strlen ( hr ) == 1 )
                strcat ( temp, hr ) ;
            else
                strcpy ( temp, hr ) ;

            writestring ( temp, row, col + 45, 112 ) ;
            writechar ( row, col + 47, ':', 112 ) ;

            strcpy ( temp, "0" ) ;

            itoa ( min, m, 10 ) ;
            if ( strlen ( m ) == 1 )
                strcat ( temp, m ) ;
            else
                strcpy ( temp, m ) ;

            writestring ( temp, row, col + 48, 112 ) ;

            strcpy ( temp, "0" ) ;
    }
    else
        writestring ( "<DIR>", row, col + 15, 112 ) ;

    /* find the next file matching the skeleton */
    done = findnext ( &file ) ;

    /* if screen is full */
    if ( row == 18 )
    {
        row = 8 ;
        writestring ( messages[28], 22, 14, 112 ) ;
        getch( ) ;
```

```
                        menubox ( 5, 5, 20, 70, 112, 66 ) ;
                        writestring ( "Directory listing", 6, 28, 112 ) ;
                        writestring ( "-----------------", 7, 28, 112 ) ;
                    }
                }
            }
        else
            writestring ( "File not found!", 9, 8, 112 ) ;

        writestring ( messages[28], 22, 14, 112 ) ;
        getch( ) ;

        writestring ( messages[1], 22, 14, 112 ) ;
        restorevideo ( 5, 5, 20, 70, p ) ;
        free ( p ) ;
}

/* global variables required by the function dirtree( ) and tree( ) */
char dirname[40], dir[32], name[32], attb, entirepath[40] ;
int dirtree_row, in ;

dirtree( )
{
    char *p, current_dir[32] ;
    int area ;

    area = ( 25 - 0 + 1 ) * ( 80 - 0 + 1 ) * 2 ;
    p = malloc ( area ) ;
    if ( p == NULL )
    {
        writestring ( messages[29], 22, 14, 112 ) ;
        getch( ) ;

        writestring ( messages[1], 22, 14, 112 ) ;
        return ;
    }
```

```
savevideo ( 0, 0, 24, 79, p ) ;

menubox ( 0, 0, 1, 79, 7, 7 ) ;
menubox ( 0, 0, 24, 79, 112, 32 ) ;
drawbox ( 0, 0, 23, 78, 112 ) ;
drawbox ( 0, 0, 21, 78, 112 ) ;
writechar ( 21, 0, 204, 112 ) ;
writechar ( 21, 78, 185, 112 ) ;

writestring ( "Directory tree", 1, 20, 112 ) ;
writestring ( "==============", 2, 20, 112 ) ;

/* store current working directory and switch over to root directory */
getcwd ( current_dir, 32 ) ;
chdir ( "\\" ) ;

/* initialise the variables used for storing the components of the path */
name[0] = '\0' ;
dir[0] = '\0' ;

entirepath[0] = '\0' ;

/* initialise the row at which the display should start */
dirtree_row = 3 ;

/* initialise the level of sub-directory */
in = 0 ;

/* if in root directory */
if ( strlen ( current_dir ) == 3 )
    attb = 159 ;  /* set attribute to highlight the word ROOT */
else
{
    /* if in sub-directory */
    attb = 112 ;  /* set normal attribute for displaying ROOT */

/* split the components of the path */
```

```
        fnsplit ( current_dir, 0, dir, name, 0 ) ;

        /* create the entire path of the sub-directory being considered */
        strcpy ( entirepath, dir ) ;
        strcat ( entirepath, name ) ;
    }

    /* display ROOT vertically in the appropriate attribute */
    writestring ( "R", 3, 2, attb ) ;
    writestring ( "O", 4, 2, attb ) ;
    writestring ( "O", 5, 2, attb ) ;
    writestring ( "T", 6, 2, attb ) ;

    tree ( "*.*" ) ;
    chdir ( current_dir ) ;  /* restore current working directory */

    writestring ( "         Press any key to return...           ", 22, 14, 112 ) ;
    getch( ) ;

    restorevideo ( 0, 0, 24, 79, p ) ;
    free ( p ) ;
}

tree ( ptr )
char *ptr ;
{
    struct ffblk file ;
    int flag, i, len ;
    static char path[40] = "" ;
    char str1[9] = "        ", str2[9] = "        ", str3[9] = "      " ;
    char str4[9] = "        ", str5[4] = "   " ;

    /* set up strings with appropriate characters */
    strnset ( str1, 196, 8 ) ;
    strnset ( str1, 195, 1 ) ;

    strnset ( str2, 32, 8 ) ;
```

```
        strnset ( str2, 179, 1 ) ;

        strnset ( str3, 196, 8 ) ;
        strnset ( str3, 192, 1 ) ;

        strnset ( str5, 196, 3 ) ;
        str5[2] = 197 ;

        /* find first entry which matches the specification *.* */
        flag = findfirst ( ptr, &file, FA_DIREC ) ;

        /* continue search for rest of the directories */
        while ( flag == 0 )
        {
            /* if directory entry */
            if ( ( ( file.ff_attrib & 16 ) == 16 ) && file.ff_name[0] != '.' )
            {
                /* create the entire path of the sub-directory being considered */
                if ( in == 0 )
                {
                    /* if in root directory, set path again to '\' */
                    strcpy ( path, "\\" ) ;
                    strcat ( path, file.ff_name ) ;
                }
                else
                {
                    /* else concatenate current component with already existing
                       path */
                    strcat ( path, "\\" ) ;
                    strcat ( path, file.ff_name ) ;
                }

                /* if screen is full */
                if ( dirtree_row >= 20 )
                {
                    writestring ( messages[28], 22, 17, 112 ) ;
                    getch() ;
```

```
        menubox ( 2, 1, 20, 77, 112, 0 ) ;

        writestring ( "Directory tree", 1, 20, 112 ) ;
        writestring ( "==============", 2, 20, 112 ) ;
        dirtree_row = 3 ;

        writestring ( "R", 3, 2, attb ) ;
        writestring ( "O", 4, 2, attb ) ;
        writestring ( "O", 5, 2, attb ) ;
        writestring ( "T", 6, 2, attb ) ;
    }

    in++ ;
    dirname[0] = '\0' ;
    /* concatenate appropriate string to directory name */
    if ( in == 1 )
        strcat ( dirname, str1 ) ;
    else
    {
        strcat ( dirname, str2 ) ;
        i = 2 ;
        while ( i < in )
        {
            strcat ( dirname, str4 ) ;
            i++ ;
        }
        strcat ( dirname, str3 ) ;
    }

    /* if subdirectory name is the current working directory */
    if ( strcmp ( path, entirepath ) == 0 )
    {
        writestring ( dirname, dirtree_row, 5, 112 ) ;

        /* highlight the current working directory */
```

```
                writestring ( file.ff_name, dirtree_row, 5 + strlen ( dirname ),
                159 ) ;
        }
        else
        {
                strcat ( dirname, file.ff_name ) ;
                writestring ( dirname, dirtree_row, 5, 112 ) ;
        }

        if ( dirtree_row == 3 )
                writestring ( str5, 3, 3, 112 ) ;

        dirtree_row++ ;

        /* go inside the directory found */
        chdir ( file.ff_name ) ;
        file.ff_name[0] = '\0' ;

        /* search directory entries in this directory */
        tree ( ptr ) ;
    }

    /* find the next entry matching the specification * * */
    flag = findnext ( &file ) ;
}

/* if inside a sub-directory, change over to its parent directory */
if ( in-- > 0 )
{
    chdir ( ".." ) ;

    /* update the variable path appropriately */
    len = strlen ( path ) ;
    if ( in >= 1 )
    {
        while ( path[len - 1] != '\\' )
                len-- ;
```

```
            path[len - 1] = '\0' ;
        }


    }
}

calendar( )
{
    char *months[ ] = {

                        "January",   "Feburary",   "March",
                        "April",     "May",        "June",
                        "July",      "August",     "September",
                        "October",   "November",   "December"
                    } ;

    int days[ ] = { 31, 28, 31, 30, 31, 30, 31, 31, 30, 31, 30, 31 } ;
    int m, y, leapyears, row, col, x, i, areareqd, firstday, thisyrdays ;
    long int totaldays ;
    char *p, str1[5], str2[3] ;

    areareqd = ( 20 - 3 + 1 ) * ( 70 - 3 + 1 ) * 2 ;
    p = malloc ( areareqd ) ;
    if ( p == NULL )
    {
        writestring ( messages[29], 22, 14, 112 ) ;
        getch( ) ;

        writestring ( messages[1], 22, 14, 112 ) ;
        return ;
    }

    savevideo ( 5, 5, 20, 70, p ) ;
    menubox ( 6, 5, 11, 50, 112, 66 ) ;

    writestring ( "          Display calendar service          ", 22, 14, 112 ) ;
```

```
writestring ( "Enter month ( 1 - 12 ):", 7, 8, 112 ) ;
size ( 6, 7 ) ;
gotoxy ( 33, 8 ) ;
scanf ( "%d", &m ) ;
size ( 32, 0 ) ;

writestring ( "Enter year:", 9, 8, 112 ) ;
size ( 6, 7 ) ;
gotoxy ( 21, 10 ) ;
scanf ( "%d", &y ) ;
size ( 32, 0 ) ;

while ( 1 )
{
     days[1] = 28 ;
     thisyrdays = 0 ;

     /* calculate number of leap years before the year y */
     leapyears = ( y - 1 ) / 4 - ( y - 1 ) / 100 + ( y - 1 ) / 400 ;

     /* check if y is a leap year */
     if ( y % 400 == 0 || y % 100 != 0 && y % 4 == 0 )
          days[1] = 29 ;
     else
          days[1] = 28 ;

     totaldays = leapyears + ( y - 1 ) * 365L ;

     /* calculate days before month m in year y */
     for ( i = 0 ; i <= m-2 ; i++ )
          thisyrdays = thisyrdays + days[i] ;

     /* calculate number of days that couldn't be evened out in weeks */
     firstday = (int) ( ( totaldays + thisyrdays ) % 7 ) ;

     /* write month and year */
     menubox ( 5, 5, 20, 70, 112, 66 ) ;
```

```
        writestring ( months[m-1], 6, 19, 112 ) ;
        itoa ( y, str1, 10 ) ;
        writestring ( str1, 6, 29, 112 ) ;

        writestring ( "Mon  Tue  Wed  Thu  Fri  Sat  Sun", 8, 7, 112 ) ;

        /* calculate in which column first day of the calendar is to be written */
        col = 7 + firstday * 6 ;


        row = 10 ;

        /* display calendar */
        for ( x = 1 ; x <= days[m-1] ; x++ )
        {
            itoa ( x, str2, 10 ) ;
            writestring ( str2, row, col, 112 ) ;
            col = col + 6 ;

            /* if September 1752 knock off 11 days to accomodate the
               changeover from Julian to Gregorian calendar */
            if ( y == 1752 && m == 9 && x == 2 )
                x = 13 ;

            if ( col > 43 )
            {
                row = row + 2 ;
                col = 7 ;
            }

            if ( row > 18 && col == 7 )
                row = 10 ;
        }

        writestring ( "Change using arrow keys ", 22, 28, 112 ) ;
        writestring ( "Next year      Up", 10, 49, 112 ) ;
        writestring ( "Previous year   Dn", 12, 49, 112 ) ;
        writestring ( "Next month     Rt", 14, 49, 112 ) ;
```

```
writestring ( "Previous month  Lt", 16, 49, 112 ) ;
writestring ( "Esc for exit", 18, 49, 112 ) ;
getkey( ) ;

/* check which is the next calendar required */
switch ( scan )
{
    case 72 :  /* up arrow */

        y++ ;
        break ;

    case 80 :  /* down arrow */

        y-- ;
        break ;

    case 77 :  /* right arrow */

        if ( m == 12 )
        {
            y = y + 1 ;
            m = 1 ;
        }
        else
            m = m + 1 ;

        break ;

    case 75 :  /* left arrow */

        if ( m == 1 )
        {
            y = y - 1 ;
            m = 12 ;
        }
        else
```

```
                        m = m - 1 ;

                break ;

          case 1 :  /* Esc key */

                writestring ( messages[1], 22, 14, 112 ) ;
                restorevideo ( 5, 5, 20, 70, p ) ;
                free ( p ) ;
                return ;
          }
     }
}

asciitable( )
{
     char *p, str[4] ;
     int areareqd, j, row, col ;

     areareqd = ( 20 - 5 + 1 ) * ( 70 - 5 + 1 ) * 2 ;
     p = malloc ( areareqd ) ;
     if ( p == NULL )
     {
          writestring ( messages[29], 22, 14, 112 ) ;
          getch( ) ;

          writestring ( messages[1], 22, 14, 112 ) ;
          return ;
     }

     savevideo ( 5, 5, 20, 70, p ) ;
     menubox ( 5, 5, 20, 70, 112, 66 ) ;

     writestring ( "       Display ascii table service              ", 22, 14, 112 ) ;

     row = 8 ;
     col = 10 ;
```

```
writestring ( "Value", row - 2, col - 2, 112 ) ;
writestring ( "Character", row - 2, col + 5,112) ;

/* display ascii table */
for ( j = 0 ; j <= 255 ; j++ )
{
    writechar ( row, ( col + 9 ), j, 112 ) ;  /* display character */

    itoa ( j, str, 10 ) ;
    writestring ( str, row, col, 112 ) ;  /* display value */

    row++ ;

    /* if screen is full */
    if ( row >= 18 )
    {
        row = 8 ;
        col += 19 ;

        if ( col > 48 )
        {
            writestring ( messages[28], 22, 14, 112 ) ;
            getch() ;
            row = 8 ;
            col = 10 ;
            menubox ( 5, 5, 20, 70, 112 ) ;
        }

        writestring ( "Value", row - 2, col - 2, 112 ) ;
        writestring ( "Character", row - 2, col + 5,112 ) ;
    }
}

writestring ( messages[28], 22, 14, 112 ) ;
getch() ;
```

```
        writestring ( messages[1], 22, 14, 112 ) ;
        restorevideo ( 5, 5, 20, 70, p ) ;
        free ( p ) ;
}

systeminfo( )
{
        union REGS ii, oo ;
        int areareqd, a, n ;
        char *p, str[3] ;

        areareqd = ( 20 - 5 + 1 ) * ( 70 - 5 + 1 ) * 2 ;
        p = malloc ( areareqd ) ;
        if ( p == NULL )
        {
                writestring ( messages[29], 22, 14, 112 ) ;
                getch( ) ;

                writestring ( messages[1], 22, 14, 112 ) ;
                return ;
        }

        savevideo ( 5, 5, 20, 70, p ) ;
        menubox ( 5, 5, 18, 65, 112, 66 ) ;

        writestring ( "        Display equipment list service            ", 22, 14, 112 ) ;

        writestring ( "Equipment list", 6, 16, 112 ) ;
        writestring ( "-------------", 7, 16, 112 ) ;

        /* call ROM BIOS equipment list routine */
        int86 ( 17, &ii, &oo ) ;
        a = oo.x.ax ;

        /* segregate information stored in bits and display it */

        if ( ( a & 1 ) == 0 )
```

```
        writestring ( "Disk drive: Absent", 9, 8, 112 ) ;
else
        writestring ( "Disk drive: Present", 9, 8, 112 ) ;

if ( ( a & 2 ) == 0 )
        writestring ( "Math co-processor: Absent", 10, 8, 112 ) ;
else
        writestring ( "Math co-processor: Present", 10, 8, 112 ) ;

writestring ( "Initial video mode:", 11, 8, 112 ) ;
n = ( a & 48 ) ;
switch ( n )
{
        case 48 :
                writestring ( "80 x 25 BW with mono card", 11, 28, 112 ) ;
                break ;

        case 32 :
                writestring ( "80 x 25 BW with color card", 11, 28, 112 ) ;
                break ;

        case 16 :
                writestring ( "40 x 25 BW with color card", 11, 28, 112 ) ;
}

if ( ( a & 1 ) == 1 )   /* if disk drive is present */
{
        n = ( a & 0x00C0 ) >> 6 ;
        writestring ( "No. of disk drives:", 12, 8, 112 ) ;
        writestring ( itoa ( n + 1, str, 10 ), 12, 28, 112 ) ;
}

n = ( a & 0x100 ) ;
if ( n == 0x100 )
        writestring ( "DMA: Absent", 16, 8, 112 ) ;
else
        writestring ( "DMA: Present", 16, 8, 112 ) ;
```

```
        n = ( a << 4 ) >> 13 ;
        writestring ( "No. of serial ports present:", 13, 8, 112 ) ;
        writestring ( itoa ( n, str, 10 ), 13, 37, 112 ) ;

        if ( ( a & 0x1000 ) == 0 )
            writestring ( "Game adapter: Absent", 14, 8, 112 ) ;
        else
            writestring ( "Game adapter: Present", 14, 8, 112 ) ;

        n = a >> 14 ;
        writestring ( "No. of parallel ports present:", 15, 8, 112 ) ;
        writestring ( itoa ( n, str, 10 ), 15, 39, 112 ) ;

        writestring ( messages[28], 22, 14, 112 ) ;
        getch( ) ;

        restorevideo ( 5, 5, 20, 70, p ) ;
        free ( p ) ;
}

/* 2-D array for setting up the grid in Shuffle */
int num [4][4] = {
                        2, 11, 15, 1,
                        6, 4, 3, 14,
                        8, 7, 9, 10,
                        5, 12, 13, 0
                } ;

shuffle( )
{
    int r = 3, c = 3, t, flag, areareqd ;

    /* number of moves in which the numbers are arranged in ascending
       order */
    int no_moves = 0 ;
```

```c
char *p, str[5] ;

areareqd = ( 25 - 0 + 1 ) * ( 80 - 0 + 1 ) * 2 ;
p = malloc ( areareqd ) ;
if ( p == NULL )
{
    writestring ( messages[29], 22, 14, 112 ) ;
    getch( ) ;

    writestring ( messages[1], 22, 14, 112 ) ;
    return ;
}

savevideo ( 0, 0, 24, 79, p ) ;
menubox ( 5, 14, 19, 65, 112, 66 ) ;

writestring ( "     Video game service     ", 22, 20, 112 ) ;

/* draw 16 squares */
shufflebox( ) ;

writestring ( "Hit arrow keys to shift numbers", 16, 23, 112 ) ;
writestring ( "Press Esc to abort", 17, 23, 112 ) ;

while ( 1 )
{
    /* display numbers in the grid */
    display( ) ;

    /* get user's response */
    getkey( ) ;

    switch ( scan )
    {
        case 80 :  /* down arrow key */

            /* if space is not present in top row */
```

```
                  if ( r != 0 )
                  {
                      t = num [r][c] ;
                      num[r][c] = num[r-1][c] ;
                      num[r-1][c] = t ;
                      r-- ;

                      /* increment the number of moves made */
                      no_moves++ ;
                  }

                  break ;

          case 72 :  /* up arrow key */

                  /* if space is not present in bottom row */
                  if ( r != 3 )
                  {
                      t = num[r][c] ;
                      num[r][c] = num[r+1][c] ;
                      num[r+1][c] = t ;
                      r++ ;

                      /* increment the number of moves made */
                      no_moves++ ;
                  }

                  break ;

          case 75 :  /* left arrow key */

                  /* if space is not present in rightmost column */
                  if ( c != 3 )
                  {
                      t = num[r][c] ;
                      num[r][c] = num[r][c+1] ;
                      num[r][c+1] = t ;
```

```
            c++ ;

            /* increment the number of moves made */
            no_moves++ ;
        }

        break ;

    case 77 :  /* right arrow key */

        /* if space is not present in leftmost column */
        if ( c != 0 )
        {
            t = num[r][c] ;
            num[r][c] = num[r][c-1] ;
            num[r][c-1] = t ;
            c-- ;

            /* increment the number of moves made */
            no_moves++ ;
        }

        break ;

    case 1 :  /* Esc key */

        writestring ( "        Goodbye!        ", 16, 23, 112 ) ;
        writestring ( "   Better luck next time   ", 17, 23, 112 ) ;
        writestring ( messages[28], 22, 14, 112 ) ;
        getch( ) ;

        writestring ( messages[1], 22, 14, 112 ) ;
        restorevideo ( 0, 0, 24, 79, p ) ;
        free ( p ) ;
        return ;

}
```

```
            /* check whether numbers have been arranged in ascending order */
            flag = check( ) ;

            if ( flag == 0 )
            {
                display( ) ;
                writestring ( "Success! You have done it!!   ", 16, 23, 112 ) ;
                writestring ( "No. of moves -   ", 17, 23, 112 ) ;
                itoa ( no_moves, str, 10 ) ;
                writestring ( str, 17, 38, 112 ) ;
                writestring ( messages[28], 22, 14, 112 ) ;
                getch( ) ;

                restorevideo ( 0, 0, 24, 79, p ) ;
                free ( p ) ;
                return ;
            }
        }
}

/* draw 16 squares (4 x 4 grid) for displaying the numbers */
shufflebox( )
{
    int row, col ;

    for ( col = 32 ; col <= 44 ; col++ )
    {
        for ( row = 6 ; row <= 14 ; row += 2 )
            writechar ( row, col, 196, 112 ) ;
    }

    for ( row = 7 ; row <= 13 ; row += 2 )
    {
        for ( col = 32 ; col <= 44 ; col += 3 )
            writechar ( row, col, 179, 112 ) ;
    }
```

```
    for ( row = 8 ; row <= 12 ; row += 2 )
    {
        for ( col = 35 ; col <= 41 ; col += 3 )
            writechar ( row, col, 197, 112 ) ;
    }

    for ( row = 8 ; row <= 12 ; row += 2 )
    {
        writechar ( row, 32, 195, 112 ) ;
        writechar ( row, 44, 180, 112 ) ;
    }

    for ( col = 35 ; col <= 41 ; col += 3 )
    {
        writechar ( 6, col, 194, 112 ) ;
        writechar ( 14, col, 193, 112 ) ;
    }

    writechar ( 6, 32, 218, 112 ) ;
    writechar ( 6, 44, 191, 112 ) ;
    writechar ( 14, 32, 192, 112 ) ;
    writechar ( 14, 44, 217, 112 ) ;
}

/* displays numbers within the 4 x 4 grid */
display( )
{
    int i, j, row = 7, col = 33 ;
    char str[5] ;

    for ( i = 0 ; i <= 3 ; i++ )
    {
        for ( j = 0 ; j <= 3 ; j++ )
        {
            /* if the array element is 0, write spaces */
            if ( num[i][j] == 0 )
                writestring ( "   ", row, col, 112 ) ;
```

```
            else
            {
                itoa ( num[i][j], str, 10 ) ;
                writestring ( str, row, col, 112 ) ;
            }

            col += 3 ;
            if ( col > 42 )
            {
                col = 33 ;
                row += 2 ;
            }
        }
    }
}

check( )
{
    int row, col ;

    int result[4][4] = {
                        1, 2, 3, 4,
                        5, 6, 7, 8,
                        9, 10, 11, 12,
                        13, 14, 15, 0
                    } ;

    for ( row = 0 ; row <= 3 ; row++ )
    {
        for ( col = 0 ; col <= 3 ; col++ )
        {
            /* if there is a mismatch return to receive user's next move */
            if ( num[row][col] != result[row][col] )
                return ( 1 ) ;
        }
    }
```

```
        return ( 0 ) ;
}

/* finds out memory capacity of the computer */
memsize( )
{
        union REGS ii, oo ;
        int areareqd, n ;
        char *p, str[6] ;

        areareqd = ( 20 - 5 + 1 ) * ( 70 - 5 + 1 ) * 2 ;
        p = malloc ( areareqd ) ;
        if ( p == NULL )
        {
            writestring ( messages[29], 22, 14, 112 ) ;
            getch( ) ;

            writestring ( messages[1], 22, 14, 112 ) ;
            return ;
        }

        savevideo ( 5, 5, 20, 70, p ) ;
        menubox ( 9, 15, 12, 47, 112, 66 ) ;

        /* issue interrupt for getting the base memory size */
        int86 ( 18, &ii, &oo ) ;
        n = oo.x.ax ;

        writestring ( "Base memory size:", 10, 18, 112 ) ;
        itoa ( n, str, 10 ) ;
        writestring ( str, 10, 36, 112 ) ;
        writestring ( "KB", 10, 40, 112 ) ;

        writestring ( messages[28], 22, 14, 112 ) ;
        getch( ) ;

        writestring ( messages[1], 22, 14, 112 ) ;
```

```
    restorevideo ( 5, 5, 20, 70, p ) ;
    free ( p ) ;
}

/* displays the logo on the screen */
logo( )
{
    int i, j ;

    for ( i = 2 ; i <= 20 ; i++ )
    {
        for ( j = 2 ; j <= 77 ; j++ )
            writechar ( i, j, 176, 7 ) ;
    }

    writestring ("      Designed & Written     ", 13, 26, 112 ) ;
    writestring ("            by               ", 14, 26, 112 ) ;
    writestring ("     Yashavant Kanetkar       ", 15, 26, 112 ) ;
    writestring ("            At               ", 16, 26, 112 ) ;
    writestring ("    ICIT, 44-A, Gokulpeth     ", 17, 26, 112 ) ;
    writestring ("     Nagpur-440010, India     ", 18, 26, 112 ) ;
    writestring ("     Ph. 531046, 535809       ", 19, 26, 112 ) ;
    writestring ("      Press any key...        ", 22, 26, 112 ) ;

    writestring ("                                              ", 3, 5, 77 ) ;
    writestring (" ** ** ****** **    ****** *** *** ******* ******** ****** ",
        4, 5, 77 ) ;
    writestring (" ** ** ** **    **    ** ** ** * * ** **   **    **   ",
        5, 5, 77 ) ;
    writestring (" ** ** ** **    **    ** ** ** *** ** **   **    **   ",
        6, 5, 77 ) ;
    writestring (" ****** ***** **    ****** ** * ** *******   **    ***** ",
        7, 5, 77 ) ;
    writestring (" ** ** ** **    **    **    ** * ** ** **   **    **   ",
        8, 5, 77 ) ;
    writestring (" ** ** ** **    **    **    ** ** ** **   **    **  ",
        9, 5, 77 ) ;
```

```
writestring ( " **  **  *****  *****  **     **    **  **  **    **     ***** ",
     10, 5, 77 ) ;
writestring ( "                                                    ", 11, 5, 77 ) ;
getch( ) ;
}
```

User Defined Functions

asciitable( )	Displays the characters and their ascii values.
calendar( )	Displays the calendar for the specified month and year. Arrow keys help you browse through the calendar monthwise or yearwise.
changedir( )	Changes the default directory to the specified directory on a specified drive.
check( )	Checks whether the user has succeeded in arranging the numbers in the Shuffle game in ascending order. If so, flashes a congratulatory message.
compress( )	Removes all blank spaces in a file so as to reduce the size of the file.
copyfile( )	Copies the contents of a source file into a target file.
decompress( )	Restores all the blank spaces in a file which has been previously compressed.
decryptfile( )	Decrypts an encoded file to get back the original file.
deletefile( )	Deletes a file from the specified/default drive and directory. Only one file can be deleted at a time. Wildcard characters are not allowed in the file specification.
dirtree( )	Displays the directory tree, starting from the root. The current working directory is highlighted.
display( )	Displays the numbers within the box created by **shufflebox**( ). This function is called after every move made by the user to update the current position of the numbers.
displayfile( )	Acts like the TYPE command of DOS. Additional features include page-by-page display and the display of the page number and the name of the file.
displaymenu( )	Displays the specified menu.

drawbox( )	Draws a double-lined rectangle with the specified attribute.
dserver( )	Displays Directory Services menu, receives user's choice and passes control to the appropriate function for performing the directory service requested by the user.
encryptfile( )	Encrypts a file. Each character is read from the source file, encoded and then stored in the target file.
fserver( )	Displays File Services menu, and depending on the choice made by the user calls the appropriate function for performing a file service.
getfileattb( )	Displays the current attributes of a file.
getkey( )	Reads a character from the keyboard, returns the ascii code and keyboard scan code of the character read.
getresponse( )	Gets the user's response after the menu has been popped up. Returns either when the user selects an option by hitting the Enter key or the hot key, or if the user abandons the menu by pressing Esc.
listdir( )	Functions like the DIR/p command of DOS.
logo( )	Displays the opening screen as soon as Helpmate is run.
mainscreen( )	Draws boxes using **drawbox**( ) and fills the inner box with character whose ascii value is 177. It also displays messages at the top and bottom of the screen.
makedir( )	Creates a new subdirectory on the specified drive and path.
memsize( )	Reports the amount of memory in the computer.
menubox( )	Fills a rectangular area with the specified color. Creates shadow for this rectangular area as per the value of **shad**.
mserver( )	Pops up the Miscellaneous Services menu, receives the user's choice and switches control to the appropriate function.
popupmenu( )	Pops up the specified menu at a specified position

	on the screen. Provides context sensitive help for the menu being displayed. Calls function **getresponse( )** to get the user's choice from the menu items displayed.
removedir( )	Deletes a directory from the specified drive and path.
restorevideo( )	Copies contents of a block of memory (RAM) to the specified rectangular portion on the screen. The rectangle is defined by its corner coordinates and the area in memory by a pointer to the memory chunk.
savevideo( )	Copies text and its attribute from a specified rectangular portion of the screen to a block of memory.
setfileattb( )	Changes the current attributes of a file.
setmode( )	Sets the specified video mode, by issuing interrupt 16.
shuffle( )	Calls **shufflebox( )** and **display( )** to construct the grid and to display the numbers in it. Depending on the arrow key hit, swaps the numbers till **check( )** reports that they have been arranged in ascending order.
shufflebox( )	Draws a grid of 16 squares.
size( )	Changes the size of the cursor by specifying the starting and ending scan lines for the cursor. To turn off the cursor the starting scan line is set to a value greater than the ending scan line.
systeminfo( )	Displays the list of equipment attached to the computer.
tree( )	Searches the entries matching the skeleton "*.*". Displays the matching entry if it happens to be a sub-directory name.
writeattr( )	Displays the attributes of the specified file. Used by functions **getfileattb( )** and **setfileattb( )**.
writechar( )	Writes a character and its attribute into VDU memory. Unlike the standard library functions,

	this can control the color of the character being displayed.
writestring( )	Uses function **writechar**( ) to write entire strings into VDU memory. Since the attribute of individual characters can be controlled, the hot key of the menu item can be displayed in a different attribute than the rest of the string.

2

Easyedit

Wordprocessors have a stimulating history of their own. At the beginning of it stand line editors like "EX" and "ED" (Unix based) and EDLIN (DOS based). However, these line editors had one big disadvantage - while using them, the screen of the computer didn't look exactly like the file contents. Moreover, some of these editors were so elementary that the user was required to use one program for entering a document and another for printing it. And then a new star, 'WordStar' was born on the horizon, which changed the entire wordprocessing scenario. Here was a program which could edit and print a document, which could do cut and paste operations, search and replace strings, merge and proofread files, and many more activities. WordStar enjoys a star status even today in the world of wordprocessing, primarily because it is a screen editor unlike all its predecessors. A screen editor always displays the text as it occurs in the file. So much so, that one often overlooks the efforts that go into its development. This chapter intends to unveil what lies below these user-friendly programs. I am sure you would enjoy the journey.

The screen editor that we will create - Easyedit - supports several features. These have been grouped under five menus as shown in the following figure.

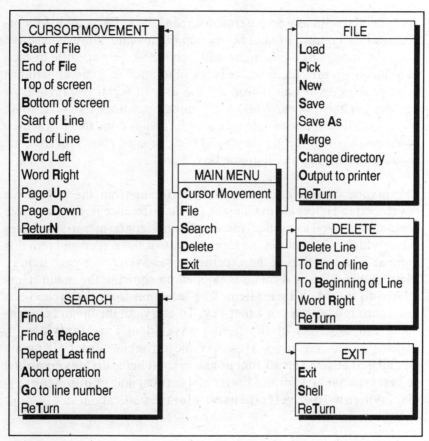

Figure 2.1

All developers of screen editors are faced with two important decisions when they set out to develop such a program. How much maximum line length and maximum file size should the editor support. We have chosen the line length to be 250. The maximum file size depends on the memory of the computer on which Easyedit is being run. To decide the maximum file size, firstly the amount of memory available for application programs is found out using the function **coreleft( )**. This memory size minus 5000 is then used as the maximum file size.

As expected with any professional screen editor, Easyedit too incorporates two common features - popup menus and context sensitive help. For menus like File menu and Exit menu, help specific to each item has been provided, whereas for other menus, general help has been provided with an option for the user to scroll to previous or subsequent help pages. While performing operations like save, load, print, etc. file names have to be entered. This is done in a box which is popped upon currently displayed file contents. Here onwards, we would call this box as 'dialogue box'.

The menus of Easyedit are a little different from the menus we developed in Helpmate in Chapter 1. The difference is, here we have horizontal as well as vertical menus. The horizontal menu is the Main menu which is laid out in the topmost row of the screen and remains there at all times during the execution of Easyedit. For each item in Main menu, a vertical menu is popped up showing the menu items related to the Main menu item. The selection from the menu is as usual through hotkeys or Enter key. To carry out the menu management, the usual set of functions - **savevideo( )**, **restorevideo( )**, **getkey( )**, etc. are used. However the difference from Helpmate menus is that two sets of functions are used here; **displaymenuh( )** & **getresponseh( )** for the horizontal menus, and **popupmenuv( )**, **displaymenuv( )** & **getresponsev( )** for the vertical ones.

Current Locations

One of the most imporant tasks in writing a screen editor is to keep the contents of the file and the contents of the screen synchronised at all times. To do so, we must understand the concept of 'current location'. For lack of a better term, the current location is the point at which the next action will take place. But whatever we do - type text, or delete text, or simply move the cursor - the action should take place in the file as well as on the screen. It means it is necessary to maintain two linked, but physically separate concepts of the 'current location'. There are several things which complicate the linkage between the screen's current location and the file's current location. These are as follows:

(a) The file is a linear entity, whereas the screen is two- dimensional.

(b) The entire file is available at all times, whereas the screen can hold only a portion of the file.

(c) A tab is stored as a single character in the file, whereas it is represented as 8 spaces on the screen. This makes the matter more complicated, since while traversing the file, skipping of a tab in the file requires skipping 8 columns on the screen.

(d) Since Easyedit accepts a maximum line length of 250 characters, if the cursor is to be positioned after the 78th column, the entire screen contents have to be scrolled horizontally.

To tackle these complications, some global variables are used in Easyedit. Its crucial for you to understand the significance of these variables. They are listed below:

Pointer	Significance
startloc	Points to the first character of the file
endloc	Points immediately after the last character in the file
currow	Points to the first character in the line in which the cursor is currently present
curscr	Points to the first character in the topmost line of current screen

Figure 2.2

The file being edited is always stored in the buffer. Therefore the pointers listed in the above figure, really speaking, point to this buffer. The user must not be allowed to move past the beginning or the end of the buffer while moving the cursor around using PgUp, PgDn or other cursor movement keys. As you will see, there is significant code in Easyedit dedicated to preventing the current location from backing up over the beginning of the buffer, or moving past its end. This may look like a minor detail, but believe me, horrible errors can creep in quite easily unless these boundaries are maintained at all times.

Throughout the program you would time and again encounter two sets of variables, **logr**, **logc**, and **curr**, **curc**. These variables basically represent the current cursor position. Remember that Easyedit allows a maximum line length of 250 characters, whereas the screen can at a time display only 78 characters. Hence, it is quite possible that the cursor is present on the 200th character in the line, whereas with respect to the left edge of the screen, this character may only be in the 15th column (earlier characters in the line having wrapped around the left edge). Therefore, cursor position needs to be maintained with reference to the screen's left edge, as well as with respect to the beginning of the line. Precisely for this purpose, the two sets of variables mentioned above are used. **logc** relates the cursor position to the left edge of the screen, whereas **curc** relates it to the beginning of the line. Similarly, to monitor the cursor position with respect to the top edge of the screen and the beginning of the file, the variables **logr** and **curr** respectively are used. The current values of **curr** and **curc** are displayed at all times in lower right corner of the screen using functions **writerow( )** and **writecol( )**.

Another important variable used in Easyedit is **skip**. Whenever the screen contents scroll horizontally, the variable **skip** is set up with a value equal to the number of columns the matter has scrolled.

The Easyedit Main Loop

Easyedit is driven by a main loop which performs two basic functions. First it receives keyboard input using the function **getkey( )**, and, second, it takes appropriate action based on what the user has typed. Basically there are two categories of keys that the user can hit: those

those which are characters to be entered into the current file, and those which are commands to the editor to perform a specific operation. The keystrokes which Easyedit recognises as command keys are shown in the following figure.

Key	Meaning
F1	Display help
F2	Save current file
Alt-X	Exit from Easyedit
Alt-C	Display Cursor Movement menu
Alt-F	Display File menu
Alt-S	Display Search menu
Alt-D	Display Delete menu
Alt-E	Display Exit menu
F10	Activate Main menu
Sh-F10	Display product information
Up/Down	Move cursor one line up/down
Left/Right	Move cursor one character left/right
PgUp/PgDn	Display previous/next file page
Home/End	Move cursor to beginning/end of line
Ctrl-PgUp/PgDn	Move cursor to beginning/end of file
Ctrl-Home/End	Move cursor to top/bottom of screen
Ctrl-Left/Right	Move cursor one word left/right
Del	Delete character at cursor
Backspace	Delete character to the left of cursor
Ctrl-T	Delete word to the right of cursor
Ctrl-Y	Delete line in which cursor is present
Ctrl-L	Repeat last search operation

Figure 2.3

The editor's main loop is contained in **main**( ) which is shown below.

```
main ( argc, argv )
int argc ;
char *argv[ ] ;
{
    int flag ;

    /* if more than one filename is supplied at DOS prompt */
    if ( argc > 2 )
    {
        printf ( "\nInvalid number of parameters!" ) ;
        printf ( "\nPress any key..." ) ;
        fflush ( stdin ) ;
        getch() ;
        exit ( 1 ) ;
    }

    #ifdef CGA
    {
        vid_mem = ( char far * ) 0xb8000000L ;
        textmode ( 3 ) ;
    }
    #else
    {
        vid_mem = ( char far * ) 0xb0000000L ;
        textmode ( 7 ) ;
    }
    #endif

    /* capture Ctrl - C interrupt */
    old23 = getvect ( 0x23 ) ;
    setvect ( 0x23, handler ) ;

    /* capture Ctrl - Break interrupt */
    old1b = getvect ( 0x1b ) ;
    setvect ( 0x1b, handler ) ;
```

```
/* calculate the maximum buffer size */
maxsize = coreleft( ) - 5000 ;

/* allocate memory, check if successful */
buf = malloc ( maxsize ) ;
if ( buf == NULL )
    error_exit( ) ;

/* initialise pointers to point to buf */
startloc = endloc = curscr = currow = buf ;

/* set Ins key to on */
*ins |= 0x80 ;

/* set default file name as 'NONAME' */
strcpy ( filespec, "NONAME" ) ;

workscreen( ) ;  /* display working screen */
displaymenuh ( mainmenu, 5 ) ;  /* display the main menu */
about( ) ;  /* display product information message */

/* if file name to be edited is specified in the command line */
if ( argc == 2 )
{
    /* load specified file */
    strcpy ( filespec, argv[1] ) ;
    flag = load( ) ;

    /* if unsuccessful in loading file */
    if ( flag == 0 )
    {
        strcpy ( filespec, "NONAME" ) ;
        write_fname( ) ;
    }
}
```

```
while ( 1 )
{
    gotoxy ( logc + 1, logr + 2 ) ;  /* position cursor */
    getkey( ) ;  /* receive key */

    /* display status of Insert key */
    if ( *ins & 0x80 )
        writestring ( "Insert", 24, 73, 47 ) ;
    else
        writestring ( "    ", 24, 73, 112 ) ;

    /* if special key has been hit */
    if ( ascii == 0 )
    {
        /* check which special key */
        switch ( scan )
        {
            case 59 :  /* F1 key */

                    displayhelp ( 1 ) ;
                    break ;

            case 60 :  /* F2 key */

                    save( ) ;
                    break ;

            case 45 :  /* Alt - X */

                    check_saved( ) ;
                    exit ( 0 ) ;

            case 46 :  /* Alt - C */

                    /* highlight the menu item */
                    writestring ( mainmenu[0], 0, 2, 15 ) ;
```

```
                    /* call cursor movement services */
                    cserver( ) ;

                    /* make highlighted item normal */
                    writestring ( mainmenu[0], 0, 2, 112 ) ;

                    break ;

            case 33 :  /* Alt - F */

                    /* highlight the menu item */
                    writestring ( mainmenu[1], 0, 25, 15 ) ;

                    /* call file services */
                    fserver( ) ;

                    /* make highlighted item normal */
                    writestring ( mainmenu[1], 0, 25, 112 ) ;

                    break ;

            case 31 :  /* Alt - S */

                    writestring ( mainmenu[2], 0, 37, 15 ) ;
                    sserver( ) ;
                    writestring ( mainmenu[2], 0, 37, 112 ) ;
                    break ;

            case 32 :  /* Alt - D */

                    writestring ( mainmenu[3], 0, 51, 15 ) ;
                    dserver( ) ;
                    writestring ( mainmenu[3], 0, 51, 112 ) ;
                    break ;

            case 18 :  /* Alt - E */
```

```
                    writestring ( mainmenu[4], 0, 65, 15 ) ;
                    eserver( ) ;
                    writestring ( mainmenu[4], 0, 65, 112 ) ;
                    break ;

            case 68 :  /* F10 key */

                    mm_server( ) ;
                    break ;

            case 93 :  /* Shift F10 */

                    about( ) ;
                    break ;

            case 75 :  /* left arrow key */

                    left( ) ;
                    break ;

            case 77 :  /* right arrow key */

                    right( ) ;
                    break ;

            case 72 :  /* up arrow key */

                    up_line ( 1 ) ;
                    break ;

            case 80 :  /* down arrow key */

                    down_line ( 1 ) ;
                    break ;

            case 73 :  /* PgUp key */
```

```
        page_up ( 1 ) ;
        break ;

case 81 :  /* PgDn key */

        page_down( ) ;
        break ;

case 71 :  /* Home key */

        start_line( ) ;
        break ;

case 79 :  /* End key */

        end_line( ) ;
        break ;

case 132 :  /* Ctrl - PgUp */

        start_file( ) ;
        break ;

case 118 :  /* Ctrl - PgDn */

        end_file( ) ;
        break ;

case 119 :  /* Ctrl - Home */

        top_screen( ) ;
        break ;

case 117 :  /* Ctrl - End */

        bottom_screen( ) ;
        break ;
```

```
                case 115 :  /* Ctrl - left arrow */

                    word_left( ) ;
                    break ;

                case 116 :  /* Ctrl - right arrow */

                    word_right( ) ;
                    break ;

                case 83 :  /* Del key */

                    del_char( ) ;
                    break ;
            }
        }
        else
        {
            switch ( ascii )
            {
                case 8 : /* backspace key */

                    backspace( ) ;
                    break ;

                case 20 :  /* Ctrl - T */

                    del_word_rt( ) ;
                    break ;

                case 25 :  /* Ctrl - Y */

                    del_line( ) ;
                    break ;

                case 12 :  /* Ctrl - L */
```

```
                    repeat_last( ) ;
                    break ;

            default :

                    /* if the character is valid character */
                    if ( ( ascii >= 32 && ascii <= 126 ) || ascii == 13  ||
                        ascii == 9 )
                        displaychar ( ascii ) ;
                }
            }
        }
}
```

When Easyedit starts executing, firstly the opening screen is prepared by the function **workscreen( )** and then the product information is displayed through the function **about( )**. Really speaking, the product information doesn't have anything to do with the actual working of Easyedit. It has been included just to give Easyedit a professional look.

Next, Easyedit checks whether the file to be edited has been entered as a command line argument by the user. If so, this file is searched and loaded into the buffer using the function **load( )**. Once loaded, the pointers **startloc, currow** and **curscr** are set to point to the beginning of the buffer, whereas the pointer **endloc** is set to point beyond the last character in the file. Having set up the pointers, one screenful of text is displayed. If the file specified at command line doesn't exist, then **load( )** permits the user to create a new file with the same name.

If no command line argument is specified, then Easyedit assumes 'NONAME' as the file name. Note that this file is not created on the disk. Once the user has typed in the matter, he can save the contents by using the option Save from the File menu. While saving,

'NONAME' is changed to whichever name the user specifies for saving.

After the initialisation of the file, the main loop begins. At each pass it waits for the key press and then processes the key stroke. As you might be aware, everytime a key is pressed, its ascii code and scan code gets generated. However, for the arrow keys, function keys, End, Home, PgUp, PgDn, etc. ascii values are zero. This is the reason that these keys are treated separately from the others, using their own **switch** statement. Each time one of these keys is pressed, the corresponding function is called. When a normal key is pressed, the **default** case of the second **switch** statement executes, which calls the function **displaychar( )**. This function checks whether there is room for another character in the buffer and whether the line length is less than 250. **displaychar( )** has to take into account the following possibilities:

(a)   Cursor is at or beyond the end of file or end of line, and a space bar is hit. In such a case the cursor is just moved one position to the right.

(b)   Cursor is at or beyond the end of file or end of line, and any character other than space is hit. In such a case irrespective of the status of the Ins key, the character is inserted at current cursor position. Naturally, if the current cursor position is say five columns to the right of end of line, then four spaces would be inserted before the character. The entire line is then reprinted using the function **displayline( )**. The reprinting of the line is necessary for the screen to reflect the current state of the file.

(c)   Cursor is somewhere in the middle of a line and a key is pressed with Ins on. This case is tackled by first making space in the buffer to accommodate the character and then inserting the character in the buffer. The space is created in the buffer by moving its contents at the current location using the function **memmove( )**.

If Ins is off, then the character hit overwrites the character at current cursor location. This change made in the buffer is then reflected on the screen using the function **writechar( )**.

Finally, the pointer **endloc** is updated appropriately in all the above cases.

When the user hits the Enter key, a somewhat more complicated sequence of actions occurs. The action taken varies depending on the status of Ins key. If Ins is on, then the part of the line after current cursor location is shifted to the next line. To accommodate this part in the next line, firstly the screen contents below the current line are scrolled down using the function **scrolldown( )**. Next the current line and the next line are updated using the function **displayline( )**. Thus instead of rewriting the entire screen, only the modified part is rebuilt. This makes the editor faster and gives it a snappier feel. However, if the Enter is pressed at the bottom of the screen, the entire display is scrolled up using the function **scrollup( )**, and the necessary part rebuilt. If Ins is off when Enter key is hit, the cursor is just placed at the beginning of the next line.

If the user presses Backspace or Del, a character is removed from the file and the screen refreshed to reflect this change. Pressing Backspace removes the character present immediately to the left of current cursor position. Pressing Del removes the character at the current cursor position. The editing process continues till the user either selects New option from the File menu, or hits Alt-X to exit from Easyedit.

Moving the Cursor around

Any editor should have facilities to take the cursor to a desired position in shortest time. To this effect Easyedit provides a number of cursor movement commands like Beginning of file, End of file, Page up, Page down, Top of screen, Bottom of screen, Beginning of line, End of line, and so on. While using these commands, the pointers **currow** and **curscr** are appropriately updated. Since while moving the cursor the file contents are not modified, the value of the pointer **endloc** doesn't change. At all times care is taken to prevent the cursor from moving past the last line in the file.

If the cursor is moved beyond the last line or before the first line of the screen, the contents are scrolled by invoking ROM BIOS routines through the functions **scrollup( )** and **scrolldown( )**. If cursor is moved beyond the 78th character in the line, the screen contents wrap around the left edge of the screen. By how many columns the wrapping takes place is monitored by the variable **skip**.

Of all the cursor movement commands, the ones you would find most difficult to understand are possibly Word left and Word right. This is because they involve a lot many considerations. Like where to place the cursor if the cursor is currently at the end of the line, and Word right is selected - at the beginning of the next line or on the first alphanumeric character of the next line? The fact that the next alphanumeric character may not be in the immediately next line, further complicates the matters. A different treatment has to be meted out depending on whether the character at current cursor location is alphanumeric or non-alphanumeric. An easier way to sort out these possibilities would be to select a paragraph, assume a cursor position and then follow the logic given in the functions **word_left( )** and **word_right( )**.

Deleting Characters, Words and Lines

Easyedit lets you delete a character, an entire word, an entire line or a part of it. On deleting any of these entities, contents of the buffer are readjusted using the function **memmove( )**. The pointer **endloc** is decremented by the number of characters deleted. This change in buffer should now be displayed on the screen. For this the function **displayline( )** is called. If in the process of deletion a '\n' gets deleted, the screen below the current line is scrolled up using the function **scrollup( )**, and if necessary, the last line on the screen is displayed by calling **displayline( )** again.

Find and Replace

Easyedit lets you find a string everywhere it occurs in a file. The search string can have a maximum of 30 characters, which may be any combination of alphabets, numbers or special characters. The search string keyed in by the user is collected by the function **find( )** using **getstring( )**. Once collected, this string is passed on to the function **search( )** to carry out the search from current cursor location onwards. If the search is indeed successful, the cursor is positioned at the end of the searched string. The next occurrence of the string can be found out by either hitting Ctrl-L, or by selecting 'Repeat last find' from the Search menu.

A provision has also been made to replace the searched string with another string if desired. This is achieved by first collecting the search string and the replace string using the function **replace( )**. Then **search( )** goes to work and locates the string to be replaced. Next, the function **f_and_r( )** is called, which actually carries out the replacement, if confirmed by the user.

displayline( ) and displayscreen( )

As their names suggest, these functions display either one line of text or one screenful of text. **displayscreen( )** always displays the next 21 lines from the line at which **curscr** is pointing. As against this, **displayline( )** doesn't necessarily display the line at which **currow** is pointing. Not only are these functions called when the file contents are modified, but also when some cursor movement keys are pressed. For example, if the cursor is at the bottom of the screen and a down arrow key is pressed, then after scrolling the screen contents **displayline( )** is called to display the line in the last row.

The Pick Utility

What if the user loads a file, edits it, loads another file, and now wants to once again load the previous file? Does he have to go through the rigmarole of Load-Save-Load cycle? To avoid this clerical stuff the Pick utility has been provided. It pops up on the screen the names of five most recently edited files and lets the user pick up any one file which he intends to work on. This is managed by storing the file names in an array **pickfile[ ]**. This array is updated whenever the user works with a new file.

save( ) and save_as( )

save( ) is used whenever current file contents are to be stored on the disk. What does the user do if having saved the file, he further edits it and now wants to keep on the disk both the versions of the file. In such cases the option 'Save as' can be used. Exercising this option allows the current file contents to be saved under a different name. Whenever these file saving functions are used, a global variable **saved** is set to YES so that other functions in the editor would know the current status of the file. Any time the file contents are changed, this variable is set to NO. When the user attempts to either load a new file or exit from Easyedit, a function **check_saved( )** is called, which uses the variable **saved** to determine whether the user be given a chance to save the file or not.

Merging Files

The contents of two files can be merged by selecting the Merge option from the File menu. It reads in the contents of the specified file at current cursor location. On doing this the buffer contents are adjusted accordingly, and the change is reflected on the screen. Care has been taken to truncate the file if the combined contents of the two files exceed the maximum buffer size allowed.

The Status of Ins

Easyedit works either in insert mode or in overwrite mode. Naturally, the meaning of the key pressed would change as per the current status of the Ins key. Since all key presses are handled by Easyedit independently, the responsibility of changing the status of Ins key also lies with it. This it does by toggling the status bit (bit number 7) of Ins key stored at location 0x417 in memory.

The Ctrl-C Trap

Normally execution of any program in DOS gets terminated any time the user hits Ctrl-C or Ctrl-Break. What if these keys are hit in the middle of an editing session when you have not saved your work? Would the execution be immediately terminated and all the changes that you made since the last save be lost? No. Easyedit reacts to this eventuality intelligently. Normally interrupt numbers 0x23 and 0x1b get generated on hitting Ctrl-C and Ctrl-Break respectively, and the corresponding DOS routines get called, which then terminate the program execution. Easyedit prevents the calling of these DOS routines by capturing the aforesaid interrupts. As a result of this, hitting of Ctrl-C or Ctrl-Break causes the control to reach the function

handler( ). This function is a 'do nothing' function and therefore doesn't do anything except setting up a flag to tell the function **getkey**( ) that one of these keys have been hit. In turn, **getkey**( ) wipes out from the screen the '^C' generated as a result of pressing Ctrl-C.

Dialogue Boxes and Button Bars

At many places in the editor, it is necessary for the program to interact with the user. For example, while saving a file the name of the file has to be keyed in by the user. Similarly, while searching a string the name of the string has to be entered by the user. Whenever such a dialogue is sought with the user, a 'dialogue box' is popped up on the screen. This box pops off the screen once the interaction is over and the original screen contents are then restored. In Easyedit, this dialogue box is managed by the function **ask_name**( ).

Also, often during execution, a typical answer in the form Yes/No/Cancel is sought from the user. To achieve this interaction a function **message**( ) is used. This function displays Yes, No and Cancel in the form of what are popularly called 'button bars'. The speciality of the button bars is the type of shadow effect which goes with them. These shadows are created by writing graphic characters in appropriate attributes. In Easyedit this is achieved by the function **menubox**( ).

Program

The entire screen editor program has been split into three files, namely UTIL.C, CURSOR.C, EDITOR.C. The listings of these three files are given below.

UTIL.C

```c
# define CGA 1
# define ESC 27
# define YES 1
# define NO 0
# define NO_SHADOW 0
# define HALF_SHADOW -1

/* various menu definitions */
/* character following '^' is a hot key */
char *mainmenu[ ] =   {
                    "^Cursor Movement",
                    "^File",
                    "^Search",
                    "^Delete",
                    "^Exit"
                } ;

char *cursormenu[ ] = {
                    "^Start of File",
                    "End of ^File",
                    "^Top of screen",
                    "^Bottom of screen",
                    "Start of ^Line",
                    "^End of Line",
                    "^Word Left",
                    "Word ^Right",
```

```
                              "Page ^Up",
                              "Page ^Down",
                              "Retur^N"
                      } ;

char *filemenu[ ] = {
                      "^Load",
                      "^Pick",
                      "^New",
                      "^Save",
                      "Save ^As",
                      "^Merge",
                      "^Change dir",
                      "^Output to printer",
                      "Re^Turn"
                          } ;


char *searchmenu[ ] = {
                          "^Find",
                          "Find & ^Replace",
                          "Repeat ^Last find",
                          "^Abort operation",
                          "^Go to line no",
                          "Re^Turn"
                          } ;

char *deletemenu[ ] = {
                          "^Delete line",
                          "To ^End of line",
                          "To ^Beginning of Line",
                          "Word ^Right",
                          "Re^Turn"
                          } ;

char *exitmenu[ ] = {
                      "^Exit",
                      "^Shell",
```

```
                      "Re^Turn"
                } ;

/* most recent files edited */
char *pickfile[5] = {
                    "        ",
                    "        ",
                    "        ",
                    "        ",
                    "        "
                } ;


/* buffer in which files are loaded and manipulated */
char *buf ;

unsigned int maxsize ;
char *startloc, *curscr, *currow, *endloc ;
char searchstr[31], replacestr[31], filespec[30], filename[17] ;

void interrupt (*old1b)( ) ;
void interrupt handler( ) ;
void interrupt (*old23)( ) ;
char *search ( char * ) ;

int ascii, scan, pickfileno, no_tab ;
int curr = 2, curc = 1, logc = 1, logr = 1 ;
int skip, findflag, frflag, saved = YES, ctrl_c_flag = 0 ;

char far *vid_mem ;
char far *ins = ( char far * ) 0x417 ;

/* writes a character in specified attribute */
writechar ( r, c, ch, attb )
int r, c, attb ;
char ch ;
{
      char far *v ;
```

```
        v = vid_mem + r * 160 + c * 2 ;  /* calculate address corresponding to
                                        row r and column c */
        *v = ch ;  /* store ascii value of character */
        v++ ;
        *v = attb ;  /* store attribute of character */
}

/* writes a string in specified attribute */
writestring ( s, r, c, attb )
int r, c, attb ;
char *s ;
{
        while ( *s != '\0' )
        {
            /* if next character is the hot key of menu item */
            if ( *s == '^' )
            {
                s++ ;

                /* if hot key of highlighted bar */
                if ( attb == 15 )
                    writechar ( r, c, *s, 15 ) ;
                else
                    writechar ( r, c, *s, 113 ) ;
            }
            else
            {
                /* if next character is hot key of "Yes", "No", "Cancel", etc. */
                if ( *s == '$' )
                {
                    s++ ;
                    writechar ( r, c, *s, 47 ) ;
                }
                else
                    writechar ( r, c, *s, attb ) ;  /* normal character */
            }
```

```
            c++ ;
            s++ ;
        }
}

/* saves screen contents into allocated memory */
savevideo ( sr, sc, er, ec, buffer )
int sr, sc, er, ec ;
char *buffer ;
{
    char far *v ;
    int i, j ;

    for ( i = sr ; i <= er ; i++ )
    {
        for ( j = sc ; j <= ec ; j++ )
        {
            v = vid_mem + i * 160 + j * 2 ;
            *buffer = *v ;  /* store character */
            v++ ;
            buffer++ ;
            *buffer = *v ;  /* store attribute */
            buffer++ ;
        }
    }
}

/* restores screen contents from allocated memory */
restorevideo ( sr, sc, er, ec, buffer )
int sr, sc, er, ec ;
char *buffer ;
{
    char far *v ;
    int i, j ;

    for ( i = sr ; i <= er ; i++ )
```

```c
    {
        for ( j = sc ; j <= ec ; j++ )
        {
            v = vid_mem + i * 160 + j * 2 ;
            *v = *buffer ;  /* restore character */
            v++ ;
            buffer++ ;
            *v = *buffer ;  /* restore attribute */
            buffer++ ;
        }
    }
}

/* displays filled box with or without shadow */
menubox ( sr, sc, er, ec, fil, shad )
int sr, sc, er, ec ;
char fil, shad ;
{
    int i, j ;

    for ( i = sr ; i < er ; i++ )
        for ( j = sc ; j < ( ec - 1 ) ; j++ )
            writechar ( i, j, ' ', fil ) ;

    /* if no shadow is required for the filled box */
    if ( shad == NO_SHADOW )
    {
        for ( i = sr; i <= er ; i++ )
        {
            writechar ( i, ec, ' ', fil ) ;
            writechar ( i, ( ec - 1 ), ' ', fil ) ;
        }

        for ( j = sc ; j <= ec ; j++ )
            writechar ( er, j, ' ', fil ) ;
    }
    else
```

```
    {
            /* if half shadow required for the filled box */
            if ( shad == HALF_SHADOW )
            {
                for ( i = sr ; i <= er ; i++ )
                    writechar ( i, ( ec - 1 ), 220, 112 ) ;

                for ( j = sc + 1 ; j < ec ; j++ )
                    writechar ( er, j, 223, 112 ) ;
            }
            else
            {
                /* create normal shadow */
                for ( i = sr + 1 ; i <= er ; i++ )
                {
                    writechar ( i, ec, ' ', shad ) ;
                    writechar ( i, ( ec - 1 ), ' ', shad ) ;
                }

                for ( j = sc + 2 ; j <= ec ; j++ )
                writechar ( er, j, ' ', shad ) ;
            }
    }
}

/* draws a double-lined box */
drawbox ( sr, sc, er, ec, attr )
int sr, sc, er, ec, attr ;
{
    int i ;

    /* draw horizontal lines */
    for ( i = sc + 1 ; i < ec ; i++ )
    {
        writechar ( sr, i , 205, attr ) ;
        writechar ( er, i, 205, attr ) ;
    }
```

```
        /* draw vertical lines */
        for ( i = sr + 1 ; i < er ; i++ )
        {
             writechar ( i, sc, 186, attr ) ;
             writechar ( i, ec, 186, attr ) ;
        }

        /* display corner characters */
        writechar ( sr, sc, 201, attr ) ;
        writechar ( sr, ec, 187, attr ) ;
        writechar ( er, sc, 200, attr ) ;
        writechar ( er, ec, 188, attr ) ;
}

/* displays or hides cursor */
size ( ssl, esl )
int ssl, esl ;
{
        union REGS i, o ;

        i.h.ah = 1 ;  /* service number */
        i.h.ch = ssl ;  /* starting scan line */
        i.h.cl = esl ;  /* ending scan line */
        i.h.bh = 0 ;  /* video page number */

        /* issue interrupt for changing the size of the cursor */
        int86 ( 16, &i, &o ) ;
}

/* gets ascii and scan code of key pressed */
getkey( )
{
        union REGS i, o ;

        /* wait till a key is hit */
        while ( !kbhit( ) )
```

```
        {
            /* if Ctrl - C has been hit */
            if ( ctrl_c_flag )
            {
                /* erase the characters ^C */
                displayline ( currow, logr + 1 ) ;
                gotoxy ( logc + 1, logr + 2 ) ;
                ctrl_c_flag = 0 ;
            }
        }

        i.h.ah = 0 ;  /* service number */

        /* issue interrupt */
        int86 ( 22, &i, &o ) ;

        ascii = o.h.al ;
        scan = o.h.ah ;
    }

/* pops up a menu vertically */
popupmenuv ( menu, count, sr, sc, hotkeys, helpnumber )
int count, sr, sc, helpnumber ;
char **menu, *hotkeys ;
{
    int er, i, ec, l, len = 0, area, choice ;
    char *p ;

    size ( 32, 0 ) ;  /* hide cursor */

    /* calculate ending row for menu */
    er = sr + count + 2 ;

    /* find longest menu item */
    for ( i = 0 ; i < count ; i++ )
    {
        l = strlen ( menu[i] ) ;
```

```
        if ( l > len )
            len = l ;
}

/* calculate ending column for menu */
ec = sc + len + 5 ;

/* calculate area required to save screen contents where menu is to be
   popped up */
area = ( er - sr + 1 ) * ( ec - sc + 1 ) * 2 ;

p = malloc ( area ) ;  /* allocate memory */

/* if allocation fails */
if ( p == NULL )
    error_exit( ) ;

/* save screen contents into allocated memory */
savevideo ( sr, sc, er, ec, p ) ;

/* draw filled box with shadow */
menubox ( sr, sc + 1, er, ec, 112, 15 ) ;

/* draw a double lined box */
drawbox ( sr, sc + 1, er - 1, ec - 2, 112 ) ;

/* display the menu in the filled box */
displaymenuv ( menu, count, sr + 1, sc + 3 ) ;

/* receive user's choice */
choice = getresponsev ( menu, hotkeys, sr, sc + 2, count, helpnumber ) ;

/* restore original screen contents */
restorevideo ( sr, sc, er, ec, p ) ;

/* free allocated memory */
free ( p ) ;
```

```c
        size ( 5, 7 ) ;  /* set cursor to normal size */
        return ( choice ) ;
}


/* displays menu vertically */
displaymenuv ( menu, count, sr, sc )
int count, sr, sc ;
char **menu ;
{
    int i ;

    for ( i = 0 ; i < count ; i++ )
    {
        writestring ( menu[i], sr, sc, 112 ) ;
        sr++ ;
    }
}

/* receives user's choice for the vertical menu displayed */
getresponsev ( menu, hotkeys, sr, sc, count, helpnumber )
char **menu, *hotkeys ;
int sr, sc, count, helpnumber ;
{
    int choice = 1, len, hotkeychoice ;

    /* calculate number of hot keys for the menu */
    len = strlen ( hotkeys ) ;

    /* highlight the first menu item */
    writestring ( menu[choice - 1], sr + choice, sc + 1, 15 ) ;

    while ( 1 )
    {
        /* receive key */
        getkey( ) ;
```

```
/* if special key is hit */
if ( ascii == 0 )
{
    switch ( scan )
    {
        case 80 :  /* down arrow key */

            /* make highlighted item normal */
            writestring ( menu[choice - 1], sr + choice, sc + 1, 112 ) ;

            choice++ ;
            break ;

        case 72 :  /* up arrow key */

            /* make highlighted item normal */
            writestring ( menu[choice - 1], sr + choice, sc + 1, 112 ) ;

            choice-- ;
            break ;

        case 77 :  /* right arrow key */
            return ( 77 ) ;

        case 75 :  /* left arrow key */
            return ( 75 ) ;

        case 59 :  /* function key F1 for help */

            /* if current menu is file menu */
            if ( helpnumber == 3 )
            {
                /* if highlighted bar is not on return */
                if ( choice != 9 )
                {
                    /* call with appropriate help screen number */
                    displayhelp ( 8 + choice - 1 ) ;
```

```
                                }
                                break ;
                        }

                        /* if current menu is exit menu */
                        if ( helpnumber == 6 )
                        {
                                /* if highlighted bar is not on Return */
                                if ( choice != 3 )
                                {
                                        /* call with appropriate help screen number */
                                        displayhelp ( 16 + choice - 1 ) ;
                                }
                                break ;
                        }

                        /* if current menu is other than file menu or exit menu */
                        displayhelp ( helpnumber ) ;
                }

                /* if highlighted bar is on first item and up arrow key is hit */
                if ( choice == 0 )
                        choice = count ;

                /* if highlighted bar is on last item and down arrow key is hit */
                if ( choice > count )
                        choice = 1 ;

                /* highlight the appropriate menu item */
                writestring ( menu[choice - 1], sr + choice, sc + 1, 15 ) ;
        }
        else
        {
                if ( ascii == 13 )  /* Enter key */
                        return ( choice ) ;

                if ( ascii == ESC )
```

```
                {
                        displaymenuh ( mainmenu, 5 ) ;
                        return ( ESC ) ;
                }

                hotkeychoice = 1 ;
                ascii = toupper ( ascii ) ;

                /* check whether hot key has been pressed */
                while ( *hotkeys != '\0' )
                {
                        if ( *hotkeys == ascii )
                                return ( hotkeychoice ) ;
                        else
                        {
                                hotkeys++ ;
                                hotkeychoice++ ;
                        }
                }

                /* reset variable to point to the first hot key character */
                hotkeys = hotkeys - len ;
            }
        }
}

/* displays menu horizontally */
displaymenuh ( menu, count )
int count ;
char **menu ;
{
    int col = 2, i ;

    size ( 32, 0 ) ;
    menubox ( 0, 0, 0, 79, 112, NO_SHADOW ) ;

    for ( i = 0 ; i < count ; i++ )
```

```
        {
            writestring ( menu[i], 0, col, 112 ) ;
            col = col + ( strlen ( menu[i] ) ) + 7 ;
        }

        size ( 5, 7 ) ;
}

/* receives user's choice for the horizontal menu displayed */
getresponseh ( menu, hotkeys, count )
char *hotkeys, **menu ;
int count ;
{
        int choice = 1, hotkeychoice, len, col ;

        size ( 32, 0 ) ;
        col = 2 ;

        /* calculate number of hot keys for the menu */
        len = strlen ( hotkeys ) ;

        /* highlight the first menu item */
        writestring ( menu[choice - 1], 0, col, 15 ) ;

        while ( 1 )
        {
            /* receive key */
            getkey( ) ;

            /* if special key is hit */
            if ( ascii == 0 )
            {
                switch ( scan )
                {
                    case 77 :  /* right arrow key */

                        /* make highlighted item normal */
```

```
                    writestring ( menu[choice - 1], 0, col, 112 ) ;

                    col += strlen ( menu[choice - 1] ) + 7 ;
                    choice++ ;
                    break ;

            case 75 :  /* left arrow key */

                    /* make highlighted item normal */
                    writestring ( menu[choice - 1], 0, col, 112 ) ;

                    col -= ( strlen ( menu[choice - 2] ) + 7 ) ;
                    choice-- ;
                    break ;

            case 59 :  /* function key F1 for help */
                    if ( choice == 1 )
                            displayhelp ( 1 ) ;
                    else
                            displayhelp ( choice + 1 ) ;
    }

    /* if highlighted bar is on the first item and left arrow key is hit */
    if ( choice == 0 )
    {
            choice = count ;
            col = 65 ;
    }

    /* if highlghted bar is on the last item and right arrow key is hit */
    if ( choice > count )
    {
            choice = 1 ;
            col = 2 ;
    }

    /* highlight the appropriate menu item */
```

```
            writestring ( menu[choice - 1], 0, col, 15 ) ;
     }
     else
     {
         if ( ascii == 13 )  /* Enter key */
         {
             size ( 5, 7 ) ;
             return ( choice ) ;
         }

         if ( ascii == ESC )  /* Esc key */
         {
             /* make highlighted item normal */
             writestring ( menu[choice - 1], 0, col, 112 ) ;

             size ( 5, 7 ) ;
             return ( ESC ) ;
         }

         hotkeychoice = 1 ;
         ascii = toupper ( ascii ) ;

         /* check whether hot key has been pressed */
         while ( *hotkeys != '\0' )
         {
             if ( *hotkeys == ascii )
             {
                 size ( 5, 7 ) ;
                 return ( hotkeychoice ) ;
             }
             else
             {
                 hotkeys++ ;
                 hotkeychoice++ ;
             }
         }
     }
```

```
            /* reset variable to point to the first hot key character */
            hotkeys = hotkeys - len ;
        }
    }
}

/* displays context sensitive help */
displayhelp ( index )
int index ;
{
    char *p ;
    int areareqd, i, row ;

    /* help messages */
    char *help[ ] = {
                "Cursor Movement Commands",
                "------------------------------------------------------------- ",
                "Character left            Left arrow         ",
                "Character right           Right arrow        ",
                "Word left                 Ctrl - Left arrow  ",
                "Word right                Ctrl - Right arrow ",
                "Line up                   Up arrow           ",
                "Line down                 Down arrow         ",
                "Page up                   PgUp               ",
                "",
                "Cursor Movement Commands     ( Contd. )      ",
                "------------------------------------------------------------- ",
                "Page down                 PgDn               ",
                "Start of file             Ctrl - PgUp        ",
                "End of file               Ctrl - PgDn        ",
                "Top of screen             Ctrl - Home        ",
                "Bottom of screen          Ctrl - End         ",
                "Start of line             Home               ",
                "End of line               End                ",
                "",
```

```
"File Commands",
"------------------------------------------------------------------   ",
"Load a file                        Alt - F L              ",
"Pick recently edited file          Alt - F P              ",
"Open new file                      Alt - F N              ",
"Save and resume                    Alt - F S              ",
"Save under another name            Alt - F A              ",
"Merge another file                 Alt - F M              ",
"Change diirectory                  Alt - F C              ",
"Output to printer                  Alt - F O              ",
"Search Commands",
"------------------------------------------------------------------   ",
"find                            .  Alt - S F              ",
"Find & replace                     Alt - S R              ",
"Repeat last search                 Alt - S L              ",
"Abort search                       Alt - S A              ",
"Go to line number                  Alt - S G              ",
""
,
""
,
""
,
"Insert & Delete Commands",
"------------------------------------------------------------------   ",
"Insert mode on/off                 Ins                    ",
"Delete line                        Ctrl - Y               "
"Delete character to left of cursor Backspace              ",
"Deletere character at cursor       Del                    ",
"Delete word to right of cursor     Ctrl - T               ",
""
,
""
,
""
,
"Exit commands",
"------------------------------------------------------------------   ",
"Permanent exit to DOS              Alt - X,Alt - E E      ",
"Temporary exit to DOS              Alt - E S              "
```

```
                 "",
                 "",
                 "",
                 "",
                 "",
                 "",
                 "Miscellaneous Commands",
                 "---------------------------------------------------------------------",
                 "Main menu                         F10                    ",
                 "Take cursor to next tab stop      Tab                    ",
                 "Help                              F1                     ",
                 "Save                              F2                     ",
                 "Display product information       Sh - F10               ",
                 "Exit from Easyedit                Alt - X                ",
                 "",
                 ""
           };

/* specific help messages for file menu */
char *filehlp[ ] = {
                 "                Load",
                 "              ( Alt - F L )",
                 "",
                 "Loads  or  creates  a  file.  You  have to type in",
                 "the  name of the file. If the file does not exist,",
                 "you have the option of creating a new file of that",
                 "name.",
                 "                Pick",
                 "              ( Alt - F P )",
                 "",
                 "Lets you pick a file from the \"pick list\", which",
                 "is  a list of the five most recently edited files.",
                 "Selecting a file from the list loads it in memory.",
                 "",
                 "                New",
```

```
"                ( Alt - F N )",
"",
"Allows you to create a file called NONAME and work",
"with it.  While saving the file, you are prompted",
"to rename it.",
"",
"                        Save",
"                ( Alt - F S )",
"",
"Saves  the  current  file  to disk. If the current",
"file is NONAME, you are asked to  rename it.",
"Pressing  F2  from anywhere in the system does the",
"same thing.",
"                Save As",
"                ( Alt - F A )",
"",
"Saves  the current file contents under a new name.",
"The  original  file  contents remain intact on the",
"disk. The new file now becomes the current file.",
"",
"                        Merge",
"                ( Alt - F M )",
"",
"Merges  the  contents  of  a file on disk into the",
"currently  loaded file at current cursor location.",
"If the file to be merged does not exist, a warning",
"is issued.",
"                Change Dir",
"                ( Alt - F C )",
"",
"Displays the current directory and lets you change",
"to the drive and directory specified at the prompt",
"",
"",
"                Output to printer",
"                ( Alt - F O )",
"",
```

```
                              "Lets you specify a file to be printed. The margins",
                              "and  the page length can be specified. If the file",
                              "does not exist, a warning is issued.",
                              ""
                        } ;

/* specific help messages for exit menu */
char *exithlp[ ] = {
                        "                      Exit",
                        "                 ( Alt - E E )",
                        "",
                        "Use  this  option to exit from Easyedit. If you've",
                        "Modified  a  workfile  without saving it, you are",
                        "prompted to do so now. The hot key Alt - X, allows",
                        "you to exit Easyedit from anywhere in the system.",
                        "                 OS Shell",
                        "                 ( Alt - E S )",
                        "",
                        "Leaves Easyedit temporarily & takes you to the DOS",
                        "prompt. To return to Easyedit, type \"exit\" & press",
                        "Enter at DOS prompt. Use this to run a DOS command",
                        "without quitting Easyedit.",
                        } ;

/* calculate area required to save screen contents where help box is to be
   popped up */
areareqd = ( 20 - 4 + 1 ) * ( 67 - 12 + 1 ) * 2 ;

p = malloc ( areareqd ) ;  /* allocate memory */

/* if memory allocation fails */
if ( p == NULL )
     error_exit( ) ;

/* save screen contents */
savevideo ( 4, 12, 20, 67, p ) ;
```

```
/* draw a filled box */
menubox ( 4, 12, 20, 67, 112, 07 ) ;

/* draw a double-lined box */
drawbox ( 4, 12, 19, 65, 112 ) ;

/* display 'Help' in a box with shadow */
menubox ( 4, 35, 5, 44, 32, HALF_SHADOW ) ;
writestring ( "Help", 4, 37, 32 ) ;

/* if one of the first six help screens is to be displayed */
if ( index <= 6 )
{
    /* calculate number of starting help message to be displayed */
    i = ( index - 1 ) * 10 ;

    row = 6 ;

    while ( 1 )
    {
        writestring ( help[i], row, 14, 112 ) ;
        i++ ;
        row++ ;

        if ( row > 15 )
        {
            /* display PgDn/PgUp/OK buttons depending on help
               screen number */
            switch ( i )
            {
                case 10 :  /* first help screen */

                        menubox ( 17, 22, 18, 31, 32, HALF_SHADOW ) ;
                        writestring ( "Pg$Dn", 17, 24, 32 ) ;
                        menubox ( 17, 48, 18, 55, 32, HALF_SHADOW ) ;
                        writestring ( "$OK", 17, 50, 32 ) ;
                        break ;
```

```
            case 70 :  /* last help screen */

                    menubox ( 17, 22, 18, 31, 32, HALF_SHADOW ) ;
                    writestring ( "Pg$Up", 17, 24, 32 ) ;
                    menubox ( 17, 48, 18, 55, 32, HALF_SHADOW ) ;
                    writestring ( "$OK", 17, 50, 32 ) ;
                    break ;

            default :  /* intermediate help screen */

                    menubox ( 17, 20, 18, 29, 32, HALF_SHADOW ) ;
                    writestring ( "Pg$Dn", 17, 22, 32 ) ;
                    menubox ( 17, 35, 18, 44, 32, HALF_SHADOW ) ;
                    writestring ( "Pg$Up", 17, 37, 32 ) ;
                    menubox ( 17, 50, 18, 57, 32, HALF_SHADOW ) ;
                    writestring ( "$OK", 17, 52, 32 ) ;
    }

    /* continue till either PgUp, PgDn, OK or Esc is hit */
    while ( 1 )
    {
        getkey( ) ;

        /* if Esc is hit or OK is selected */
        if ( ascii == 27 || ascii == 'o' || ascii == 'O' )
        {
            restorevideo ( 4, 12, 20, 67, p ) ;
            free ( p ) ;
            return ;
        }

        /* if PgDn is selected and it is not the last help screen */
        if ( ( scan == 81 || ascii == 'd' || ascii == 'D' ) && ( i != 70 ) )
        {
            menubox ( 6, 13, 18, 64, 112, 0 ) ;
            row = 6 ;
```

```
                    break ;
              }

              /* if PgUp is selected and it is not the first help screen */
              if ( ( scan == 73 || ascii == 'U' || ascii == 'u' ) && i != 10 )
              {
                    i -= 20 ;  /* go back by 20 lines */
                    menubox ( 6, 13, 18, 64, 112, 0 ) ;
                    row = 6 ;
                    break ;
              }
          }
       }
    }
}
else
{
    /* if specific file help is to be displayed */
    if ( index <= 15 )
    {
        /* calculate number of starting help message to be displayed */
        i = ( index - 8 ) * 7 ;

        /* display help screen */
        for ( row = 7 ; row < 14 ; row++ )
        {
            writestring ( filehlp[i], row, 14, 112 ) ;
            i++ ;
        }
    }
    else
    {
        /* calculate number of starting help message to be displayed */
        i = ( index - 16 ) * 7 ;

        /* display help screen */
        for ( row = 7 ; row < 14 ; row++ )
```

```
            {
                writestring ( exithlp[i], row, 14, 112 ) ;
                i++ ;
            }
        }

    /* display OK button */
    menubox ( 15, 34, 16, 43, 32, HALF_SHADOW ) ;
    writestring ( " $OK ", 15, 36, 32 ) ;

    /* continue till Esc is hit or OK is selected */
    while ( 1 )
    {
        getkey( ) ;

        if ( ascii == 27 || ascii == 'o' || ascii == 'O' )
        {
            restorevideo ( 4, 12, 20, 67, p ) ;
            free ( p ) ;
            break ;
        }
    }
}
```

CURSOR.C

```
/* positions cursor at the beginning of the file */
start_file( )
{
    int display = YES ;

    /* if first page of the file is being currently displayed */
    if ( curscr == startloc && skip == 0 )
        display = NO ;

    /* reset variables */
    curr = 2 ;
    curc = 1 ;
    logr = 1 ;
    logc = 1 ;
    skip = 0 ;
    curscr = startloc ;
    currow = startloc ;

    /* display first page of file, if necessary */
    if ( display == YES )
    {
        menubox ( 2, 1, 22, 78, 27, NO_SHADOW ) ;
        displayscreen ( curscr ) ;
    }

    /* display current cursor location */
    writerow( ) ;
    writecol( ) ;
}

/* positions cursor at the end of the file */
end_file( )
{
    char *temp ;
```

```
int i, status ;

size ( 32, 0 ) ;  /* hide cursor */

/* count the total number of lines in the file */
logr = 1 ;
curr = 2 ;
temp = startloc ;
while ( temp != endloc )
{
    if ( *temp == '\n' )
        curr++ ;
    temp++ ;
}

/* set up current screen and current row pointers */
curscr = endloc ;
currow = endloc ;

/* display the last page of the file */
page_up ( 0 ) ;

/* position cursor 20 lines after current row */
for ( i = 0 ; i < 20 ; i++ )
{
    status = down_line ( 0 ) ;

    /* if end of file is reached */
    if ( status == 1 )
        break ;
}

/* position cursor at the end of the last line */
end_line( ) ;

size ( 5, 7 ) ;  /* show cursor */
```

```
    /* display current cursor row */
    writerow( ) ;
}

/* positions cursor in the first row of current screen */
top_screen( )
{
    size ( 32, 0 ) ;

    /* go up until the first row is encountered */
    while ( logr != 1 )
        up_line ( 0 ) ;

    /* display current cursor row */
    writerow( ) ;

    size ( 5, 7 ) ;
}

/* positions cursor in the last row of current screen */
bottom_screen( )
{
    int status ;

    size ( 32, 0 ) ;

    /* go down until the last row or end of file is encountered */
    while ( logr != 21 )
    {
        status = down_line ( 0 ) ;

        /* if end of file is reached */
        if ( status == 1 )
            break ;
    }

    writerow( ) ;
```

```
    size ( 5, 7 ) ;
}

/* positions cursor at the beginning of current row */
start_line( )
{
    /* if there exist characters to the left of currently displayed line */
    if ( skip != 0 )
    {
        skip = 0 ;
        menubox ( 2, 1, 22, 78, 27, NO_SHADOW ) ;
        displayscreen ( curscr ) ;
    }

    logc = 1 ;
    curc = 1 ;

    /* display current cursor column */
    writecol( ) ;
}

/* positions cursor at the end of current row */
end_line( )
{
    char *temp ;
    int count, display = YES ;

    temp = currow ;
    count = 1 ;

    /* count the number of characters in current line */
    while ( *temp != '\n' )
    {
        /* if end of file is encountered */
        if ( temp >= endloc )
            break ;
```

```
        if ( *temp == '\t' )
            count += 8 ;
        else
            count++ ;

        temp++ ;
}

/* backtrace across the \t's and spaces which may be present at the end
   of the line */
while ( * ( temp - 1 ) == '\t' || * ( temp - 1 ) == ' ' )
{
    if ( * ( temp - 1 ) == '\t' )
        count -= 8 ;
    else
        count++ ;

    temp-- ;
}

/* if the number of characters in the line is less than 78 */
if ( count <= 78 )
{
    /* if no characters exist to the left of currently displayed line */
    if ( skip == 0 )
        display = NO ;
    else
        skip = 0 ;

    logc = count ;
}
else
{
    skip = count - 78 ;
    logc = 78 ;
}
```

```
        if ( display == YES )
        {
            menubox ( 2, 1, 22, 78, 27, NO_SHADOW ) ;
            displayscreen ( curscr ) ;
        }

        curc = count ;
        writecol( ) ;
}

/* positions cursor one word to the left */
word_left( )
{
    char *temp ;
    int col, count = 0, condition1, condition2, condition3 ;

    /* increment 'temp' to point to character at current cursor location */
    temp = currow ;
    for ( col = 1 ; col < curc ; col++ )
    {
        /* if end of file is encountered */
        if ( temp >= endloc )
            break ;

        if ( *temp == '\t' )
            col += 7 ;

        /* if end of line is encountered before current cursor column */
        if ( *temp == '\n' )
        {
            end_line( ) ;
            break ;
        }

        temp++ ;
    }
```

```
/* if end of file is encountered */
if ( temp >= endloc )
    temp-- ;

/* if characters at current cursor location and to its left are alphanumeric */
condition1 = isalnum ( *temp ) && isalnum ( * ( temp - 1 ) ) ;

/* if character at current cursor location is alphanumeric and the previous
   character is not alphanumeric */
condition2 = isalnum ( *temp ) && !isalnum ( * ( temp - 1 ) ) ;

/* if character at current cursor location.is not alphanumeric */
condition3 = !isalnum ( *temp ) ;

if ( *temp == '\n' )
    temp-- ;

if ( condition2 )
    temp-- ;

if ( condition1 )
{
    /* move left so long as alphanumeric characters are found */
    while ( isalnum ( *temp ) )
    {
        if ( temp == startloc )
            break ;

        temp-- ;
        count++ ;
    }
}

if ( condition2 || condition3 )
{
    /* move left till an alphanumeric character is found */
    while ( ! ( isalnum ( *temp ) ) )
```

```
        {
            if ( temp <= startloc )
                break ;

            if ( *temp == '\t' )
                count += 7 ;

            /* if end of previous line is encountered */
            if ( *temp == '\n' )
            {
                /* position cursor at the end of previous line */
                up_line ( 0 ) ;
                end_line( ) ;

                return ;
            }

            temp-- ;
            count++ ;
        }

        /* move left till a non-alphanumeric character is found */
        while ( isalnum ( *temp ) )
        {
            if ( temp == startloc )
                oreak ;

            temp-- ;
            count++ ;
        }
    }

    /* if beginning of file is encountered */
    if ( temp == startloc )
    {
        logc = 1 ;
        curc = 1 ;
```

```
        }
        else
        {
            logc -= count ;
            curc -= count ;

            /* if screen needs to be scrolled horizontally */
            if ( curc > 78 )
            {
                logc = 78 ;
                skip = curc - 78 ;
                menubox ( 2, 1, 22, 78, 27, NO_SHADOW ) ;
                displayscreen ( curscr ) ;
            }
        }

        writecol( ) ;
        writerow( ) ;
}

/* positions cursor one word to the right */
word_right( )
{
        char *temp ;
        int col, count = 0 ;

        /* increment 'temp' to point to character at current cursor location */
        temp = currow ;
        for ( col = 1 ; col < curc ; col++ )
        {
            /* if end of file is encountered */
            if ( temp >= endloc )
                return ;

            if ( *temp == '\t' )
                col += 7 ;
```

```
    /* if end of line is encountered before current cursor column */
    if ( *temp == '\n' )
        break ;

    temp++ ;
}

if ( temp >= endloc )
    return ;

/* if cursor is at the end of current line */
if ( *temp == '\n' )
{
    /* continue till an alphanumeric character is found */
    while ( ! ( isalnum ( *temp ) ) )
    {
        /* if end of file is encountered */
        if ( temp >= endloc )
            break ;

        if ( *temp == '\t' )
            count += 7 ;

        /* if end of line is encountered */
        if ( *temp == '\n' )
        {
            /* position cursor in the next line */
            down_line ( 0 ) ;

            /* position cursor at the beginning of the line */
            start_line( ) ;

            temp = currow ;
            count = 0 ;
            continue ;
        }
```

```
            temp++ ;
            count++ ;
        }
    }
    else
    {
        /* there exists a word to the right of cursor */
        count = 0 ;

        /* move right so long as alphanumeric characters are found */
        while ( isalnum ( *temp ) )
        {
            if ( temp >= endloc )
                break ;

            temp++ ;
            count++ ;
        }

        /* move right till a non-alphanumeric character or end of line is met */
        while ( ! ( isalnum ( *temp ) || *temp == '\n' ) )
        {
            if ( temp >= endloc )
                break ;

            if ( *temp == '\t' )
                count += 7 ;

            temp++ ;
            count++ ;
        }
    }

    logc += count ;
    curc += count ;

    /* if screen needs to be scrolled horizontally */
```

```
        if ( curc > 78 )
        {
            logc = 78 ;
            skip = curc - 78 ;
            menubox ( 2, 1, 22, 78, 27, NO_SHADOW ) ;
            displayscreen ( curscr ) ;
        }

        writecol( ) ;
        writerow( ) ;
}

/* displays previous file page */
page_up ( display )
int display ;
{
        int row ;

        /* if first page is currently displayed */
        if ( curscr == startloc )
            return ;

        /* position the 'curscr' pointer 20 lines before */
        for ( row = 1 ; row <= 20 ; row++ )
        {
            /* go to end of previous line */
            curscr -= 2 ;

            /* if beginning of file is encountered */
            if ( curscr <= startloc )
            {
                /* reset variables */
                curscr = startloc ;
                currow = startloc ;
                logr = 1 ;
                curr = 2 ;
                logc = 1 ;
```

```
        curc = 1 ;

        menubox ( 2, 1, 22, 78, 27, NO_SHADOW ) ;
        displayscreen ( curscr ) ;

        if ( display )
        {
            writecol( ) ;
            writerow( ) ;
        }

        return ;
    }

    /* go to the beginning of previous line */
    while ( *curscr != '\n' )
    {
        if ( curscr <= startloc )
        {
            curscr = startloc ;
            break ;
        }

        curscr-- ;
    }
    if ( curscr != startloc && *( curscr + 1 ) != '\n' )
        curscr++ ;
}

/* display the previous screen */
menubox ( 2, 1, 22, 78, 27, NO_SHADOW ) ;
displayscreen ( curscr ) ;

/* position cursor 20 lines before */
for ( row = 1 ; row <= 20 ; row++ )
{
    currow -= 2 ;
```

```
            if ( currow < startloc )
                currow = startloc ;

            while ( *currow != '\n' )
                currow-- ;

            if ( currow != startloc || * ( currow + 1 ) == '\n' )
                currow++ ;
        }

        curr -= 20 ;

        /* position cursor in appropriate column */
        gotocol( ) ;

        if ( display )
        {
            writerow( ) ;
            writecol( ) ;
        }
    }

/* displays next file page */
page_down( )
{
    char *p ;
    int row = 1, i, col ;

    /* position the 'curscr' pointer 20 lines hence */
    p = curscr ;
    for ( row = 1 ; row <= 20 ; row++ )
    {
        /* go to the end of current line */
        while ( *curscr != '\n' )
        {
            /* if end of file is encountered */
            if ( curscr >= endloc )
```

```
        {
            curscr = p ;
            return ;
        }

        curscr++ ;
    }

    if ( curscr >= endloc )
    {
        curscr = p ;
        return ;
    }

    /* go to the beginning of next line */
    curscr++ ;
}

/* display the next screen */
menubox ( 2, 1, 22, 78, 27, NO_SHADOW ) ;
displayscreen ( curscr ) ;

/* position cursor 20 lines hence */

size ( 32, 0 ) ;

/* continue till first row on the screen is reached */
row = 1 ;
while ( currow != curscr )
{
    if ( *currow == '\n' )
    {
        curr++ ;
        row++ ;
    }
    currow++ ;
}
```

```
        logr = 1 ;
        col = curc ;

        for ( i = row ; i <= 20 ; i++ )
            down_line ( 0 ) ;

        curc = col ;

        /* position cursor in appropriate column */
        gotocol( ) ;

        writerow( ) ;
        writecol( ) ;

        size ( 5, 7 ) ;
}

/* positions cursor one column to the right */
right( )
{
        char *temp ;
        int col ;

        /* if current column exceeds 249, beep */
        if ( curc >= 249 )
        {
            curc = 249 ;
            printf ( "\a" ) ;
            return ;
        }

        /* increment 'temp' to point to character at current cursor location */
        temp = currow ;
        for ( col = 1 ; col < curc ; col++ )
        {
            if ( *temp == '\t' )
```

```
            col += 7 ;

        if ( *temp == '\n' )
            break ;

        temp++ ;
    }

    /* if next character is a tab */
    if ( *temp == '\t' )
    {
        logc += 7 ;
        curc += 7 ;
    }

    curc++ ;

    /* if cursor is in the last column , scroll screen horizontally */
    if ( logc >= 78 )
    {
        skip = curc - 78 ;
        menubox ( 2, 1, 22, 78, 27, NO_SHADOW ) ;
        displayscreen ( curscr ) ;
        logc = 78 ;
    }
    else
        logc++ ;

    writecol( ) ;
}

/* positions cursor one column to the left */
left( )
{
    int col = 1 ;
    char *temp ;
```

```c
/* if cursor is in the first column */
if ( curc == 1 )
    return ;

/* increment 'temp' to point to character at current cursor location */
temp = currow ;
for ( col = 1 ; col < curc ; col++ )
{
    if ( *temp == '\t' )
        col += 7 ;

    if ( *temp == '\n' )
        break ;

    temp++ ;
}

/* if previous character is a tab */
if ( * ( temp - 1 ) == '\t' )
{
    logc -= 7 ;
    curc -= 7 ;
}

/* if cursor is in the first column and if there exist characters to the left of
   currently displayed line, scroll screen horizontally */
if ( logc <= 1 && skip != 0 )
{
    logc = 1 ;
    curc-- ;
    skip = curc - logc ;
    menubox ( 2, 1, 22, 78, 27, NO_SHADOW ) ;
    displayscreen ( curscr ) ;
}
else
{
    curc-- ;
```

```
            logc-- ;
        }

        writecol( ) ;
}

/* positions cursor one line up */
up_line ( display )
int display ;
{
        /* if cursor is in the first line of the file */
        if ( curr == 2 )
            return ;

        /* remove spaces and tabs at the end of the line */
        del_whitespace( ) ;

        logr-- ;
        curr-- ;

        /* go to the beginning of previous line */
        currow -= 2 ;
        if ( curscr < startloc )
            curscr = startloc ;
        while ( *currow != '\n' )
        {
            if ( currow <= startloc )
                break ;

            currow-- ;
        }
        if ( currow != startloc || *( currow + 1 ) == '\n' )
            currow++ ;

        /* if vertical scrolling is required */
        if ( logr < 1 )
        {
```

```
            logr = 1 ;
            curscr = currow ;
            scrolldown ( 2, 1, 22, 78 ) ;
            displayline ( curscr, 2 ) ;
        }

    /* position cursor in appropriate column */
    gotocol( ) ;

    /* if current cursor row and column is to be displayed */
    if ( display )
    {
        writecol( ) ;
        writerow( ) ;
    }
}

/* positions cursor one line down */
down_line ( display )
int display ;
{
    char *p ;

    /* remove spaces and tabs at the end of the line */
    del_whitespace( ) ;

    /* go to the beginning of next line */
    p = currow ;
    while ( *currow != '\n' )
    {
        /* if end of file is encountered */
        if ( currow >= endloc )
        {
            currow = p ;
            return ( 1 ) ;
        }
```

```
                currow++ ;
        }
        if ( currow == endloc )
        {
                currow = p ;
                return ( 1 ) ;
        }
        currow++ ;
        logr++ ;
        curr++ ;

        /* if vertical scrolling is required */
        if ( logr >= 22 )
        {
                logr = 21 ;
                scrollup ( 2, 1, 22, 78 ) ;
                displayline ( currow, 22 ) ;

                /* position 'curscr' pointer at the beginning of current screen */
                while ( *curscr != '\n' )
                        curscr++ ;
                curscr++ ;
        }

        /* position cursor in appropriate column */
        gotocol( ) ;

        /* if current cursor row and column is to be displayed */
        if ( display )
        {
                writecol( ) ;
                writerow( ) ;
        }

        return ( 0 ) ;
}
```

```
/* scrolls the screen contents down */
scrolldown ( sr, sc, er, ec )
int sr, sc, er, ec ;
{

    union REGS ii, oo ;

    ii.h.ah = 7 ;  /* service number */
    ii.h.al = 1 ;  /* number of lines to scroll */
    ii.h.ch = sr ;  /* starting row */
    ii.h.cl = sc ;  /* starting column */
    ii.h.dh = er ;  /* ending row */
    ii.h.dl = ec ;  /* ending column */
    ii.h.bh = 27 ; /* display attribute of blank line created at top */
    int86 ( 16, &ii, &oo ) ;  /* issue interrupt */
}

/* scrolls the screen contents up */
scrollup ( sr, sc, er, ec )
int sr, sc, er, ec ;
{
    union REGS ii, oo ;

    ii.h.ah = 6 ;  /* service number */
    ii.h.al = 1 ;   /* number of lines to scroll */
    ii.h.ch = sr ;  /* starting row */
    ii.h.cl = sc ;  /* starting column */
    ii.h.dh = er ;  /* ending row */
    ii.h.dl = ec ;  /* ending column */
    ii.h.bh = 27 ; /* display attribute of blank line created at bottom */
    int86 ( 16, &ii, &oo ) ;  /* issue interrupt */
}

/* positions cursor in appropriate column */
gotocol( )
{
    char *temp ;
```

```
    int col ;

    /* increment 'temp' to point to character at current cursor location */
    temp = currow ;
    for ( col = 1 ; col < curc ; col++ )
    {
        if ( *temp == '\t' )
            col += 7 ;

        if ( *temp == '\n' )
            break ;

        temp++ ;
    }

    /* if the character at current cursor location is a tab */
    if ( col > curc )
    {
        /* go to the end of tab */
        logc += ( col - curc ) ;
        curc = col ;

        /* if screen needs to be scrolled horizontally */
        if ( curc > 78 )
        {
            logc = 78 ;
            skip = curc - 78 ;
            menubox ( 2, 1, 22, 78, 27, NO_SHADOW ) ;
            displayscreen ( curscr ) ;
        }
    }
}
```

EDITOR.C

```c
# include "math.h"
# include "dos.h"
# include "process.h"
# include "alloc.h"
# include "stdlib.h"
# include "stdio.h"
# include "ctype.h"

# include "util.c"
# include "cursor.c"

main ( argc, argv )
int argc ;
char *argv[ ] ;
{
    int flag ;

    /* if more than one filename is supplied at DOS prompt */
    if ( argc > 2 )
    {
        printf ( "\nInvalid number of parameters!" ) ;
        printf ( "\nPress any key..." ) ;
        fflush ( stdin ) ;
        getch( ) ;
        exit ( 1 ) ;
    }

    #ifdef CGA
    {
        vid_mem = ( char far * ) 0xb8000000L ;
        textmode ( 3 ) ;
    }
    #else
    {
```

```
    vid_mem = ( char far * ) 0xb0000000L ;
    textmode ( 7 ) ;
}
#endif

/* capture Ctrl - C interrupt */
old23 = getvect ( 0x23 ) ;
setvect ( 0x23, handler ) ;

/* capture Ctrl - Break interrupt */
old1b = getvect ( 0x1b ) ;
setvect ( 0x1b, handler ) ;

/* calculate the maximum buffer size */
maxsize = coreleft( ) - 5000 ;

/* allocate memory, check if successful */
buf = malloc ( maxsize ) ;
if ( buf == NULL )
    error_exit( ) ;

/* initialise pointers to point to buf */
startloc = endloc = curscr = currow = buf ;

/* set Ins key to on */
*ins |= 0x80 ;

/* set default file name as 'NONAME' */
strcpy ( filespec, "NONAME" ) ;

workscreen( ) ;  /* display working screen */
displaymenuh ( mainmenu, 5 ) ;  /* display the main menu */
about( ) ;  /* display product information message */

/* if file name to be edited is specified in the command line */
if ( argc == 2 )
{
```

```
            /* load specified file */
            strcpy ( filespec, argv[1] ) ;
            flag = load( ) ;

            /* if unsuccessful in loading file */
            if ( flag == 0 )
            {
                strcpy ( filespec, "NONAME" ) ;
                write_fname( ) ;
            }
    }

    while ( 1 )
    {
        gotoxy ( logc + 1, logr + 2 ) ;  /* position cursor */
        getkey( ) ;  /* receive key */

        /* display status of Insert key */
        if ( *ins & 0x80 )
            writestring ( "Insert", 24, 73, 47 ) ;
        else
            writestring ( "     ", 24, 73, 112 ) ;

        /* if special key has been hit */
        if ( ascii == 0 )
        {
            /* check which special key */
            switch ( scan )
            {
                case 59 :  /* F1 key */

                    displayhelp ( 1 ) ;
                    break ;

                case 60 :  /* F2 key */

                    save( ) ;
```

```
            break ;

    case 45 :  /* Alt - X */

            check_saved( ) ;
            exit ( 0 ) ;

    case 46 :  /* Alt - C */

            /* highlight the menu item */
            writestring ( mainmenu[0], 0, 2, 15 ) ;

            /* call cursor movement services */
            cserver( ) ;

            /* make highlighted item normal */
            writestring ( mainmenu[0], 0, 2, 112 ) ;

            break ;

    case 33 :  /* Alt - F */

            /* highlight the menu item */
            writestring ( mainmenu[1], 0, 25, 15 ) ;

            /* call file services */
            fserver( ) ;

            /* make highlighted item normal */
            writestring ( mainmenu[1], 0, 25, 112 ) ;

            break ;

    case 31 :  /* Alt - S */

            writestring ( mainmenu[2], 0, 37, 15 ) ;
            sserver( ) ;
```

```
        writestring ( mainmenu[2], 0, 37, 112 ) ;
        break ;

    case 32 :  /* Alt - D */

        writestring ( mainmenu[3], 0, 51, 15 ) ;
        dserver( ) ;
        writestring ( mainmenu[3], 0, 51, 112 ) ;
        break ;

    case 18 :  /* Alt - E */

        writestring ( mainmenu[4], 0, 65, 15 ) ;
        eserver( ) ;
        writestring ( mainmenu[4], 0, 65, 112 ) ;
        break ;

    case 68 :  /* F10 key */

        mm_server( ) ;
        break ;

    case 93 :  /* Shift F10 */

        about( ) ;
        break ;

    case 75 :  /* left arrow key */

        left( ) ;
        break ;

    case 77 :  /* right arrow key */

        right( ) ;
        break ;
```

```
case 72 :  /* up arrow key */

    up_line ( 1 ) ;
    break ;

case 80 :  /* down arrow key */

    down_line ( 1 ) ;
    break ;

case 73 :  /* PgUp key */

    page_up ( 1 ) ;
    break ;

case 81 :  /* PgDn key */

    page_down( ) ;
    break ;

case 71 :  /* Home key */

    start_line( ) ;
    break ;

case 79 :  /* End key */

    end_line( ) ;
    break ;

case 132 :  /* Ctrl - PgUp */

    start_file( ) ;
    break ;

case 118 :  /* Ctrl - PgDn */
```

```
                        end_file( ) ;
                        break ;

                case 119 :  /* Ctrl - Home */

                        top_screen( ) ;
                        break ;

                case 117 :  /* Ctrl - End */

                        bottom_screen( ) ;
                        break ;

                case 115 :  /* Ctrl - left arrow */

                        word_left( ) ;
                        break ;

                case 116 :  /* Ctrl - right arrow */

                        word_right( ) ;
                        break ;

                case 83 :  /* Del key */

                        del_char( ) ;
                        break ;
            }
    }
    else
    {
        switch ( ascii )
        {
            case 8 : /* backspace key */

                        backspace( ) ;
                        break ;
```

```
            case 20 :  /* Ctrl - T */

                    del_word_rt( ) ;
                    break ;

            case 25 :  /* Ctrl - Y */

                    del_line( ) ;
                    break ;

            case 12 :  /* Ctrl - L */

                    repeat_last( ) ;
                    break ;

            default :

                    /* if the character is valid character */
                    if ( ( ascii >= 32 && ascii <= 126 ) || ascii == 13  ||
                        ascii == 9 )
                        displaychar ( ascii ) ;
                }
            }
        }
}

/* displays Main Menu, receives choice and branches control to appropriate
   function */
mm_server( )
{
    int mchoice, esc_flag ;

    while ( 1 )
    {
        displaymenuh ( mainmenu, 5 ) ;
        mchoice = getresponseh ( mainmenu, "CFSDE", 5 ) ;
```

```
        switch ( mchoice )
        {
            case 1 :
                esc_flag = cserver( ) ;
                break ;

            case 2 :
                esc_flag = fserver( ) ;
                break ;

            case 3 :
                esc_flag = sserver( ) ;
                break ;

            case 4 :
                esc_flag = dserver( ) ;
                break ;

            case 5 :
                esc_flag = eserver( ) ;
                break ;

            case ESC :  /* if Esc key is hit when in horizontal main menu */
                esc_flag = ESC ;
        }

        /* if Esc key has been hit in vertical or horizontal menu */
        if ( esc_flag == ESC )
            return ( esc_flag ) ;
    }
}

/* displays Cursor Movement menu, receives choice and branches control to
   appropriate function */
cserver( )
{
```

```
int cchoice, esc_flag = 0 ;

/* pop up Cursor Movement menu */
cchoice = popupmenuv ( cursormenu, 11, 1, 0, "SFTBLEWRUDN", 1 ) ;

/* call appropriate functions to position cursor */
switch ( cchoice )
{
    case 1 :
        start_file( ) ;
        break ;

    case 2 :
        end_file( ) ;
        break ;

    case 3 :
        top_screen( ) ;
        break ;

    case 4 :
        bottom_screen( ) ;
        break ;

    case 5 :
        start_line( ) ;
        break ;

    case 6 :
        end_line( ) ;
        break ;

    case 7 :
        word_left( ) ;
        break ;

    case 8 :
```

```
        word_right( ) ;
        break ;

case 9 :
        page_up ( 1 ) ;
        break ;

case 10 :
        page_down( ) ;
        break ;

case 11 :

        /* call main menu services */
        esc_flag = mm_server( ) ;

        break ;

case 75 :  /* left arrow key */

        /* make the 'Cursor Movement' menu item normal */
        writestring ( mainmenu[0], 0, 2, 112 ) ;

        /* highlight the 'Exit' menu item */
        writestring ( mainmenu[4], 0, 65, 15 ) ;

        /* call exit services */
        esc_flag = eserver( ) ;

        /* make the 'Exit' menu item normal */
        writestring ( mainmenu[4], 0, 65, 112 ) ;

        break ;

case 77 :  /* right arrow key */

        /* make the 'Cursor Movement' menu item normal */
```

```
                    writestring ( mainmenu[0], 0, 2, 112 ) ;

                    /* highlight the 'File' menu item */
                    writestring ( mainmenu[1], 0, 25, 15 ) ;

                    /* call file services */
                    esc_flag = fserver( ) ;

                    /* make the 'File' menu item normal */
                    writestring ( mainmenu[1], 0, 25, 112 ) ;

                    break ;

                case ESC :
                    esc_flag = ESC ;
        }

        return ( esc_flag ) ;
}

/* displays File menu, receives choice and branches control to appropriate
   function */
fserver( )
{
        int fchoice, flag, esc_flag = 0 ;
        char fname[30] ;

        fchoice = popupmenuv ( filemenu, 9, 1, 23, "LPNSAMCOT", 3 ) ;

        switch ( fchoice )
        {
            case 1 :

                    check_saved( ) ;  /* check if current file has been saved */
                    strcpy ( fname, filespec ) ;

                    /* get the name of the file to be loaded */
```

```
            esc_flag = ask_name ( "Enter file name", filespec ) ;
            if ( esc_flag == ESC )
                break ;

            flag = load( ) ;  /* load file */

            /* if unsuccessful in loading file */
            if ( flag == 0 )
            {
                strcpy ( filespec, fname ) ;
                write_fname( ) ;
            }

            break ;

        case 2 :
            pick( ) ;  /* load a file from the pick list */
            break ;

        case 3 :
            new( ) ;  /* create a new file */
            break ;

        case 4 :
            save( ) ;  /* save current file */
            break ;

        case 5 :
            save_as( ) ;  /* save current file under a new name */
            break ;

        case 6 :
            merge( ) ;  /* read another file into current file */
            break ;

        case 7 :
            change_dir( ) ;  /* change the default directory */
```

```
            break ;

    case 8 :
            print( ) ;  /* print a file */
            break ;

    case 9 :

            /* call main menu services */
            esc_flag = mm_server( ) ;

            break ;

    case 75 :  /* left arrow key */

            /* display Cursor Movement menu */
            writestring ( mainmenu[1], 0, 25, 112 ) ;
            writestring ( mainmenu[0], 0, 2, 15 ) ;
            esc_flag = cserver( ) ;
            writestring ( mainmenu[0], 0, 2, 112 ) ;

            break ;

    case 77 :  /* right arrow key */

            /* display Search menu */
            writestring ( mainmenu[1], 0, 25, 112 ) ;
            writestring ( mainmenu[2], 0, 37, 15 ) ;
            esc_flag = sserver( ) ;
            writestring ( mainmenu[2], 0, 37, 112 ) ;

            break ;

    case ESC :
            esc_flag = ESC ;
}
```

```
      return ( esc_flag ) ;
}

/* displays Search menu, receives choice and branches control to appropriate
   function */
sserver( )
{
      int schoice, esc_flag = 0 ;

      schoice = popupmenuv ( searchmenu, 6, 1, 35, "FRLAGT", 4 ) ;

      switch ( schoice )
      {
            case 1 :

                  /* set appropriate flags */
                  findflag = 1 ;
                  frflag = 0 ;

                  find( ) ;  /* search string */
                  break ;

            case 2 :

                  /* set appropriate flags */
                  findflag = 0 ;
                  frflag = 1 ;

                  replace( ) ;  /* search and replace string */
                  break ;

            case 3 :
                  repeat_last( ) ;  /* repeat last search operation */
                  break ;

            case 4 :
                  abort_find( ) ;  /* abandon search operation */
```

```
        break ;

    case 5 :
        gotoline( ) ;  /* go to the specified line */
        break ;

    case 6 :

        /* call main menu services */
        esc_flag = mm_server( ) ;

        break ;

    case 75 :  /* left arrow key */

        /* display File menu */
        writestring ( mainmenu[2], 0, 37, 112 ) ;
        writestring ( mainmenu[1], 0, 25, 15 ) ;
        esc_flag = fserver( ) ;
        writestring ( mainmenu[1], 0, 25, 112 ) ;

        break ;

    case 77 :  /* right arrow key */

        /* display Delete menu */
        writestring ( mainmenu[2], 0, 37, 112 ) ;
        writestring ( mainmenu[3], 0, 51, 15 ) ;
        esc_flag = dserver( ) ;
        writestring ( mainmenu[3], 0, 51, 112 ) ;

        break ;

    case ESC :
        esc_flag = ESC ;
}
```

```
        return ( esc_flag ) ;
}

/* displays Delete menu, receives choice and branches control to appropriate
   function */
dserver( )
{
        int dchoice, esc_flag = 0 ;

        dchoice = popupmenuv ( deletemenu, 5, 1, 49, "DEBRT", 5 ) ;

        switch ( dchoice )
        {
            case 1 :
                del_line( ) ;  /* delete one line */
                break ;

            case 2 :
                del_line_rt( ) ;  /* delete line to right of cursor */
                break ;

            case 3 :
                del_line_lt( ) ;  /* delete line to left of cursor */
                break ;

            case 4 :
                del_word_rt( );  /* delete word to the right of cursor */
                break ;

            case 5 :

                /* call main menu services */
                esc_flag = mm_server( ) ;

                break ;

            case 75 :  /* left arrow key */
```

```
                    /* display Search menu */
                    writestring ( mainmenu[3], 0, 51, 112 ) ;
                    writestring ( mainmenu[2], 0, 37, 15 ) ;
                    esc_flag = sserver( ) ;
                    writestring ( mainmenu[2], 0, 37, 112 ) ;

                    break ;

              case 77 :  /* right arrow key */

                    /* display Exit menu */
                    writestring ( mainmenu[3], 0, 51, 112 ) ;
                    writestring ( mainmenu[4], 0, 65, 15 ) ;
                    esc_flag = eserver( ) ;
                    writestring ( mainmenu[4], 0, 65, 112 ) ;

                    break ;

              case ESC :
                    esc_flag = ESC ;
        }

        return ( esc_flag ) ;
}

/* displays Exit menu, receives choice and branches control to appropriate
   function */
eserver( )
{
        int fchoice, esc_flag ;

        fchoice = popupmenuv ( exitmenu, 3, 1, 62, "EST", 6 ) ;

        switch ( fchoice )
        {
              case 1 :
```

```
              /* check if current file has been saved */
              check_saved( ) ;

              /* restore interrupt vectors */
              setvect ( 0x23, old23 ) ;
              setvect ( 0x1b, old1b ) ;

              /* exit permanently to DOS */
              exit ( 0 ) ;

      case 2 :
              shell( ) ;  /* exit temporarily to DOS */
              break ;

      case 3 :

              /* call main menu services */
              esc_flag = mm_server( ) ;

              break ;

      case 75 :  /* left arrow key */

              /* display Delete menu */
              writestring ( mainmenu[4], 0, 65, 112 ) ;
              writestring ( mainmenu[3], 0, 51, 15 ) ;
              esc_flag = dserver( ) ;
              writestring ( mainmenu[3], 0, 51, 112 ) ;

              break ;

      case 77 :  /* right arrow key */

              /* display Cursor Movement menu */
              writestring ( mainmenu[4], 0, 65, 112 ) ;
              writestring ( mainmenu[0], 0, 2, 15 ) ;
```

```
            esc_flag = cserver( ) ;
            writestring ( mainmenu[0], 0, 2, 112 ) ;

            break ;

        case ESC :
            esc_flag = ESC ;
    }

    return ( esc_flag ) ;
}

/* creates working screen */
workscreen( )
{
    size ( 32, 0 ) ;

    /* draw filled box in editing portion of screen */
    menubox ( 1, 0, 23, 79, 27, NO_SHADOW ) ;

    /* draw a box around editing portion of screen */
    drawbox ( 1, 0, 23, 79, 27 ) ;

    /* display the name of the current file i.e. "NONAME" */
    write_fname( ) ;

    /* draw box of different color in bottommost row */
    menubox ( 24, 0, 24, 79, 112, NO_SHADOW ) ;

    /* display certain special keys and their significance */
    status_line( ) ;

    size ( 5, 7 ) ;
}

/* displays product information */
about( )
```

```
{
    int area ;
    char *p ;

    size ( 32, 0 ) ;   /* hide cursor */

    /* allocate memory, if unsuccessful terminate execution */
    area = ( 17 - 6 + 1 ) * ( 60 - 19 + 1 ) * 2 ;
    p = malloc ( area ) ;
    if ( p == NULL )
        error_exit( ) ;

    /* create dialogue box */
    savevideo ( 6, 19, 17, 60, p ) ;
    menubox ( 6, 19, 17, 60, 112, 7 ) ;
    drawbox ( 6, 19, 16, 58 , 112 ) ;

    writestring ( "Easyedit", 7, 35, 112 ) ;
    writestring ( "Version 1.00", 9, 33, 112 ) ;
    writestring ( "Designed and developed at", 10, 27, 112 ) ;
    writestring ( "ICIT, 44-A, Gokulpeth", 11, 28, 112 ) ;
    writestring ( "Nagpur, India", 12, 32, 112 ) ;

    /* display OK button */
    menubox ( 14, 36, 15, 43, 32, HALF_SHADOW ) ;
    writestring ( "OK", 14, 38, 47 ) ;

    /* continue till either Esc is hit or OK is selected */
    while ( 1 )
    {
        getkey( ) ;

        if ( ascii == ESC || ascii != 'O' || ascii == 'o' )
            break ;
    }

    restorevideo ( 6, 19, 17, 60, p ) ;
```

```
    free ( p ) ;

    size ( 5, 7 ) ;  /* show cursor */
}

/* writes the name of the file */
write_fname( )
{
    int len ;
    char drive[2], fname[9], ext[5] ;

    size ( 32, 0 ) ;  /* hide cursor */

    /* draw the enclosing box */
    drawbox ( 1, 0, 23, 79, 27 ) ;

    /* display current cursor location */
    writecol( ) ;
    writerow( ) ;

    /* find drive name */
    if ( filespec[1] == ':' )
        drive[0] = filespec[0] ;
    else
        drive[0] = getdisk( ) + 65 ;
    drive[1] = '\0' ;

    fnsplit ( filespec, "", "", fname, ext ) ;

    strcpy ( filename, " " ) ;
    strcat ( filename, drive ) ;
    strcat ( filename, ":" ) ;
    strcat ( filename, fname ) ;

    /* if extension exists */
    if ( ext[0] )
        strcat ( filename, ext ) ;
```

```
        strcat ( filename, " " ) ;
        strupr ( filename ) ;

        /* display file name */
        len = strlen ( filename ) ;
        writestring ( filename, 1, 39 - len / 2, 27 ) ;

        size ( 5, 7 ) ;  /* show cursor */
}

/* displays current row number */
writerow( )
{
        int i ;
        char s[10] ;

        /* overwrite currently displayed  row number */
        for ( i = 0 ; i <= 3 ; i++ )
            writechar ( 23, 60 + i, 205, 27 ) ;

        /* display current row number */
        itoa ( curr - 1, s, 10 ) ;
        writestring ( s, 23, 64 - strlen ( s ), 15 ) ;
        writechar ( 23, 64, ':', 15 ) ;

        /* position the cursor */
        gotoxy ( logc + 1, logr + 2 ) ;
}

/* displays current column number */
writecol( )
{
        int i ;
        char s[10] ;

        /* overwrite currently displayed column number */
```

```
        for ( i = 0 ; i <= 2 ; i++ )
            writechar ( 23, 65 + i, 205, 27 ) ;

        /* display current column number */
        itoa ( curc, s, 10 ) ;
        writestring ( s, 23, 65, 15 ) ;
        writechar ( 23, 64, ':', 15 ) ;

        /* position the cursor */
        gotoxy ( logc + 1, logr + 2 ) ;
}

/* displays certain special keys and their significance */
status_line( )
{
        menubox ( 24, 0, 24, 79, 112, NO_SHADOW ) ;
        writestring ( "^F^1-Help   ^F^2-Save   ^S^h^-^F^1^0-Product Info
                    ^A^l^t^-^X-Exit", 24, 1, 112 ) ;

        /* display current status of Ins key */
        if ( *ins & 0x80 )
            writestring ( "Insert", 24, 73, 47 ) ;
}

/* displays a message and collects the string entered in response */
ask_name ( str, name )
char *str, *name ;
{
        int area, esc_flag, len ;
        char *p, currentdir[31] ;

        /* allocate memory, if unsuccessful terminate execution */
        area = ( 17 - 7 + 1 ) * ( 62 - 17 + 1 ) * 2 ;
        p = malloc ( area ) ;
        if ( p == NULL )
            error_exit( ) ;
```

```
/* create dialogue box */
savevideo ( 7, 17, 17, 62, p ) ;
menubox ( 7, 17, 17, 62, 112, 7 ) ;
drawbox ( 7, 17, 16, 60 , 112 ) ;

len = strlen ( str ) ;
writestring ( str, 9, 39 - len / 2, 112 ) ;

menubox ( 11, 21, 12, 56, 32, HALF_SHADOW ) ;

/* if directory name is to be entered, display current directory */
if ( strcmp ( str, "Enter directory name" ) == 0 )
{
      getcwd ( currentdir, 30 ) ;
      writestring ( currentdir, 11, 22, 47 ) ;
}

menubox ( 14, 27, 15, 51, 32, HALF_SHADOW ) ;
writestring ( "Press Esc to cancel", 14, 29, 47 ) ;

/* collect the string entered */
esc_flag = getname ( 11, 22, name ) ;

restorevideo ( 7, 17, 17, 62, p ) ;
free ( p ) ;
return ( esc_flag ) ;
}

/* collects a string from keyboard */
getname ( row, col, p )
int row, col ;
char *p ;
{
      int i = 0 ;
      char str[30] ;

      size ( 5, 7 ) ;
```

```
/* continue to collect characters until Esc or Enter key is hit */
while ( 1 )
{
    gotoxy ( col + i + 1, row + 1 ) ;
    getkey( ) ;

    if ( ascii == 27 )
        return ( ESC ) ;

    /* if current directory name is displayed, erase it */
    if ( i == 0 )
        menubox ( 11, 21, 12, 56, 32, HALF_SHADOW ) ;

    /* if Enter is hit or more than 30 characters have been entered */
    if ( ascii == 13 || i > 30 )
        break ;

    /* if backspace key is hit */
    if ( ascii == '\b' )
    {
        /* if at least one character has been entered */
        if ( i != 0 )
        {
            i-- ;
            writechar ( row, col + i, ' ', 47 ) ;
        }
    }

    /* if a valid ascii character and not a control character */
    if ( isascii ( ascii ) && ! iscntrl ( ascii ) )
    {
        str[i] = ascii ;
        writechar ( row, col + i, ascii, 47 ) ;
        i++ ;
    }
}
```

```
        str[i] = '\0' ;  /* terminate string */
        strcpy ( p, str ) ;
        size ( 32, 0 ) ;
        return ( 0 ) ;
}

/* displays message strings passed to it */
message ( str1, str2 )
char *str1, *str2 ;
{
        int area, len ;
        char *p ;

        size ( 32, 0 ) ;

        /* allocate memory, if unsuccessful terminate execution */
        area = ( 17 - 8 + 1 ) * ( 60 - 19 + 1 ) * 2 ;
        p = malloc ( area ) ;
        if ( p == NULL )
            error_exit( ) ;

        /* create dialogue box */
        savevideo ( 8, 19, 16, 60, p ) ;
        menubox ( 8, 19, 16, 60, 112, 7 ) ;
        drawbox ( 8, 19, 15, 58 , 112 ) ;

        writestring ( filename, 10, 25, 112 ) ;

        /* display the two strings */
        writestring ( str1, 10, 26 + strlen ( filename ), 112 ) ;
        len = strlen ( str2 ) ;
        writestring ( str2, 11, 39 - len / 2, 112 ) ;

        /* display Yes, No and Cancel buttons */
        menubox ( 13, 24, 14, 30, 32, HALF_SHADOW ) ;
        writestring ( " $Yes ", 13, 24, 32 ) ;
```

```
        menubox ( 13, 44, 14, 53, 32, HALF_SHADOW ) ;
        writestring ( " $Cancel ", 13, 44, 32 ) ;
        menubox ( 13, 34, 14, 39, 32, HALF_SHADOW ) ;
        writestring ( " $No ", 13, 34, 32 ) ;

        /* continue till Y, N or C is hit */
        while ( 1 )
        {
            getkey( ) ;
            ascii = toupper ( ascii ) ;
            if ( ascii == 'Y' || ascii == 'N' || ascii == 'C' )
                break ;
        }

        restorevideo ( 8, 19, 16, 60, p ) ;
        free ( p ) ;

        size ( 5, 7 ) ;
        return ( ascii ) ;
}

/* loads the specified file in memory */
load( )
{
        FILE *fp ;
        int i = 0, flag = 0 ;
        char ans = 'N', *temp ;

        temp = endloc ;
        saved = YES ;
        menubox ( 24, 0, 24, 79, 112, NO_SHADOW ) ;
        write_fname( ) ;  /* write the name of the file */
        writestring ( "Loading Editor File...", 24, 1, 112 ) ;

        /* initialise endloc so that it points to the beginning of buffer */
        endloc = buf ;
```

```c
/* open the specified file */
fp = fopen ( filespec, "r" ) ;

/* if unable to open file */
if ( fp == NULL )
{
    menubox ( 24, 0, 24, 79, 112, NO_SHADOW ) ;

    /* ask whether to create a new file */
    ans = message ( "does not exist...", "Create ?" ) ;
}
else
{
    /* read file contents into buffer */
    while ( ( buf[i] = getc ( fp ) ) != EOF )
    {
        i++ ;

        /* if the file size exceeds the buffer size */
        if ( i == maxsize )
        {
            ans = message ( "too large!", "Truncate ?" ) ;

            /* if file is to be truncated */
            if ( ans == 'Y' )
                break ;
            else
            {
                endloc = temp ;
                status_line( ) ;
                return ( 0 ) ;
            }
        }

        endloc++ ;
    }
}
```

```
/* if loading was successful or if new file is to be created */
if ( fp != NULL || ans == 'Y' )
{
    /* reset variables */
    curr = 2 ;
    curc = 1 ;
    logr = 1 ;
    logc = 1 ;
    skip = 0 ;
    startloc = curscr = currow = buf ;

    /* display current cursor location */
    writerow( ) ;
    writecol( ) ;

    /* clear previous screen contents */
    menubox ( 2, 1, 22, 78, 27, NO_SHADOW ) ;

    /* display one screen-full (or less) of loaded file */
    displayscreen ( curscr ) ;

    /* store the name of the file in the pick list */
    strcpy ( pickfile[pickfileno], filespec ) ;

    pickfileno++ ;  /* increment the number of pick files */

    if ( pickfileno > 4 )  /* a maximum of 5 files are present in the pick list */
        pickfileno = 0 ;

    flag = 1 ;
    status_line( ) ;
}
else
{
    endloc = temp ;
    status_line( ) ;
```

```
            return ( 0 ) ;
    }

    /* close the file */
    fclose ( fp ) ;

    return ( flag ) ;
}

/* checks if current file is saved or not */
check_saved( )
{
    char ans ;

    /* if file is not saved */
    if ( saved == NO )
    {
        ans = message ( "is not saved...", "Save ?" ) ;

        if ( ans == 'Y' )
            save( ) ;
    }
}

/* displays a line and returns 0 if end of file is encountered while printing that
    line and returns 1 otherwise */
displayline ( p, row )
char *p ;
int row ;
{
    int col, tabflag = 0, i, num ;

    if ( p >= endloc )
        return ( 0 ) ;

    num = skip ;
```

```
/* skip past 'skip' number of characters at the beginning of the line */
for ( i = 1 ; i <= skip ; i++ )
{
    /* if a newline is encountered */
    if ( *p == '\n' )
        return ( 1 ) ;

    /* if a tab is encountered */
    if ( *p == '\t' )
    {
        /* if less than 8 characters remain to be skipped */
        if ( num <= 8 )
            tabflag = 1 ;
        else
        {
            /* skip past the tab */
            i += 7 ;
            num -= 8 ;

            p++ ;
            if ( p >= endloc )
                return ( 0 ) ;
        }
    }
    else
    {
        p++ ;
        if ( p >= endloc )
            return ( 0 ) ;
    }
}

/* display the line */
for ( col = 1 ; col < 79 ; col++ )
{
    if ( *p == '\n' )
        return ( 1 ) ;
```

```
        if ( *p == '\t' )
        {
            if ( tabflag )
            {
                /* leave  spaces representing part of the tab not scrolled
                    past horizontally */
                col += ( 7 - num ) ;
                tabflag = 0 ;
            }
            else
                col += 7 ;
        }
        else
            writechar ( row, col, *p, 27 ) ;

        p++ ;
        if ( p >= endloc )
            return ( 0 ) ;
    }

    return ( 1 ) ;
}

/* displays one screen full (or less) of file contents on screen */
displayscreen ( p )
char *p ;
{
    int row, status ;

    for ( row = 2 ; row < 23 ; row++ )
    {
        /* print one line */
        status = displayline ( p, row ) ;

        /* if end of file is reached while printing the line */
        if ( status == 0 )
```

```
                return ( 0 ) ;

        /* increment the pointer to point to the beginning of next line */
        while ( *p != '\n' )
        {
                p++ ;

                /* if p reaches beyond the last character in the file */
                if ( p >= endloc )
                        return ( 0 ) ;
        }
        p++ ;

        /* if p reaches beyond the last character in the file */
        if ( p >= endloc )
                return ( 0 ) ;
    }
}

/* loads selected file from the pick list */
pick( )
{
    int choice, flag ;
    char fname[31] ;

    /* if pick list is empty */
    if ( pickfileno == 0 )
        return ;

    strcpy ( fname, filespec ) ;

    /* pop up pick file list */
    choice = popupmenuv ( pickfile, pickfileno, 1, 23, "", 7 ) ;

    /* if file is selected from the popped pick list */
    if ( choice != ESC )
    {
```

```
            /* check if current file has been saved */
            check_saved( ) ;
            strcpy ( filespec, pickfile[choice - 1] ) ;

            /* load file into buffer */
            flag = load( ) ;

            /* if unable to load file */
            if ( flag == 0 )
            {
                strcpy ( filespec, fname ) ;
                write_fname( ) ;
            }
        }
}

/* sets up a new file for editing */
new( )
{
    /* check if current file has been saved */
    check_saved( ) ;

    /* set up 'NONAME' as the default file name */
    strcpy ( filespec, "NONAME" ) ;
    write_fname( ) ;

    /* reset variables */
    curr = 2 ;
    curc = 1 ;
    logr = 1 ;
    logc = 1 ;
    saved = YES ;

    /* initialise pointers so that they point to the beginning of buffer */
    startloc = endloc = curscr = currow = buf ;

    /* clear previous screen contents */
```

```
        menubox ( 2, 1, 22, 78, 27, NO_SHADOW ) ;

        /* display current cursor location */
        writecol( ) ;
        writerow( ) ;
}

/* stores a file on disk */
save( )
{
        FILE *fp ;
        char *p ;

        size ( 32, 0 ) ;

        /* if current file name is 'NONAME' */
        if ( strcmp ( filespec, "NONAME" ) == 0 )
        {
                /* ask for the new file name */
                ask_name ( "Enter file name", filespec ) ;

                /* write new file name */
                write_fname( ) ;

                /* add new file name to pick list */
                strcpy ( pickfile[pickfileno], filespec ) ;
                pickfileno++ ;
                if ( pickfileno > 4 )
                        pickfileno = 0 ;
        }

        /* open file for writing and check if successful */
        fp = fopen ( filespec, "w" ) ;
        if ( fp == NULL )
        {
                message ( "File creation error", "Return ?" ) ;
                return ( 0 ) ;
```

```
        }

        menubox ( 24, 0, 24, 79, 112, NO_SHADOW ) ;
        writestring ( "Saving Editor File...", 24, 1, 112 ) ;

        p = startloc ;

        /* write each character in the buffer into file */
        while ( p != endloc )
        {
            putc ( *p, fp ) ;
            p++ ;
        }

        fclose ( fp ) ;
        saved = YES ;
        status_line( ) ;  /* display status line */
        size ( 5, 7 ) ;
        return ( 1 ) ;
}

/* saves the curent file under a new name */
save_as( )
{
    int success ;

    size ( 32, 0 ) ;

    /* receive the new file name */
    ask_name ( "Enter new file name", filespec ) ;

    success = save( ) ;  /* save the file under new name */

    if ( success )
    {
        /* display new file name */
        write_fname( ) ;
```

```
        /* update pick list */
        strcpy ( pickfile[pickfileno], filespec ) ;
        pickfileno++ ;
        if ( pickfileno > 4 )
            pickfileno = 0 ;
    }

    size ( 5, 7 ) ;
}

/* merges another file into current file at current cursor location */
merge( )
{
    int col, i ;
    unsigned count = 0 ;
    unsigned long totalsize ;
    FILE *fp ;
    char ans, str[17], *temp ;

    size ( 32, 0 ) ;

    strcpy ( str, filename ) ;

    /* receive name of file to merge */
    ask_name ( "Enter file name", filename ) ;

    /* open file and check if successful in opening */
    fp = fopen ( filename, "r" ) ;
    if ( fp == NULL )
    {
        message ( "does not exist...", "OK ?" ) ;
        strcpy ( filename, str ) ;
        return ;
    }

    /* count characters in file to be merged */
```

```
while ( getc ( fp ) != EOF )
    count++ ;

totalsize = ( unsigned ) ( endloc - startloc ) ;
totalsize += count ;

/* check would  the file size exceed the buffer size on merging */
if ( totalsize >= maxsize )
{
    ans = message ( "too large!", "Truncate ?" ) ;

    /* if file is to be truncated */
    if ( ans == 'Y' )
        count = maxsize - ( unsigned ) ( endloc - startloc ) ;
    else
        return ;
}

/* increment 'temp' to point to character at current cursor location */
temp = currow ;
for ( col = 1 ; col < curc ; col++ )
{
    if ( *temp == '\t' )
        col += 7 ;

    if ( *temp == '\n' || temp == endloc )
        break ;

    temp++ ;
}

/* move characters after 'temp' ahead by 'count' bytes */
memmove ( temp + count , temp, endloc - temp ) ;

/* update ending location pointer */
endloc += count ;
```

```
        saved = NO ;

        /* read the file to be merged into the buffer */
        rewind ( fp ) ;
        for ( i = 0 ; i < count ; i++ )
        {
            *temp = getc ( fp ) ;
            temp++ ;
        }

        /* clear screen contents from current row onwards */
        menubox ( logr + 1, 1, 22, 78, 27, NO_SHADOW ) ;

        /* update screen contents */
        displayscreen ( curscr ) ;

        strcpy ( filename, str ) ;

        size ( 5, 7 ) ;
}

/* changes default directory */
change_dir( )
{
        char dirname[31], *p ;
        int status, area, esc_flag ;

        /* collect directory name */
        esc_flag = ask_name ( "Enter directory name", dirname ) ;
        if ( esc_flag )
            return ;

        status = chdir ( dirname ) ;

        /* allocate memory, if unsuccessful terminate execution */
        area = ( 17 - 8 + 1 ) * ( 60 - 19 + 1 ) * 2 ;
        p = malloc ( area ) ;
```

```
            if ( p == NULL )
                error_exit( ) ;

            /* create dialogue box */
            savevideo ( 8, 19, 16, 60, p ) ;
            menubox ( 8, 19, 16, 60, 112, 7 ) ;
            drawbox ( 8, 19, 15, 58 , 112 ) ;

            menubox ( 10, 21, 11, 56, 32, HALF_SHADOW ) ;
            menubox ( 13, 21, 14, 56, 32, HALF_SHADOW ) ;

            /* check if successful in changing directory */
            if ( status == 0 )
            {
                writestring ( "Directory sucessfully changed", 10, 22, 47 ) ;
                write_fname( ) ;
            }
            else
                writestring ( "Error in changing directory", 10, 22, 47 ) ;

            writestring ( "Press any key...", 13, 22, 47 ) ;
            fflush ( stdin ) ;
            getch( ) ;

            restorevideo ( 8, 19, 16, 60, p ) ;
            free ( p ) ;
}

/* prints the file on printer */
print( )
{
        int area, tm, bm, pl, i, row = 1, esc_flag, top_of_page = 1 ;
        char *p, ch, topmargin[3], botmargin[3], pagelength[3], fname[31] ;
        FILE *fs ;

        /* receive the file name */
        esc_flag = ask_name ( "Enter file name", fname ) ;
```

```
if ( esc_flag )
    return ;

/* allocate memory, if unsuccessful terminate execution */
area = ( 17 - 8 + 1 ) * ( 60 - 19 + 1 ) * 2 ;
p = malloc ( area ) ;
if ( p == NULL )
    error_exit( ) ;

/* create dialogue box */
savevideo ( 8, 19, 16, 60, p ) ;
menubox ( 8, 19, 15, 60, 112, 7 ) ;
drawbox ( 8, 19, 14, 58 , 112 ) ;

/* open file and check if successful */
fs = fopen ( fname, "r" ) ;
if ( fs == NULL )
{
    writestring ( "Unable to open", 10, 25, 112 ) ;
    writestring ( fname, 10, 40, 112 ) ;
    writestring ( "Press any key to return...", 11, 24, 112 ) ;
    fflush ( stdin ) ;
    getch( ) ;
    restorevideo ( 8, 19, 16, 60, p ) ;
    free ( p ) ;
    return ;
}

/* collect page specifications */
esc_flag = ask_name ( "Top Margin", topmargin ) ;
esc_flag = ask_name ( "Bottom Margin", botmargin ) ;
esc_flag = ask_name ( "Page Length", pagelength ) ;

tm = atoi ( topmargin ) ;
bm = atoi ( botmargin ) ;
pl = atoi ( pagelength ) ;
```

```
writestring ( "Set up the printer", 9, 27, 112 ) ;
writestring ( "Press any key when ready...", 10, 25, 112 ) ;
menubox ( 12, 27, 13, 51, 32, HALF_SHADOW ) ;
writestring ( "Press Esc to cancel", 12, 29, 47 ) ;
getkey( ) ;
restorevideo ( 8, 19, 16, 60, p ) ;
free ( p ) ;

if ( ascii == ESC )
    return ;

/* continue printing till end of file is reached */
while ( ( ch = fgetc ( fs ) ) != EOF )
{
    /* if at top of page */
    if ( top_of_page )
    {
        /* skip top margin */
        for ( i = 0 ; i < tm ; i++ )
            putc ( '\n', stdprn ) ;

        top_of_page = 0 ;
    }

    putc ( ch, stdprn ) ;

    /* if end of line is encountered */
    if ( ch == '\n' )
    {
        row++ ;

        /* if at end of page */
        if ( row == pl - tm - bm )
        {
            /* skip bottom margin */
            for ( i = 0 ; i < bm ; i++ )
                putc ( '\n', stdprn ) ;
```

```
                        top_of_page = 1 ;
                        row = 1 ;
                }
            }
        }
}

/* searches a string in current file */
find( )
{
    int esc_flag ;

    /* collect the string to be searched */
    esc_flag = ask_name ( "Enter search string", searchstr ) ;
    if ( esc_flag )
        return ( esc_flag ) ;

    search ( searchstr ) ;
}

/* searches string and returns a pointer to it */
char *search ( searchstr )
char *searchstr ;
{
    char *p, *temp, *t_loc ;
    int len, area, col, tr, tc, tlr, tlc ;

    /* initialise temporary variables */
    t_loc = currow ;
    tr = curr ;
    tc = curc ;
    tlr = logr ;
    tlc = logc ;

    len = strlen ( searchstr ) ;
```

```
/* increment 'temp' to point to character at current cursor location */
temp = currow ;
for ( col = 1 ; col < curc ; col++ )
{
    if ( *temp == '\t' )
        col += 7 ;

    if ( *temp == '\n' || temp >= endloc )
        break ;

    temp++ ;
}

/* search string until end of file is reached or string is found */
while ( strncmp ( searchstr, temp, len ) != 0 )
{
    /* if end of file is reached */
    if ( temp >= endloc )
    {
        /* allocate memory, if unsuccessful terminate execution */
        area = ( 17 - 8 + 1 ) * ( 60 - 19 + 1 ) * 2 ;
        p = malloc ( area ) ;
        if ( p == NULL )
            error_exit( ) ;

        /* create dialogue box */
        savevideo ( 8, 19, 16, 60, p ) ;
        menubox ( 8, 19, 16, 60, 112, 7 ) ;
        drawbox ( 8, 19, 15, 58 , 112 ) ;

        menubox ( 10, 21, 11, 56, 32, HALF_SHADOW ) ;
        menubox ( 13, 21, 14, 56, 32, HALF_SHADOW ) ;
        writestring ( "Search unsuccessful!", 10, 22, 47 ) ;
        writestring ( "Press any key...", 13, 22, 47 ) ;
        fflush ( stdin ) ;
        getch( ) ;
```

```
        /* reset the variables */
        currow = t_loc ;
        curr = tr ;
        curc = tc ;
        logr = tlr ;
        logc = tlc ;

        restorevideo ( 8, 19, 16, 60, p ) ;
        free ( p ) ;
        size ( 5, 7 ) ;
        return ( 0 ) ;
    }
    else
    {
        if ( *temp == '\t' )
        {
            curc += 8 ;
            temp++ ;
        }
        else
        {
            if ( *temp == '\n' )
            {
                /* go to beginning of next row */
                curr++ ;
                curc = 1 ;
                temp++ ;
                currow = temp ;
            }
            else
            {
                curc++ ;
                temp++ ;
            }
        }
    }
}
```

```
        logr = 1 ;

        /* position cursor at the end of search string */
        curc += ( len - 1 ) ;

        /* if the string searched lies beyond 78th column on that line */
        if ( curc > 78 )
        {
            skip = curc - 78 ;
            logc = 78 ;
        }
        else
        {
            skip = 0 ;
            logc = curc ;
        }

        /* display the file from the line which contains the search string */
        curscr = currow ;
        menubox ( 2, 1, 22, 78, 27, NO_SHADOW ) ;
        displayscreen ( curscr ) ;
        writecol( ) ;
        writerow( ) ;

        size ( 5, 7 ) ;
        return ( temp ) ;
}

/* searches for a string and replaces it with another string */
replace( )
{
    int esc_flag ;

    /* collect string to be searched */
    esc_flag = ask_name ( "Enter search string", searchstr ) ;
    if ( esc_flag )
```

```
        return ;

    /* collect string to be substituted */
    esc_flag = ask_name ( "Replace with", replacestr ) ;
    if ( esc_flag )
        return ;

    f_and_r ( searchstr, replacestr ) ;
}

/* searches a string and replaces it with the specified string */
f_and_r ( searchstr, replacestr )
char *searchstr, *replacestr ;
{
    int area, ls, lr, i ;
    char *p, *temp, *wherefr, ans ;

    /* search string and set up a pointer pointing to its beginning */
    wherefr = search ( searchstr ) ;

    /* if search is unsuccessful */
    if ( wherefr == 0 )
        return ( 0 ) ;

    /* allocate memory, if unsuccessful terminate execution */
    area = ( 17 - 8 + 1 ) * ( 60 - 19 + 1 ) * 2 ;
    p = malloc ( area ) ;
    if ( p == NULL )
        error_exit( ) ;

    /* create dialogue box */
    savevideo ( 8, 19, 16, 60, p ) ;
    menubox ( 9, 19, 15, 60, 112, 7 ) ;
    drawbox ( 9, 19, 14, 58 , 112 ) ;

    menubox ( 11, 29, 12, 48, 32, HALF_SHADOW ) ;
    writestring ( "Replace (Y/N)", 11, 30, 47 ) ;
```

```
size ( 5, 7 ) ;

/* alternate cursor between searched string and message till a key is hit */
while ( !kbhit( ) )
{
    gotoxy ( 45, 12 ) ;
    delay ( 10 ) ;
    gotoxy ( logc + 1, logr + 2 ) ;
    delay ( 10 ) ;
}

fflush ( stdin ) ;
ans = getch( ) ;
restorevideo ( 8, 19, 16, 60, p ) ;
free ( p ) ;

if ( ! ( ans == 'y' || ans == 'Y' ) )
    return ( 0 ) ;

saved = NO ;

ls = strlen ( searchstr ) ;
lr = strlen ( replacestr ) ;

if ( exceed_size ( ( unsigned ) ( endloc - startloc + lr - ls ) ) )
    return ( 1 ) ;

/* move the contents of the file after the search string to accomodate the
   replace string */
memmove ( wherefr + lr, wherefr + ls, endloc - ( wherefr + ls ) ) ;
endloc += ( lr - ls ) ;

/* substitute the search string with the replace string */
temp = wherefr ;
for ( i = 0 ; i < lr ; i++ )
{
```

```
                *temp = replacestr[i] ;
                temp++ ;
           }

           curc += ( lr - ls ) ;

           /* if the replaced string lies beyond 78th column on that line */
           if ( curc > 78 )
           {
                skip = curc - 78 ;
                logc = 78 ;
           }
           else
           {
                skip = 0 ;
                logc = curc ;
           }

           /* display the file from the line which contains the replaced string */
           curscr = currow ;
           menubox ( 2, 1, 22, 78, 27, NO_SHADOW ) ;
           displayscreen ( curscr ) ;
           writecol( ) ;
     }

/* continues the last search operation */
repeat_last( )
{
     /* if find flag is set, search the next occurrence of the string */
     if ( findflag )
          search ( searchstr ) ;

     /* if find and replace flag is set, search and replace the next occurrence
        of the string */
     if ( frflag )
          f_and_r ( searchstr, replacestr ) ;
}
```

```
/* abandons search operation */
abort_find( )
{
    frflag = 0 ;
    findflag = 0 ;
}

/* displays file contents from specified line onwards */
gotoline( )
{
    char lineno[31], *temp ;
    int number, esc_flag ;

    /* collect the line number */
    esc_flag = ask_name ( "Enter line number", lineno ) ;
    if ( esc_flag )
        return ;

    number = atoi ( lineno ) ;
    currow = startloc ;
    temp = currow ;
    curr = 2 ;
    curc = 1 ;

    /* continue till the required line is reached */
    while ( curr != ( number + 1 ) )
    {
        /* if end of file is reached */
        if ( temp >= endloc )
            break ;

        /* if end of line is reached */
        if ( *temp == '\n' )
        {
            curr++ ;
            temp++ ;
```

```
                  currow = temp ;
           }
        else
             temp++ ;
   }

   /* display file contents starting from the specified line */
   skip = 0 ;
   curscr = currow ;
   menubox ( 2, 1, 22, 78, 27, NO_SHADOW ) ;
   displayscreen ( curscr ) ;

   /* display current cursor position */
   logr = 1 ;
   logc = 1 ;
   writerow( ) ;
   writecol( ) ;

   size ( 5, 7 ) ;
}

/* deletes character to the left of cursor */
backspace( )
{
   char *temp ;
   int col ;

   /* if cursor is at the first character in file */
   if ( curc == 1 && curr == 2 )
        return ;

   /* increment 'temp' to point to character at current cursor location */
   temp = currow ;
   for ( col = 1 ; col < curc ; col++ )
   {
        if ( *temp == '\t' )
             col += 7 ;
```

```
            /* if cursor is beyond the end of line */
            if ( *temp == '\n' )
            {
                left( ) ;
                return ;
            }

            temp++ ;
        }

        /* if the character to the left of cursor is '\n' */
        if ( *( temp - 1 ) == '\n' )
        {
            /* position cursor in the previous line */
            up_line ( 1 ) ;

            /* position cursor at the end of the line */
            end_line( ) ;

            /* delete the '\n' at the end of the line */
            del_char( ) ;
        }
        else
        {
            /* position cursor one column to the left */
            left( ) ;

            /* delete the character at current cursor location */
            del_char( ) ;
        }
    }

/* deletes the character at current cursor position */
del_char( )
{
    char *temp ;
```

```
int col, row, count = 0 ;

/* if cursor is at end of file */
if ( currow >= endloc )
    return ;

/* increment 'temp' to point to character at current cursor location */
temp = currow ;
for ( col = 1 ; col < curc ; col++ )
{
    if ( temp >= endloc )
        return ;

    if ( *temp == '\t' )
        col += 7 ;

    /* if cursor is beyond the end of line */
    if ( *temp == '\n' )
        break ;

    temp++ ;
}

if ( temp >= endloc )
    return ;

/* if cursor is at the end of the line or beyond the end of line */
if ( *temp == '\n' )
{
    /* count number of spaces from end of line to current cursor position */
    count = curc - col ;

    /* rearrange buffer to move the end of line to current cursor position */
    memmove ( temp + count, temp + 1, endloc - temp ) ;

    /* put spaces from last character in the line till current cursor position */
    memset ( temp, 32, count ) ;
```

```
endloc += ( count - 1 ) ;
saved = NO ;

/* display the modified line */
menubox ( logr + 1, 1, logr + 1, 78, 27, NO_SHADOW ) ;
displayline ( currow, logr + 1 ) ;

/* scroll the screen after current line */
scrollup ( logr + 2, 1, 22, 78 ) ;

/* display the line in the last row */
temp = currow ;
for ( row = logr + 1 ; row < 22 ; row++ )
{
    /* go to the beginning of next line */
    while ( *temp != '\n' )
    {
        if ( temp >= endloc )
            return ;
        temp++ ;
    }
    temp++ ;

    if ( temp >= endloc )
        return ;
}
displayline ( temp, row ) ;
}
else
{
    /* rearrange buffer to delete the character */
    memmove ( temp, temp + 1, endloc - temp ) ;

    endloc-- ;
    saved = NO ;
```

```
            /* display the modified line */
            menubox ( logr + 1, 1, logr + 1, 78, 27, NO_SHADOW ) ;
            displayline ( currow, logr + 1 ) ;
    }
}

/* deletes the line in which cursor is currently present */
del_line( )
{
    char *temp ;
    int count = 1, row ;

    /* if cursor is at end of file */
    if ( currow == endloc )
        return ( 0 ) ;

    /* count number of characters in the line to be deleted */
    temp = currow ;
    while ( *temp != '\n' )
    {
        /* if end of file is encountered */
        if ( temp >= endloc )
            break ;

        count++ ;
        temp++ ;
    }

    /* if the line to be deleted is the last line and there is no Enter at the end
       of the line */
    if ( temp >= endloc )
    {
        /* position 'endloc' */
        endloc -= count ;

        /* erase last line */
        menubox ( logr + 1, 1, logr + 1, 78, 27, NO_SHADOW ) ;
```

```
        /* position cursor at the beginning of previous line */
        up_line ( 1 ) ;
        start_line( ) ;

        return ( 0 ) ;
    }

    temp++ ;

    /* rearrange the buffer so that current line is deleted */
    memmove ( currow, temp, endloc - temp ) ;

    endloc -= count ;
    saved = NO ;

    /* scroll the screen after current line */
    scrollup ( logr + 1, 1, 22, 78 ) ;

    /* display the line in the last row */
    temp = currow ;
    for ( row = logr + 1 ; row < 22 ; row++ )
    {
        /* go to the beginning of next line */
        while ( *temp != '\n' )
        {
            if ( temp >= endloc )
                return ( 0 ) ;
            temp++ ;
        }
        temp++ ;

        if ( temp >= endloc )
            return ( 0 ) ;
    }
    displayline ( temp, row ) ;
}
```

```
/* deletes line to the left of current cursor position */
del_line_lt( )
{
    char *temp ;
    int count, col ;

    /* if cursor is at end of file */
    if ( currow >= endloc )
        return ;

    /* count the number of characters to the left of cursor */
    temp = currow ;
    count = 0 ;
    for ( col = 1 ; col < curc ; col++ )
    {
        if ( *temp == '\t' )
            col += 7 ;

        /* if cursor is to the right of the end of current line */
        if ( *temp == '\n' )
        {
            del_line( ) ;  /* delete the entire line */
            return ;
        }

        temp++ ;
        count++ ;
    }

    /* rearrange the buffer so that line to the left of cursor is deleted */
    memmove ( currow, temp, endloc - temp ) ;

    endloc -= count ;
    saved = NO ;

    /* display the modified line */
```

```
        menubox ( logr + 1, 1, logr + 1, 78, 27, NO_SHADOW ) ;
        displayline ( currow, logr + 1 ) ;

        /* position cursor at the beginning of the line */
        start_line( ) ;
}

/* deletes line to the right of current cursor position */
del_line_rt( )
{
        char *temp, *temp1 ;
        int col, count = 0 ;

        /* if cursor is at end of file */
        if ( currow >= endloc )
            return ;

        /* increment 'temp' to point to character at current cursor location */
        temp = currow ;
        for ( col = 1 ; col < curc ; col++ )
        {
            if ( temp >= endloc )
                return ;

            if ( *temp == '\t' )
                col += 7 ;

            /* if cursor is to the right of the end of current line */
            if ( *temp == '\n' )
                return ;

            temp++ ;
        }

        /* if cursor is at the end of line */
        if ( *temp == '\n' )
            return ;
```

```
        /* count the number of characters to the right of cursor */
        temp1 = temp ;
        count = 0 ;
        while ( *temp1 != '\n' )
        {
            if ( temp1 >= endloc )
                break ;

            temp1++ ;
            count++ ;
        }

        /* rearrange the buffer so that line to the right of cursor is deleted */
        memmove ( temp, temp1, endloc - temp1 ) ;

        endloc -= count ;
        saved = NO ;

        /* display the modified line */
        menubox ( logr + 1, 1, logr + 1, 78, 27, NO_SHADOW ) ;
        displayline ( currow, logr + 1 ) ;
}

/* deletes the word to the right of current cursor position */
del_word_rt( )
{
        char *temp, *temp1 ;
        int col, row, count = 0 ;

        /* if cursor is at end of file */
        if ( currow >= endloc )
            return ;

        /* increment 'temp' to point to character at current cursor location */
        temp = currow ;
        for ( col = 1 ; col < curc ; col++ )
```

```
        {
                if ( temp >= endloc )
                        return ;

                if ( *temp == '\t' )
                        col += 7 ;

                /* if cursor is beyond the end of line */
                if ( *temp == '\n' )
                        break ;

                temp++ ;
        }

        if ( temp >= endloc )
                return ;

        /* if cursor is at the end of the line or beyond the end of line */
        if ( *temp == '\n' )
        {
                /* count number of spaces from end of line to current cursor position */
                count = curc - col ;

                /* rearrange buffer to move the end of line to current cursor position */
                memmove ( temp + count, temp + 1, endloc - temp ) ;

                /* put spaces from last character in line till current cursor position */
                memset ( temp, 32, count ) ;

                endloc += ( count - 1 ) ;
                saved = NO ;

                /* display the modified line */
                menubox ( logr + 1, 1, logr + 1, 78, 27, NO_SHADOW ) ;
                displayline ( currow, logr + 1 ) ;

                /* scroll the screen after current line */
```

```
        scrollup ( logr + 2, 1, 22, 78 ) ;

        /* display the line in the last row */
        temp = currow ;
        for ( row = logr + 1 ; row < 22 ; row++ )
        {
            /* go to the beginning of next line */
            while ( *temp != '\n' )
            {
                if ( temp >= endloc )
                    return ;
                temp++ ;
            }
            temp++ ;
            if ( temp >= endloc )
                return ;
        }
        displayline ( temp, row ) ;
    }
    else
    {
        temp1 = temp ;

        /* if character at current cursor position is alphanumeric */
        if ( isalnum ( *temp1 ) )
        {
            /* continue till a non-alphanumeric character is encountered */
            while ( isalnum ( *temp1 ) )
            {
                if ( temp1 == endloc )
                    break ;

                temp1++ ;
                count++ ;
            }
        }
        else
```

```
        {
            /* go to the next character */
            temp1++ ;
            count++ ;
        }

        /* skip consecutive spaces */
        while ( *temp1 == ' ' )
        {
            if ( temp1 == endloc )
                break ;

            temp1++ ;
            count++ ;
        }

        /* rearrange buffer so that word to the right of cursor is deleted */
        memmove ( temp, temp1, endloc - temp1 ) ;
        endloc -= count ;

        /* display the modified line */
        menubox ( logr + 1, 1, logr + 1, 78, 27, NO_SHADOW ) ;
        displayline ( currow, logr + 1 ) ;
    }
}

/* takes control temporarily to DOS */
shell( )
{
    int area, status ;
    char *p ;

    /* allocate memory, if unsuccessful terminate execution */
    area = ( 24 - 0 + 1 ) * ( 79 - 0 + 1 ) * 2 ;
    p = malloc ( area ) ;
    if ( p == NULL )
        error_exit( ) ;
```

```
        /* create dialogue box */
        savevideo ( 0, 0, 24, 79, p ) ;
        menubox ( 0, 0, 24, 79, 7, NO_SHADOW ) ;
        menubox ( 8, 21, 16, 60, 127, 47 ) ;

        drawbox ( 9, 23, 14, 56, 127 ) ;

        writestring ( "Quitting temporarily to DOS", 11, 25, 127 ) ;
        writestring ( "Type EXIT to return...", 13, 25, 127 ) ;

        gotoxy ( 7, 1 ) ;
        status = system ( "C:\\COMMAND.COM" ) ;

        /* if unable to load 'COMMAND.COM' */
        if ( status == -1 )
        {
            writestring ( "Oops! Cannot load COMMAND.COM!", 11, 25, 127 ) ;
            writestring ( "Press any key...", 13, 25, 127 ) ;
            fflush ( stdin ) ;
            getch( ) ;
        }

        restorevideo ( 0, 0, 24, 79, p ) ;
        free ( p ) ;
}

/* ensures that no action takes place if Ctrl - C or Ctrl - Break is hit */
void interrupt handler( )
{
        ctrl_c_flag = 1 ;
}

/* places a character on the screen */
displaychar ( ch )
char ch ;
{
```

```
char *temp ;
int col = 1, insert ;

/* if current column exceeds 249, beep */
if ( curc >= 249 )
{
    printf ( "\a" ) ;
    return ;
}

/* check the status of Ins key */
if ( *ins & 0x80 )
    insert = YES ;
else
    insert = NO ;

/* if Enter key is hit replace it with newline */
if ( ch == '\r' )
    ch = '\n' ;

/* increment 'temp' to point to character at current cursor location */
temp = currow ;
for ( col = 1 ; col < curc ; col++ )
{
    /* if cursor is beyond the end of line or the end of file is reached */
    if ( *temp == '\n' || temp >= endloc )
    {
        /* if spacebar was hit */
        if ( ch == ' ' )
        {
            /* position cursor one column to the right */
            right( ) ;
            return ;
        }

        /* if Enter key was hit */
        if ( ch == '\n' )
```

```
            break ;

        if ( exceed_size ( ( unsigned )( endloc - startloc + curc - col + 1 )))
            return ;

        /* rearrange buffer to move end of line to current cursor position */
        memmove ( temp + curc - col, temp, endloc - temp ) ;

        /* put spaces from last character in line till current cursor position */
        memset ( temp, 32, curc - col ) ;

        /* position 'temp' at the end of these spaces */
        temp += curc - col ;

        endloc += curc - col ;
        saved = NO ;

        /* rearrange the buffer to accomodate the character hit */
        memmove ( temp + 1, temp, endloc - temp ) ;

        /* store the character in the buffer */
        *temp = ch ;

        endloc++ ;

        /* display the character */
        writechar ( logr + 1, logc, ch, 27 ) ;

        /* position cursor one column to the right */
        if ( ch == '\t' )
        {
            curc += 8 ;
            logc += 8 ;

            /* position cursor at appropriate column */
            gotocol( ) ;
        }
```

```
            else
                right( ) ;

            return ;
        }

        if ( *temp == '\t' )
            col += 7 ;

        temp++ ;
    }

    /* if Enter key is hit */
    if ( ch == '\n' )
    {
        /* if cursor is at or beyond the last character in the file */
        if ( temp >= endloc )
        {
            if ( exceed_size ( ( unsigned ) ( endloc - startloc + 1 ) ) )
                return ;

            /* put the character in the buffer */
            *temp = ch ;

            endloc++ ;
            saved = NO ;

            /* erase the current line */
            menubox ( logr + 1, logc, logr + 1, 78, 27, NO_SHADOW ) ;

            /* display the modified line */
            displayline ( currow, logr + 1 ) ;

            /* position cursor at the beginning of the next line */
            down_line ( 1 ) ;
            start_line( ) ;
            return ;
```

```
        }

    /* if Ins is off */
    if ( insert == NO )
    {
        /* position cursor at the beginning of the next line */
        down_line ( 1 ) ;
        start_line( ) ;

        /* position cursor on the first non-whitespace character */
        temp = currow ;
        while ( *temp == ' ' || *temp == '\t' )
        {
            if ( *temp == '\t' )
                curc += 7 ;

            temp++ ;
            curc++ ;
        }

        /* if the first non-whitespace character is beyond the first 78
           columns */
        if ( curc > 78 )
        {
            /* scroll the screen horizontally */
            logc = 78 ;
            skip = curc - 78 ;
            menubox ( 2, 1, 22, 78, 27, NO_SHADOW ) ;
            displayscreen ( curscr ) ;
        }
        else
            logc = curc ;

        writecol( ) ;
        return ;
    }
}
```

```
/* if Ins is on or end of file is encountered */
if ( insert == YES || temp == endloc || *temp == '\n' )
{
    if ( exceed_size ( ( unsigned ) ( endloc - startloc+ 1 ) ) )
        return ;

    /* rearrange the buffer to accomodate the character */
    memmove ( temp + 1, temp, endloc - temp ) ;

    endloc++ ;
}

/* place the character in the buffer */
*temp = ch ;

saved = NO ;

/* if Enter is hit (Ins is on) */
if ( ch == '\n' )
{
    /* remove spaces and tabs at the end of the line */
    del_whitespace( ) ;

    /* erase the current row */
    menubox ( logr + 1, logc, logr + 1, 78, 27, NO_SHADOW ) ;

    /* scroll down the screen below the current line */
    scrolldown ( logr + 2, 1, 22, 78 ) ;

    /* position cursor at the beginning of the next line */
    down_line ( 1 ) ;
    start_line( ) ;

    /* display the modified current line */
    displayline ( currow, logr + 1 ) ;
}
```

```
            else
            {
                /* erase the current line */
                menubox ( logr + 1, logc, logr + 1, 78, 27, NO_SHADOW ) ;

                /* display the modified line */
                displayline ( currow, logr + 1 ) ;

                /* if tab key is hit */
                if ( ch == '\t' )
                {
                    curc += 8 ;
                    logc += 8 ;

                    /* position cursor at appropriate column */
                    gotocol( ) ;
                }
                else
                    right( ) ;  /* position cursor in the next column */
            }
}

/* displays error message and terminates execution */
error_exit( )
{
    writestring ( "Memory Allocation Error! Press any key...", 22, 14, 112) ;
    fflush ( stdin ) ;
    getch( ) ;
    exit ( 2 ) ;
}

/* removes spaces and tabs at the end of the line */
del_whitespace( )
{
    char *temp ;

    /* go to the end of the line */
```

```
        temp = currow ;
        while ( *temp != '\n' )
        {
            if ( temp >= endloc )
                return ;

            temp++ ;
        }

        /* remove tabs and spaces after the end of the line */
        while ( * ( temp - 1 ) == '\t' || * ( temp - 1 ) == ' ' )
        {
            memmove ( temp - 1, temp, endloc - temp ) ;
            temp-- ;
            endloc-- ;
        }
    }


/* checks whether the maximum buffer size is exceeded */
exceed_size ( size )
unsigned int size ;
{
    int area ;
    void *p ;

    if ( size >= maxsize )
    {
        /* allocate memory, if unsuccessful terminate execution */
        area = ( 14 - 11 + 1 ) * ( 64 - 15 + 1 ) * 2 ;
        p = malloc ( area ) ;
        if ( p == NULL )
            error_exit( ) ;

        /* create dialogue box */
        savevideo ( 9, 15, 15, 65, p ) ;
        menubox ( 9, 15, 15, 65, 112, 7 ) ;
        drawbox ( 9, 15, 14, 63, 112 ) ;
```

```
        writestring ( "File size too large! Delete some characters!!", 11, 17, 112 ) ;
        writestring ( "Press any key...", 12, 17, 112 ) ;
        getch( ) ;

        restorevideo ( 9, 15, 15, 65, p ) ;
        return ( 1 ) ;
    }

    return ( 0 ) ;
}
```

User Defined Functions

abort_find( )	Abandons search operation.
about( )	Displays product information.
ask_name( )	Displays a message and collects the string entered in response.
backspace( )	Deletes character to the left of cursor.
bottom_screen( )	Positions cursor in the last row of current screen.
change_dir( )	Changes default directory.
check_saved( )	Checks if current file is saved or not.
cserver( )	Displays Cursor Movement menu, receives choice and branches control to appropriate function.
del_char( )	Deletes the character at current cursor position.
del_line( )	Deletes the line in which cursor is currently present.
del_line_lt( )	Deletes line to the left of current cursor position.
del_line_rt( )	Deletes line to the right of current cursor position.
del_whitespace( )	Removes spaces and tabs at the end of the line.
del_word_rt( )	Deletes the word to the right of current cursor position.
displaychar( )	Places a character on the screen.
displayhelp( )	Displays context sensitive help.
displayline( )	Displays a line and returns 0 if end of file is encountered while printing that line and returns 1 otherwise.
displaymenuh( )	Displays menu horizontally.
displaymenuv( )	Displays menu vertically.
displayscreen( )	Displays one screen full(or less) of file contents on screen.
down_line( )	Positions cursor one line down.
drawbox( )	Draws a double-lined box.
dserver( )	Displays Delete menu, receives choice and branches control to appropriate function.
end_file( )	Positions cursor at the end of the file.

end_line( )	Positions cursor at the end of current row.
error_exit( )	Displays error message and terminates execution.
eserver( )	Displays Exit menu, receives choice and branches control to appropriate function.
exceed_size( )	Checks whether the maximum buffer size is exceeded.
f_and_r( )	Searches a string and replaces it with the specified string.
find( )	Searches a string in current file.
fserver( )	Displays File menu, receives choice and branches control to appropriate function.
getkey( )	Gets ascii and scan code of key pressed.
getname( )	Collects a string from keyboard.
getresponseh( )	Receives user's choice for the horizontal menu displayed.
getresponsev( )	Receives user's choice for the vertical menu displayed.
gotocol( )	Positions cursor in appropriate column.
gotoline( )	Displays file contents from specified line onwards.
handler( )	Ensures that no action takes place if Ctrl-C or Ctrl-Break is hit.
left( )	Positions cursor one column to the left.
load( )	Loads the specified file in memory.
menubox( )	Displays filled box with or without shadow.
merge( )	Merges another file into current file at current cursor location.
message( )	Displays message strings passed to it.
mm_server( )	Displays Main Menu, receives choice and branches control to appropriate function.
new( )	Sets up a new file for editing.
page_down( )	Displays next file page.
page_up( )	Displays previous file page.
pick( )	Loads selected file from the pick list.
popupmenuv( )	Pops up a menu vertically.
print( )	Prints the file on printer.
repeat_last( )	Continues the last search operation.

replace( )	Searches for a string and replaces it with another string.
restorevideo( )	Restores screen contents from allocated memory.
right( )	Positions cursor one column to the right.
save( )	Stores a file on disk.
save_as( )	Saves the current file under a new name.
savevideo( )	Saves screen contents into allocated memory.
scrolldown( )	Scrolls the screen contents down.
scrollup( )	Scrolls the screen contents up.
search( )	Searches string and returns a pointer to it.
shell( )	Takes control temporarily to DOS.
size( )	Displays or hides cursor.
sserver( )	Displays Search menu, receives choice and branches control to appropriate function.
start_file( )	Positions cursor at the beginning of the file.
start_line( )	Positions cursor at the beginning of current row.
status_line( )	Displays certain special keys and their significance.
top_screen( )	Positions cursor in the first row of current screen.
up_line( )	Positions cursor one line up.
word_left( )	Positions cursor one word to the left.
word_right( )	Positions cursor one word to the right.
workscreen( )	Creates working screen.
write_fname( )	Writes the name of the file.
writechar( )	Writes a character in specified attribute.
writecol( )	Displays current column number.
writerow( )	Displays current row number.
writestring( )	Writes a string in specified attribute.

3

Chart Master

Numbers in financial, statistical or other numerical information have a limited reach in the sense that it may be difficult to extract subtle trends or notice gradual changes in performance from rows and columns of numerical data. Numerical results are often skimmed over quickly with just a few cursory glances at the numbers. In the process one may miss fundamental conclusions about performance. An illustrative picture - a graph - showing results as they change helps one to recognise patterns and trends one would otherwise overlook.

However, plotting and drawing graphs can prove to be quite a task! Specially so if there's an abundance of data, as is bound to be in any industrial, economical or any such analysis. With computers, however, the whole exercise of drawing graphs is reduced to a few key hits. And Chart Master will show you what goes into the making of this convenient utility. You will learn how to create a software that offers different graph types as may be required in different situations.

Throughout the program, we switch between the graphics and text modes with the help of standard library functions **initgraph( )** and **restorecrtmode( )**. The graphs are drawn in graphics mode, while the remaining operations like menu management, entry of data etc. are carried out in the text mode. Naturally, Chart Master won't work on computers which do not support graphics capabilities. Very often while switching from text to graphics mode or vice versa it is necessary to save the screen contents in memory. Saving text screen image is **savevideo( )**'s job, whereas **getimage( )** is employed to save graphics image. However, there is a catch here. For saving the text screen we need 4000 bytes in memory, since every character's ascii value and attribute needs to be saved, and there are 2000 characters on the screen. However, for saving the graphics image the number of bytes required is obtained using the formula:

$$4 + (\text{ number of pixels per scan line} + 7) / 8 * \text{number of scan lines}$$

In high resolution graphics mode (Chart Master draws all graphs in this mode) the number of scan lines is 200 and pixels across scan lines are 640. Once the number of bytes is calculated, **malloc( )** is put to work to reserve memory for saving the text/graphics screen. The function **alloc_error_exit( )** is called should **malloc( )** fail to do the job. As the name suggests, this function displays a memory allocation error message and terminates execution.

Menu management

Life would have been miserable had software not been menu driven. Highlighted bars, hot keys, context sensitive help, all have become part of a C programmer's daily routine. Therefore any C programmer who wishes to manage menus has to have his customised tool-box comprising small but useful functions. As you may have realised over the last two chapters, our menu management tool-kit consists of functions like **popupmenu( )**, **getresponse( )**, **displaymenu( )**, **menubox( )**, **drawbox( )**, **writestring( )**, **writechar( )**, **getkey( )**, **savevideo( )**, **restorevideo( )**, etc. We first developed these functions in Chapter 1 and thereafter have been using them more or less faithfully for all types of menus. Here we would avoid the explanation of these functions. Should you wish to have a closer look at these functions, you are referred to Chapter 1.

Data Services

In Chart Master, the graphs can be drawn for a maximum of 6 different y axes. Hence, for each x axis entry, there can be from 1 to 6 corresponding sets of y axis entries. Further, you can have upto 15 such x axis entries.

The function **data_options( )** is called for supplying data for the graph to be drawn. The user may enter data directly from the keyboard, or initialise it from a file created beforehand. For the former case, the values entered by the user are collected by the function **getnum( )**. This function stores the entered number as a string and then converts it back to a value using the function **atof( )**. Examine **getnum( )** closely. It would help you understand how back space, Escape, Enter, decimal point, minus sign, etc. are managed by standard library functions while inputting numbers. As each x axis and y axis entry is received using **getnum( )**, it is displayed and stored appropriately in the arrays **xrange[ ]** and **yrange[ ][ ]** respectively. Once a given number of x axis entries have been input, the program takes care that for different y axes (minimum 1, maximum 6) those many y axis entries are provided.

If you wish to make any modifications in the entered data, you can do so using the Edit option of the Data Entry submenu. The function **editdata( )** is used for this purpose. Whenever current data is edited or fresh data is either entered from keyboard or read from file, a function **verifydata( )** is called. This function gets the data okayed from the user and optionally saves it in a file using the function **storedata( )**.

Giving Legends

Legends add to the clarity of a graph. Apart from giving descriptions to the symbol of each data type, this option allows you to give a title to the graph as well as to the x and y axes. The function **legend( )**

uses **getstr( )**, written on the lines of **getnum( )**, in order to read a string of limited characters from the keyboard. Once the legends have been entered, the user is given a choice to save the data as well as the legends in a file. Thus, the next time the same graph is to be viewed, the data and legends need not be re-entered.

The Omnipresent data_type

What if the user attempts to give legends without having entered the data? Or what if the user tries to draw a graph without entering the data and/or legend? Well, no problem! A global variable **data_type** keeps track of the current status of data and legend entries and thus manages to avoid the above pitfalls. The following figure shows the different values that **data_type** may contain and their significance.

data_type	Source of data	Source of legend
1	File	Legend not available
2	File	File
3	Keyboard	Keyboard
4	Keyboard	Legend not available

Figure 3.1

Two more global variables that are used at a number of places are **max_x_entries** and **max_y_sets**. The first one signifies the number of x axis entries made and the second signifies the number of y axes employed. Another global variable of significance is **graph_ptr**. Whenever a graph is drawn, it is saved in a portion of memory, which is pointed to by this pointer variable.

Drawing Graphs

Having initialised the data, the Graph option gives you a choice between 5 types of graphs - Bar, Stacked Bar, Pie, XY, and Line chart. These graphs are shown in Figures 3.3 through 3.6. The sample data used for drawing these graphs is as shown in Figure 3.2.

Yr.	Baseball	Basketball	Football	Golf
1991	16000.00	42000.00	9000.00	28000.00
1992	31500.00	20000.00	37000.00	46000.00
1993	20500.00	30000.00	36000.00	16500.00
1994	8050.00	13500.00	5500.00	19000.00

Figure 3.2 Consolidated Sales figures

Bar Chart

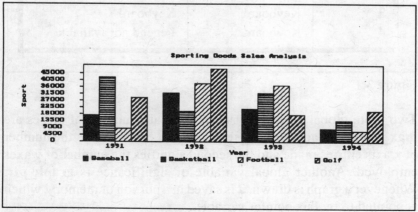

Figure 3.3

A bar chart is usually used to compare related data at a certain time or to show the trend of numeric data across time. As shown in Figure 3.3, it is made up of rectangles filled with different patterns, their dimensions depending on the data entered. Hence, with the available data, we first determine the value of the largest and smallest y axis entry. This information is the deciding factor for the scale to which the y axis is reduced or enlarged. The number of bars required is calculated as the number of x axis entries multiplied by the number of y axis values for each. Next, depending on the number of bars to be drawn and the magnitude of each y entry, the width and height respectively of each bar is calculated. This done, the bars are drawn using the function **bar3d( )**, whose arguments include the coordinates of the diagonal of the rectangular bar. For different y axis values pertaining to the same x axis entry, these bars are filled with different patterns. If there are any negative y axis entries, then the program appropriately adjusts the position of the x axis and the bars.

Stacked Bar Chart

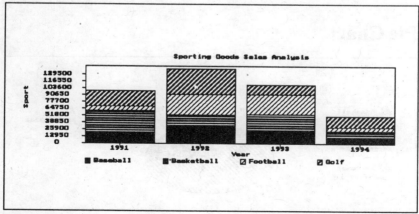

Figure 3.4

The stacked bar chart comes in useful while comparing two or more data ranges and the proportion of the total contributed by each data point. In this type of graph, all data values corresponding to a single x axis entry are depicted as bars of appropriate height stacked one above the other. Hence, here we draw only as many bars as there are x axis entries, as the various y axis values are represented along the height of the bar for each x axis value.

We begin by adding separately the positive and negative values of each set of y axis entries, i.e. the positive and negative values specified for A, B, C, etc. for each x. Now the scaling factor for the y axis is determined, so that the maximum positive sum lies at the top end of the y axis, and the maximum negative one at the bottom. Thus, care is taken of the stray instances of plotting a stacked bar graph with negative values. Calculating the width of each bar is simple. Next, bars filled in various patterns are drawn in such a way that the base of each consecutive bar coincides with the top of the one drawn prior to it. If some values are negative, obviously the bar for these would be displayed below the x axis.

For both bar and stacked bar type of graphs, legends appear at the bottom describing the pattern used for each data type.

Pie Chart

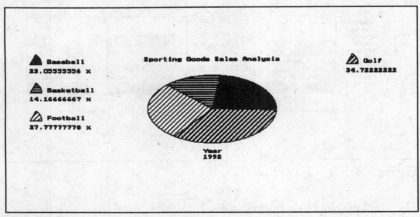

Figure 3.5

A pie chart is used when the data is to be analysed on the basis of percentage taken up by each y axis value for an individual x axis entry. Thus, we regard the sum of all y axis entries for a single x axis value as 100%, and show the component sectors in keeping with the area shared by each of the data values A, B, C, etc. Starting from the positive x axis as reference, the sectors are marked successively, and description of each is depicted on either side of the pie diagram. Since a pie chart shows component sectors of a circle, it is not equipped to handle negative values.

XY and Line Charts

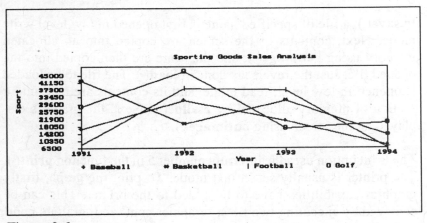

Figure 3.6

In these charts, we first determine both the minimum as well as maximum x and y axis entries. If all values are positive, instead of starting from the origin, we start our x and y axes from the minimum required values as specified by their respective entries. In case of data comprising of negative values, we scale our axes appropriately in order to accommodate either sides of both the axes. Next, the x axis entries are sorted in ascending order, and the corresponding y axis values are rearranged. Note that the sorting is not done in Bar, Stacked Bar or Pie chart. This is because these graphs are used essentially for comparisons, rather than for evaluating trends. For an XY chart, only plotting the coordinates is sufficient, while a line chart requires these points to be joined by straight lines. The standard library function **line( )** is used for doing this. The sorted x-coordinates allow proper joining of consecutive points.

File Operations

Once the graphs have been created and the legends added, you would surely want to save your work, review it from time to time or get a hard copy of it. File menu offers to do all this for you.

In **save( )**, a file of specified name is first opened in low level write mode. Next, contents of the screen are copied into an allocated memory using **getimage( )**, and the same are then copied into the opened file. Just the reverse is done in **load( )**. The file to be loaded is opened in low level, read mode, and its contents are read into a section of memory allocated by **malloc( )**. Next, the graph is displayed on the screen using **putimage( )**.

The Print option uses the interrupt number 5 in the function **print( )**. The printer is usually set in text mode. To print the graph, firstly graphics capabilities have to be added to the printer. This can be achieved by executing two files, 'graphics.com' and 'graftabl.com' in that order at the DOS prompt.

Exit options

This option allows the user either to quit Chart Master permanently or to work in a DOS shell. If DOS shell is selected the DOS prompt is displayed and normal DOS commands can then be executed. You may resume working with Chart Master by typing 'EXIT' at the DOS prompt.

The Timekeeper

Be it a normal exit (when you select exit option) or an abnormal exit (when memory allocation fails), Chart Master always informs you for how much time you were using it. This is achieved by noting the time at the beginning of the execution of Chart Master, and then calling the function **activetime( )** just before the termination. **activetime( )** calculates the time difference and converts it to the format of hours, minutes and seconds. On exiting, these are then displayed in the top row on the screen.

Program

For ease in handling the entire code, it has been split in two files, namely CHARTHDR.C and CHART.C. The listings of these files are given below.

CHARTHDR.C

```c
# include "graphics.h"
# include "dos.h"
# include "math.h"
# include "process.h"
# include "alloc.h"
# include "stdlib.h"
# include "stdio.h"
# include "fcntl.h"
# include "ctype.h"
# include "types.h"
# include "stat.h"

# define CGA 1
# define ENTRYOVER 1
# define ENTRYSTART 0
# define ESCAPE 27
# define END 79
# define LINE 1
# define XY 2

/* various menu definitions */
/* character following ^ symbol is the hot key */
char *mainmenu[ ] =   {
                        " ^Data ",
                        " ^Graph ",
                        " ^Files ",
```

```
                                 " ^Exit "
                          } ;

char *datamenu[ ] =    {
                                 " ^File ",
                                 " ^Keyboard ",
                                 " ^Return "
                          } ;

char *graphmenu[ ] =  {
                                 " ^Bar chart ",
                                 " ^Stacked bar ",
                                 " ^Pie chart ",
                                 " ^X Y chart ",
                                 " ^Line chart ",
                                 " ^Return "
                          } ;

char *filesmenu[ ] = {
                                 " ^Load ",
                                 " ^Save ",
                                 " ^Print ",
                                 " ^Return "
                          } ;

char *keyboardmenu[ ] =   {
                                    " ^New data ",
                                    " ^Edit data ",
                                    " ^Legend ",
                                    " ^Return "
                            } ;

char *exitmenu[ ] =    {
                                 " ^Exit ",
                                 " ^Shell ",
                                 " ^Return "
                          } ;
```

```c
char *messages[ ] =   {
                        "Main Menu",
                        "Allows entry of data from file / keyboard",
                        "Draws bar / stacked / X Y / line / pie chart",
                        "Loads / Saves / Prints a graph",
                        "Exit to DOS",
                        "Data Menu",
                        "Reads data from a file",
                        "Entry of data from keyboard",
                        "Return to main menu",
                        "Graph Menu",
                        "Draws bar chart",
                        "Draws stacked bar chart",
                        "Draws pie chart",
                        "Draws X Y chart",
                        "Draws line chart",
                        "Return to main menu",
                        "File Menu",
                        "Loads a graph",
                        "Saves a graph",
                        "Prints a graph",
                        "Return to main menu",
                        "Keyboard Menu",
                        "Enter fresh data",
                        "Edit current data",
                        "Entry of legend",
                        "Return to Data menu",
                        "Exit Menu",
                        "Exit to DOS",
                        "OS Shell",
                        "Return to main menu",
                        "   Chart Master   ",
                      "Memory allocation error",
                      "Press any key to continue...",
```

```
int count, ascii, scan, data_type, max_x_entries, max_y_sets, area, gd, gm ;
long starttime, endtime ;
char y_sets_desc[6][31], titles[3][31], filename[31], arr[ ] = "ABCDEF" ;
char *graph_ptr ;
char far *vid_mem ;
double yrange[15][6], xrange[15] ;

/* symbols used for indicating points while drawing XY/Line chart */
char *symbol[ ] = { "+", "*", "█", "O", "|", "#" } ;

/* pops up a menu on the existing screen contents */
popupmenu ( menu, count, hotkeys, helpnumber )
int count, helpnumber ;
char **menu, *hotkeys ;
{
    int sr, sc, er, ec, srmenu, scmenu, i, l = 0, len, areareqd, choice ;
    char *p ;

    /* calculate starting row and ending row of menu box */
    sr = ( 25 - ( count + 10 ) ) / 2 ;
    er = 24 - sr ;
    if ( count % 2 )
        er++ ;

    /* find the longest help message */
    for ( i = 1 ; i <= count ; i++ )
    {
        len = strlen ( messages[helpnumber + i] ) ;
        if ( len > l )
            l = len ;
    }

    /* calculate starting column of menu box depending on longest help
      message */
    sc = ( 80 - ( l + 9 ) ) / 2 ;

    /* calculate ending column of menu box */
```

```
ec = 80 - sc ;

/* calculate area required to save screen contents where menu is to be
   popped up */
areareqd = ( er - sr + 1 ) * ( ec - sc + 1 ) * 2 ;

/* allocate memory, if unsuccessful display error and terminate execution */
p = malloc ( areareqd ) ;
if ( p == NULL )
    alloc_error_exit( ) ;

/* save screen contents into allocated memory */
savevideo ( sr, sc, er, ec, p ) ;

/* give the effect of zooming menus */
delay ( 15 ) ;
menubox ( 9, 37, 15, 42, 127, 0 ) ;
drawbox ( 9, 37, 15, 42, 127 ) ;
delay ( 15 ) ;
menubox ( sr, sc, er, ec, 127, 07 ) ;
drawbox ( sr + 1, sc + 2, er - 2, ec - 4, 127 ) ;

/* determine length of current menu name */
l = strlen ( messages[helpnumber] ) ;

/* calculate column from where the menu name is to be displayed */
l = 39 - l / 2 ;

/* display menu name */
writestring ( messages[helpnumber], sr + 2, l, 127 ) ;

/* draw two horizontal lines */
for ( i = sc + 3 ; i <= ec - 4 ; i++ )
{
    writechar ( sr + 3, i, 196, 127 ) ;
    writechar ( er - 4, i, 196, 127 ) ;
}
```

```
/* display corner characters */
writechar ( sr + 3, sc + 2, 199, 127 ) ;
writechar ( er - 4, sc + 2, 199, 127 ) ;
writechar ( sr + 3, ec - 4, 182, 127 ) ;
writechar ( er - 4, ec - 4, 182, 127 ) ;

/* find the longest menu item in current menu */
l = 0 ;
for ( i = 0 ; i < count ; i++ )
{
    len = strlen ( menu[i] ) ;
    if ( len > l )
        l = len ;
}

/* calculate starting row and starting column for displaying menu items */
srmenu = ( ( 25 - count ) / 2 ) - 1 ;
scmenu = ( ( 80 - ( l + 6 ) ) / 2 ) - 1 ;

/* display the menu in the menu box drawn earlier */
displaymenu ( menu, count, srmenu, scmenu ) ;

/* display help message */
writestring ( messages[helpnumber + 1], er - 3, sc + 4, 127 ) ;

/* receive user's choice */
choice = getresponse ( menu, hotkeys, srmenu, scmenu, count,
                                helpnumber + 1, er, sc ) ;

/* restore original screen contents */
restorevideo ( sr, sc, er, ec, p ) ;

/* free allocated memory */
free ( p ) ;

return ( choice ) ;
}
```

```
/* writes a character and its attribute in VDU memory */
writechar ( r, c, ch, attb )
int r, c, attb ;
char ch ;
{
    char far *v ;

    /* calculate address in VDU memory corresponding to row r and column c */
    v = vid_mem + r * 160 + c * 2 ;
    *v = ch ;  /* store character */
    v++ ;
    *v = attb ;  /* store attribute */
}

/* writes a string into VDU memory in the desired attribute */
writestring ( s, r, c, attb )
int r, c, attb ;
char *s ;
{
    while ( *s != '\0' )
    {
        /* if the next character is a hot key, write in different attribute,
           otherwise in normal attribute */
        if ( *s == '^' )
        {
            s++ ;
            writechar ( r, c, *s, 113 ) ;
        }
        else
            writechar ( r, c, *s, attb ) ;
        s++ ;
        c++ ;
    }
}

/* saves screen contents into allocated memory in RAM */
```

```
savevideo ( sr, sc, er, ec, buffer )
int sr, sc, er, ec ;
char *buffer ;
{
     char far *v ;
     int i, j ;

     for ( i = sr ; i <= er ; i++ )
     {
         for ( j = sc ; j <= ec ; j++ )
         {
             /* calculate address in VDU memory corresponding to row r and column c */
             v = vid_mem + i * 160 + j * 2 ;
             *buffer = *v ;  /* store character */
             v++ ;
             buffer++ ;
             *buffer = *v ;  /* store attribute */
             buffer++ ;
         }
     }
}


/* restores screen contents from allocated memory in RAM */
restorevideo ( sr, sc, er, ec, buffer )
int sr, sc, er, ec ;
char *buffer ;
{
     char far *v ;
     int i, j ;

     for ( i = sr ; i <= er ; i++ )
     {
         for ( j = sc ; j <= ec ; j++ )
         {
             /* calculate address in VDU memory corresponding to row r and column c */
             v = vid_mem + i * 160 + j * 2 ;
             *v = *buffer ;  /* restore character */
```

```
                v++ ;
                buffer++ ;
                *v = *buffer ;  /* restore attribute */
                buffer++ ;
            }
        }
}

/* draws a filled box with or without shadow */
menubox ( sr, sc, er, ec, fill, shadow )
int sr, sc, er, ec, fill, shadow ;
{
    int i, j ;

    /* draw filled box */
    for ( i = sr ; i < er ; i++ )
        for ( j = sc ; j < ( ec - 1 ) ; j++ )
            writechar ( i, j, ' ', fill ) ;

    /* if shadow is desired */
    if ( shadow != 0 )
    {
        /* draw a column with different attribute */
        for ( i = sr + 1 ; i <= er ; i++ )
        {
            writechar ( i, ec, ' ', shadow ) ;
            writechar ( i, ec - 1, ' ', shadow ) ;
        }

        /* draw a row with different attribute */
        for ( j = sc + 2 ; j <= ec ; j++ )
            writechar ( er, j, ' ', shadow ) ;
    }
    else
    {
        /* draw a column with same attribute as menu box */
        for ( i = sr ; i <= er ; i++ )
```

```
        {
            writechar ( i, ec, ' ', fill ) ;
            writechar ( i, ec - 1, ' ', fill ) ;
        }

        /* draw a row with same attribute as menu box */
        for ( j = sc ; j <= ec ; j++ )
            writechar ( er, j, ' ', fill ) ;
    }
}

/* displays the menu in the box drawn by menubox( ) */
displaymenu ( menu, count, sr, sc )
int sr, sc, count ;
char **menu ;
{
    int i ;

    for ( i = 0 ; i < count ; i++ )
    {
        /* write menu item in VDU memory */
        writestring ( menu[i], sr + 1, sc + 1, 127 ) ;
        sr++ ;
    }
}

/* draws a double lined box */
drawbox ( sr, sc, er, ec, attr )
int sr, sc, er, ec, attr ;
{
    int i ;

    /* draw vertical lines */
    for ( i = sc + 1 ; i < ec ; i++ )
    {
        writechar ( sr, i , 205, attr ) ;
        writechar ( er, i, 205, attr ) ;
```

```
        }

        /* draw horizontal lines */
        for ( i = sr + 1 ; i < er ; i++ )
        {
            writechar ( i, sc, 186, attr ) ;
            writechar ( i, ec, 186, attr ) ;
        }

        /* draw four corners */
        writechar ( sr, ec, 187, attr ) ;
        writechar ( er, sc, 200, attr ) ;
        writechar ( er, ec, 188, attr ) ;
        writechar ( sr, sc, 201, attr ) ;
}

/* gets user's response for the current menu */
getresponse ( menu, hotkeys, sr, sc, count, helpnumber, ermenu, scmenu )
char **menu, *hotkeys ;
int sr, sc, ermenu, scmenu, count, helpnumber ;
{
        int choice = 1, len, hotkeychoice, i, l = 0 ;

        /* find the longest help message */
        for ( i = 0 ; i < count ; i++ )
        {
            len = strlen ( messages[helpnumber + i] ) ;
            if ( len > l )
                l = len ;
        }

        /* highlight first menu item */
        writestring ( menu[choice - 1], sr + choice, sc + 1, 15 ) ;

        while ( 1 )
        {
            getkey( ) ;  /* receive key */
```

```
/* if special key is hit */
if ( ascii == 0 )
{
    switch ( scan )
    {
        case 80 :  /* down arrow key */

                /* make highlighted item normal */
                writestring ( menu[choice - 1], sr + choice, sc + 1, 127 ) ;

                choice++ ;
                helpnumber++ ;
                break ;

        case 72 :  /* up arrow key */

                /* make highlighted item normal */
                writestring ( menu[choice - 1], sr + choice, sc + 1, 127 ) ;

                choice-- ;
                helpnumber-- ;
                break ;

        default :
                break ;
    }

    /* if highlighted bar is on first item and up arrow key is hit */
    if ( choice == 0 )
    {
        choice = count ;
        helpnumber = helpnumber + count ;
    }

    /* if highlighted bar is on last item and down arrow key is hit */
    if ( choice > count )
```

```
                {
                    choice = 1 ;
                    helpnumber = helpnumber - count ;
                }

                /* highlight the appropriate menu item */
                writestring ( menu[choice - 1], sr + choice, sc + 1, 15 ) ;

                /* clear previous help message */
                for ( i = scmenu + 4 ; i < ( scmenu + 4 + l ) ; i++ )
                    writechar ( ermenu - 3, i, ' ', 127 ) ;

                /* write the corresponding help message */
                writestring ( messages[helpnumber], ermenu - 3, scmenu + 4,
                        127 ) ;
        }
        else
        {
                if ( ascii == 13 )  /* Enter key */
                    return ( choice ) ;

                ascii = toupper ( ascii ) ;
                hotkeychoice = 1 ;
                len = strlen ( hotkeys ) ;

                /* check whether hot key has been pressed */
                while ( *hotkeys != '\0' )
                {
                    if ( *hotkeys == ascii )
                        return ( hotkeychoice ) ;
                    else
                    {
                        hotkeys++ ;
                        hotkeychoice++ ;
                    }
                }
                /* reset variable to point to the first hot key character */
```

```
                hotkeys = hotkeys - len ;
            }
        }
}

/* gets ascii and scan codes of key pressed */
getkey( )
{
    union REGS i, o ;

    /* wait till a key is hit */
    while ( !kbhit( ) )
        ;

    i.h.ah = 0 ;  /* service number */

    /* issue interrupt */
    int86 ( 22, &i, &o ) ;

    ascii = o.h.al ;
    scan = o.h.ah ;
}

/* displays or hides the cursor */
size ( ssl, esl )
int ssl, esl ;
{
    union REGS i, o ;

    i.h.ah = 1 ;  /* service number */
    i.h.ch = ssl ;  /* starting scan line */
    i.h.cl = esl ;  /* ending scan line */
    i.h.bh = 0 ;  /* video page number */

    /* issue interrupt for changing the size of the cursor */
    int86 ( 16, &i, &o ) ;
}
```

CHART.C

```
# include "charthdr.c"
main( )
{
     int mchoice ;

     /* collect the time at which execution of the program begins */
     time ( &starttime ) ;

     /* determine graphics driver by checking the hardware */
     detectgraph ( &gd, &gm ) ;

     /* if hardware doesn't support graphics */
     if ( gd == -2 )
     {
          printf ( "\nThis program requires hardware with graphics capability to
                         operate successfully" ) ;
          printf ( "\nPlease use this program on such a system" ) ;
          printf ( "\nPress any key..." ) ;
          fflush ( stdin ) ;  /* flush the keyboard buffer */
          getch( ) ;
          activetime( ) ;  /* calculate and display active time */
          exit ( 1 ) ;  /* terminate program execution */
     }

     /* store base address of VDU memory */
     vid_mem = ( char far * ) 0xb8000000L ;

     /* set video mode to text mode */
     textmode ( 3 ) ;

     /* calculate area required to save entire screen contents in graphics mode */
     area = 4 + ( 640 + 7 ) / 8 * 200 ;

     /* allocate memory, if unsuccessful display error and terminate execution */
```

```
graph_ptr = malloc ( area ) ;
if ( graph_ptr == NULL )
    alloc_error_exit( ) ;

/* prepare the screen on which the different menus are popped up */
size ( 32, 0 ) ;
menubox ( 0, 0, 24, 79, 47, 0 ) ;
drawbox ( 0, 0, 24, 79, 47 ) ;
writestring ( messages[30], 0, 31, 48 ) ;

while ( 1 )
{
    /* pop up Main menu and collect choice made by user */
    mchoice = popupmenu ( mainmenu, 4, "DGFE", 0 ) ;

    /* test choice received */
    switch( mchoice)
    {
        case 1 :
            data_options( ) ;
            break ;

        case 2 :
            graph_options( ) ;
            break ;

        case 3 :
            file_options( ) ;
            break ;

        case 4 :
            exit_options( ) ;
    }
}
}

/* pops up Data menu, receives choice, branches to appropriate function */
```

```
data_options( )
{
    int dchoice ;

    while ( 1 )
    {
        dchoice = popupmenu ( datamenu, 3, "FKR", 5 ) ;

        switch ( dchoice )
        {
            case 1 :  /* read data from a file */
                data_from_file( ) ;
                break ;

            case 2 :  /* receive data from the keyboard */
                data_from_kb( ) ;
                break ;

            case 3 :  /* return to main menu */
                return ;
        }
    }
}

/* pops up Graph menu, receives choice, branches to appropriate function */
graph_options( )
{
    int gchoice ;

    while ( 1 )
    {
        gchoice = popupmenu ( graphmenu, 6, "BSPXLR", 9 ) ;

        switch ( gchoice )
        {
            case 1 :  /* bar  chart */
                bar_chart( ) ;
```

```
            break ;

        case 2 :  /* stacked bar chart */
            stack_bar_chart( ) ;
            break ;

        case 3 :  /* pie chart */
            pie_chart( ) ;
            break ;

        case 4 :  /* XY chart */
            xy_or_line ( XY ) ;
            break ;

        case 5 :  /* line chart */
            xy_or_line ( LINE ) ;
            break ;

        case 6 :  /* return to main menu */
            return ;
        }
    }
}

/* pops up File menu, receives choice, branches to appropriate function */
file_options( )
{
    int fchoice ;

    while ( 1 )
    {
        fchoice = popupmenu ( filesmenu, 4, "LSPR", 16 ) ;

        switch ( fchoice )
        {
            case 1 :  /* load a graph from a file */
                load( ) ;
```

```
                    break ;

               case 2 :  /* save the current graph into a file */
                    save( ) ;
                    break ;

               case 3 :  /* print the current graph on the printer */
                    print( ) ;
                    break ;

               case 4 :  /* return to main menu */
                    return ;
          }
     }
}

/* pops up Exit menu, receives choice, branches to appropriate function */
exit_options( )
{
     int fchoice ;

     while ( 1 )
     {
          fchoice = popupmenu ( exitmenu, 3, "ESR", 26 ) ;

          switch ( fchoice )
          {
               case 1 :  /* exit permanently to DOS */
                    activetime( ) ;  /* calculate and display active time */
                    exit ( 0 ) ;

               case 2 :  /* exit temporarily to DOS */
                    shell( ) ;
                    break ;

               case 3 :  /* return to main menu */
                    return ;
```

```
            }
        }
    }

/* pops up Keyboard Entry menu, receives choice, branches to appropriate
   function */
data_from_kb( )
{
    int kchoice ;

    while ( 1 )
    {
        kchoice = popupmenu ( keyboardmenu, 4, "NELR", 21 ) ;

        switch ( kchoice )
        {
            case 1 :  /* enter new data values */
                newdata( ) ;
                break ;

            case 2 :  /* edit existing data values */
                editdata( ) ;
                break ;

            case 3 :  /* enter legend values */
                legendentry( ) ;
                break ;

            case 4 :  /* return to Data menu */
                return ;
        }
    }
}

/* Initialises the graphics system */
graphicsmode( )
{
```

```
    int g_error ;

    /* initialise the graphics system */
    initgraph ( &gd, &gm, "c:\\tc\\bgi" ) ;

    /* determine success/failure of initialisation operation */
    g_error = graphresult( ) ;

    /* if failure */
    if ( g_error != 0 )
    {
        /* print error message string */
        printf ( "\ninitgraph error: %s.\n", grapherrormsg ( g_error ) ) ;
        exit ( 1 ) ;
    }
}

/* clears the last row on the screen */
cleartext( )
{
    int i ;
    for ( i = 1 ; i <= 78 ; i++ )
        writechar ( 23, i, ' ', 32 ) ;
}

/* accepts fresh data from keyboard */
newdata( )
{
    double num ;
    int areareqd, i, entry, flag, indicator = 0 ;
    int col[7] = { 13, 24, 35, 46, 57, 68, 2 } ;
    char *p ;

    /* calculate area required to save entire screen contents */
    areareqd = ( 24 - 0 + 1 ) * ( 79 - 0 + 1 ) * 2 ;

    /* allocate memory, if unsuccessful display error and terminate execution */
```

```
p = malloc ( areareqd ) ;
if ( p == NULL )
    alloc_error_exit( ) ;

/* save screen contents */
savevideo ( 0, 0, 24, 79, p ) ;

/* set up data_type to indicate that data is being entered from keyboard */
data_type = 4 ;

/* draw the box used for entry of data */
draw_entrybox( ) ;

/* clear last row and display message */
cleartext( ) ;
writestring ( "Press Enter on empty entry to stop", 23, 1, 32) ;
writestring ( "Esc to abort", 23, 66, 32) ;

/* accept x axis values, maximum 15 */
for ( i = 0 ; i <= 14 ; i++ )
{
    /* store the value entered in num; getnum will respond to the Esc key
       in a special way */
    getnum ( &flag, &num, i, 2, ESCAPE ) ;

    /* if user hits Esc or Enter on an empty entry */
    if ( flag == ENTRYOVER || flag == ESCAPE )
        break ;

    /* assign the number entered to the global variable xrange[ ] */
    xrange[i] = num ;
}

/* store the total number of x axis entries made */
max_x_entries = i ;

/* abandon all data entered if Esc key is hit */
```

```
if ( flag == ESCAPE )
    max_x_entries = 0 ;

/* accept sets of data values, maximum 6 sets */
for ( i = 0 ; i <= 5 ; i++ )
{
    /* accept as many y axis values as there are x axis entries */
    for ( entry = 0 ; entry < max_x_entries ; entry++ )
    {
        getnum ( &flag, &num, entry, col[i], ESCAPE ) ;

        /* if Esc key is hit */
        if ( flag == ESCAPE )
        {
            indicator = 1 ;
            break ;
        }

        /* if user hits Enter on a blank entry */
        if ( flag == ENTRYOVER )
        {
            /* if at least one set of y axis values is entered */
            if ( entry == 0 && i != 0 )
            {
                indicator = 1 ;
                break ;
            }

            /* if Enter is hit before supplying even one set of y axis
               values or at an entry other than the first */
            if ( ( ( entry == 0 && i == 0 ) || entry != 0 )
            {
                cleartext( ) ;
                writestring ( "Enter all values!", 23, 1, 32 ) ;
                writestring ( "Press any key to continue...", 23, 47, 32 ) ;
                fflush ( stdin ) ;
                getch( ) ;
```

```
                      cleartext( ) ;
                      writestring ( "Press Enter on empty entry to stop", 23,
                                1, 32 ) ;
                      writestring ( "Esc to abort", 23, 66, 32 ) ;
                      entry-- ;
                      continue ;
            }
        }

        /* assign the received number to the global variable yrange[ ][ ] */
        yrange[entry][i] = num ;
    }

    /* if Esc key was hit or if Enter was hit after supplying complete sets
       of y axis values */
    if ( indicator )
        break ;
}

/* store the total number of sets of y axis entries made */
max_y_sets = i ;

/* abandon all data entered if Esc key is hit */
if ( flag == ESCAPE )
{
    max_y_sets = 0 ;
    max_x_entries = 0 ;
}

/* if any entries are made, get them okayed */
if ( max_x_entries > 0 )
    verifydata( ) ;

/* restore original screen contents and free allocated memory */
restorevideo ( 0, 0, 24, 79, p ) ;
free ( p ) ;
}
```

```c
/* draws a box used for entering, editing or displaying data */
draw_entrybox( )
{
    int i, j ;

    /* display a filled box */
    menubox ( 0, 0, 24, 79, 47, 0 ) ;

    /* draw a double lined box */
    drawbox ( 0, 0, 24, 79, 47 ) ;
    writestring ( "  Data Entry  ", 0, 33, 48 ) ;

    /* draw the horizontal lines */
    for ( i = 0 ; i <= 2 ; i++ )
    {
        for ( j = 2 ; j <= 77 ; j++ )
        {
            writechar ( 2, j, 196, 32 ) ;
            writechar ( 5, j, 196, 32 ) ;
            writechar ( 22, j, 196, 32 ) ;
        }
    }

    /* draw the vertical lines */
    for ( j = 1 ; j <= 78 ; j += 11 )
    {
        for ( i = 4 ; i <= 21 ; i++ )
            writechar ( i, j, 179, 32 ) ;
    }
    for ( j = 1 ; j <= 13 ; j += 11 )
        writechar ( 3, j, 179, 32 ) ;
    writechar ( 3, 78, 179, 32 ) ;

    /* complete the box by drawing the appropriate characters at the edges */
    i = 0 ;
    for ( j = 17 ; j < 78 ; j += 11 )
```

```
        {
                writechar ( 4, j, arr[i], 32 ) ;
                writechar ( 5, j - 5, 197, 32 ) ;
                writechar ( 22, j - 5, 193, 32 ) ;
                i++ ;
        }
        writechar ( 2, 1, 218, 32 ) ;
        writechar ( 22, 1, 192, 32 ) ;
        writechar ( 2, 78, 191, 32 ) ;
        writechar ( 22, 78, 217, 32 ) ;
        writechar ( 2, 12, 194, 32 ) ;
        writechar ( 5, 1, 195, 32 ) ;
        writechar ( 5, 78, 180, 32 ) ;

        writestring ( "X-axis", 3, 4, 32 ) ;
        writestring ( "Values", 4, 4, 32 ) ;
        writestring ( "Y-axis values", 3, 38, 32 ) ;
}

/* accepts a number from the keyboard */
getnum ( pf, num, row, col, key )
int *pf, row, col, key ;
double *num ;
{
        int ch, j = 0 ;
        char str[12] ;

        *pf = ENTRYSTART ;
        size ( 5, 7 ) ;  /* display cursor */

        while ( 1 )
        {
                gotoxy ( col + i + 1, 7 + row ) ;

                /* get a character */
                fflush ( stdin ) ;
                ch = getch( ) ;
```

```
/* if the key hit is a special key, get the scan code */
if ( ch == 0 )
    ch = getch( ) ;

/* if the key hit is Esc or End as specified by the calling function */
if ( ch == key )
{
    *pf = ch ;
    size ( 32, 0 ) ;  /* hide cursor */
    return ;
}

/* if the Backspace key is hit */
if ( ch == '\b' )
{
    /* if the cursor is not on the first column */
    if ( i != 0 )
    {
        i-- ;

        /* erase previous character */
        writechar ( row + 6, col + i, ' ', 47 ) ;
    }
}

/* if the Enter key is hit */
if ( ch == '\r' )
{
    /* if the Enter key is hit on a blank entry */
    if ( i == 0 )
    {
        *pf = ENTRYOVER ;  /* set up flag */
        size ( 32, 0 ) ;  /* hide cursor */
        return ;
    }
    else
```

```
            break ;
        }

    /* display the character only if it is a digit, a decimal point or a minus
       sign entered in the first column */
    if ( isdigit ( ch ) || ch == '.' || ( ch == '-' && i == 0 ) )
    {
        /* clear the columns for receiving a fresh entry */
        if ( i == 0 )
            writestring ( "        ", row + 6, col + i, 47 ) ;

        str[i] = ch ;
        writechar ( row + 6, col + i, ch, 47 ) ;
        i++ ;

        /* if the number entered exceeds 10 digits */
        if ( i > 9 )
            break ;
    }
}

str[i] = '\0' ;  /* terminate the string */

/* convert the input string to a floating point number */
*num = atof ( str ) ;

size ( 32, 0 ) ;
}

/* gets the data okayed */
verifydata( )
{
    int entry, flag, i, areareqd ;
    int col[7] = { 13, 24, 35, 46, 57, 68, 2 } ;
    char ans, *p ;
    FILE *fp ;
```

```
/* so long as data is not okay */
while ( 1 )
{
     /* erase the last row, display the message, get user's response */
     cleartext( ) ;
     writestring ( "Is the data OK (Y/N) ?", 23, 16, 32 ) ;
     fflush ( stdin ) ;  /* flush the keyboard buffer */
     ans = getch( ) ;

     /* if data is okay, terminate the loop */
     if ( ans == 'Y' || ans == 'y' )
         break ;

     /* erase the last row, display the message */
     cleartext( ) ;
     writestring ( "Press Enter if current entry is OK.", 23, 1, 32 ) ;
     writestring ( "Press End to finish.", 23, 58, 32 ) ;

     /* get all the x axis entries okayed */
     for ( entry = 0 ; entry < max_x_entries ; entry++ )
     {
         getnum ( &flag, &xrange[entry], entry, col[6], END ) ;

         /* if END key is hit, terminate the loop */
         if ( flag == END )
             break ;
     }

     /* get all sets of y axis entries okayed */
     if ( flag != END )
     {
         for ( i = 0 ; i < max_y_sets ; i++ )
         {
             for ( entry = 0 ; entry < max_x_entries ; entry++ )
             {
                 getnum ( &flag, &yrange[entry][i], entry, col[i], END ) ;
```

```
                        /* if End key is hit, break out of the loop */
                        if ( flag == END )
                                break ;
                }

                if ( flag == END )
                        break ;
        }
}

        /* if verification of data is over, terminate the loop */
        if ( flag == END )
                break ;
}

/* erase the last row, display message, receive user's response */
cleartext( ) ;
writestring ( "Do you want to save the data in a file (Y/N) ?", 23, 12, 32 ) ;
fflush ( stdin ) ;
ans = getch( ) ;

if ( ans == 'Y' || ans == 'y' )
{
        /* calculate area required to save screen contents where box is to be
          popped up */
        areareqd = ( 16 - 9 + 1 ) * ( 75 - 3 + 1 ) * 2 ;

        /* allocate memory, if unsuccessful display error and terminate
          execution */
        p = malloc ( areareqd ) ;
        if ( p == NULL )
                alloc_error_exit( ) ;

        savevideo ( 9, 3, 16, 75, p ) ;  /* save screen contents */
        menubox ( 9, 3, 16, 75, 127, 07 ) ;  /* display a filled box */
```

```
/* if data and legend or only data have been entered from keyboard
   (i.e. not saved to a file so far) */
if ( data_type == 3 || data_type == 4 )
{
    /* ask for file name */
    writestring ( "Enter name of the file:", 10, 5, 127 ) ;

    size ( 5, 7 ) ;  /* display cursor */

    /* collect the file name entered */
    getstring ( filename, 10, 31, 127 ) ;

    size ( 32, 0 ) ;  /* hide cursor */

    fp = fopen ( filename, "w" ) ;

    /* if unsuccessful in opening file */
    if ( fp == NULL )
    {
        writestring ( "Error in opening file!", 12, 5, 127 ) ;
        writestring ( "Press any key...", 14, 5, 127 ) ;
        fflush ( stdin ) ;
        getch( ) ;

        restorevideo ( 9, 3, 16, 75, p ) ;
        free ( p ) ;
        return ;
    }
}

/* if data and legend or only data have been read from the file */
if ( data_type == 1 || data_type == 2 )
{
    writestring ( "Overwriting existing data...", 10, 5, 127 ) ;

    fp = fopen ( filename, "r+" ) ;
```

```
      /* if unsuccessful in opening file */
      if ( fp == NULL )
      {
           writestring ( "Error in opening file!", 12, 5, 127 ) ;
           writestring ( "Press any key...", 14, 5, 127 ) ;
           fflush ( stdin ) ;
           getch( ) ;

           restorevideo ( 9, 3, 16, 75, p ) ;
           free ( p ) ;
           return ;
      }
}

writestring ( "Please wait...", 12, 5, 127 ) ;

/* store the data in the file */
storedata ( fp ) ;

fclose ( fp ) ;

/* if legend has also been entered, append it after data */
if ( data_type == 3 )
{
      storelegend ( fp ) ;

      /* set data_type to indicate that data and legend are saved */
      data_type = 2 ;
}

if ( data_type == 4 )
      data_type = 1 ;  /* set data_type to indicate that data is saved */

writestring ( "Data values successfully stored!", 12, 5, 127 ) ;
writestring ( "Press any key...", 14, 5, 127 ) ;
fflush ( stdin ) ;
getch( ) ;
```

```
        /* restore original screen contents */
        restorevideo ( 9, 3, 16, 75, p ) ;

        /* free allocated memory */
        free ( p ) ;
    }
}

/* accepts a string from the keyboard */
getstring ( str, row, col, color )
int row, col, color ;
char *str ;
{
    int ch, i = 0 ;

    str[0] = '\0' ;
    size ( 5, 7 ) ;

    while ( 1 )
    {
        gotoxy ( col + i + 1, row + 1 ) ;

        fflush ( stdin ) ;
        ch = getch( ) ;

        if ( ch == '\r' )
            break ;

        if ( ch == '\b' )
        {
            if ( i != 0 )
            {
                i-- ;
                writechar ( row, col + i, ' ', color ) ;
            }
        }
```

```
        /* display the character only if it is an ascii character and not a
          control character */
        if ( isascii ( ch ) && !iscntrl ( ch ) )
        {
            str[i] = ch ;
            writechar ( row, col + i, ch, color ) ;
            i++ ;

            /* if the string entered exceeds 30 characters */
            if ( i > 29 )
                break ;
        }
    }

    str[i] = '\0' ;  /* terminate the string */
    size ( 32, 0 ) ;  /* hide cursor */
}

/* saves the data in a file in a predetermined format */
storedata ( fp )
FILE *fp ;
{
    int i, j ;

    fprintf ( fp, "%d\n", max_x_entries ) ;
    fprintf ( fp, "%d\n", max_y_sets ) ;

    /* store x axis entries */
    for ( i = 0 ; i < max_x_entries ; i++ )
        fprintf ( fp, "%lf\n", xrange[i] ) ;

    /* store y axis entries */
    for ( i = 0 ; i < max_x_entries ; i++ )
    {
        for ( j = 0 ; j < max_y_sets ; j++ )
            fprintf ( fp, "%lf\n", yrange[i][j] ) ;
```

```
        }
}

/* allows changes in current data */
editdata( )
{
        int areareqd ;
        char *p ;

        /* calculate area required to save entire screen contents */
        areareqd = ( 24 - 0 + 1 ) * ( 79 - 0 + 1 ) * 2 ;

        /* allocate memory, if unsuccessful display error and terminate execution */
        p = malloc ( areareqd ) ;
        if ( p == NULL )
                alloc_error_exit( ) ;

        savevideo ( 0, 0, 24, 79, p ) ;

        /* display current data */
        displaydata( ) ;

        /* if any data exists, get it okayed */
        if ( max_x_entries > 0 )
                verifydata( ) ;

        restorevideo ( 0, 0, 24, 79, p ) ;
        free ( p ) ;
}

/* displays current data on screen */
displaydata( )
{
        int col[7] = { 13, 24, 35, 46, 57, 68, 2 }, i, j ;
        char str[12] ;

        /* draw the box used for displaying the data */
```

```
        draw_entrybox( ) ;

        /* if no entries have been supplied so far */
        if ( max_x_entries < 1 )
        {
            writestring ( "Oops! No data. Go back to Data menu.", 23, 1, 47 ) ;
            writestring ( "Press any key...", 23, 62, 47 ) ;
            fflush ( stdin ) ;
            getch( ) ;

            return ;
        }

        /* display all the x axis entries */
        for ( i = 0 ; i < max_x_entries ; i++ )
        {
            /* convert floating point number to string and display it */
            gcvt ( xrange[i], 10, str ) ;
            writestring ( str, i + 6, col[6], 47 ) ;
        }

        /* display all sets of y axis entries */
        for ( i = 0 ; i < max_x_entries ; i++ )
        {
            for ( j = 0 ; j < max_y_sets ; j++ )
            {
                gcvt ( yrange[i][j], 10, str ) ;
                writestring ( str, i + 6, col[j], 47 ) ;
            }
        }
    }

    /* accepts legend entries */
    legendentry( )
    {
        int row, i, areareqd ;
        char *p, ans ;
```

```
FILE *fp ;

/* calculate area required to save entire screen contents */
areareqd = ( 24 - 0 + 1 ) * ( 79 - 0 + 1 ) * 2 ;

/* allocate memory, if unsuccessful display error and terminate execution */
p = malloc ( areareqd ) ;
if ( p == NULL )
    alloc_error_exit( ) ;

/* save screen contents */
savevideo ( 0, 0, 24, 79, p ) ;

/* draw a filled box */
menubox ( 0, 0, 24, 79, 47, 0 ) ;

/* draw a double lined box */
drawbox ( 0, 0, 24, 79, 47 ) ;

/* draw a horizontal line */
for ( i = 1 ; i <= 78 ; i++ )
    writechar ( 22, i, 205, 47 ) ;
writechar ( 22, 0, 204, 47 ) ;
writechar ( 22, 79, 185, 47 ) ;

writestring ( "  Legend Entry  ", 0, 32, 48 ) ;

/* if no data has been entered so far */
if ( max_x_entries < 1 )
{
    writestring ( "Oops! No data. Go back to Data menu.", 23, 1, 32 ) ;
    writestring ( "Press any key...", 23, 62, 32 ) ;
    fflush ( stdin ) ;
    getch( ) ;

    restorevideo ( 0, 0, 24, 79, p ) ;
    free ( p ) ;
```

```
        return ;
}


writestring ( "Graph Title   :", 2, 10, 47 ) ;
writestring ( "Enter the title of the graph", 23, 2, 32 ) ;
fflush ( stdin ) ;
getstring ( titles[0], 2, 27, 32 ) ;


writestring ( "X-axis Title  :", 4, 10, 47 ) ;
writestring ( "Enter the title of X - axis ", 23, 2, 32 ) ;
fflush ( stdin ) ;
getstring ( titles[1], 4, 27, 32 ) ;


writestring ( "Y-axis Title  :", 6, 10, 47 ) ;
writestring ( "Enter the title of Y - axis ", 23, 2, 32 ) ;
fflush ( stdin ) ;
getstring ( titles[2], 6, 27, 32 ) ;


writestring ( "-----: LEGEND :-----", 8, 10, 32 ) ;
writestring ( "Entry for legend          ", 23, 2, 32 ) ;
row = 10 ;

/* receive legends for different sets of y axis values */
for ( i = 0 ; i < max_y_sets ; i++ )
{
    writechar ( row, 15, arr[i], 47 ) ;
    writechar ( row, 17, ':', 47 ) ;
    fflush ( stdin ) ;
    getstring ( y_sets_desc[i], row, 19, 32 ) ;
    row += 2 ;
}


size ( 32, 0 ) ;

/* if data is entered from keyboard */
if ( data_type == 4 )
{
```

```
        /* set up data_type to indicate that data and legend have been
            entered  from keyboard */
        data_type = 3 ;
}


/* erase last row, display message, receive user's choice */
cleartext( ) ;
writestring ( "Do you want to save the data in a file (Y/N) ?", 23, 12, 32 ) ;
fflush ( stdin ) ;
ans = getch( ) ;

if ( ans == 'Y' || ans == 'y' )
{
    /* restore original screen contents and free allocated memory */
    restorevideo ( 0, 0, 24, 79, p ) ;
    free ( p ) ;

    /* calculate area required to save screen contents where box is to be
       popped up */
    areareqd = ( 16 - 9 + 1 ) * ( 75 - 3 + 1 ) * 2 ;

    /* allocate memory, if unsuccessful display error and terminate
       execution */
    p = malloc ( areareqd ) ;
    if ( p == NULL )
        alloc_error_exit( ) ;

    savevideo ( 9, 3, 16, 75, p ) ;
    menubox ( 9, 3, 16, 75, 127, 07 ) ;

    /* if data and legend have not been saved */
    if ( data_type == 3 )
    {
        writestring ( "Enter name of the file:", 10, 5, 127 ) ;
        size ( 5, 7 ) ;
        getstring ( filename, 10, 31, 127 ) ;
        size ( 32, 0 ) ;
```

```
        }

        /* if data and legend have already been saved */
        if ( data_type == 2 )
        {
            writestring ( "Legend already saved! Overwrite (Y/N) ?", 10,5,127);
            fflush ( stdin ) ;
            ans = getch( ) ;
            writechar ( 10, 47, ans, 127 ) ;
        }

        if ( ans == 'y' || ans == 'Y' || data_type == 3 )
        {
            fp = fopen ( filename, "w" ) ;

            /* if unsuccessful in opening file */
            if ( fp == NULL )
            {
                writestring ( "Error in opening file!", 12, 5, 127 ) ;
                writestring ( "Press any key...", 14, 5, 127 ) ;
                fflush ( stdin ) ;
                getch( ) ;

                restorevideo ( 9, 3, 16, 75, p ) ;
                free ( p ) ;
                return ;
            }

            writestring ( "Please wait...", 12, 5, 127 ) ;

            /* store data in the file */
            storedata ( fp ) ;

            /* add the legend entries at the end of the file */
            storelegend ( fp ) ;

            fclose ( fp ) ;
```

```
        /* set up data_type to indicate that data and legend have been
           saved */
        data_type = 2 ;

        restorevideo ( 9, 3, 16, 75, p ) ;
        free ( p ) ;
}

if ( data_type == 1 )
{
    writestring ( "Appending to file containing data...", 10, 5, 127 ) ;
    fp = fopen ( filename, "a" ) ;

    /* if unable to open file */
    if ( fp == NULL )
    {
        writestring ( "Error in opening file!", 12, 5, 127 ) ;
        writestring ( "Press any key...", 14, 5, 127 ) ;
        fflush ( stdin ) ;
        getch() ;

        restorevideo ( 9, 3, 16, 75, p ) ;
        free ( p ) ;
        return ;
    }

    writestring ( "Please wait...", 12, 5, 127 ) ;

    /* add legend entries at the end of data values */
    storelegend ( fp ) ;

    fclose ( fp ) ;

    /* set up data_type to indicate that data and legend have been
       saved */
    data_type = 2 ;
```

```
            restorevideo ( 9, 3, 16, 75, p ) ;
            free ( p ) ;
        }
    }
    else
    {
        /* control reaches here if user doesn't wish to save the legend entries */

        restorevideo ( 0, 0, 24, 79, p ) ;
        free ( p ) ;
    }
}

/* saves the current legend entries into a file in a predetermined format */
storelegend ( fp )
FILE *fp ;
{
    int i ;

    /* take file pointer to the end */
    fseek ( fp, 0, SEEK_END ) ;

    for ( i = 0 ; i <= 2 ; i++ )
        fprintf ( fp, "%s\n", titles[i] ) ;

    for ( i = 0 ; i < max_y_sets ; i++ )
        fprintf ( fp, "%s\n", y_sets_desc[i] ) ;

    writestring ( "Data values & Legend entries successfully stored!", 12,
                5, 127 ) ;
    writestring ( "Press any key...", 14, 5, 127 ) ;
    fflush ( stdin ) ;
    getch( ) ;
}

/* reads data stored in a file */
```

```
data_from_file( )
{
     int i, j, areareqd, len ;
     FILE *fp ;
     char *p ;

     /* calculate area required to save screen contents where box is to be
       popped up */
     areareqd = ( 16 - 9 + 1 ) * ( 75 - 3 + 1 ) * 2 ;

     /* allocate memory, if unsuccessful display error and terminate execution */
     p = malloc ( areareqd ) ;
     if ( p == NULL )
          alloc_error_exit( ) ;

     savevideo ( 9, 3, 16, 75, p ) ;
     menubox ( 9, 3, 16, 75, 127, 07 ) ;

     writestring ( "Enter name of the file:", 10, 5, 127 ) ;
     size ( 5, 7 ) ;
     getstring ( filename, 10, 31, 127 ) ;
     size ( 32, 0 ) ;

     fp = fopen ( filename, "r" ) ;

     /* if unsuccessful in opening file */
     if ( fp == NULL )
     {
          writestring ( "Error in opening file!", 12, 5, 127 ) ;
          writestring ( "Press any key...", 14, 5, 127 ) ;
          fflush ( stdin ) ;
          getch( ) ;

          restorevideo ( 9, 3, 16, 75, p ) ;
          free ( p ) ;
          return ;
     }
```

```
writestring ( "Please wait...", 12, 5, 127 ) ;

data_type = 1 ;  /* set up data_type to indicate that data is read from file */

/* read maximum number of x entries and maximum sets of y entries */
fscanf ( fp, "%d", &max_x_entries ) ;
fscanf ( fp, "%d", &max_y_sets ) ;

/* read x entries from the file */
for ( i = 0 ; i < max_x_entries ; i++ )
    fscanf ( fp, "%lf", &xrange[i] ) ;

/* read y entries from the file */
for ( i = 0 ; i < max_x_entries ; i++ )
{
    for ( j = 0 ; j < max_y_sets ; j++ )
        fscanf ( fp, "%lf", &yrange[i][j] ) ;
}

/* bypass the newline character separating the data values from the
   legend entries */
fgetc ( fp ) ;

/* check whether legend entries are present in file */
if ( fgets ( titles[0], 80, fp ) == NULL )
    writestring ( "Legend not set...", 12, 5, 127 ) ;
else
{
    /* set up data_type to indicate that data and legend have been read
       from the file */
    data_type = 2 ;

    /* terminate string */
    len = strlen ( titles[0] ) ;
    titles[0][len - 1] = '\0' ;
```

```
        /* read legend entries */
        for ( i = 1 ; i <= 2 ; i++ )
        {
            fgets ( titles[i], 80, fp ) ;
            len = strlen ( titles[i] ) ;
            titles[i][len - 1] = '\0' ;
        }

        for ( i = 0 ; i < max_y_sets ; i++ )
        {
            fgets ( y_sets_desc[i], 80, fp ) ;
            len = strlen ( y_sets_desc[i] ) ;
            y_sets_desc[i][len - 1] = '\0' ;
        }
    }

    writestring ( "Values successfully set up!", 13, 5, 127 ) ;
    writestring ( "Press any key...",14, 5, 127 ) ;
    fflush ( stdin ) ;
    getch( ) ;

    fclose ( fp ) ;
    restorevideo ( 9, 3, 16, 75, p ) ;
    free ( p ) ;
}

/* draws a bar chart */
bar_chart( )
{
    char *p, str[13] ;
    double big, small, scale_factor, incr_val, total ;
    int areareqd, xright, xleft, ytop, ybottom, total_bars, endx, posi_of_xaxis ;
    int i, j, xincr, bar_width, y_incr, boxheight, graphwidth, graphheight ;

    /* calculate area required to save screen contents where chart is to be
       drawn */
    areareqd = ( 24 - 0 + 1 ) * ( 79 - 0 + 1 ) * 2 ;
```

```
/* allocate memory, if unsuccessful display error and terminate execution */
p = malloc ( areareqd ) ;
if ( p == NULL )
     alloc_error_exit( ) ;

/* save screen contents into allocated memory */
savevideo ( 0, 0, 24, 79, p ) ;

/* if data doesn't exist */
if ( max_x_entries < 1 )
{
     menubox ( 11, 8, 16, 71, 127, 07 ) ;
     writestring ( "Oops! No data. Go back to Data menu.", 12, 9, 127 ) ;
     writestring ( "Press any key...", 14, 9, 127 ) ;
     fflush ( stdin ) ;
     getch( ) ;

     restorevideo ( 0, 0, 24, 79, p ) ;
     free ( p ) ;
     return ;
}

/* the chart is drawn within a box with dimensions 528 x 136 */
/* corner coordinates of the box are (104, 24) and (631, 163) */
boxheight = 163 - 24 + 1 ;
graphwidth = 528 ;

/* find the biggest and smallest y axis entry */
small = big = yrange[0][0] ;
for ( i = 0 ; i < max_x_entries ; i++ )
{
     for ( j = 0 ; j < max_y_sets ; j++ )
     {
          if ( big < yrange[i][j] )
               big = yrange[i][j] ;
```

```
            if ( small > yrange[i][j] )
                small = yrange[i][j] ;
        }
    }


/* if all data values are positive */
if ( small >= 0 )
{
    total = big ;
    graphheight = boxheight - 10 ;

    /* calculate the position where x axis is to be placed */
    posi_of_xaxis = 163 ;
}
else
{
    /* if all data values are negative */
    if ( big < 0 )
    {
        big = 0 ;
        total = big - small ;
        graphheight = boxheight - 20 ;

        /* calculate the position where x axis is to be placed */
        posi_of_xaxis = 22 + 10 ;
    }
    else
    {
        /* some data values are positive and some are negative */
        total = big - small ;
        graphheight = boxheight - 20 ;

        /* calculate the position where x axis is to be placed */
        posi_of_xaxis = 163 - 10 - graphheight / ( ( big / -small ) + 1 ) ;
    }
}
```

```
/* calculate the y axis scaling factor */
scale_factor = total / graphheight ;

/* calculate the total number of bar widths required */
total_bars = max_x_entries * max_y_sets + ( max_x_entries - 1 ) ;

/* calculate the width of each bar */
bar_width = graphwidth / total_bars ;

/* calculate the exact x coordinate of right corner of the box */
endx = bar_width * total_bars + 104 ;

/* change to graphics mode */
graphicsmode( ) ;

/* draw the box */
rectangle ( 104, 22, endx, 163 ) ;

/* draw the x axis */
line ( 104, posi_of_xaxis, endx, posi_of_xaxis ) ;

/* set the variables for drawing the first bar */
xleft = 104 ;
xright = 104 + bar_width ;

for ( i = 0 ; i < max_x_entries ; i++ )
{
     for ( j = 0 ; j < max_y_sets ; j++ )
     {
          /* if the data value is negative */
          if ( yrange[i][j] >= 0 )
          {
               /* set the y coordinate from which the bar should begin */
               ybottom = posi_of_xaxis ;

               /* calculate the height of the bar */
               ytop = ybottom - yrange[i][j] / scale_factor ;
```

```
            }
            else
            {
                /* set the y coordinate from which the bar should begin */
                ytop = posi_of_xaxis ;

                /* calculate the height of the bar */
                ybottom = ytop - yrange[i][j] / scale_factor ;
            }

            /* set up the fill style for the bar to be drawn */
            setfillstyle ( 1 + j, WHITE ) ;

            /* draw a bar in the current fill style */
            bar3d ( xleft, ytop, xright, ybottom, 0, 0 ) ;

            /* update the variables for the next bar */
            xright += bar_width ;
            xleft += bar_width ;
        }

        /* leave space (equal to one bar width) between two consecutive
           clusters of bars */
        xright += bar_width ;
        xleft += bar_width ;
    }

    /* set up text justification */
    settextjustify ( CENTER_TEXT, TOP_TEXT ) ;

    /* calculate the number of pixels for each division along the y axis */
    y_incr = graphheight / 10 ;

    /* calculate the magnitude of each division */
    incr_val = total / 10 ;

    /* if all data values are positive */
```

```
if ( small >= 0 )
{
    for ( i = 0 ; i <= 10 ; i++ )
    {
        /* convert the floating point magnitude to a string */
        gcvt ( incr_val * i , 10, str ) ;

        /* display the string along the y axis */
        moveto ( 52, ( 163 - 4 - ( y_incr * i ) ) ) ;
        outtext ( str ) ;

        /* mark the corresponding y axis division */
        line ( 99, 163 - ( y_incr * i ), 99 + 4, 163 - ( y_incr * i ) ) ;
    }
}
else
{
    /* mark the divisions along the positive direction of y axis */
    i = 0 ;
    while ( posi_of_xaxis - ( y_incr * i ) >= 22 )
    {
        /* convert the floating point magnitude to a string */
        gcvt ( incr_val * i , 10, str ) ;

        /* display the string along the y axis */
        moveto ( 52, ( posi_of_xaxis - 4 - ( y_incr * i ) ) ) ;
        outtext ( str ) ;

        line ( 99, posi_of_xaxis - ( y_incr * i ), 99 + 4, posi_of_xaxis -
                ( y_incr * i ) ) ;
        i++ ;
    }

    /* mark the divisions along the negative direction of y axis */
    i = 1 ;
    while ( posi_of_xaxis + ( y_incr * i ) <= 163 )
    {
```

```
                    /* convert the floating point magnitude to a string */
                    gcvt ( - ( incr_val * i ) , 10, str ) ;

                    /* display the string along the y axis */
                    moveto ( 52, ( posi_of_xaxis - 4 + ( y_incr * i ) ) ) ;
                    outtext ( str ) ;

                    line ( 99, posi_of_xaxis + ( y_incr * i ), 99 + 4, posi_of_xaxis +
                            ( y_incr * i ) ) ;
                    i++ ;
            }
    }

    /* calculate the number of pixels for each division along the x axis */
    xincr = 104 + ( bar_width * max_y_sets ) / 2 ;

    /* display the x axis entries */
    for ( i = 0 ; i < max_x_entries ; i++ )
    {
            /* convert the floating point x axis entry to a string */
            gcvt ( xrange[i], 10, str ) ;

            /* write the string */
            moveto ( xincr, 168 ) ;
            outtext ( str ) ;

            /* mark the corresponding x axis division */
            line ( xincr, 163, xincr, 163 + 4 ) ;

            /* go to the next division along x axis */
            xincr += ( bar_width * ( max_y_sets + 1 ) ) ;
    }

    /* if legend entries exist, display them */
    if ( data_type == 2 || data_type == 3 )
            displaylegend ( 1 ) ;
```

```
        /* store the current graph in allocated memory */
        getimage ( 0, 0, 639, 199, graph_ptr ) ;

        /* wait till a key is hit */
        fflush ( stdin ) ;
        getch( ) ;

        /* return to text mode */
        closegraph( ) ;
        restorecrtmode( ) ;
        size ( 32, 0 ) ;
        restorevideo ( 0, 0, 24, 79, p ) ;
        free ( p ) ;
}

/* displays legend entries */
displaylegend ( graph_type )
int graph_type ;
{
        int xincr, i, graphwidth = 528 ;

        /* display the title of the graph */
        moveto ( 368, 8 ) ;
        settextjustify ( CENTER_TEXT, TOP_TEXT ) ;
        settextstyle ( DEFAULT_FONT, HORIZ_DIR, 1 ) ;
        outtext ( titles[0] ) ;

        /* display the label given to the x axis */
        moveto ( 368, 178 ) ;
        outtext ( titles[1] ) ;

        settextjustify ( LEFT_TEXT, TOP_TEXT ) ;
        xincr = graphwidth / max_y_sets ;

        /* if a bar chart or a stacked bar chart is being drawn */
        if ( graph_type == 1 || graph_type == 2 )
        {
```

```
                /* display the description of each fill pattern */
                for ( i = 0 ; i < max_y_sets ; i++ )
                {
                        setfillstyle ( 1 + i, WHITE ) ;
                        bar3d ( 104 + i * xincr, 190, 104 + i * xincr + 8, 198, 0, 0 ) ;
                        outtextxy ( 104 + i * xincr + 15, 190, y_sets_desc[i] ) ;
                }
        }
        else
        {
                /* if an XY chart or a line chart is being drawn */
                for ( i = 0 ; i < max_y_sets ; i++ )
                {
                        /* display the description of each symbol */
                        outtextxy ( 104 + i * xincr, 190, symbol[i] ) ;
                        outtextxy ( 104 + i * xincr + 15, 190, y_sets_desc[i] ) ;
                }
        }

        /* display the label for the y axis */
        moveto ( 8, 84 ) ;
        settextjustify ( RIGHT_TEXT, CENTER_TEXT ) ;
        settextstyle ( DEFAULT_FONT, VERT_DIR, 1 ) ;
        outtext ( titles[2] ) ;
}

/* draws a stacked bar chart */
stack_bar_chart( )
{
        char *p, str[13] ;
        double big, scale_factor, positivesum, negativesum, incr_val, small, total ;
        int i, j, areareqd, xright, xleft, neg_ytop, neg_ybottom, pos_ytop,
            pos_ybottom, endx, posi_of_xaxis ;
        int xincr, bar_width, y_incr, graphheight, graphwidth, boxheight ;

        /* calculate area required to save screen contents where chart is to be
           drawn */
```

```
areareqd = ( 24 - 0 + 1 ) * ( 79 - 0 + 1 ) * 2 ;

/* allocate memory, if unsuccessful display error and terminate execution */
p = malloc ( areareqd ) ;
if ( p == NULL )
    alloc_error_exit( ) ;

/* save screen contents into allocated memory */
savevideo ( 0, 0, 24, 79, p ) ;

/* if data doesn't exist */
if ( max_x_entries < 1 )
{
    menubox ( 11, 8, 16, 71, 127, 07 ) ;
    writestring ( "Oops! No data. Go back to Data menu.", 12, 9, 127 ) ;
    writestring ( "Press any key...", 14, 9, 127 ) ;
    fflush ( stdin ) ;
    getch( ) ;

    restorevideo ( 0, 0, 24, 79, p ) ;
    free ( p ) ;
    return ;
}


/* the chart is drawn within a box with dimensions 528 x 136 */
/* corner coordinates of the box are (104, 24) and (631, 163) */
boxheight = 163 - 24 + 1 :
graphwidth = 528 ;


small = 0 ;
big = 0 ;

/* calculate the largest positive sum and largest negative sum of all
   y axis entries */
for   ( i = 0 ; i < max_x_entries ; i++ )
{
    /* find the positive sum and the negative sum of all y axis entries for
```

```
        a given x axis entry */
    positivesum = 0 ;
    negativesum = 0 ;
    for ( j = 0 ; j < max_y_sets ; j++ )
    {
        if ( yrange[i][j] > 0 )
            positivesum += yrange[i][j] ;
        else
            negativesum += yrange[i][j] ;
    }

    if ( big < positivesum )
        big = positivesum ;

    if ( small > negativesum )
        small = negativesum ;
}
/* if all data values are positive */
if ( small >= 0 )
{
    total = big ;
    graphheight = boxheight - 10 ;

    /* calculate the position where x axis is to be placed */
    posi_of_xaxis = 163 ;
}
else
{
    total = big - small ;
    graphheight = boxheight - 20 ;

    if ( big == 0 )
    {
        /* if all data values are negative */
        posi_of_xaxis = 22 + 10 ;
    }
```

```
    else
    {
        /* some data values are positive and some are negative */
        posi_of_xaxis = 163 - 10 - graphheight / ( ( big / -small ) + 1 ) ;
    }
}

/* calculate the y axis scaling factor */
scale_factor = total / graphheight ;

/* calculate the width of each bar */
bar_width = ( graphwidth - 20 * ( max_x_entries - 1 ) ) / max_x_entries ;

/* initialise the variable xincr such that 20 pixels are left between
   adjacent bars */
xincr = bar_width + 20 ;

/* calculate the exact x-coordinate of right corner of the box */
endx = bar_width * max_x_entries + 20 * ( max_x_entries - 1 ) + 104 ;

/* change to graphics mode */
graphicsmode( ) ;

/* draw the box */
rectangle ( 104, 24, endx, 163 ) ;

/* draw the x axis */
line ( 104, posi_of_xaxis, endx, posi_of_xaxis ) ;

/* set the variables for drawing the first bar */
xleft = 104 ;
xright = 104 + bar_width ;

for ( i = 0 ; i < max_x_entries ; i++ )
{
    /* set the y coordinate from which the stacked bar should begin */
    neg_ytop = posi_of_xaxis ;
```

```
pos_ybottom = posi_of_xaxis ;

for ( j = 0 ; j < max_y_sets ; j++ )
{
    if ( yrange[i][j] >= 0 )
    {
        /* calculate the height of each bar */
        pos_ytop = pos_ybottom - yrange[i][j] / scale_factor ;

        /* draw a bar in the current fill pattern */
        setfillstyle ( 1 + j, WHITE ) ;
        bar3d ( xleft, pos_ytop, xright, pos_ybottom, 0, 0 ) ;

        /* set the base of the next bar to the top of the previous one */
        pos_ybottom = pos_ytop ;
    }
    else
    {
        /* calculate the height of the bar */
        neg_ybottom = neg_ytop - yrange[i][j] / scale_factor ;

        /* draw a bar in the current fill pattern */
        setfillstyle ( 1 + j, WHITE ) ;
        bar3d ( xleft, neg_ytop, xright, neg_ybottom, 0, 0 ) ;

        /* set the top of next bar to the bottom of previous one */
        neg_ytop = neg_ybottom ;
    }
}

/* update the variables for the next bar */
xright += xincr ;
xleft += xincr ;
}

/* set up text justification */
settextjustify ( CENTER_TEXT, TOP_TEXT ) ;
```

```
/* calculate the number of pixels for each division along the y axis */
y_incr = graphheight / 10 ;

/* calculate the appropriate magnitude of each division */
incr_val = total / 10 ;

/* if all data values are positive */
if ( small >= 0 )
{
     for ( i = 0 ; i <= 10 ; i++ )
     {
          /* convert the floating point magnitude to a string */
          gcvt ( incr_val * i, 10, str ) ;
          moveto ( 56, ( 163 - 4 - ( y_incr * i ) ) ) ;

          /* display the string along the y axis */
          outtext ( str ) ;

          /* mark the corresponding y axis division */
          line ( 99, 163 - ( y_incr * i ), 99 + 4, 163 - ( y_incr * i ) ) ;
     }
}
else
{
     /* mark the divisions along the positive direction of y axis */
     i = 0 ;
     while ( posi_of_xaxis - ( y_incr * i ) >= 22 )
     {
          /* convert the floating point magnitude to a string */
          gcvt ( incr_val * i , 10, str ) ;

          /* display the string along the y axis */
          moveto ( 52, ( posi_of_xaxis - 4 - ( y_incr * i ) ) ) ;
          outtext ( str ) ;

          /* mark the corresponding y axis division */
```

```
                line ( 99, posi_of_xaxis - ( y_incr * i ), 99 + 4, posi_of_xaxis -
                        ( y_incr * i ) ) ;
            i++ ;
        }

    /* mark the divisions along the negative direction of y axis */
    i = 1 ;
    while ( posi_of_xaxis + ( y_incr * i ) <= 163 )
    {
            /* convert the floating point magnitude to a string */
            gcvt ( - ( incr_val * i ) , 10, str ) ;

            /* display the string along the y axis */
            moveto ( 52, ( posi_of_xaxis - 4 + ( y_incr * i ) ) ) ;
            outtext ( str ) ;

            /* mark the corresponding y axis division */
            line ( 99, posi_of_xaxis + ( y_incr * i ), 99 + 4, posi_of_xaxis +
                    ( y_incr * i ) ) ;
            i++ ;
        }
    }

/* calculate the number of pixels for each division along the x axis */
xincr = 104 + bar_width / 2 ;

settextjustify ( CENTER_TEXT, TOP_TEXT ) ;

/* display the x axis entries */
for ( i = 0 ; i < max_x_entries ; i++ )
{
    gcvt ( xrange[i], 10, str ) ;
    moveto ( xincr, 168 ) ;
    outtext ( str ) ;

    /* mark the corresponding x axis division */
    line ( xincr, 163, xincr, 163 + 4 ) ;
```

```
            xincr += ( bar_width + 20 ) ;
        }

        /* if legend entries exist, display them */
        if ( data_type == 2 || data_type == 3 )
            displaylegend ( 2 ) ;

        /* store the current graph in allocated memory */
        getimage ( 0, 0, 639, 199, graph_ptr ) ;

        fflush ( stdin ) ;
        getch( ) ;

        /* return to text mode */
        closegraph( ) ;
        restorecrtmode( ) ;

        size ( 32, 0 ) ;
        restorevideo ( 0, 0, 24, 79, p ) ;
        free ( p ) ;
}

/* draws a pie chart */
pie_chart( )
{
        char *p, str[12] ;
        double sum = 0, percent[15] ;
        int i, j, areareqd, xc, yc, start_angle, end_angle ;

        /* calculate area required to save screen contents where chart is to be
           drawn */
        areareqd = ( 24 - 0 + 1 ) * ( 79 - 0 + 1 ) * 2 ;

        /* allocate memory, if unsuccessful display error and terminate execution */
        p = malloc ( areareqd ) ;
        if ( p == NULL )
```

```
        alloc_error_exit( ) ;

/* save screen contents into allocated memory */
savevideo ( 0, 0, 24, 79, p ) ;

/* if data doesn't exist */
if ( max_x_entries < 1 )
{
    menubox ( 11, 8, 16, 71, 127, 07 ) ;
    writestring ( "Oops! No data. Go back to Data menu.", 12, 9, 127 ) ;
    writestring ( "Press any key...", 14, 9, 127 ) ;
    fflush ( stdin ) ;
    getch( ) ;

    restorevideo ( 0, 0, 24, 79, p ) ;
    free ( p ) ;
    return ;
}

/* change to graphics mode */
graphicsmode( ) ;

/* draw as many pie charts as there are x entries */
for ( i = 0 ; i < max_x_entries ; i++ )
{
    /* calculate sum of all y axis entries for each x axis entry */
    sum = 0 ;
    for ( j = 0 ; j < max_y_sets ; j++ )
        sum += fabs ( yrange[i][j] ) ;

    /* set the variable for drawing the first sector of the chart */
    start_angle = 0 ;

    for ( j = 0 ; j < max_y_sets ; j++ )
    {
        /* determine the magnitude of the angle of each sector */
        end_angle = ceil ( ( fabs ( yrange[i][j] ) * 360.0 ) / sum ) ;
```

```
        /* calculate the percentage of the chart occupied by each sector */
        percent[j] = 100.0 * end_angle / 360 ;

        /* determine the angle at which each sector should end */
        end_angle += start_angle ;

        /* if last sector, round off ending angle to 360 */
        if ( j == max_y_sets - 1 )
            end_angle = 360 ;

        if ( percent[j] != 0 )
        {
            /* draw a sector in the current fill style */
            setfillstyle ( 1 + j, WHITE ) ;
            sector ( 319, 99, start_angle, end_angle, 110, 60 ) ;
        }
        else
            pieslice ( 319, 99, start_angle, end_angle, 110 ) ;

        /* set the start of next sector at the end of the previous one */
        start_angle = end_angle ;
    }

    /* display the legend entries */

    xc = 10 ;
    yc = 20 ;

    /* set up text justification */
    settextjustify ( LEFT_TEXT, TOP_TEXT ) ;

    for ( j = 0 ; j < max_y_sets ; j++ )
    {
        /* draw a sector depicting fill style used */
        setfillstyle ( 1 + j, WHITE ) ;
        sector ( xc, yc, 0, 60, 20, 20 ) ;
```

```
        /* if legend entries exist, display them */
        if ( data_type == 2 || data_type == 3 )
        {
                /* display the description of each fill style */
                moveto ( xc + 30, yc - 8 ) ;
                outtext ( y_sets_desc[j] ) ;
        }

        /* display the percentage of chart occupied by each y axis entry */
        gcvt ( percent[j], 10, str ) ;
        moveto ( xc, yc + 8 ) ;
        outtext ( str ) ;
        outtext ( " % " ) ;

        /* update the coordinates for the next sector */
        yc += 50 ;
        if ( j == 2 )
        {
                xc = 550 ;
                yc = 20 ;
        }
}

/* if legend entries exist, display them */
if ( data_type == 2 || data_type == 3 )
{
        /* display the title of the graph */
        moveto ( 319, 8 ) ;
        settextjustify ( CENTER_TEXT, TOP_TEXT ) ;
        settextstyle ( DEFAULT_FONT, HORIZ_DIR, 1 ) ;
        outtext ( titles[0] ) ;

        /* display the label given to the x axis */
        moveto ( 319, 170 ) ;
        outtext ( titles[1] ) ;
```

```
                        /* display the x axis entry */
                        moveto ( 319, 180 ) ;
                        gcvt ( xrange[i], 10, str ) ;
                        outtext ( str ) ;
                }

                /* store the current graph in allocated memory */
                getimage ( 0, 0, 639, 199, graph_ptr ) ;

                gotoxy ( 1, 25 ) ;
                printf ( "Press any key for Pie chart of next X range value...
                        Esc to return" ) ;
                fflush ( stdin ) ;
                if ( getch( ) == 27 )
                        break ;

                clearviewport( ) ;
        }

        /* return to text mode */
        closegraph( ) ;
        restorecrtmode( );

        size ( 32, 0 ) ;
        restorevideo ( 0, 0, 24, 79, p ) ;
        free ( p ) ;
}

/* draws an XY chart or a line chart depending on the argument passed */
xy_or_line ( graph_type )
int graph_type ;
{
        char *p, str[12] ;
        double scale_factor_x, scale_factor_y, small_x, small_y, big_x, big_y,
                incr_val ;
        int i, j, k, areareqd, x, y, xincr, y_incr, endx, xc[15], yc[15][16], temp,
                graphheight, graphwidth, boxheight, posi_of_xaxis, posi_of_yaxis ;
```

```
/* calculate area required to save screen contents where chart is to be
   drawn */
areareqd = ( 24 - 0 + 1 ) * ( 79 - 0 + 1 ) * 2 ;

/* allocate memory, if unsuccessful display error and terminate execution */
p = malloc ( areareqd ) ;
if ( p == NULL )
    alloc_error_exit( ) ;

/* save screen contents into allocated memory */
savevideo ( 0, 0, 24, 79, p ) ;

/* if data doesn't exist */
if ( max_x_entries < 1 )
{
    menubox ( 11, 8, 16, 71, 127, 07 ) ;
    writestring ( "Oops! No data. Go back to Data menu.", 12, 9, 127 ) ;
    writestring ( "Press any key...", 14, 9, 127 ) ;
    fflush ( stdin ) ;
    getch( ) ;

    restorevideo ( 0, 0, 24, 79, p ) ;
    free ( p ) ;
    return ( 0 ) ;
}

boxheight = 163 - 24 + 1 ;
graphwidth = 496 ;

/* find the biggest and the smallest y axis entry */
big_y = yrange[0][0] ;
small_y = yrange[0][0] ;
for   ( i = 0 ; i < max_x_entries ; i++ )
{
    for ( j = 0 ; j < max_y_sets ; j++ )
    {
```

```
            if ( big_y < yrange[i][j] )
                big_y = yrange[i][j] ;

            if ( small_y > yrange[i][j] )
                small_y = yrange[i][j] ;
        }
    }

    /* if all y axis values are same */
    if ( big_y == small_y )
    {
        /* if that entry is positive */
        if ( big_y > 0 )
            small_y = 0 ;
        else
            big_y = 0 ;
    }

    /* if all y axis entries are positive */
    if ( small_y >= 0 )
    {
        graphheight = boxheight - 10 ;

        /* calculate the position where x axis is to be placed */
        posi_of_xaxis = 163 ;
    }
    else
    {
        /* if all y axis entries are negative */
        if ( big_y < 0 )
        {
            big_y = 0 ;
            graphheight = boxheight - 20 ;

            /* calculate the position where x axis is to be placed */
            posi_of_xaxis = 22 + 10 ;
        }
```

```
        else
        {
                /* control reaches here if some y axis entries are positive and
                    some are negative */

                graphheight = boxheight - 20 ;

                /* calculate the position where x axis is to be placed */
                posi_of_xaxis = 163 - 10 - graphheight / ( ( big_y / -small_y ) + 1 ) ;
        }
}

/* calculate the y axis scaling factor */
scale_factor_y = ( big_y - small_y ) / graphheight ;

/* find the biggest and the smallest x axis entry */
big_x = small_x = xrange[0] ;
for ( i = 0 ; i < max_x_entries ; i++ )
{
        if.( big_x < xrange[i] )
                big_x = xrange[i] ;

        if ( small_x > xrange[i] )
                small_x = xrange[i] ;
}

/* if all x axis values are same */
if ( big_x == small_x )
{
        if ( big_x > 0 )
                small_x = 0 ;
        else
                big_x = 0 ;
}

/* if all x axis entries are positive */
if ( small_x >= 0 )
```

```
{
    /* calculate the position where y axis is to be placed */
    posi_of_yaxis = 104 ;
}
else
{
    /* if all x axis entries are negative */
    if ( big_x < 0 )
    {
        big_x = 0 ;

        /* set the position where y axis is to be placed */
        posi_of_yaxis = 104 + graphwidth ;
    }
    else
    {
        /* some x axis entries are positive and some are negative */
        posi_of_yaxis = 104 + graphwidth / ( ( big_x / -small_x ) + 1 ) ;
    }
}

/* calculate the x axis scaling factor */
scale_factor_x = ( big_x - small_x ) / graphwidth ;

/* calculate the exact x-coordinate of right corner of the box */
endx = ( big_x - small_x ) / scale_factor_x + 104 ;

/* change to graphics mode */
graphicsmode( ) ;

/* draw the box */
rectangle ( 104, 22, endx, 163 ) ;

/* draw the x axis and the y axis */
line ( 104, posi_of_xaxis, endx, posi_of_xaxis ) ;
line ( posi_of_yaxis, 22, posi_of_yaxis, 163 ) ;
```

```
/* plot all the points on the graph */
for ( i = 0 ; i < max_x_entries ; i++ )
{
    /* find the coordinate corresponding to each x axis entry */
    if ( small_x > 0 )
        x = posi_of_yaxis + ( xrange[i] - small_x ) / scale_factor_x ;
    else
        x = posi_of_yaxis + xrange[i] / scale_factor_x ;

    xc[i] = x ;

    /* find all the y coordinates for each x axis entry */
    for ( j = 0 ; j < max_y_sets ; j++ )
    {
        /* find the coordinate corresponding to each x axis entry */
        if ( small_y > 0 )
            y = posi_of_xaxis - ( yrange[i][j] - small_y ) / scale_factor_y ;
        else
            y = posi_of_xaxis - yrange[i][j] / scale_factor_y ;

        yc[i][j] = y ;

        /* mark the point using appropriate symbol */
        outtextxy ( x - 4, y - 4, symbol[j] ) ;
    }
}

/* calculate the number of pixels for each division along the y axis */
y_incr = graphheight / 10 ;

/* calculate the magnitude of each division */
incr_val = ( big_y - small_y ) / 10 ;

settextjustify ( CENTER_TEXT, TOP_TEXT ) ;

/* if all y axis values are positive */
if ( small_y >= 0 )
```

```
{
    for ( i = 0 ; i <= 10 ; i++ )
    {
        /* convert the floating point magnitude to a string */
        gcvt ( small_y + ( incr_val * i ), 10, str ) ;

        /* display the string along the y axis */
        moveto ( 56, ( 163 - 4 - ( y_incr * i ) ) ) ;
        outtext ( str ) ;

        /* mark the corresponding y axis division */
        line ( 99, 163 - ( y_incr * i ), 99 + 4, 163 - ( y_incr * i ) ) ;
    }
}
else
{
    /* mark the divisions along the positive direction of y axis */
    i = 0 ;
    while ( posi_of_xaxis - ( y_incr * i ) >= 22 )
    {
        /* convert the floating point magnitude to a string */
        gcvt ( incr_val * i , 10, str ) ;

        /* display the string along the y axis */
        moveto ( 52, ( posi_of_xaxis - 4 - ( y_incr * i ) ) ) ;
        outtext ( str ) ;

        line ( 99, posi_of_xaxis - ( y_incr * i ), 99 + 4, posi_of_xaxis -
                ( y_incr * i ) ) ;
        i++ ;
    }

    /* mark the divisions along the negative direction of y axis */
    i = 1 ;
    while ( posi_of_xaxis + ( y_incr * i ) <= 163 )
    {
        /* convert the floating point magnitude to a string */
```

```
            gcvt ( - ( incr_val * i ) , 10, str ) ;

            /* display the string along the y axis */
            moveto ( 52, ( posi_of_xaxis - 4 + ( y_incr * i ) ) ) ;
            outtext ( str ) ;

            line ( 99, posi_of_xaxis + ( y_incr * i ), 99 + 4, posi_of_xaxis +
                    ( y_incr * i ) ) ;
            i++ ;
        }
    }

    if ( small_x >= 0 && max_x_entries > 1 )
    {
        /* calculate the number of pixels for each division along the x axis */
        xincr = ( endx - 104 + 1 ) / ( max_x_entries - 1 ) ;

        /* calculate the magnitude of each division */
        incr_val = ( big_x - small_x ) / ( max_x_entries - 1 ) ;
    }
    else
    {
        /* calculate the number of pixels for each division along the x axis */
        xincr = ( endx - 104 + 1 ) / 8 ;

        /* calculate the magnitude of each division */
        incr_val = ( big_x - small_x ) / 8 ;
    }

    settextjustify ( CENTER_TEXT, TOP_TEXT ) ;

    /* display the x axis entries */
    if ( small_x > 0 )
    {
        for ( i = 0 ; i < max_x_entries ; i++ )
        {
            /* convert the floating point magnitude to a string */
```

```
            gcvt ( small_x + ( incr_val * i ), 10, str ) ;

            /* display the string along the x axis */
            moveto ( 104 + xincr * i , 168 ) ;
            outtext ( str ) ;

            /* mark the corresponding x axis division */
            line ( 104 + xincr * i, 163, 104 + xincr * i, 163 + 4 ) ;
        }
}
else
{
        /* mark the divisions along the positive direction of x axis */
        i = 0 ;
        while ( posi_of_yaxis + xincr * i <= endx )
        {
            /* convert the floating point magnitude to a string */
            gcvt ( incr_val * i, 10, str ) ;

            /* display the string along the x axis */
            moveto ( posi_of_yaxis + xincr * i , 168 ) ;
            outtext ( str ) ;

            /* mark the corresponding x axis division */
            line ( posi_of_yaxis + xincr * i, 163, posi_of_yaxis + xincr * i,
                    163 + 4 ) ;
            i++ ;
        }

        /* mark the divisions along the negative direction of x axis */
        i = 1 ;
        while ( posi_of_yaxis - xincr * i >= 104 )
        {
            /* convert the floating point magnitude to a string */
            gcvt ( - ( incr_val * i ), 10, str ) ;

            /* display the string along the x axis */
```

```
            moveto ( posi_of_yaxis - xincr * i , 168 ) ;
            outtext ( str ) ;

            /* mark the corresponding x axis division */
            line ( posi_of_yaxis - xincr * i, 163, posi_of_yaxis - xincr * i,
                    163 + 4 ) ;
            i++ ;
        }
    }


    /* if a line chart is to be drawn */
    if ( graph_type == LINE )
    {
        /* arrange the x axis entries in ascending order */
        for ( i = 0 ; i < max_x_entries - 1 ; i++ )
        {
            for ( j = i + 1 ; j < max_x_entries ; j++ )
            {
                if ( xc[i] > xc[j] )
                {
                    temp = xc[i] ;
                    xc[i] = xc[j] ;
                    xc[j] = temp ;

                    /* swap corresponding y axis entries */
                    for ( k = 0 ; k < max_y_sets ; k++ )
                    {
                        temp = yc[i][k] ;
                        yc[i][k] = yc[j][k] ;
                        yc[j][k] = temp ;
                    }
                }
            }
        }

        /* join the points of each line on the graph */
        for ( i = 0 ; i < max_x_entries - 1 ; i++ )
```

```
        {
            for ( j = 0 ; j < max_y_sets ; j++ )
                line ( xc[i], yc[i][j], xc[i + 1], yc[i + 1][j] ) ;
        }
    }

    /* if legend entries exist, display them */
    if ( data_type == 2 || data_type == 3 )
        displaylegend ( 3 ) ;

    /* store the current graph in allocated memory */
    getimage ( 0, 0, 639, 199, graph_ptr ) ;

    fflush ( stdin ) ;
    getch( ) ;

    /* return to text mode */
    closegraph( ) ;
    restorecrtmode( ) ;

    size ( 32, 0 ) ;
    restorevideo ( 0, 0, 24, 79, p ) ;
    free ( p ) ;
}

/* saves the graph present in memory into a file */
save( )
{
    char fname[31], *p ;
    int out, areareqd ;

    /* calculate area required to save entire screen contents */
    areareqd = ( 24 - 0 + 1 ) * ( 79 - 0 + 1 ) * 2 ;

    /* allocate memory, if unsuccessful display error and terminate execution */
    p = malloc ( areareqd ) ;
    if ( p == NULL )
```

```
        alloc_error_exit( ) ;

savevideo ( 0, 0, 24, 79, p ) ;
menubox ( 9, 3, 16, 75, 127, 07 ) ;

/* if data doesn't exist */
if ( max_x_entries < 1 )
{
        writestring ( "Oops! No data. Go back to Data menu.", 10, 5, 127 ) ;
        writestring ( "Press any key...", 12, 5, 127 ) ;
        fflush ( stdin ) ;
        getch( ) ;

        restorevideo ( 0, 0, 24, 79, p ) ;
        free ( p ) ;
        return ;
}

writestring ( "Enter name of the file:", 10, 5, 127 ) ;
size ( 5, 7 ) ;
getstring ( fname, 10, 31, 127 ) ;
size ( 32, 0 ) ;

/* open the file in appropriate mode */
out = open ( fname, O_BINARY | O_CREAT | O_RDWR, S_IWRITE ) ;

/* if unable to open file */
if ( out == -1 )
{
        writestring ( "Error in opening file!", 12, 5, 127 ) ;
        writestring ( "Press any key...", 14, 5, 127 ) ;
        fflush ( stdin ) ;
        getch( ) ;

        restorevideo ( 0, 0, 24, 79, p ) ;
        free ( p ) ;
        return ;
```

```
        }

        /* calculate the area occupied by the graph in memory */
        area = 4 + ( ( 640 + 7 ) / 8 ) * 200 ;

        /* copy the graph from memory into the specified file */
        write ( out, graph_ptr, area ) ;

        /* close the file */
        close ( out ) ;

        writestring ( "Graph successfully saved!", 12, 5, 127 ) ;
        writestring ( "Press any key...", 14, 5, 127 ) ;
        fflush ( stdin ) ;
        getch( ) ;

        restorevideo ( 0, 0, 24, 79, p ) ;
        free ( p ) ;
}

/* loads the graph from the file into memory, and displays it */
load( )
{
        char fname[31], *p ;
        int in, areareqd ;

        /* calculate area required to save entire screen contents */
        areareqd = ( 24 - 0 + 1 ) * ( 79 - 0 + 1 ) * 2 ;

        /* allocate memory, if unsuccessful display error and terminate execution */
        p = malloc ( areareqd ) ;
        if ( p == NULL )
                alloc_error_exit( ) ;

        savevideo ( 0, 0, 24, 79, p ) ;
        menubox ( 9, 3, 16, 75, 127, 07 ) ;
```

```
writestring ( "Enter name of the file:", 10, 5, 127 ) ;
size ( 5, 7 ) ;
getstring ( fname, 10, 31, 127 ) ;
size ( 32, 0 ) ;

/* open the file in appropriate mode */
in = open ( fname, O_BINARY | O_RDONLY ) ;

/* if unable to open file */
if ( in == -1 )
{
    writestring ( "Error in opening file!", 12, 5, 127 ) ;
    writestring ( "Press any key...", 14, 5, 127 ) ;
    fflush ( stdin ) ;
    getch( ) ;

    restorevideo ( 0, 0, 24, 79, p ) ;
    free ( p ) ;
    return ;
}

/* calculate area required to store the graph in memory */
area = 4 + ( ( 640 + 7 ) / 8 ) * 200 ;

/* read the contents from the file into allocated memory */
read ( in, graph_ptr, area ) ;

/* close the file */
close ( in ) ;

/* switch to graphics mode */
graphicsmode( ) ;
clearviewport( ) ;

/* put the contents of the allocated memory on the screen */
putimage ( 0, 0, graph_ptr, OR_PUT ) ;
```

```
            fflush ( stdin ) ;
            getch() ;

            /* switch back to text mode */
            closegraph( ) ;
            restorecrtmode( ) ;

            size ( 32, 0 ) ;
            restorevideo ( 0, 0, 24, 79, p ) ;
            free ( p ) ;
}

/* prints the graph on printer */
print( )
{
            char ch, *p ;
            union REGS i, o ;
            int areareqd, status ;

            /* calculate area required to save entire screen contents */
            areareqd = ( 24 - 0 + 1 ) * ( 79 - 0 + 1 ) * 2 ;

            /* allocate memory, if unsuccessful display error and terminate execution */
            p = malloc ( areareqd ) ;
            if ( p == NULL )
                    alloc_error_exit( ) ;

            savevideo ( 0, 0, 24, 79, p ) ;
            menubox ( 9, 3, 16, 75, 127, 07 ) ;

            /* if data doesn't exist */
            if ( max_x_entries < 1 )
            {
                    writestring ( "Oops! No data. Go back to Data menu.", 10, 5, 127 ) ;
                    writestring ( "Press any key...", 12, 5, 127 ) ;
                    fflush ( stdin ) ;
                    getch( ) ;
```

```
        restorevideo ( 0, 0, 24, 79, p ) ;
        free ( p ) ;
        return ;
}


writestring ( "Set up the printer and press any key.", 10, 5, 127 ) ;
writestring ( "Press Esc to return", 12, 5, 127 ) ;

fflush ( stdin ) ;
ch = getch( ) ;

if ( ch == 27 )  /* Escape key */
{
        restorevideo ( 0, 0, 24, 79, p ) ;
        free ( p ) ;
        return ;
}

menubox ( 9, 3, 16, 75, 127, 07 ) ;
writestring ( "Please wait...", 10, 12, 127 ) ;
delay ( 20 ) ;

/* switch to graphics mode */
graphicsmode( ) ;

/* put the contents of the allocated memory on the screen */
putimage ( 0, 0, graph_ptr, OR_PUT ) ;

/* issue interrupt to print the screen contents on the printer */
int86 ( 5, &i, &o ) ;

closegraph( ) ;
restorecrtmode( ) ;
size ( 32, 0 ) ;
restorevideo ( 0, 0, 24, 79, p ) ;
free ( p ) ;
```

```
}
/* takes control to DOS temporarily */
shell( )
{
    int areareqd, status ;
    char *p ;

    /* calculate area required to save entire screen contents */
    areareqd = ( 24 - 0 + 1 ) * ( 79 - 0 + 1 ) * 2 ;

    /* allocate memory, if unsuccessful display error and terminate execution */
    p = malloc ( areareqd ) ;
    if ( p == NULL )
        alloc_error_exit( ) ;

    savevideo ( 0, 0, 24, 79, p ) ;
    menubox ( 0, 0, 24, 79, 7, 0 ) ;

    menubox ( 8, 21, 16, 60, 127, 47 ) ;
    drawbox ( 9, 23, 14, 56, 127 ) ;
    writestring ( "Quitting temporarily to DOS   ", 11, 25, 127 ) ;
    writestring ( "Type EXIT to return...", 13, 25, 127 ) ;

    gotoxy ( 7, 1 ) ;
    size ( 5, 7 ) ;

    status = system ( "C:\\COMMAND.COM" ) ;

    if ( status == -1 )
    {
        writestring ( "Oops! Cannot load COMMAND.COM!", 11, 25, 127 ) ;
        writestring ( "Press any key to return...", 13, 25, 127 ) ;
        fflush ( stdin ) ;
        getch( ) ;
    }
```

```
        size ( 32, 0 ) ;
        restorevideo ( 0, 0, 24, 79, p ) ;
}

/* calculates time for which Chart Master was active */
activetime( )
{
        int hr = 0, min = 0, sec = 0 ;
        long duration ;

        /* find time at end of execution */
        time ( &endtime ) ;

        /* calculate time for which Chart Master was active */
        duration = ( long ) difftime ( endtime, starttime ) ;
        hr = ( int ) duration / 3600 ;
        duration = duration % 3600 ;
        min = ( int ) duration / 60 ;
        sec = ( int ) duration % 60 ;

        /* display the calculated time */
        clrscr( ) ;
        size ( 5, 7 ) ;
        gotoxy ( 1, 1 ) ;
        printf ( "Thanks for using Chart Master. You were with us for " ) ;
        printf ( "%d hr(s) %d min(s) %d sec(s).\n", hr, min, sec ) ;
}

/* displays memory allocation error and terminates execution */
alloc_error_exit( )
{
        writestring ( messages[31], 22, 14, 127 ) ;
        writestring ( messages[32], 23, 14, 127 ) ;
        fflush ( stdin ) ;
        getch( ) ;

        activetime( ) ;
```

```
    exit ( 3 ) ;
}
```

User Defined Functions

activetime( )	Calculates the time for which Chart Master is active.
alloc_error_exit( )	Displays the memory allocation error and terminates program execution.
bar_chart( )	Draws a bar chart.
cleartext( )	Clears the line used for displaying instructions.
data_options( )	Displays the data entry menu and calls either the function **data_from_kb( )** or **data_from_file( )** as per the user's choice.
data_from_file( )	Reads data and/or legend entries from a file.
data_from_kb( )	Displays Keyboard menu, receives choice and branches control to appropriate function.
display_legend( )	Displays the current legend entries.
displaydata( )	Displays the current data.
displaymenu( )	Displays the specified menu.
drawbox( )	Draws a double-lined box in the specified attribute.
draw_entrybox( )	Creates the data entry screen.
editdata( )	Allows editing of current data.
exit_options( )	Displays Exit menu, receives choice and branches control to appropriate function.
file_options( )	Displays File menu, receives choice and branches control to appropriate function.
getkey( )	Reads a character from the keyboard and returns the ascii code and scan code of the character read.
getnum( )	Reads in a numeric value at the position specified by row and column.
getresponse( )	Gets the user's response after the menu has been popped up.
getstring( )	Reads a string of limited characters from the keyboard.
graph_options( )	Displays Graph menu, receives choice and branches control to appropriate function.

graphicsmode( )	Initialises the graphics system and terminates execution if initialisation fails.
legendentry( )	Allows entry of graph title, x and y axis titles, etc.
load( )	Reads a graph from file and displays it on screen.
menubox( )	Fills a rectangular area with the specified color.
newdata( )	Allows entry of fresh data from the keyboard.
pie_chart( )	Draws a pie chart. One pie chart is drawn for each value of x.
popupmenu( )	Pops up the specified menu at a specified position on the screen.
print( )	Prints the graph displayed on the screen.
restorevideo( )	Copies contents of a block of memory (RAM) to the specified rectangular portion on the screen.
save( )	Saves the current graph into a file.
savevideo( )	Copies text and its attribute from a specified rectangular portion of the screen to a block of memory.
shell( )	Exits temporarily from Chart Master.
size( )	Changes the size of the cursor.
stack_bar_chart( )	Draws a stacked bar chart.
storedata( )	Saves the current data in a file.
storelegend( )	Saves legend entries in a file.
verifydata( )	Gets the data okayed.
writechar( )	Writes a character and its attribute into VDU memory.
writestring( )	Uses function **writechar( )** to write entire strings into VDU memory.
xy_or_line( )	Draws an XY chart or a line chart.

4

Mycad

One of the most fascinating concepts to develop on this side of the century is Computer Graphics and Computer Aided Design or CAD. Graphics and CAD is the world where our imagination is the limit. It's like an extension of the mind which allows you to draw, edit, cut, paste, enhance, zoom and instantly visualise even the most complicated designs. Animation, special effects, Mechanical drafting, Architectural designs, pollution control models, fractals, flight simulation, are some of the areas where CAD plays a major role. All this may sound daunting to begin with, but it will all flow perfectly as we go along. Through C we get a rare glimpse into the working of these applications. In fact, through Mycad we aim to show you how such a slick software can be created using C. In Mycad, however, we have limited the virtually unlimited field of CAD to drawing and editing of regular and irregular shapes. So lets get into the rough and tumble and meet the concept head on.

The Graphics Mode

The video system on microcomputers works in one of the two fundamental modes - text or graphics. With most of the systems the text mode is the default working mode. Drawing images is entirely a job involving graphics, hence we use the function **initgraph( )** to transport us to the graphics mode. But there are several graphics modes for different configurations of the IBM compatible PCs. So to which graphics mode does the **initgraph( )** function really takes us to? **initgraph( )** sorts this matter out by calling another function **detectgraph( )** which returns the graphics driver and the highest resolution graphics mode available with the computer on which it is being run. Note that **initgraph( )** calls **detectgraph( )** only if one of its arguments is set up with a macro DETECT.

Mycad has been programmed to work in CGA high resolution graphics mode (640 x 200). However, with a few small changes it can be adapted to work with any of the modes available with high calibre EGA or VGA adapters.

The Graphics Cursor

Once **initgraph( )** transports us to the graphics mode, the first change we can notice is that the cursor has vanished. And if Mycad is to retain its interactive drawing feature, the first job at hand is to construct a cursor. The function **drawcursor( )** manages to do this. It employs 7 scan lines vertically and 7 pixels across to construct the cursor. In fact, **drawcursor( )** is a double sided phenomenon - it manages to either draw or erase the cursor depending on the argument passed to it. The current position of the cursor is always monitored by two global variables, **x** and **y**. We can move the cursor (through the function **movecursor( )**) in any direction using selected keys on the numeric keypad. In the program, the function **getkey( )** collects the ascii and scan codes of the key pressed, and the function **testkeys( )** updates the coordinates of the cursor appropriately. With every key-hit the cursor is erased from its current position and placed at the updated one. What if we attempt to move the cursor beyond the drawing area? We would not be allowed to do so, as the function **testkeys( )** has provision for restricting our graphics excursions to a predefined area. This area is set up using the standard library function **setviewport( )**.

Mycad Menus

Any drawing or designing activity on a computer would consist of four major operations, namely, drawing figures, modifying them, saving them to disk and printing them on the printer. Each of these operations comprise of different activities which can be grouped under different menus. These menus for Mycad are shown in the following figure.

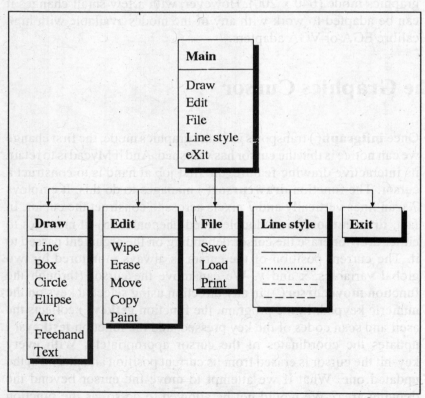

Figure 4.1

These menus are always displayed in the topmost row on the screen. For the menu displayed, the current menu item is always associated with a triangle-shaped character (ascii 16). This triangle can be moved from one item to another using arrow keys. The desired menu item can be selected either by hitting the Enter key at the option associated with the triangle or by hitting the hot key. As in the earlier chapters, here also menu management is done through functions like **displaymenu( )**, **getkey( )**, **getresponse( )**, etc.

The Draw Menu

This menu offers to draw various types of images like lines, boxes, circles, etc. interactively. All that is done is, the relevant coordinates for each figure are obtained, and then the figure is drawn using the appropriate function. The coordinates are supplied by the user by moving the cursor to the desired point on the screen and hitting Enter. On hitting Enter in the Draw mode, the current x and y coordinates of the cursor are stored for passing them to the respective functions for drawing the images. Once the required coordinates have been procured, standard functions like **line( )**, **arc( )**, **circle( )**, etc. take care of the rest.

For example, if a box is to be drawn, the user is first asked to select one corner of the rectangle. This he does by moving the cursor to the desired position on the screen and hitting the Enter key. At this instance, in the **drawbox( )** function, the starting corner coordinates are stored in variables **x1** and **y1**. Next, the user is prompted to select the diagonally opposite corner of the rectangle. As he does so by hitting the arrow keys, the control rotates in a **while** loop, performing the following operations in turn:

(a) Draw the box
(b) Collect the key hit by the user
(c) Erase the box
(d) Redraw the box at new coordinates

Each time the box is drawn, the function **rectangle( )** is called with the starting coordinates (**x1, y1**) and the current cursor coordinates (**x, y**). Obviously, first time through the loop, only a dot would be drawn in place of a box, since this time the starting and current coordinates would be same. As the user proceeds to hit the arrow keys, the current coordinates (**x, y**) change, drawing a new box in the process everytime through the loop. This draw-erase-draw cycle is broken either when the user confirms the second corner by hitting the Enter key, or he decides to abandon the drawing altogether by hitting the Esc key. What if the box is to be superimposed on an existing drawing? Would it not erase the existing drawing? No. This aspect is taken care of by the functions **getimage( )** and **putimage( )**. **getimage( )** stores the current screen contents where the box is to be drawn. After the box is drawn and the arrow keys are hit, the current cursor coordinates are updated, and the current box is erased. Now, **putimage( )** goes to work and restores the original screen contents. This cycle goes on within the **while** loop. Finally, when the user confirms the second corner coordinate, the box is made permanent and the screen contents present in memory are superimposed on this box using **putimage( )**.

An exactly similar procedure is employed for drawing other regular figures like line, circle, ellipse and arc. The only difference is in the points the user is prompted to select.

Apart from these regular figures, there's the option Freehand, wherein you can draw figures of any shapes that suit your fancy. Here once again, first the point where the Freehand drawing is to begin is selected by the user. Thereafter, depending on what key is hit by the user, **testkeys( )** updates the coordinates of the cursor (in graphics mode) accordingly, tracing out the freehand drawing as the cursor moves. This is done by lighting the pixel at the current coordinates using the function **putpixel( )**.

For producing fully comprehensible diagrams, lables are a must. The Text option in Draw menu provides this facility. Using this option, any number of strings, having a maximum length of 50 characters can be supplied and displayed anywhere in the viewport. Further, the font, size and orientation of the text can be chosen from a range of options available. The functions **settextstyle( )** and **settextjustify( )** are used for setting up the desired attributes for the text, and then **outtextxy( )** places the text at the specified location in the viewport.

The Edit Menu

The various options of the Edit Menu go a long way in making designing on the Computer so much more superior and effortless as compared to the laborious drawing, erasing and redrawing on paper. For the three editing operations - erasing a part of a drawing, or moving it to a new place on the screen, or copying it at another location, firstly the part in question is to be selected. This selection is done by enclosing the part in question within a rectangle. The drawing of this rectangle is done as usual: by first choosing the starting corner of the enclosing box, and then the ending corner. Once the enclosing box is drawn, the **erase( )** function proceeds to erase the contents of the box. Thus, erasing a part of the drawing is accomplished easily.

Selection of the part for moving or copying is same as it is for erasing. However, after selection the logic varies. While moving, the part selected is first stored in memory using **getimage( )**. Now the part is erased from the existing position and moved across the screen using the arrow keys. Finally it is made permanent at the new position by hitting the Enter key. This movement is achieved through the repeated use of **putimage( )** within a **while** loop. Everytime through the loop, the first call to **putimage( )** erases the part and the second call draws it at a new position. When Enter key is hit **putimage( )** is called for the last time to confirm the final position.

The copying procedure is exactly same as moving, except for one small difference. Here, first time through the loop, the part selected is not erased from its initial position. During subsequent times, however, the erasing and redrawing procedure proceeds exactly as it does while moving.

How come the same **putimage( )** can sometimes draw the image and at other times erase it? This is managed by an argument supplied to **putimage( )**. The value of this argument and its significance is given in the following figure.

Argument passed	Status of image		Resultant image on screen
	Memory	Screen	
XOR_PUT	Present	Present	Erased
XOR_PUT	Present	Absent	Drawn
OR_PUT	Present	Present	Superimposed
OR_OUT	Present	Absent	Superimposed
COPY_PUT	Present	Present	Replaced
COPY_PUT	Present	Absent	Replaced

Figure 4.2

The other two editing operations are quite simple. The Wipe option wipes out the current viewport contents using the standard library function **clearviewport( )**. The Paint option fills a bounded region with the current fill pattern and fill color using another standard library function **floodfill( )**.

The File Menu

This menu offers various file operations for the designs created and edited using Draw and Edit menus. The Save operation is completed in a two step process after specifying the file name. The first step consists of storing the contents of the screen using **getimage( )** in an area allocated by **malloc( )**. In the second step, these screen contents from memory are written into the file using **write( )**. Loading a file involves just the reverse action - firstly read data from the file using **read( )** and then display it on the screen using **putimage( )**.

For a hard copy of the design, the Print option of the File menu is used. The printing is managed by calling a ROM BIOS routine using **int86( )**. Before exercising this option ensure that the two DOS files 'graphics.com' and 'graftabl.com' have been executed. On execution of these files at the DOS prompt the printer is able to print graphics output.

Line Styles

By passing different arguments to the function **setlinestyle( )**, we can have different types of lines. Using a loop, we display four types of lines, and allow the user to decide on the type of lines needed for the drawing. Once set, all the lines and boxes you draw will appear in the chosen line style, until you change the setting again.

Enhancing Mycad

Mycad includes a considerable number of designing operations. Still, there's a lot more that can be added to it. Like the facility of rotating an object, obtaining its mirror image, or zooming into a part of the drawing. Similarly, in the Draw menu, the Line option can be enhanced to draw lines of various thicknesses. A polygon option can also be added to the Draw menu. Like many professional softwares, instead of drawing interactively through keyboard, mouse interfacing can be added. Interaction with mouse is discussed in Chapter 5.

Program

```
# include "graphics.h"
# include "math.h"
# include "dos.h"
# include "process.h"
# include "alloc.h"
# include "stdlib.h"
# include "ctype.h"
# include "stdio.h"
# include "fcntl.h"
# include "types.h"
# include "stat.h"


/* macro definitions for various keys and their scan/ascii codes */
# define ESC              27
# define ENTER            13
# define DOWN             80
# define LEFT             75
# define RIGHT            77
# define UP               72
# define HOME             71
# define END              79
# define PGUP             73
# define PGDN             81
# define TAB              9
# define SH_TAB           15
# define CTRL_RIGHT       116
# define CTRL_LEFT        115
# define CTRL_PGDN        118
# define CTRL_PGUP        132
# define CTRL_HOME        119
# define CTRL_END         117

/* various menu definitions */
```

```
char *mainmenu[ ] = {
                    "Draw",
                    "Edit",
                    "File",
                    "Line style",
                    "eXit"
              } ;

char *drawmenu[ ] = {
                    "Line",
                    "Box",
                    "Circle",
                    "Ellipse",
                    "Arc",
                    "Freehand",
                    "Text"
               } ;

char *editmenu[ ] = {
                    "Wipe",
                    "Erase",
                    "Move",
                    "Copy",
                    "Paint"
                } ;

char *filemenu[ ] = {
                    "Save",
                    "Load",
                    "Print"
                 } ;

void *p, *q, *r ;
int x = 10, y = 10, ascii, scan ;

main( )
{
```

```
int choice, gm, gd = DETECT ;
size_t area, cursorarea ;

/* initialise the graphics system */
initgraph ( &gd, &gm, "c:\\tc\\bgi" ) ;

/* allocate memory in RAM for saving screen contents */
area = imagesize ( 0, 0, 637, 177 ) ;
p = malloc ( area ) ;

/* allocate memory in RAM for saving screen contents while drawing
   lines, boxes, circles etc. */
r = malloc ( area ) ;

/* allocate memory in RAM for saving area of screen on which the cursor
   is to be placed */
cursorarea = imagesize ( 0, 0, 7, 7 ) ;
q = malloc ( cursorarea ) ;

/* if memory allocation fails, terminate execution */
if ( p == NULL || q == NULL || r == NULL )
{
    printf ( "Insufficient memory! Press any key..." ) ;
    fflush ( stdin ) ;
    getch( ) ;

    closegraph( ) ;  /* shut down graphics system */
    restorecrtmode( ) ;  /* restore original video mode */

    exit ( 1 ) ;
}

/* create opening screen display */
mainscreen( ) ;

/* clear the screen contents */
clearviewport( ) ;
```

```
/* define the drawing area */
rectangle ( 0, 10, 639, 189 ) ;
setviewport ( 1, 11, 638, 188, 1 ) ;

/* display current cursor position */
gotoxy ( 68, 25 ) ;
printf ( "X:%3d  Y:%3d", x, y ) ;

while ( 1 )
{
    /* display main menu in topmost row */
    displaymenu ( mainmenu, 5 ) ;

    /* receive user's response */
    choice = getresponse ( "DEFLX", 5 ) ;

    /* call appropriate function */
    switch ( choice )
    {
        case 1 :
            draw( ) ;
            break ;

        case 2 :
            edit( ) ;
            break ;

        case 3 :
            file( ) ;
            break ;

        case 4 :
            linetype( ) ;
            break ;

        case 5 :
```

```
                        closegraph( ) ;  /* shut down graphics system */
                        restorecrtmode( ) ;  /* restore original video mode */
                        exit ( 0 ) ;
                }
        }
}

/* creates the opening screen display */
mainscreen( )
{
        int maxx, maxy, in, area ;

        /* get maximum x, y coordinates of the screen */
        maxx = getmaxx( ) ;
        maxy = getmaxy( ) ;

        /* draw rectangles */
        setcolor ( WHITE ) ;
        rectangle ( 0, 0, maxx, maxy ) ;
        rectangle ( 0, 10, 639, 189 ) ;

        /* open the file */
        in = open ( "screen.dwg", O_BINARY | O_RDONLY ) ;
        if ( in == -1 )
                return ;

        /* find area required to accomodate file contents in memory */
        area = imagesize ( 0, 0, 637, 177 ) ;

        /* read the file contents into allocated memory */
        read ( in, p, area ) ;

        /* close the file */
        close ( in ) ;

        /* display the contents of allocated memory on the screen */
        putimage ( 1, 11, p, COPY_PUT ) ;
```

```
        /* set line style and text justification */
        settextstyle ( DEFAULT_FONT, HORIZ_DIR, 0 ) ;
        settextjustify ( CENTER_TEXT, TOP_TEXT ) ;

        /* output text */
        outtextxy ( maxx / 2, 2, "MYCAD" ) ;
        outtextxy ( 39 * 8, 24 * 8 - 1, "Press any key to continue..." ) ;

        fflush ( stdin ) ;
        getch( ) ;

        /* clear the viewport area */
        clearviewport( ) ;
}

/* displays Draw menu, receives choice and branches control to appropriate
   function */
draw( )
{
        int dchoice ;

        while ( 1 )
        {
             displaymenu ( drawmenu, 7 ) ;

             gotoxy ( 1, 25 ) ;
             printf ( "Press Esc to return to previous menu" ) ;

             dchoice = getresponse ( "LBCEAFT", 7 ) ;

             switch ( dchoice )
             {
                  case 1 :
                       drawline( ) ;
                       break ;
```

```
        case 2 :
            drawbox( ) ;
            break ;

        case 3 :
            drawcircle( ) ;
            break ;

        case 4 :
            drawellipse( ) ;
            break ;

        case 5 :
            drawarc( ) ;
            break ;

        case 6 :
            freehand( ) ;
            break ;

        case 7 :
            text( ) ;
            break ;

        case ESC :
            return ;
        }
    }
}

/* displays Edit menu, receives choice and branches control to appropriate
   function */
edit( )
{
    int echoice ;

    while ( 1 )
```

```
{
    displaymenu ( editmenu, 5 ) ;

    gotoxy ( 1, 25 ) ;
    printf ( "Press Esc to return to previous menu" ) ;

    echoice = getresponse ( "WEMCP", 5 ) ;

    switch ( echoice )
    {
        case 1 :
            wipe( ) ;
            break ;

        case 2 :
            erase( ) ;
            break ;

        case 3 :
            move( ) ;
            break ;

        case 4 :
            copy( ) ;
            break ;

        case 5 :
            paint( ) ;
            break ;

        case ESC :
            return ;
    }
}
}
```

/* displays File menu, receives choice and branches control to appropriate

```
    function */
file( )
{
    int fchoice ;

    while ( 1 )
    {
        displaymenu ( filemenu, 3 ) ;

        gotoxy ( 1, 25 ) ;
        printf ( "Press Esc to return to previous menu" ) ;

        fchoice = getresponse ( "SLP", 3 ) ;

        switch ( fchoice )
        {
            case 1 :
                save( ) ;
                break ;

            case 2 :
                load( ) ;
                break ;

            case 3 :
                print( ) ;
                break ;

            case ESC :
                return ;
        }
    }
}

/* displays the given menu in topmost row */
displaymenu ( menu, count )
int count ;
```

```
char **menu ;
{
    int col = 2, i ;

    cleartext ( 2 ) ;  /* erase the top and bottom row */

    for ( i = 0 ; i < count ; i++ )
    {
        gotoxy ( col, 1 ) ;
        printf ( "%s", menu[i] ) ;
        col = col + 79 / count ;
    }
}

/* receives user's choice */
getresponse ( hotkeys, count )
char *hotkeys ;
int count ;
{
    int col, choice = 1, hotkeychoice, len ;

    while ( 1 )
    {
        /* calculate the column in which the triangle is to be placed */
        col = ( choice - 1 ) * ( 79 / count ) + 1 ;

        /* display triangle to indicate current menu item */
        gotoxy ( col, 1 ) ;
        putchar ( 16 ) ;

        /* receive a key from keyboard */
        getkey( ) ;

        /* if special key is hit */
        if ( ascii == 0 )
        {
            /* erase triangle */
```

```
                    gotoxy ( col, 1 ) ;
                    putchar ( ' ' ) ;

                    /* test if left or right arrow key is hit */
                    switch ( scan )
                    {
                        case RIGHT :
                            choice++ ;
                            break ;

                        case LEFT :
                            choice-- ;
                    }

                    /* if triangle is on last item and right arrow key is hit */
                    if ( choice > count )
                        choice = 1 ;

                    /* if triangle is on first item and left arrow key is hit */
                    if ( choice == 0 )
                        choice = count ;
            }
        else
            {
                if ( ascii == ENTER )
                    return ( choice ) ;

                if ( ascii == ESC )
                    return ( ESC ) ;

                /* check whether a hot key has been pressed */

                len = strlen ( hotkeys ) ;
                hotkeychoice = 1 ;
                ascii = toupper ( ascii ) ;

                while ( *hotkeys )
```

```
                    {
                        if ( *hotkeys == ascii )
                            return ( hotkeychoice ) ;
                        else
                        {
                            hotkeys++ ;
                            hotkeychoice++ ;
                        }
                    }

                    /* reset hotkeys pointer */
                    hotkeys = hotkeys - len ;

                    /* beep to indicate invalid choice */
                    printf ( "\a" ) ;
                }
        }
}

/* gets ascii and scan codes of the key pressed */
getkey( )
{
    union REGS i, o ;

    /* wait till a key is pressed */
    while ( !kbhit( ) )


    i.h.ah = 0 ;  /* service number */

    /* issue interrupt */
    int86 ( 22, &i, &o ) ;

    ascii = o.h.al ;
    scan = o.h.ah ;
}
```

```
/* clears top and/or bottom row on the screen */
cleartext ( n )
int n ;
{
    int i ;

    switch ( n )
    {
        case 0 :  /* erase top row */
            for ( i = 1 ; i <= 80 ; i++ )
            {
                gotoxy ( i, 1 ) ;
                putchar ( ' ' ) ;
            }
            break ;

        case 1 :  /* erase bottom row */
            for ( i = 1 ; i <= 67 ; i++ )
            {
                gotoxy ( i, 25 ) ;
                putchar ( ' ' ) ;
            }
            break ;

        case 2 :  /* erase top and bottom row */
            cleartext ( 0 ) ;
            cleartext ( 1 ) ;
            break ;
    }
}

drawline()
{
    int lchoice, x1, y1, x2, y2 ;

    cleartext ( 2 ) ;
    gotoxy ( 1, 1 ) ;
```

```
printf ( "LINE" ) ;
gotoxy ( 69, 1 ) ;
printf ( "Esc to exit" ) ;

while ( 1 )
{
    cleartext ( 1 ) ;
    gotoxy ( 1, 25 ) ;
    printf ( "Select the starting point" ) ;

    /* save current screen contents */
    getimage ( 0, 0, 637, 177, p ) ;

    /* allow movement of cursor and selection of starting point */
    lchoice = movecursor( ) ;

    if ( lchoice == ESC )
        return ;

    /* save starting point coordinates */
    x1 = x ;
    y1 = y ;

    cleartext ( 1 ) ;
    gotoxy ( 1, 25 ) ;
    printf ( "Use arrow keys to draw, Enter to confirm" ) ;

    /* allow interactive drawing of line */
    while ( 2 )
    {
        /* store the image of screen where line is to be drawn */
        getimage ( x1, y1, x, y, r ) ;

        /* draw line */
        moveto ( x1, y1 ) ;
        lineto ( x, y ) ;
```

```
            /* receive key */
            getkey( ) ;

            /* erase line */
            setcolor ( BLACK ) ;
            moveto ( x1, y1 ) ;
            lineto ( x, y ) ;
            setcolor ( WHITE ) ;

            /* assign to x2 the smaller of x1 and x, and to y2 that of y1 and y */
            x2 = x1 < x ? x1 : x ;
            y2 = y1 < y ? y1 : y ;

            /* restore the image on screen where line was drawn */
            putimage ( x2, y2, r, OR_PUT ) ;

            /* test the key that has been pressed */
            lchoice = testkeys( ) ;

            /* if Esc key is pressed, abandon line drawing */
            if ( lchoice == ESC )
                return ;

            /* if Enter key is pressed, make the line permanent */
            if ( lchoice == ENTER )
            {
                moveto ( x1, y1 ) ;
                lineto ( x, y ) ;

                /* line completed, hence start with a new line */
                break ;
            }
        }
    }
}
}
```

/* allow movement of cursor until Enter or Esc key is pressed */

```
movecursor( )
{
    int choice ;

    while ( 1 )
    {
        /* draw the cursor at current x, y coordinates */
        drawcursor ( 1 ) ;

        /* receive key */
        getkey( ) ;

        /* erase the cursor from current x, y coordinates */
        drawcursor ( 0 ) ;

        /* test the key that has been hit */
        choice = testkeys( ) ;

        if ( choice == ESC || choice == ENTER )
            return ( choice ) ;
    }
}

/* draws or erases cursor as per the value of color */
drawcursor ( color )
int color ;
{
    int xx, yy ;

    /* save image if cursor is to be drawn */
    if ( color == 1 )
        getimage ( x - 3, y - 3, x + 3, y + 3, q ) ;

    /* draw horizontal line of the cursor */
    for ( xx = x - 3 ; xx <= x + 3 ; xx++ )
        putpixel ( xx, y, color ) ;
```

```
    /* draw vertical line of the cursor */
    for ( yy = y - 3 ; yy <= y + 3 ; yy++ )
        putpixel ( x, yy, color ) ;

    /* restore image if the cursor has been erased */
    if ( color == 0 )
        putimage ( x - 3, y - 3, q, OR_PUT ) ;
}

/* tests which key has been hit */
testkeys( )
{
    /* if cursor movement key is hit, update values of x, y */
    if ( ascii == 0 )
    {
        switch ( scan )
        {
            case DOWN :
                y++ ;
                break ;

            case UP :
                y-- ;
                break ;

            case LEFT :
                x-- ;
                break ;

            case RIGHT :
                x++ ;
                break ;

            case HOME :
                y-- ;
                x-- ;
                break ;
```

```
        case END :
            x-- ;
            y++ ;
            break ;

        case PGUP :
            x++ ;
            y-- ;
            break ;

        case PGDN :
            x++ ;
            y++ ;
            break ;

        case SH_TAB :
            x -= 10 ;
            break ;

        case CTRL_RIGHT :
            x = 636 ;
            break ;

        case CTRL_LEFT :
            x = 2 ;
            break ;

        case CTRL_PGDN :
            y += 5 ;
            break ;

        case CTRL_PGUP :
            y -= 5 ;
            break ;

        case CTRL_HOME :
```

```
                    x = 2 ;
                    y = 2 ;
                    break ;

            case CTRL_END :
                x = 636 ;
                y = 176 ;
    }
}
else
{
    if ( ascii == ENTER )
        return ( ENTER ) ;

    if ( ascii == ESC )
    {
        putimage ( 0, 0, p, OR_PUT ) ; /* restore screen contents */
        return ( ESC ) ;
    }

    if ( ascii == TAB )
        x += 10 ;
}

/* readjust x, y if their values exceed the limits */

if ( x > 635 )
    x = 635 ;

if ( x < 3 )
    x = 3 ;

if ( y > 175 )
    y = 175 ;

if ( y < 3 )
    y = 3 ;
```

```
        /* display new x, y coordinates */
        gotoxy ( 68, 25 ) ;
        printf ( "X:%3d  Y:%3d", x, y ) ;

        /* if a key other than Enter or Esc is pressed */
        return ( 100 ) ;
}

drawbox( )
{
        int bchoice, x1, y1, x2, y2 ;

        cleartext ( 2 ) ;
        gotoxy ( 1, 1 ) ;
        printf ( "BOX" ) ;
        gotoxy ( 69, 1 ) ;
        printf ( "Esc to exit" ) ;

        while ( 1 )
        {
            cleartext ( 1 ) ;
            gotoxy ( 1, 25 ) ;
            printf ( "Select the first corner" ) ;

            /* save current screen contents */
            getimage ( 0, 0, 637, 177, p ) ;

            /* allow movement of cursor and selection of starting corner */
            bchoice = movecursor( ) ;

            if ( bchoice == ESC )
                return ;

            /* save coordinates of starting corner */
            x1 = x ;
            y1 = y ;
```

```
cleartext ( 1 ) ;
gotoxy ( 1, 25 ) ;
printf ( "Use arrow keys to select other corner, Enter to confirm" ) ;

/* allow interactive drawing of box */
while ( 2 )
{
    /* store the image of screen where box is to be drawn */
    getimage ( x1, y1, x, y, r ) ;

    /* draw box */
    rectangle ( x1, y1, x, y ) ;

    /* receive key */
    getkey( ) ;

    /* erase box */
    setcolor ( BLACK ) ;
    rectangle ( x1, y1, x, y ) ;
    setcolor ( WHITE ) ;

    /* assign to x2 the smaller of x1 and x, and to y2 that of y1 and y */
    x2 = x1 < x ? x1 : x ;
    y2 = y1 < y ? y1 : y ;

    /* restore the image on screen where box was drawn */
    putimage ( x2, y2, r, OR_PUT ) ;

    /* test the key that has been pressed */
    bchoice = testkeys( ) ;

    /* if Esc key is pressed, abandon box drawing */
    if ( bchoice == ESC )
        return ;

    /* if Enter key is pressed, make the box permanent */
```

```
            if ( bchoice == ENTER )
            {
                    rectangle ( x1, y1, x, y ) ;

                    /* box completed, hence start with a new box */
                    break ;
            }
        }
    }
}

drawcircle( )
{
    int cchoice, radius, xc, yc, x1, x2, y1, y2 ;

    cleartext ( 2 ) ;
    gotoxy ( 1, 1 ) ;
    printf ( "CIRCLE" ) ;
    gotoxy ( 69, 1 ) ;
    printf ( "Esc to exit" ) ;

    while ( 1 )
    {
        cleartext ( 1 ) ;
        gotoxy ( 1, 25 ) ;
        printf ( "Select the centre of circle" ) ;

        /* save current screen contents */
        getimage ( 0, 0, 637, 177, p ) ;

        /* allow movement of cursor and selection of the centre of circle */
        cchoice = movecursor( ) ;

        if ( cchoice == ESC )
            return ;

        /* save coordinates of centre of circle */
```

```
xc = x ;
yc = y ;

cleartext ( 1 ) ;
gotoxy ( 1, 25 ) ;
printf ( "Use Left & Right arrow keys to draw circle, Enter to confirm" ) ;

/* allow interactive drawing of circle */
while ( 2 )
{
    /* calculate radius of circle */
    radius = abs ( x - xc ) ;

    /* calculate coordinates of the rectangle in which the circle is to
       be inscribed */
    x1 = xc - radius ;
    x2 = xc + radius ;
    y1 = yc - 0.5 * radius ;
    y2 = yc + 0.5 * radius ;

    /* readjust x1, y1, x2, y2 if their values exceed the limits */

    if ( x1 < 2 )
        x1 = 2 ;

    if ( x2 > 636 )
        x2 = 636 ;

    if ( y1 < 2 )
        y1 = 2 ;

    if ( y2 > 176 )
        y2 = 176 ;

    /* store the image of screen where circle is to be drawn */
    getimage ( x1, y1, x2, y2, r ) ;
```

```
        /* draw circle */
        circle ( xc, yc, radius ) ;

        /* receive key */
        getkey( ) ;

        /* erase circle */
        setcolor ( BLACK ) ;
        circle ( xc, yc, radius ) ;
        setcolor ( WHITE ) ;

        /* restore the image on screen where circle was drawn */
        putimage ( x1, y1, r, OR_PUT ) ;

        /* test the key that has been pressed */
        cchoice = testkeys( ) ;

        /* if Esc key is pressed, abandon circle drawing */
        if ( cchoice == ESC )
            return ;

        /* if Enter key is pressed, make the circle permanent */
        if ( cchoice == ENTER )
        {
            circle ( xc, yc, radius ) ;

            /* circle completed, hence start with a new circle */
            break ;
        }
      }
    }
}

drawellipse( )
{
    int echoice, xradius, yradius, x1, y1, x2, y2, xc, yc ;
```

```
cleartext ( 2 ) ;
gotoxy ( 1, 1 ) ;
printf ( "ELLIPSE" ) ;
gotoxy ( 69, 1 ) ;
printf ( "Esc to exit" ) ;

while ( 1 )
{
    cleartext ( 1 ) ;
    gotoxy ( 1, 25 ) ;
    printf ( "Select the centre of ellipse" ) ;

    /* save current screen contents */
    getimage ( 0, 0, 637, 177, p ) ;

    /* allow movement of cursor and selection of the centre of ellipse */
    echoice = movecursor( ) ;

    if ( echoice == ESC )
        return ;

    /* save coordinates of centre of ellipse */
    xc = x ;
    yc = y ;

    cleartext ( 1 ) ;
    gotoxy ( 1, 25 ) ;
    printf ( "Use arrow keys to draw ellipse, Enter to confirm" ) ;

    /* allow interactive drawing of ellipse */
    while ( 2 )
    {
        /* calculate major and minor axes of the ellipse */
        xradius = abs ( x - xc ) ;
        yradius = abs ( y - yc ) ;

        /* calculate coordinates of the rectangle in which the ellipse is to
```

```
        be inscribed */
x1 = xc - xradius ;
x2 = xc + xradius ;
y1 = yc - yradius ;
y2 = yc + yradius ;

/* readjust x1, y1, x2, y2 if their values exceed the limits */

if ( x1 < 2 )
    x1 = 2 ;

if ( x2 > 636 )
    x2 = 636 ;

if ( y1 < 2 )
    y1 = 2 ;

if ( y2 > 176 )
    y2 = 176 ;

/* store the image of screen where ellipse is to be drawn */
getimage ( x1, y1, x2, y2, r ) ;

/* draw ellipse */
ellipse ( xc, yc, 0, 360, xradius, yradius ) ;

/* receive key */
getkey( ) ;

/* erase ellipse */
setcolor ( BLACK ) ;
ellipse ( xc, yc, 0, 360, xradius, yradius ) ;
setcolor ( WHITE ) ;

/* restore the image on screen where ellipse was drawn */
putimage ( x1, y1, r, OR_PUT ) ;
```

```
                    /* test the key that has been pressed */
                    echoice = testkeys( ) ;

                    /* if Esc key is pressed, abandon ellipse drawing */
                    if ( echoice == ESC )
                        return ;

                    /* if Enter key is pressed, make ellipse permanent */
                    if ( echoice == ENTER )
                    {
                        ellipse ( xc, yc, 0, 360, xradius, yradius ) ;

                        /* ellipse completed, hence start with new ellipse */
                        break ;
                    }
                }
            }
        }
}

drawarc( )
{
        int achoice, xc, yc, start, end, x1, y1, x2, y2 ;
        double st_angle, en_angle, radius, s, a, b ;

        cleartext ( 2 ) ;
        gotoxy ( 1, 1 ) ;
        printf ( "ARC" ) ;
        gotoxy ( 69, 1 ) ;
        printf ( "Esc to exit" ) ;

        while ( 1 )
        {
            cleartext ( 1 ) ;
            gotoxy ( 1, 25 ) ;
            printf ( "Select the centre of arc" ) ;

            /* save current screen contents */
```

```
getimage ( 0, 0, 637, 177, p ) ;

/* allow movement of cursor and selection of the centre of arc */
achoice = movecursor( ) ;

if ( achoice == ESC )
    return ;

/* save coordinates of centre of arc */
xc = x ;
yc = y ;

cleartext ( 1 ) ;
gotoxy ( 1, 25 ) ;
printf ( "Select the starting point of arc, Enter to confirm" ) ;

/* test the key that has been pressed */
achoice = movecursor( ) ;

/* if Esc key is pressed, abandon arc drawing */
if ( achoice == ESC )
    return ;

/* find absolute difference between the x-coordinates of the center
   and starting point of arc */
a = abs ( x - xc ) ;

/* find absolute difference between the y-coordinates of the center
   and starting point of arc */
b = 2 * abs ( y - yc ) ;  /* 2 takes care of the aspect ratio */

/* calculate radius of the arc */
radius = sqrt ( a * a + b * b ) ;

/* calculate the starting angle */
st_angle = asin ( b / radius ) ;
```

```
/* convert from radians to degrees */
start = st_angle * 180 / 3.14 ;

/* if the starting point of the arc lies in the second quadrant */
if ( ( x <= xc ) && ( y <= yc ) )
     start = 180 - start ;  /* take the complement of calculated angle */
else
{
     /* if the starting point of the arc lies in the third quadrant */
     if ( ( x <= xc ) && ( y > yc ) )
          start = 180 + start ;
     else
     {
          /* if the starting point of the arc lies in the fourth quadrant */
          if ( ( x > xc ) && ( y > yc ) )
               start = 360 - start ;
     }
}

cleartext ( 1 ) ;
gotoxy ( 1, 25 ) ;
printf ( "Use arrow keys to draw arc, Enter to confirm" ) ;

/* calculate coordinates of the rectangle in which the arc is to be
   inscribed */
x1 = xc - radius ;
x2 = xc + radius ;
y1 = yc - 0.5 * radius ;
y2 = yc + 0.5 * radius ;

/* readjust x1, y1, x2, y2 if their values exceed the limits */

if ( x1 < 2 )
     x1 = 2 ;

if ( x2 > 636 )
     x2 = 636 ;
```

```
if ( y1 < 2 )
    y1 = 2 ;

if ( y2 > 176 )
    y2 = 176 ;

/* allow interactive drawing of arc */
while ( 2 )
{
    /* readjust x and y in instances where attempt is made to stretch
       the arc beyond its radius */

    if ( x < xc - radius )
        x = xc - radius ;

    if ( y < yc - radius )
        y = yc - radius ;

    if ( x > xc + radius )
        x = xc + radius ;

    if ( y > yc + radius )
        y = yc + radius ;

    /* calculate ending angle */
    a = abs ( x - xc ) ;
    b = 2 * abs ( y - yc ) ;
    s = sqrt ( a * a + b * b ) ;
    en_angle = asin ( b / s ) ;
    end = en_angle * 180 / 3.14 ;

    /* readjust ending angle as per the quadrant in which the ending
       point lies */
    if ( ( x <= xc ) && ( y <= yc ) )
        end = 180 - end ;
    else
```

```
{
    if ( ( x <= xc ) && ( y > yc ) )
        end = 180 + end ;
    else
    {
        if ( ( x > xc ) && ( y > yc ) )
            end = 360 - end ;
    }
}

/* store the image of screen where arc is to be drawn */
getimage ( x1, y1, x2, y2, r ) ;

/* draw arc */
arc ( xc, yc, start, end, radius ) ;

/* receive key */
getkey( ) ;

/* erase arc */
setcolor ( BLACK ) ;
arc ( xc, yc, start, end, radius ) ;
setcolor ( WHITE ) ;

/* restore the image on screen where arc was drawn */
putimage ( x1, y1, r, OR_PUT ) ;

/* test the key that has been pressed */
achoice = testkeys( ) ;

/* if Esc key is pressed, abandon arc drawing */
if ( achoice == ESC )
    return ;

/* if Enter key is pressed, make arc permanent */
if ( achoice == ENTER )
{
```

```
                    arc ( xc, yc, start, end, radius ) ;

                    /* arc completed, hence start with a new arc */
                    break ;
                }
            }
        }
}

/* draws freehand drawing */
freehand( )
{
    int fchoice ;

    cleartext ( 2 ) ;
    gotoxy ( 1, 1 ) ;
    printf ( "FREEHAND" ) ;
    gotoxy ( 69, 1 ) ;
    printf ( "Esc to exit" ) ;

    while ( 1 )
    {
        cleartext ( 1 ) ;
        gotoxy ( 1, 25 ) ;
        printf ( "Select the starting point" ) ;

        /* save current screen contents */
        getimage ( 0, 0, 637, 177, p ) ;

        /* allow movement of cursor and selection of the starting point */
        fchoice = movecursor( ) ;

        if ( fchoice == ESC )
            return ;

        cleartext ( 1 ) ;
        gotoxy ( 1, 25 ) ;
```

```
        printf ( "Use arrow keys to draw, Enter to end" ) ;

        /* allow interactive freehand drawing */
        while ( 2 )
        {
            /* draw a pixel */
            putpixel ( x, y, 1 ) ;

            /* receive key */
            getkey( ) ;

            /* test the key that has been pressed */
            fchoice = testkeys( ) ;

            /* if Esc key is pressed, abandon freehand drawing */
            if ( fchoice == ESC )
            {
                /* restore original screen contents, thereby erasing the
                   freehand drawing */
                putimage ( 0, 0, p, COPY_PUT , ,
                return ;
            }

            /* if Enter key is pressed, make the freehand drawing permanent */
            if ( fchoice == ENTER )
            {
                /* freehand completed, hence start with a new freehand
                   drawing */
                break ;
            }
        }
    }
}

/* displays text at specified location */
text( )
{
```

```c
char ch, str[51] ;
int tchoice, j = 0 , k = 0 , l = 0 ;

cleartext ( 2 ) ;
gotoxy ( 1, 1 ) ;
printf ( "TEXT" ) ;
gotoxy ( 69, 1 ) ;
printf ( "Esc to exit" ) ;

while ( 1 )
{
    cleartext ( 1 ) ;
    gotoxy ( 1, 25 ) ;
    printf ( "Enter the text:" ) ;

    /* receive the text entered */
    tchoice = getstring ( str, 17 ) ;

    if ( tchoice == ESC )
        return ;

    cleartext ( 1 ) ;
    gotoxy ( 1, 25 ) ;
    printf ( "Select the position to place the text, Enter to confirm" ) ;

    /* save current screen contents */
    getimage ( 0, 0, 637, 177, p ) ;

    /* allow movement of cursor and selection of the starting point */
    tchoice = movecursor( ) ;

    if ( tchoice == ESC )
        return ;

    /* output the text in default style and justification */
    settextstyle ( DEFAULT_FONT, HORIZ_DIR, 0 ) ;
    settextjustify ( LEFT_TEXT, TOP_TEXT ) ;
```

```
        outtextxy ( x, y, str ) ;

        cleartext ( 1 ) ;
        gotoxy ( 1, 25 ) ;
        printf ( "Want to change the font (Y/N) ?" ) ;
        fflush ( stdin ) ;
        ch = getch( ) ;

        if ( ch == ESC )
        {
            putimage ( 0, 0, p, COPY_PUT ) ;
            return ;
        }

        /* allow interactive changing of the font of the text */
        if ( ch == 'y' || ch == 'Y' )
        {
            cleartext ( 1 ) ;
            gotoxy ( 1, 25 )
            printf ( "Press any key to examine the fonts, Enter to confirm" ) ;

            while ( 1 )
            {
                fflush ( stdin ) ;
                ch = getch( ) ;

                if ( ch == ENTER )
                    break ;

                /* if Esc key is pressed, restore screen contents and return
                   to Draw menu */
                if ( ch == ESC )
                {
                    putimage ( 0, 0, p, COPY_PUT ) ;
                    return ;
                }
```

```
                    /* counter for different font styles, maximum 5 */
                    j++ ;
                    if ( j > 4 )
                         j = 0 ;

                    /* set the text style as indicated by j */
                    settextstyle ( j, HORIZ_DIR, 1 ) ;

                    /* output the text in the chosen style */
                    putimage ( 0, 0, p, COPY_PUT ) ;
                    outtextxy ( x, y, str ) ;
              }
        }

   cleartext ( 1 ) ;
   gotoxy ( 1, 25 ) ;
   printf ( "Want to change the size of text (Y/N) ?" ) ;
   fflush ( stdin ) ;
   ch = getch( ) ;

   /* if Esc key is pressed, return to Draw menu */
   if ( ch == ESC )
   {
        putimage ( 0, 0, p, COPY_PUT ) ;
        return ;
   }

   /* allow interactive changing of the size of the text */
   if ( ch == 'y' || ch == 'Y' )
   {
        cleartext ( 1 ) ;
        gotoxy ( 1, 25 ) ;
        printf ( "Press any key to examine the sizes, Enter to confirm" ) ;

        while ( 1 )
        {
             fflush ( stdin ) ;
```

```
                    ch = getch( ) ;

                    if ( ch == ENTER )
                        break ;

                    /* if Esc key is pressed, return to Draw menu */
                    if ( ch == ESC )
                    {
                        putimage ( 0, 0, p, COPY_PUT ) ;
                        return ;
                    }

                    /* counter for different character sizes, maximum 10 */
                    k++ ;
                    if ( k > 9 )
                        k = 0 ;

                    /* set style as indicated by j and size as indicated by k */
                    settextstyle ( j, HORIZ_DIR, k ) ;
                    putimage ( 0, 0, p, COPY_PUT ) ;
                    outtextxy ( x, y, str ) ;
                }
            }

        cleartext ( 1 ) ;
        gotoxy ( 1, 25 ) ;
        printf ( "Want to change the direction (Y/N) ?" ) ;
        fflush ( stdin ) ;
        ch = getch( ) ;

        /* if Esc key is pressed, restore screen contents and return to Draw
           menu */
        if ( ch == ESC )
        {
            putimage ( 0, 0, p, COPY_PUT ) ;
            return ;
        }
```

```
/* allow interactive changing of the direction of the text */
if ( ch == 'y' || ch == 'Y' )
{
    cleartext ( 1 ) ;
    gotoxy ( 1, 25 ) ;
    printf ( "Press any key to observe the directions, Enter to
             confirm" ) ;

    while ( 1 )
    {
        fflush ( stdin ) ;
        ch = getch( ) ;

        if ( ch == ENTER )
            break ;

        /* if Esc key is pressed, restore screen contents and return
           to Draw menu */
        if ( ch == ESC )
        {
            putimage ( 0, 0, p, COPY_PUT ) ;
            return ;
        }

        /* counter for different text directions, maximum 2 */
        l++ ;
        if ( l > 1 )
            l = 0 ;

        /* set style as indicated by j, size as indicated by k and
           direction as indicated by l */
        settextstyle ( j, l, k ) ;
        putimage ( 0, 0, p, COPY_PUT ) ;
        outtextxy ( x, y, str ) ;
    }
}
```

```
        }
}

/* gets a string from keyboard */
getstring ( str, col )
char *str ;
int col ;
{
    int i = 0 ;
    char ch ;

    /* receive text */
    while ( 1 )
    {
        /* receive key */
        fflush ( stdin ) ;

        /* if special key like arrow keys etc. are hit, ignore them */
        if ( ( ch = getch( ) ) == 0 )
        {
            getch( ) ;
            continue ;
        }

        /* if Enter key is hit, terminate string */
        if ( ch == ENTER )
        {
            str[i] = '\0' ;
            break ;
        }

        /* if Esc key is hit, return to Draw menu */
        if ( ch == ESC )
            return ( ESC ) ;

        /* if Backspace key is hit and some text has been entered */
        if ( ch == '\b' && i > 0 )
```

```
        {
                i-- ;

                /* erase the previously entered character */
                gotoxy ( col + i, 25 ) ;
                printf ( " " ) ;

                gotoxy ( col + i, 25 ) ;
                continue ;
        }

        /* ignore control characters */
        if ( ch < 32 )
                continue ;

        /* if not a control character, display it on the screen */
        gotoxy ( col + i, 25 ) ;
        printf ( "%c", ch ) ;

        str[i] = ch ;
        i++ ;

        /* accept a maximum of 50 characters */
        if ( i == 50 )
        {
                str[i] = '\0' ;
                break ;
        }
    }

    return ( 0 ) ;
}

/* wipes out the entire drawing */
wipe( )
{
    char ch ;
```

```
        cleartext ( 2 ) ;
        gotoxy ( 1, 1 ) ;
        printf ( "WIPE" ) ;
        gotoxy ( 69, 1 ) ;
        printf ( "Esc to exit" ) ;
        gotoxy ( 1, 25 ) ;
        printf ( "Are you sure (Y/N) ?" ) ;

        fflush ( stdin ) ;
        ch = getch( ) ;

        /* if Esc key is pressed, return to Edit menu */
        if ( ch == ESC )
            return ;

        /* clear the viewport */
        if ( ch == 'y' || ch == 'Y' )
            clearviewport( ) ;
    }

/* erases the selected portion (here onwards called 'object') on the screen */
erase( )
{
        int echoice, x1, y1, x2, y2 ;
        struct linesettingstype linfo ;

        cleartext ( 2 ) ;
        gotoxy ( 1, 1 ) ;
        printf ( "ERASE" ) ;
        gotoxy ( 69, 1 ) ;
        printf ( "Esc to exit" ) ;
        gotoxy ( 1, 25 ) ;
        printf ( "Select the first corner" ) ;

        /* save current screen contents */
        getimage ( 0, 0, 637, 177, p ) ;
```

```
/* allow movement of cursor and selection of starting corner */
echoice = movecursor( ) ;

if ( echoice == ESC )
    return ;

/* save coordinates of the starting corner */
x1 = x ;
y1 = y ;

/* get the current line settings */
getlinesettings ( &linfo ) ;

/* set the line settings to the default values */
setlinestyle ( SOLID_LINE, 0, NORM_WIDTH ) ;

cleartext ( 1 ) ;
gotoxy ( 1, 25 ) ;
printf ( "Use arrow keys to draw rectangle, Enter to confirm" ) ;

/* allow interactive drawing of box */
while ( 2 )
{
    /* store the image of screen where box is to be drawn */
    getimage ( x1, y1, x, y, r ) ;

    /* draw box */
    rectangle ( x1, y1, x, y ) ;

    /* receive key */
    getkey( ) ;

    /* erase box */
    setcolor ( BLACK ) ;
    rectangle ( x1, y1, x, y ) ;
    setcolor ( WHITE ) ;
```

```
        /* assign to x2 the smaller of x1 and x, and to y2 that of y1 and y */
        x2 = x1 < x ? x1 : x ;
        y2 = y1 < y ? y1 : y ;

        /* restore the image on screen where box was drawn */
        putimage ( x2, y2, r, OR_PUT ) ;

        /* test the key that has been pressed */
        echoice = testkeys( ) ;

        /* if Esc key is pressed, abandon erasing operation */
        if ( echoice == ESC )
            break ;

        /* if Enter key is pressed, erase object */
        if ( echoice == ENTER )
        {
            putimage ( x2, y2, r, XOR_PUT ) ;
            break ;
        }
    }

    /* restore the original line settings */
    setlinestyle ( linfo.linestyle, linfo.upattern, linfo.thickness ) ;
}

/* moves an 'object' on screen to a new place */
move( )
{
    int mchoice, x1, x2, y1, y2 ;
    struct linesettingstype linfo ;

    cleartext ( 2 ) ;
    gotoxy ( 1, 1 ) ;
    printf ( "MOVE" ) ;
    gotoxy ( 69, 1 ) ;
```

```
    printf ( "Esc to exit" ) ;
    gotoxy ( 1, 25 ) ;
    printf ( "Select the first corner" ) ;

    /* save current screen contents */
    getimage ( 0, 0, 637, 177, p ) ;

    /* allow movement of cursor and selection of starting corner */
    mchoice = movecursor( ) ;

    if ( mchoice == ESC )
        return ;

    /* save coordinates of starting corner */
    x1 = x ;
    y1 = y ;

    /* get the current line settings */
    getlinesettings ( &linfo ) ;

    /* set the line settings to the default values */
    setlinestyle ( SOLID_LINE, 0, NORM_WIDTH ) ;

    cleartext ( 1 ) ;
    gotoxy ( 1, 25 ) ;
    printf ( "Use arrow keys to draw rectangle, Enter to confirm" ) ;

    /* allow interactive drawing of box */
    while ( 2 )
    {
        /* store the image of screen where box is to be drawn */
        getimage ( x1, y1, x, y, r ) ;

        /* draw box */
        rectangle ( x1, y1, x, y ) ;

        /* receive key */
```

```
getkey( ) ;

/* erase box */
setcolor ( BLACK ) ;
rectangle ( x1, y1, x, y ) ;
setcolor ( WHITE ) ;

/* assign to x2 the smaller of x1 and x, and to y2 that of y1 and y */
x2 = x1 < x ? x1 : x ;
y2 = y1 < y ? y1 : y ;

/* restore the image on screen where box was drawn */
putimage ( x2, y2, r, OR_PUT ) ;

/* test the key that has been pressed */
mchoice = testkeys( ) ;

/* if Esc key is pressed, abandon the move */
if ( mchoice == ESC )
{
    /* restore the original line settings */
    setlinestyle ( linfo.linestyle, linfo.upattern, linfo.thickness ) ;
    return ;
}

/* if Enter key is pressed */
if ( mchoice == ENTER )
{
    /* assign to x1 the greater of x1 and x, and to y1 that of y1 and y */
    x1 = x1 > x ? x1 : x ;
    y1 = y1 > y ? y1 : y ;

    /* save coordinates of starting position of object to be moved */
    x = x2 ;
    y = y2 ;

    cleartext ( 1 ) ;
```

```
gotoxy ( 1, 25 ) ;
printf ( "Use arrow keys to move to final position, Enter to
            confirm" ) ;

/* allow interactive movement of the object */
while ( 3 )
{
    /* receive key */
    getkey( ) ;

    /* erase object */
    putimage ( x, y, r, XOR_PUT ) ;

    /* test the key that has been pressed */
    mchoice = testkeys( ) ;

    /* if the object being moved exceeds limits, readjust its
       position */

    if ( x > 636 - abs ( x1 - x2 ) )
        x = 636 - abs ( x1 - x2 ) ;

    if ( y > 176 - abs ( y1 - y2 ) )
        y = 176 - abs ( y1 - y2 ) ;

    /* if Esc key is pressed, abandon the movement */
    if ( mchoice == ESC )
    {
        /* restore the original line settings */
        setlinestyle ( linfo.linestyle, linfo.upattern,
                        linfo.thickness ) ;

        return ;
    }

    /* if Enter key is pressed, make the object permanent */
    if ( mchoice == ENTER )
```

```
                {
                        /* restore the original line settings */
                        setlinestyle ( linfo.linestyle, linfo.upattern,
                                        linfo.thickness ) ;

                        putimage ( x, y, r, XOR_PUT ) ;
                        return ;
                }

                /* draw object */
                putimage ( x, y, r, XOR_PUT ) ;
            }
        }
    }
}

/* copies an 'object' on screen to a new place */
copy( )
{
    int cchoice, x1, x2, y1, y2, flag = 1 ;
    struct linesettingstype linfo ;

    cleartext ( 2 ) ;
    gotoxy ( 1, 1 ) ;
    printf ( "COPY" ) ;
    gotoxy ( 69, 1 ) ;
    printf ( "Esc to exit" ) ;

    gotoxy ( 1, 25 ) ;
    printf ( "Select the first corner" ) ;

    /* save current screen contents */
    getimage ( 0, 0, 637, 177, p ) ;

    /* allow movement of cursor and selection of starting corner */
    cchoice = movecursor( ) ;
```

```
if ( cchoice == ESC )
    return ;

/* save coordinates of starting corner */
x1 = x ;
y1 = y ;

/* get the current line settings */
getlinesettings ( &linfo ) ;

/* set the line settings to the default values */
setlinestyle ( SOLID_LINE, 0, NORM_WIDTH ) ;

cleartext ( 1 ) ;
gotoxy ( 1, 25 ) ;
printf ( "Use arrow keys to draw rectangle, Enter to confirm" ) ;

/* allow interactive drawing of box */
while ( 1 )
{
    /* store the image of screen where box is to be drawn */
    getimage ( x1, y1, x, y, r ) ;

    /* draw box */
    rectangle ( x1, y1, x, y ) ;

    /* receive key */
    getkey( ) ;

    /* erase box */
    setcolor ( BLACK ) ;
    rectangle ( x1, y1, x, y ) ;
    setcolor ( WHITE ) ;

    /* test the key that has been pressed */
    cchoice = testkeys( ) ;
```

```
/* assign to x2 the smaller of x1 and x, and to y2 that of y1 and y */
x2 = x1 < x ? x1 : x ;
y2 = y1 < y ? y1 : y ;

/* restore the image on screen where box was drawn */
putimage ( x2, y2, r, OR_PUT ) ;

/* if Esc key is pressed, abandon copying operation */
if ( cchoice == ESC )
{
     /* restore the original line settings */
     setlinestyle ( linfo.linestyle, linfo.upattern, linfo.thickness ) ;

     return ;
}

/* if Enter key is pressed */
if ( cchoice == ENTER )
{
     /* assign to x1 the greater of x1 and x, and to y1 that of y1 and y */
     x1 = x1 > x ? x1 : x ;
     y1 = y1 > y ? y1 : y ;

     /* save coordinates of starting position of the object to be copied */
     x = x2 ;
     y = y2 ;

     cleartext ( 1 ) ;
     gotoxy ( 1, 25 ) ;
     printf ( "Use arrow keys to move, Enter to confirm" ) ;

     /* allow interactive copying of the object */
     while ( 3 )
     {
          /* receive key */
          getkey( ) ;
```

```
/* erase the object except when in original position */
if ( flag != 1 )
     putimage ( x, y, r, XOR_PUT ) ;

flag = 0 ;

/* test the key that has been pressed */
cchoice = testkeys( ) ;

/* if the object being moved exceeds limits, readjust its
   position */

if ( x > 636 - abs ( x1 - x2 ) )
     x = 636 - abs ( x1 - x2 ) ;

if ( y > 176 - abs ( y1 - y2 ) )
     y = 176 - abs ( y1 - y2 ) ;

/* if Esc key is pressed, abandon the copying operation */
if ( cchoice == ESC )
{
     /* restore the original line settings */
     setlinestyle ( linfo.linestyle, linfo.upattern,
                    linfo.thickness ) ;

     return ;
}

/* if Enter key is pressed, make the copy permanent */
if ( cchoice == ENTER )
{
     /* restore the original line settings */
     setlinestyle ( linfo.linestyle, linfo.upattern,
                    linfo.thickness ) ;

     putimage ( x, y, r, OR_PUT ) ;
     return ;
```

```
                }

                /* draw the image */
                putimage ( x, y, r, XOR_PUT ) ;
            }
        }
    }
}

/* fills a bounded area */
paint( )
{
    int pchoice, i = 1 ;
    char ch ;

    cleartext ( 2 ) ;
    gotoxy ( 1, 1 ) ;
    printf ( "PAINT" ) ;
    gotoxy ( 69, 1 ) ;
    printf ( "Esc to exit" ) ;

    gotoxy ( 1, 25 ) ;
    printf ( "Place cursor within the boundary to be painted, Enter to confirm" ) ;

    /* save current screen contents */
    getimage ( 0, 0, 637, 177, p ) ;

    /* allow movement of cursor and selection of the area to be painted */
    pchoice = movecursor( ) ;

    /* if Esc key is pressed, abandon the painting operation */
    if ( pchoice == ESC )
        return ;

    /* if Enter key is pressed, fill the selected area */
    if ( pchoice == ENTER )
    {
```

```
        setfillstyle ( SOLID_FILL, WHITE ) ;
        floodfill ( x, y, WHITE ) ;
}

cleartext ( 1 ) ;
gotoxy ( 1, 25 ) ;
printf ( "Want to change the fill pattern (Y/N) ?" ) ;

fflush ( stdin ) ;
ch = getch( ) ;

if ( ch == ESC )
{
        putimage ( 0, 0, p, COPY_PUT ) ;
        return ;
}

/* allow interactive changing of the fill style */
if ( ch == 'y' || ch == 'Y' )
{
        cleartext ( 1 ) ;
        gotoxy ( 1, 25 ) ;
        printf ( "Press any key to examine the fill pattern, Enter to confirm" ) ;

        while ( 1 )
        {
                fflush ( stdin ) ;
                ch = getch( ) ;

                if ( ch == ENTER )
                        break ;

                /* counter for different fill styles, maximum 12 */
                i++ ;
                if ( i > 11 )
                        i = 0 ;
```

```
                /* if Esc key is pressed, abandon the painting operation */
                if ( ch == ESC )
                {
                    putimage ( 0, 0, p, COPY_PUT ) ;
                    return ;
                }

                /* set fill style as indicated by i */
                setfillstyle ( i, WHITE ) ;

                /* restore original image and fill bounded region */
                putimage ( 0, 0, p, COPY_PUT ) ;
                floodfill ( x, y, WHITE ) ;
            }
        }
}

/* saves the current drawing into a file */
save( )
{
    char fname[30] ;
    int out, area, retvalue ;

    cleartext ( 2 ) ;
    gotoxy ( 1, 1 ) ;
    printf ( "SAVE" ) ;
    gotoxy ( 69, 1 ) ;
    printf ( "Esc to exit" ) ;

    gotoxy ( 1, 25 ) ;
    printf ( "Enter the file name:" ) ;

    /* get the name of the file */
    retvalue = getstring ( fname, 22 ) ;
    if ( retvalue == ESC )
        return ;
```

```
/* open the file */
out = open ( fname, O_BINARY | O_CREAT | O_RDWR, S_IWRITE ) ;

/* if unable to open file */
if ( out == -1 )
{
    cleartext ( 1 ) ;
    gotoxy ( 1, 25 ) ;
    printf ( "Unable to open the file! Press any key..." ) ;
    fflush ( stdin ) ;
    getch( ) ;

    return ;
}

/* store the screen contents into allocated memory */
getimage ( 0, 0, 637, 177, p ) ;

/* find area occupied by screen image in memory */
area = imagesize ( 0, 0, 637, 177 ) ;

/* copy the stored contents into the file */
write ( out, p, area ) ;

/* close the file */
close ( out ) ;
}

/* loads a drawing from file into memory */
load( )
{
    char fname[30] ;
    int area, in, retvalue ;

    cleartext ( 2 ) ;
    gotoxy ( 1, 1 ) ;
    printf ( "LOAD" ) ;
```

```
gotoxy ( 69, 1 ) ;
printf ( "Esc to exit" ) ;

gotoxy ( 1, 25 ) ;
printf ( "Enter the file name:" ) ;

/* get the name of the file */
retvalue = getstring ( fname, 22 ) ;
if ( retvalue == ESC )
    return ;

/* open the file */
in = open ( fname, O_BINARY | O_RDONLY ) ;

/* if unable to open file */
if ( in == -1 )
{
    cleartext ( 1 ) ;
    gotoxy ( 1, 25 ) ;
    printf ( "Unable to open the file! Press any key..." ) ;
    fflush ( stdin ) ;
    getch() ;

    return ;
}

/* find area required to accomodate file contents in memory */
area = imagesize ( 0, 0, 637, 177 ) ;

/* read the file contents into allocated memory */
read ( in, p, area ) ;

/* close the file */
close ( in ) ;

/* display the contents of allocated memory on the screen */
putimage ( 0, 0, p, COPY_PUT ) ;
```

```
}

/* prints the current drawing on the printer */
print( )
{
    char ch ;
    union REGS i, o ;

    cleartext ( 2 ) ;
    gotoxy ( 1, 1 ) ;
    printf ( "PRINT" ) ;
    gotoxy ( 69, 1 ) ;
    printf ( "Esc to exit" ) ;

    gotoxy ( 1, 25 ) ;
    printf ( "Set up the printer and press any key" ) ;

    fflush ( stdin ) ;
    ch = getch( ) ;

    /* if Esc key is pressed return to File menu */
    if ( ch == ESC )
        return ;

    /* issue interrupt for printing the graphic screen */
    int86 ( 5, &i, &o ) ;
}


/* displays Line style menu, receives choice & sets up appropriate line style */
linetype( )
{
    int typechoice ;
    struct linesettingstype linfo ;

    /* get the current line settings */
    getlinesettings ( &linfo ) ;
```

```
        cleartext ( 2 ) ;

        /* display Line style menu in topmost row */
        displaylinemenu( ) ;

        gotoxy ( 1, 25 ) ;
        printf ( "Press Esc to return to previous menu" ) ;

        /* receive user's response */
        typechoice = getresponse ( "", 4 ) ;

        /* if Esc key is pressed return to Draw menu */
        if ( typechoice == ESC )
        {
            /* restore the original line settings */
            setlinestyle ( linfo.linestyle, linfo.upattern, linfo.thickness ) ;

            return ;
        }

        /* set line style as indicated by variable typechoice */
        setlinestyle ( typechoice - 1, 0, NORM_WIDTH ) ;
}

/* displays Line style menu */
displaylinemenu( )
{
        int incr, j, col = 11 ;

        setviewport ( 0, 0, 639, 199, 1 ) ;
        incr = 540 / 4 ;

        /* display available line styles */
        for ( j = 0 ; j < 4 ; j++ )
        {
            setlinestyle ( j, 0, NORM_WIDTH ) ;
            moveto ( col, 4 ) ;
```

```
        lineto ( col + incr, 4 ) ;
        col = col + incr + 17 ;
}

/* set viewport back to normal */
setviewport ( 1, 11, 638, 188, 1 ) ;
}
```

User defined functions

cleartext( )	Clears top and/or bottom row on the screen.
copy( )	Copies an 'object' on the screen to a new place.
displaylinemenu( )	Displays the various line styles available.
displaymenu( )	Displays the given menu in topmost row.
draw( )	Displays Draw menu, receives choice and branches control to appropriate function.
drawarc( )	Draws an arc interactively.
drawbox( )	Draws a rectangle interactively.
drawcircle( )	Draws a circle interactively.
drawcursor( )	Draws or erases cursor as per the argument passed to it.
drawellipse( )	Draws an ellipse interactively.
drawline( )	Draws a line interactively.
edit( )	Displays Edit menu, receives choice and branches control to appropriate function.
erase( )	Erases an 'object' on the screen.
file( )	Displays File menu, receives choice and branches control to appropriate function.
freehand( )	Draws freehand drawing interactively.
getkey( )	Gets ascii and scan codes of the key pressed.
getresponse( )	Receives user's choice.
getstring( )	Gets a string of limited length from keyboard.
load( )	Loads a drawing from file into memory and displays it on screen.
linetype( )	Displays Linestyle menu, receives choice and sets up appropriate line style.
mainscreen( )	Creates the opening screen display.
move( )	Moves an 'object' on screen to a new place.
movecursor( )	Moves the graphics cursor in current viewport.
paint( )	Fills a user selected bounded region.
print( )	Prints the current drawing on printer.
save( )	Stores the current drawing in a file.
testkeys( )	Tests which key has been hit.

text( )	Displays text at specified location in the chosen font, style, justification and orientation.
wipe( )	Wipes out the entire drawing.

5

Graphical

User Interface

A user interacts with the Operating System (OS) through a shell. This interface to the OS can be either textual or graphical. In textual approach the user is required to type commands, which are then interpreted by the shell and an appropriate action is taken. In a graphical OS interface much of the functionality of the OS is displayed on the screen. This is accomplished by using small symbols called 'icons', which represent certain OS functions. In other words, 'icons' are symbolic representations of the function they are tied up to. Whether a graphical OS interface is better or a textual OS interface is often debatable. And more often than not it is a matter of taste and choice. As a seasoned programmer, it might not appear very sensible to have attractive icons on the screen - some depicting the activity of renaming files, some deleting files, and so on. But look at it from the user's point of view. A normal user is more interested in the convenience of the finesse of the program he is using, than the hard work that has gone into the development of the program. He prefers visual pictures to textual commands - pictures which he can easily relate to and understand, rather than memorising commands. This is where the Graphical User Interfaces (GUIs) score. Thus, the underlying principle of any GUI is very simple - not only do pictures communicate, but sometimes they say it better than words. GUIs were first introduced by Apple on its Microcomputers, and lately by Microsoft Corp. on IBM compatibles under the name Windows.

Creating Icons

Naturally, before using the icons, they need to be created. The easiest way to create icons is to use an Icon Editor. The Icon Editor that we have developed here shows an expanded view of the icon on the screen which makes the editing process easier. The normal sized icon is also shown simultaneously. Our Icon Editor uses arrow keys to draw, but some other editors may also allow the use of a mouse.

The icons are drawn with a black background color and a light grey foreground color. The program needs to be suitably altered if you want a different color combination. A multicolored icon is also possible, but the combination that one can have depends on the graphics adapter and the monitor that is installed on your computer. We have based our editor on a CGA adapter with a soft white monitor.

The dimension chosen for each icon is 32 pixels down and 40 pixels across. This makes the icon slightly taller than it is long. The extra height (arguably) adds to the aesthetics of the icon. However, you can change the dimension if you like. Each icon has associated with it a 2-D array **icon_image[ ][ ]** which holds the status of various bits which go to construct the icon.

How the Icon Editor works

Icon Editor presents two displays on the screen. The smaller display is referred to as icon and the larger as the grid. Grid is nothing but the expanded version of the actual image of the icon shown to its left. The expansion factor is controlled by the value of a macro EXP_FACTOR. A cursor is shown in the grid which tells you where exactly you are within the icon display. Unless an existing icon has been loaded from the disk or drawn from the keyboard, neither the grid nor the icon display will show any picture.

The opening menu allows the user to either begin drawing an icon, load an existing icon from disk, or save the current icon to the disk. The drawing of a new icon is managed by the function **edit_icon( )**. Through this function, one can either draw the icon using arrow keys, move around without drawing anything, or erase an existing icon. As one proceeds with the drawing, the icon is constructed in the grid as well as in the icon display. The reason for showing it at both places is that the expanded view offered by the grid makes it much easier to actually draw the icon, whereas the normal icon image allows one to see exactly how the icon would look like when used in the GUI.

The edit_icon( ) function

This function is the heart of the Icon Editor. As mentioned earlier, it uses the array **icon_image[ ][ ]** to store the status of various pixels which form the icon. The status of a pixel could be either 'drawn' or 'erased'. The 'drawn' status is represented by the macro FORE_GND and the 'erased' status by BACK_GND_ICON. **edit_icon( )** uses an indefinite **while** loop in which a number of steps are performed. To begin with, the graphics cursor is displayed in the grid using the function **drawcursor( )**. On hitting a key, the function **getkey( )** collects the scan code of the key pressed. Before testing which key is pressed, the cursor is erased, and the pixels occupied by the cursor are restored to their original color. Next, in a **switch**, the scan code of the key hit is checked. If arrow keys are hit, then depending on whether currently we are in draw mode or erase mode, the array **icon_image[ ][ ]** is updated accordingly and the corresponding pixel in the icon display and the grid is lit or erased. This goes on until the user selects the End option, upon which the control breaks out of the **while** loop.

While drawing if the user feels that he has messed up the whole icon and wishes to start all over again, he can select the Wipe option. This calls the function **init_icon( )** to reset the status of all the pixels of the icon in **icon_image[ ][ ]** to 'erased'. Next, the functions **dis-**

play_icon( ) and **display_grid( )** are called to reflect the contents of **icon_image[ ][ ]** on the screen.

GUI

GUIs and mouse go hand in hand. Though some GUIs do exist which manage the show without a mouse, the mouse has more or less become a standard input device with any GUI worth its name. A mouse is used to point at the icons which form the menu in a GUI - much like the way a child points to something he wants. These point-and-shoot menus of GUI bring along ease and convenience alongwith all the added agility of the real life look alike of the mouse. As a result, more and more packages today are not only menu driven, but also mouse driven.

The use of a mouse requires a program to sense its presence. Just attaching the mouse to the computer is not enough. What we also need to do is load a device driver program that understands the mouse. A device driver is a program which senses the signals coming from the port to which the mouse is attached. On sensing the signals, the driver translates these into the related action on the screen. This device driver is usually available in a program called MOUSE.COM or WITTYMS.COM, which work with different variety of mice. Our GUI uses a mouse driver called WITTYMS.COM and a True mouse which is installed at the port COM2.

The mouse has a separate cursor (often called a mouse 'pointer') which looks like an arrow and functions in the same way as the normal cursor. As we move the mouse, the mouse pointer moves correspondingly. It is just like using arrow keys. The only difference being the speed at which the mouse cursor moves is much faster than that of an ordinary cursor. If desired, we can even change the speed of the mouse pointer, and even its shape.

Once the mouse driver is loaded, the various mouse functions can be accessed by issuing interrupt number 0x33. By setting up the AX register with different values (service numbers), various mouse related functions are called, some of which are listed in Figure 5 .1.

Service No.	Service
0x0000	Reset mouse and get status
0x0001	Show mouse pointer
0x0002	Hide mouse pointer
0x0003	Get mouse position and button status
0x0013	Set double speed threshold

Figure 5.1

In our program the interrupts for different services have been issued from functions like **reset_mouse( )**, **get_position( )**, etc. and the values returned, if any, are analysed for the information they signify.

Displaying Menu and Selecting Options

To keep things simple, we have used only one menu which consists of file services like deleting file, renaming file, encrypting file, and so on. As with other GUIs, these menu items are represented by appropriate icons stored in files like 'gdel.icn', 'gren.icn', 'genc.icn', etc. Each menu item is selected by pointing to it using the mouse. Let us now see how this is brought about.

First of all the mouse driver is loaded using the function **system( )**. Next the graphics system is to be initialised. As usual, we use **initgraph( )** to change over to medium resolution graphics mode.

Following this, the various icons which form our menu are loaded from the disk and displayed at appropriate positions on the screen using the function **display_icons**( ). Now the user is free to select any of the icons by pointing the mouse pointer to it. The selection of a menu item is managed by the function **getresponse**( ). But for pointing at an icon shouldn't the mouse pointer be present on the screen? That's the point. We must first display the mouse pointer, which is done by the function **show_ptr**( ).

Whether the mouse pointer is pointing to any of the icons is determined via the functions **get_position**() and **check_icon**( ). **get_position**() returns the current position of the mouse pointer and the status of its buttons. Once the mouse position is known, **check_icon**( ) checks whether the mouse pointer is within the area of any icon. This is done by comparing the coordinates of the mouse pointer with the maximum and the minimum x and y coordinates of the displayed icons. If the pointer lies within an icon, a box is displayed around the icon accompanied by a corresponding help message at the bottom.

As said earlier, **get_position**( ) also scans whether the user has pressed a mouse button on any menu option. For our program, we have used the left button of the mouse to get the user's response. How do we know which mouse button has been pressed? This is a simple affair. The value of the button pressed is always placed in the BX register. Only the lower 3 bits of this two-byte register are important. Bit 0, if it is on, indicates that the left button has been pressed, bit 1, the right button, and bit 2, the center button. Since we are interested in the left button, we isolate the last bit by ANDing the contents of BX with 1. If bit 0 is on, it means that the icon representing the menu item has been selected.

Once the position of the pointer is discerned and the button-press scanned, the rest is simple. Just as in any menu driven software, the program execution is steered appropriately to carry on with the desired activity. For example, if the mouse pointer is pointing at the 'delete file' icon and the left mouse button is pressed, the function **deletefile**( ) is called.

Program

The program has been split into two files, namely ICON.C and GUI.C. ICON.C contains the Icon Editor whereas GUI.C contains the logic to display and interact with the user through icons which have been drawn using the Icon Editor. The listing of these two files is given below.

ICON.C

```c
# include "stdio.h"
# include "dos.h"
# include "bios.h"
# include "graphics.h"
# include "process.h"


# define MAXX 40  /* maximum x-coordinate of icon */
# define MAXY 32  /* maximum y-coordinate of icon */
# define DRAW 0
# define SKIP 1
# define ERASE 2
# define EXP_FACTOR 4  /* expansion factor for grid */
# define BACK_GND_GRID 1  /* background color for grid */
# define BACK_GND_ICON 0  /* background color for icon */
# define FORE_GND 3  /* foreground color for grid and icon */

/* array to store image of the icon */
unsigned char icon_image [MAXX][MAXY] ;

int scan ;

main ( argc, argv )
int argc ;
char *argv[ ] ;
```

```
{
    int gm = 3, gd = 1 ;
    char fname[30] ;

    /* initialise graphics system in medium resolution graphics mode */
    initgraph ( &gd, &gm, "c:\\tc\\bgi" ) ;

    /* if icon to be loaded is mentioned at DOS prompt */
    if ( argc == 2 )
        load_icon ( argv[1] ) ;
    else
    {
        /* initialise icon image array */
        init_icon( ) ;
    }

    /* display the icon in the icon box */
    display_icon( ) ;

    /* display the icon in the grid */
    display_grid( ) ;

    while ( 1 )
    {
        /* display main menu */
        gotoxy ( 2, 25 ) ;
        printf ( "F1-Draw  F2-Load  F3-Save  F4-Quit" ) ;

        /* get user's choice */
        getkey( ) ;

        switch ( scan )
        {
            case 59 :  /* F1 key */
                edit_icon( ) ;
                break ;
```

```
                case 60 :  /* F2 key */

                        /* collect the file name */
                        gotoxy ( 6, 21 ) ;
                        printf ( "Enter file name: " ) ;
                        gets ( fname ) ;

                        /* erase the message line */
                        cleartext ( 21 ) ;

                        load_icon ( fname ) ;
                        display_icon( ) ;
                        display_grid( ) ;
                        break ;

                case 61 :  /* F3 key */
                        save_icon( ) ;
                        break ;

                case 62 :  /* F4 key */

                        /* restore original video mode */
                        closegraph( ) ;
                        restorecrtmode( ) ;

                        exit ( 0 ) ;
                }
        }
}

/* reads icon from file into memory */
load_icon ( name )
char *name ;
{
        FILE *fp ;

        /* open file and check if successful */
```

```
        if ( ( fp = fopen ( name, "rb" ) ) == NULL )
        {
            gotoxy ( 1, 21 ) ;
            printf ( "Unable to open file! Press any key..." ) ;
            getch( ) ;

            cleartext ( 21 ) ;
            return ;
        }

        fread ( icon_image, sizeof ( icon_image ), 1, fp ) ;
        fclose ( fp ) ;
}

/* erases the message line */
cleartext ( row )
int row ;
{
    int col ;

    for ( col = 1 ; col <= 39 ; col++ )
    {
        gotoxy ( col, row ) ;
        printf ( " " ) ;
    }
}

/* initialises the icon image array */
init_icon( )
{
    int x, y ;

    for ( x = 0 ; x < MAXX ; x++ )
    {
        for ( y = 0 ; y < MAXY ; y++ )
            icon_image[x][y] = BACK_GND_ICON ;
    }
```

```c
}

/* displays the current icon */
display_icon( )
{
    int x, y ;

    setcolor ( 3 ) ;
    rectangle ( 0, 0, 41, 33 ) ;

    for ( x = 0 ; x < MAXX ; x++ )
    {
        for ( y = 0 ; y < MAXY ; y++ )
            putpixel ( x + 1, y + 1, icon_image[x][y] ) ;
    }
}

/* constructs the grid as per the expansion factor */
display_grid( )
{
    int x, y, xgrid, ygrid ;

    for ( x = 0 ; x < MAXX ; x++ )
    {
        for ( y = 0 ; y < MAXY ; y++ )
        {
            xgrid = 100 + x * EXP_FACTOR ;
            ygrid = y * EXP_FACTOR ;

            if ( icon_image[x][y] == 0 )
                putpixel ( xgrid, ygrid, 1 ) ;
            else
                putpixel ( xgrid, ygrid, icon_image[x][y] ) ;
        }
    }
}
```

```
/* collects the scan code of the key hit */
getkey( )
{
    union REGS i, o ;

    /* wait until a key is hit */
    while ( !kbhit( ) )


    i.h.ah = 0 ;  /* service number */
    int86 ( 22, &i, &o ) ;  /* issue interrupt */

    scan = o.h.ah ;  /* collect scan code of key hit */
}

/* allows drawing/editing of the icon */
edit_icon( )
{
    int x = 0, y = 0, xgrid = 100, ygrid = 0, flag = SKIP ;

    /* display menu */
    gotoxy ( 1, 25 ) ;
    printf ( "F1-Draw F2-Skip F3-Erase F4-Wipe F5-End" ) ;

    while ( 1 )
    {
        /* draw cursor */
        drawcursor ( xgrid, ygrid, FORE_GND ) ;

        getkey( ) ;  /* receive key */

        /* erase cursor */
        drawcursor ( xgrid, ygrid, BACK_GND_ICON ) ;

        /* display the current pixel in the grid in its previous color */
        if ( icon_image[x][y] == 0 )
            putpixel ( xgrid, ygrid, BACK_GND_GRID ) ;
```

```
else
     putpixel ( xgrid, ygrid, icon_image[x][y] ) ;

switch ( scan )
{
     case 59 :  /* F1 key */

          flag = DRAW ;
          break ;

     case 60 :  /* F2 key */

          flag = SKIP ;
          break ;

     case 61 :  /* F3 key */

          flag = ERASE ;
          break ;

     case 62 :  /* F4 key */

          init_icon( ) ;
          display_icon ( ) ;
          display_grid( )  ;
          break ;

     case 63 :  /* F5 key */

          cleartext ( 25 ) ;
          return ;

     case 75 :  /* left arrow key */

          x-- ;
          break ;
```

```
case 77 :  /* right arrow key */

    x++ ;
    break ;

case 72 :  /* up arrow key */

    y-- ;
    break ;

case 80 :  /* down arrow key */

    y++ ;
    break ;

case 71 :  /* Home key */

    x-- ;
    y-- ;
    break ;

case 73 :  /* End key */

    x++ ;
    y-- ;
    break ;

case 79 :  /* PgUp key */

    x-- ;
    y++ ;
    break ;

case 81 :  /* PgDn key */

    x++ ;
    y++ ;
```

```
            break ;

        default :  /* any other key */

            printf ( "\a" ) ;
}

/* readjust x and y if they exceed the limits */

if ( x < 0 )
    x++ ;

if ( y < 0 )
    y++;

if ( x == MAXX )
    x-- ;

if ( y == MAXY )
    y-- ;

if ( flag == DRAW )
    icon_image[x][y] = FORE_GND ;

if ( flag == ERASE )
    icon_image[x][y] = BACK_GND_ICON ;

/* display the corresponding pixel in the icon box */
putpixel ( x + 1, y + 1, icon_image[x][y] ) ;

/* calculate coordinates of corresponding pixel in grid */
xgrid = 100 + x * EXP_FACTOR ;
ygrid = y * EXP_FACTOR ;

/* display the corresponding pixel in grid */
if ( icon_image[x][y] == 0 )
    putpixel ( xgrid, ygrid, BACK_GND_GRID ) ;
```

```
        else
                putpixel ( xgrid, ygrid, icon_image[x][y] ) ;
    }
}

/* saves current icon into file */
save_icon( )
{
    FILE *fp ;
    char fname[30] ;

    /* collect the file name */
    gotoxy ( 6, 21 ) ;
    printf ( "Enter the file name: " ) ;
    gets ( fname ) ;

    /* erase the message line */
    cleartext ( 21 ) ;

    /* open file, exit if unsuccessful */
    if ( ( fp = fopen ( fname, "wb" ) ) == NULL )
    {
        gotoxy ( 1, 21 ) ;
        printf ( "Unable to open file! Press any key..." ) ;
        getch( ) ;

        cleartext ( 21 ) ;
        return ;
    }

    fwrite ( icon_image, sizeof ( icon_image ), 1, fp ) ;
    fclose ( fp ) ;
}

/* draws or erases the graphics cursor */
drawcursor ( xgrid, ygrid, color )
int xgrid, ygrid, color ;
```

```
{
    int xx, yy ;

    for ( xx = xgrid - 2 ; xx <= xgrid + 2 ; xx++ )
        putpixel ( xx, ygrid, color ) ;

    for ( yy = ygrid - 2 ; yy <= ygrid + 2 ; yy++ )
        putpixel ( xgrid, yy, color ) ;
}
```

GUI.C

```c
# include "dos.h"
# include "stdio.h"
# include "graphics.h"
# include "alloc.h"

# define NO 0

int mx, my, mouse_button, maxx, maxy ;

/* array for storing icon image */
unsigned char icon_image[40][32] ;

/* flags to determine whether icon has been boxed */
int icon_flag[6] ;

/* array for storing help messages */
char *messages[ ] = {
                              "Delete a file",
                              "Rename a file",
                              "Compare two files",
                              "Encrypt a file",
                              "Decrypt a file",
                              "Exit to dos"
                      } ;

main( )
{
    int gm = 3, gd = 1, selected_icon = 0, area ;
    void *image ;

    /* load the mouse driver */
    load_mousedriver( ) ;

    /* reset the mouse */
```

```
reset_mouse( ) ;

/* initialise graphics system in CGA medium resolution graphics mode */
initgraph ( &gd, &gm, "c:\\tc\\bgi" ) ;

/* get maximum x, y coordinates of the screen */
maxx = getmaxx( ) ;
maxy = getmaxy( ) ;

/* prepare the opening screen */
rectangle ( 0, 0, maxx, maxy ) ;
rectangle ( 0, 25, maxx, maxy - 25 ) ;
settextjustify ( CENTER_TEXT, TOP_TEXT ) ;
outtextxy ( 160, 9, "Graphical User Interface" ) ;

/* load icons from disk and display them on screen */
display_icons( ) ;

/* allocate memory and check if successful */
area = imagesize ( 1, 26, 318, 173 ) ;
image = malloc ( area ) ;
if ( image == NULL )
{
    outtextxy ( 160, 184, "Insufficient memory! Press any key..." ) ;
    getch( ) ;

    exit ( 1 ) ;
}

/* save the screen contents where icons are drawn */
getimage ( 1, 26, 318, 173, image ) ;

while ( 1 )
{
    /* select icon */
    selected_icon = getresponse( ) ;
```

```
/* clear the screen where icons are drawn */
setviewport ( 1, 26, 318, 173, 1 ) ;
clearviewport( ) ;

/* reset viewport back to normal */
setviewport ( 0, 0, maxx, maxy, 1 ) ;

/* set text justification for displaying messages */
settextjustify ( LEFT_TEXT, TOP_TEXT ) ;

/* branch to appropriate function */
switch ( selected_icon )
{
    case 1 :
        deletefile( ) ;
        break ;

    case 2 :
        renamefile( ) ;
        break ;

    case 3 :
        comparefile( ) ;
        break ;

    case 4 :
        encryptfile( ) ;
        break ;

    case 5 :
        decryptfile( ) ;
        break ;

    case 6 :
        closegraph( ) ;
        restorecrtmode( ) ;
        exit ( 0 ) ;
```

```
        }

        /* restore the icons from memory */
        putimage ( 1, 26, image, COPY_PUT ) ;

        /* set text justification back to original */
        settextjustify ( CENTER_TEXT, TOP_TEXT ) ;
    }
}

/* loads mouse driver in memory, if not already loaded */
load_mousedriver( )
{
    unsigned char far *ms ;

    /* convert the segment:offset address from IVT into a far pointer */
    ms = MK_FP ( peek ( 0, 0x33 * 4 + 2 ), peek ( 0, 0x33 * 4 ) ) ;

    /* check if mouse driver isn't already loaded */
    if ( ms == NULL || *ms == 0xcf )
        system ( "wittyms -p2" ) ;
}

/* initialises the mouse driver */
reset_mouse( )
{
    union REGS i, o ;

    /* issue interrupt */
    i.x.ax = 0 ;
    int86 ( 0x33, &i, &o ) ;

    /* if unable to reset mouse */
    if ( o.x.ax == 0 )
    {
        gotoxy ( 20, 15 ) ;
        printf ( "Mouse not available! Press any key..." ) ;
```

```
            fflush ( stdin ) ;
            getch( ) ;

            exit ( 2 ) ;
        }
}

/* loads icons from disk and displays them on screen */
display_icons( )
{
    load_icon ( "gdel.icn", 51, 45 ) ;
    load_icon ( "gren.icn", 141, 45 ) ;
    load_icon ( "gcmp.icn", 231, 45 ) ;
    load_icon ( "genc.icn", 51, 125 ) ;
    load_icon ( "gdec.icn", 141, 125 ) ;
    load_icon ( "gdos.icn", 231, 125 ) ;
}


/* loads an icon from file and displays it on screen */
load_icon ( file, x, y )
int x, y  ;
char *file ;
{
    int xx, yy ;
    FILE *fp ;

    /* open the specified icon file */
    fp = fopen ( file, "rb" ) ;

    /* if unable to open file */
    if ( fp == NULL )
    {
        outtextxy ( 160, 184, "Unable to open file! Press any key..." ) ;
        getch( ) ;

        /* shut down the graphics system */
        closegraph( ) ;
```

```
        restorecrtmode( ) ;

        exit ( 3 ) ;
    }

    /* read the bit image of icon */
    fread ( icon_image, sizeof ( icon_image ), 1, fp ) ;

    /* output the icon on the screen */
    for ( xx = x ; xx < x + 40 ; xx++ )
    {
        for ( yy = y ; yy < y + 32 ; yy++ )
            putpixel ( xx, yy, icon_image[xx - x][yy - y] ) ;
    }

    fclose ( fp ) ;
}

/* displays the mouse pointer */
show_ptr( )
{
    union REGS i, o ;

    i.x.ax = 1 ;  /* service number */
    int86 ( 0x33, &i, &o ) ;  /* issue interrupt */
}

/* hides the mouse pointer */
hide_ptr( )
{
    union REGS i, o ;

    i.x.ax = 2 ;  /* service number */
    int86 ( 0x33, &i, &o ) ;  /* issue interrupt */
}

/* checks which icon is selected */
```

```
getresponse( )
{
    int icon_no, selected = NO ;

    /* display the mouse pointer */
    show_ptr( ) ;

    icon_no = 1 ;

    while ( !selected )
    {
        /* get current mouse position and status of mouse buttons */
        get_position( ) ;

        /* check whether any of the 6 icons have been selected */
        for ( icon_no = 1 ; icon_no <= 6 ; icon_no++ )
        {
            selected = check_icon ( icon_no ) ;
            if ( selected )
                break ;
        }
    }

    /* hide the mouse pointer */
    hide_ptr( ) ;

    /* return the selected icon number */
    return ( icon_no ) ;
}

/* gets current coordinates of mouse pointer and status of mouse buttons */
get_position( )
{
    union REGS i, o ;

    i.x.ax = 3 ;  /* service number */
    int86 ( 0x33, &i, &o ) ;  /* issue interrupt */
```

```
        mx = o.x.cx ;  /* x coordinate */
        my = o.x.dx ;  /* y coordinate */
        mouse_button = o.x.bx & 1 ;  /* store status of mouse buttons */
}

/* checks whether an icon has been selected */
check_icon ( icon_no )
int icon_no ;
{
        int sx, sy, ex, ey ;

        /* calculate coordinates of the icon */
        if ( icon_no <= 3 )
        {
            sx = ( 51 + ( icon_no - 1 ) * 90 ) * 2 ;
            sy = 45 ;
        }
        else
        {
            sx = ( 51 + ( icon_no - 4 ) * 90 ) * 2 ;
            sy = 125 ;
        }
        ex = sx + ( 40 * 2 ) ;
        ey = sy + 32 ;

        /* if mouse pointer lies within the boundaries of the icon */
        if ( mx >= sx && mx <= ex && my >= sy && my <= ey )
        {
            /* if box has not been drawn around the icon */
            if ( icon_flag[icon_no - 1] == 0 )
            {
                /* draw a box around the icon */
                icon_box ( sx, ex, sy, ey, 3 ) ;

                /* set flag to indicate that the icon has been boxed */
                icon_flag[icon_no - 1] = 1 ;
```

```
                        /* display help message */
                        outtextxy ( 160, 184, messages[icon_no - 1] ) ;
                }


        /* if the left button of the mouse is pressed */
        if ( mouse_button == 1 )
        {
                /* erase the box around the icon */
                icon_box ( sx, ex, sy, ey, 0 ) ;

                /* set flag to indicate that the icon is no longer boxed */
                icon_flag[icon_no - 1] = 0 ;

                /* erase help message */
                cleartext( ) ;

                return ( 1 ) ;
        }
}
else
{
        /* if box has been drawn around the icon */
        if ( icon_flag[icon_no - 1] == 1 )
        {
                /* erase the box around the icon */
                icon_box ( sx, ex, sy, ey, 0 ) ;

                /* reset flag */
                icon_flag[icon_no - 1] = 0 ;

                /* erase the help message */
                cleartext( ) ;
        }
}

return ( 0 ) ;
```

```
}

/* draws/erases the icon box */
icon_box ( sx, ex, sy, ey, color )
int sx, ex, sy, ey, color ;
{
    hide_ptr( ) ;
    setcolor ( color ) ;
    rectangle ( sx / 2 - 5, sy - 5, ex / 2 + 5, ey + 5 ) ;
    show_ptr( ) ;
}

/* erases the row used for displaying messages */
cleartext( )
{
    int col ;

    for ( col = 2 ; col <= 39 ; col++ )
    {
        gotoxy ( col, 24 ) ;
        printf ( " " ) ;
    }
}

/* deletes a file */
deletefile( )
{
    union REGS i, o ;
    char filename[30] ;

    /* collect file name */
    setcolor ( 3 ) ;
    outtextxy ( 4 * 8, 6 * 8, "Enter file name:") ;
    gotoxy ( 5, 9  ) ;
    fflush ( stdin ) ;
    gets ( filename ) ;
```

```
        i.h.ah = 65 ;  /* service number */
        i.x.dx = ( unsigned int ) filename ;  /* store base address */

        /* issue interrupt for deleting file */
        intdos ( &i, &o ) ;

        /* check if successful in deleting file */
        if ( o.x.cflag == 0 )
            outtextxy ( 4 * 8, 11 * 8, "File was successfully deleted!" ) ;
        else
            outtextxy ( 4 * 8, 11 * 8, "Unable to delete file!" ) ;

        outtextxy ( 32, 184, "Press any key..." ) ;
        fflush ( stdin ) ;
        getch( ) ;
        cleartext( ) ;
}

/* renames a file */
renamefile( )
{
        union REGS i, o ;
        char old[30], new[30] ;

        /* collect old file name */
        setcolor ( 3 ) ;
        outtextxy ( 4 * 8, 6 * 8, "Enter old file name:") ;
        gotoxy ( 5, 9 ) ;
        fflush ( stdin ) ;
        gets ( old ) ;

        /* collect new file name */
        outtextxy ( 4 * 8, 11 * 8, "Enter new file name:") ;
        gotoxy ( 5, 14 ) ;
        fflush ( stdin ) ;
        gets ( new ) ;
```

```
        i.h.ah = 86 ;  /* service number */
        i.x.dx = ( int ) old ;
        i.x.di = ( int ) new ;

        /* issue interrupt for renaming file */
        intdos ( &i, &o ) ;

        /* check if successful in renaming file */
        if ( o.x.cflag == 0 )
            outtextxy ( 4 * 8, 16 * 8, "File was successfully renamed!" ) ;
        else
            outtextxy ( 4 * 8, 16 * 8, "Unable to rename file!" ) ;

        outtextxy ( 32, 184, "Press any key..." ) ;
        fflush ( stdin ) ;
        getch( ) ;
        cleartext( ) ;
}

/* compares two files */
comparefile( )
{
        FILE *fs, *ft ;
        char c, d, file1[30], file2[30] ;

        /* collect first file name */
        setcolor ( 3 ) ;
        outtextxy ( 4 * 8, 6 * 8, "Enter first file name:") ;
        gotoxy ( 5, 9 ) ;
        fflush ( stdin ) ;
        gets ( file1 ) ;

        /* open first file and check if successful */
        fs = fopen ( file1, "r" ) ;
        if ( fs == NULL)
        {
            outtextxy ( 4 * 8, 11 * 8, "Cannot open file!" ) ;
```

```
        outtextxy ( 32, 184, "Press any key..." ) ;
        fflush ( stdin ) ;
        getch( ) ;

        return ;
    }

/* collect second file name */
outtextxy ( 4 * 8, 11 * 8, "Enter second file name:") ;
gotoxy ( 5, 14 ) ;
fflush ( stdin ) ;
gets ( file2 ) ;

/* open second file and check if successful */
ft = fopen ( file2, "r" ) ;
if ( ft == NULL )
{
        outtextxy ( 4 * 8, 16 * 8, "Cannot open file!" ) ;
        outtextxy ( 32, 184, "Press any key..." ) ;
        fflush ( stdin ) ;
        getch( ) ;

        fclose ( fs ) ;
        return ;
    }

/* compare files, character by character till a mismatch occurs */
c = getc ( fs ) ;
d = getc ( ft ) ;
while ( c == d )
{
        c = getc ( fs ) ;
        d = getc ( ft ) ;

        /* if end of any file is reached */
        if ( c == EOF || d == EOF )
            break ;
```

```
        }

        fclose ( fs ) ;
        fclose ( ft ) ;

        if ( c == d )
            outtextxy ( 4 * 8, 16 * 8, "Files match!" ) ;
        else
            outtextxy ( 4 * 8, 16 * 8, "Files do not match!" ) ;

        outtextxy ( 32, 184, "Press any key..." ) ;
        fflush ( stdin ) ;
        getch() ;
        cleartext() ;
}

/* encrypts a file using substitution cipher */
encryptfile( )
{
        char arr1[97] = "IOP{a}sdfghjkl;'ASDFGHJKL:zxcvbnm,./ZX\
                CV BNM<>?1234567890-=~!@#$%^&(*)_\
                +|qwertyuiop[Q]WERTYU\\\"\n\t" ;
        char arr2[97] = "'12345 67890-=~!@#$%^&(*)_+|qwertyuiop\
                [Q]WERTYUIOP{a}sdfghjkl;'ASDFGHJKL\
                :ZXCVBNM,./zxcvbnm<>?\\\"\n\t" ;
        char source[30], target[30], ch ;
        int i ;
        FILE *fs, *ft ;

        /* collect source file name */
        setcolor ( 3 ) ;
        outtextxy ( 4 * 8, 6 * 8, "Enter source file name:") ;
        gotoxy ( 5, 9 ) ;
        fflush ( stdin ) ;
        gets ( source ) ;

        /* open source file and check if successful */
```

```
fs = fopen ( source, "r" ) ;
if ( fs == NULL )
{
    outtextxy ( 4 * 8, 11 * 8, "Cannot open source file!" ) ;
    outtextxy ( 32, 184, "Press any key..." ) ;
    fflush ( stdin ) ;
    getch( ) ;

    return ;
}

/* collect target file name */
outtextxy ( 4 * 8, 11 * 8, "Enter target file name:" ) ;
gotoxy ( 5, 14 ) ;
fflush ( stdin ) ;
gets ( target ) ;

/* open target file and check if successful */
ft = fopen ( target, "w" ) ;
if ( ft == NULL )
{
    outtextxy ( 4 * 8, 16 * 8, "Cannot open target file!" ) ;
    outtextxy ( 32, 184, "Press any key..." ) ;
    fflush ( stdin ) ;
    getch( ) ;

    fclose ( fs ) ;
    return ;
}

/* read characters from source file till end of file is reached */
while ( ( ch = getc ( fs ) ) != EOF )
{
    /* search the character read in arr1[ ] */
    for ( i = 0 ; i <= 96 ; i++ )
    {
        if ( ch == arr1[i] )
```

```
                    break ;
            }

            /* place the corresponding character from arr2[ ] in target file */
            putc ( arr2[i], ft ) ;
        }

        fclose ( fs ) ;
        fclose ( ft ) ;

        outtextxy ( 4 * 8, 16 * 8, "File was successfully encrypted!" ) ;
        outtextxy ( 32, 184, "Press any key..." ) ;
        fflush ( stdin ) ;
        getch( ) ;
        cleartext( ) ;
}

/* decrypts an encrypted file */
decryptfile( )
{
        char arr1[97] = "IOP{a}sdfghjkl;'ASDFGHJKL:zxcvbnm,./ZX\
                    CV BNM<>?1234567890-=~!@#$%^&(*)_\
                    +|qwertyuiop[Q]WERTYU\\\"\n\t" ;
        char arr2[97] = "'12345 67890-=~!@#$%^&(*)_+|qwertyuiop\
                    [Q]WERTYUIOP{a}sdfghjkl;'ASDFGHJKL\
                    :ZXCVBNM,./zxcvbnm<>?\\\"\n\t" ;
        char source[30], target[30], ch ;
        int i ;
        FILE *fs, *ft ;

        /* collect source file name */
        setcolor ( 3 ) ;
        outtextxy ( 4 * 8, 6 * 8, "Enter source file name:") ;
        gotoxy ( 5, 9 ) ;
        fflush ( stdin ) ;
        gets ( source ) ;
```

```
/* open source file and check if successful */
fs = fopen ( source, "r" ) ;
if ( fs == NULL )
{
    outtextxy ( 4 * 8, 11 * 8, "Cannot open source file!" ) ;
    outtextxy ( 32, 184, "Press any key..." ) ;
    fflush ( stdin ) ;
    getch( ) ;

    return ;
}

/* collect target file name */
outtextxy ( 4 * 8, 11 * 8, "Enter target file name:") ;
gotoxy ( 5, 14 ) ;
fflush ( stdin ) ;
gets ( target ) ;

/* open target file and check if successful */
ft = fopen ( target, "w" ) ;
if ( ft == NULL )
{
    outtextxy ( 4 * 8, 16 * 8, "Cannot open target file!" ) ;
    outtextxy ( 32, 184, "Press any key..." ) ;
    fflush ( stdin ) ;
    getch( ) ;

    fclose ( fs ) ;
    return ;
}

/* read characters from source file till end of file is reached */
while ( ( ch = getc ( fs ) ) != EOF )
{
    /* search the character read in arr2[ ] */
    for ( i = 0 ; i <= 96 ; i++ )
    {
```

```
            if ( ch == arr2[i] )
                 break ;
        }

        /* place the corresponding character from arr1[ ] in target file */
        putc ( arr1[i], ft ) ;
    }

    fclose ( fs ) ;
    fclose ( ft ) ;

    outtextxy ( 4 * 8, 16 * 8, "File was successfully decrypted!" ) ;
    outtextxy ( 32, 184, "Press any key..." ) ;
    fflush ( stdin ) ;
    getch( ) ;
    cleartext( ) ;
}
```

User Defined Functions

Icon Editor

cleartext( )	Erases the message line.
display_grid( )	Constructs the grid as per the expansion factor.
display_icon( )	Displays the current icon.
drawcursor( )	Draws or erases the graphics cursor.
edit_icon( )	Allows drawing/editing of the icon.
getkey( )	Collects the scan code of the key hit.
init_icon( )	Initialises the icon image array.
load_icon( )	Reads icon from file into memory.
save_icon( )	Saves current icon into file.

Graphical User Interface

check_icon( )	Checks whether an icon has been selected.
cleartext( )	Erases the row used for displaying messages.
comparefile( )	Compares two files.
decryptfile( )	Decrypts an encrypted file.
deletefile( )	Deletes a file.
display_icons( )	Loads icons from disk and displays them on screen.
encryptfile( )	Encrypts a file using substitution cipher.
get_position( )	Gets the current coordinates of the mouse pointer and status of mouse buttons.
getresponse( )	Checks which icon is selected.
hide_ptr( )	Hides the mouse pointer.
icon_box( )	Draws/erases the icon box.
load_icon( )	Loads an icon from file and displays it on screen.
load_mousedriver( )	Loads mouse driver in memory, if not already loaded.
renamefile( )	Renames a file.

reset_mouse( )   Initialises the mouse driver.
show_ptr( )   Displays the mouse pointer.

6

Video Games

All work and no play... We have put C to work in a range of utilities like Easyedit, Chartmaster, Mycad, and so on. How about putting it to play now? Computers make fine adversaries for all sorts of games - be they serious as chess or light as patience - with their speed and apparent intelligence. 'Apparent', because the brain behind it is the program. It is in the programmer's power to make the computer as smart as he wants to, or is able to. So much so, he can ensure that the Computer always emerges the winner, or the other way round! In the pages to come, I present you with three games that use computer animation. Having soaked up their logic, you would in all probability be in a position to add to the list on your own.

Bricks

In this game the player is presented with a wall of bricks and a maximum of four balls with which to knock each of the bricks down. The ball is to be caught on the paddle provided for it, from where it bounces back and hits the bricks on the rebound. For every brick you strike, you are awarded 5 points, whereas you lose 15 points for every ball lost. So much for the crust. For what goes in the making of the game, read on.

The System

Our first job is to change over to the graphics mode using the function **initgraph( )**. Next, we call the function **mainscreen( )**, which displays the starting screen and returns the player's choice of the level at which he wants to play the game. There are three levels, those of novice, advanced and expert. The three differ in the speeds at which the ball moves. Having set the right speed, we now draw the bricks using two functions - **drawbrick( )** and **bricks( )**. **drawbrick( )** draws a single brick, whereas **bricks( )** draws the five rows comprising the wall. The ball and the paddle are created using standard library functions **circle( )**, **rectangle( )** and **floodfill( )**. Once created, the wall, the ball and the paddle would look as shown in the following figure.

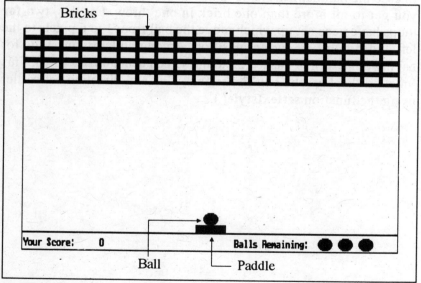

Figure 6.1

As shown in the figure, the score is displayed at the bottom left corner, whereas the balls still available at the player's disposal are displayed at the bottom right corner.

The Action

The ball and the paddle are to be moved throughout the game, the ball moving under the program's control, and the paddle under the player's. For this, we first store their images in memory which is allocated using **malloc( )**. Once this is done, the image is put on the screen at consecutive locations in the direction of motion, after erasing the previous image. The factors by which the position of the ball changes are **dx** and **dy**, which provide increments or decrements of 1, as the case may be. Whenever the ball reaches any of the boundaries of the view port, provision has been made for it to bounce inwards in the appropriate direction.

Everytime the ball hits a brick, the brick is erased from the display. In case the ball happens to be in the vicinity of more than one brick, you get to hit more than one brick in one throw. For this, two **for** loops have been set up which move the ball from 1 to 6 pixels to the left and right of its current position. A congratulatory message for having done well is flashed on to the screen using **outtextxy( )**. This function displays the text in the font, size and direction set earlier using the function **settextstyle( )**.

Program

```
# include "process.h"
# include "dos.h"
# include "stdlib.h"
# include "graphics.h"
# include "stdio.h"

# define NULL 0
# define YES 1
# define NO 0

int maxx, maxy, midx, midy ;
int bri[5][20] ;

main( )
{
    union REGS ii, oo ;
    int ballx, bally, paddlex, paddley, dx = 1, dy = -1, oldx, oldy ;
    int gm, gd = DETECT, playerlevel ;
    int i, flag = 0, speed = 250, welldone = NO, score = 0, chance = 4, area ;
    int layer[5] = { 10, 20, 30, 40, 50 }, limit = 50, currentlayer = 4 ;
    char *p1, *p2 ;

    /* initialise the graphics system */
    initgraph ( &gd, &gm, "c:\\tc\\bgi" ) ;

    /* get the maximum x and y screen coordinates */
    maxx = getmaxx( ) ;
    maxy = getmaxy( ) ;

    /* calculate center of screen */
    midx = maxx / 2 ;
    midy = maxy / 2 ;
```

```
/* display opening screen and receive player's level */
playerlevel = mainscreen( ) ;

/* set speed of ball as per the level chosen */
switch ( playerlevel )
{
    case 'A' :
    case 'a' :
        speed = 100 ;
        break ;

    case 'E' :
    case 'e' :
        speed = 0 ;
}

/* draw the bricks, the paddle and the ball */
rectangle ( 0, 0, maxx, maxy - 12 ) ;
bricks( ) ;
rectangle ( midx - 25, maxy - 7 - 12, midx + 25, maxy - 12 ) ;
floodfill ( midx, maxy - 1 - 12, 1 ) ;
circle ( midx, maxy - 13 - 12, 12 ) ;
floodfill ( midx, maxy - 10 - 12, 1 ) ;

/* allocate memory for storing the image of the paddle */
area = imagesize ( midx - 12, maxy - 18, midx + 12, maxy - 8 ) ;
p1 = malloc ( area ) ;

/* allocate memory for storing the image of the ball */
area = imagesize ( midx - 25, maxy - 7, midx + 25, maxy - 1 ) ;
p2 = malloc ( area ) ;

/* if memory allocation unsuccessful */
if ( p1 == NULL || p2 == NULL )
{
    puts ( "Insufficient memory!!" ) ;
    exit ( 1 ) ;
```

```
}

/* store the image of the paddle and the ball into allocated memory */
getimage ( midx - 12, maxy - 7 - 12 - 12 + 1, midx + 12, maxy - 8 - 12, p1 ) ;
getimage ( midx - 25, maxy - 7 - 12, midx + 25, maxy - 1 - 12, p2 ) ;

/* store current position of the paddle and ball */
paddlex = midx - 25 ;
paddley = maxy - 7 - 12 ;
ballx = midx - 12 ;
bally = maxy - 7 - 12 + 1 - 12 ;

/* display balls in hand ( initially 3 ) */
gotoxy ( 45, 25 ) ;
printf ( "Balls Remaining:" ) ;
for ( i = 0 ; i < 3 ; i++ )
{
    circle ( 515 + i * 35, maxy - 5, 12 ) ;
    floodfill ( 515 + i * 35, maxy - 5, 1 ) ;
}

/* display initial score */
gotoxy ( 1, 25 ) ;
printf ( "Your Score:   %4d", score ) ;

/* select font and alignment for displaying text */
settextjustify ( CENTER_TEXT, CENTER_TEXT ) ;
settextstyle ( SANS_SERIF_FONT, HORIZ_DIR, 4 ) ;

while ( 1 )
{
    flag = 0 ;

    /* save the current x and y coordinates of the ball */
    oldx = ballx ;
    oldy = bally ;
```

```
/* update ballx and bally to move the ball in appropriate direction */
ballx = ballx + dx ;
bally = bally + dy ;

/* as per the position of ball determine the layer of bricks to check */
if ( bally > 40 )
{
    limit = 50 ;
    currentlayer = 4 ;
}
else
{
    if ( bally > 30 )
    {
        limit = 40 ;
        currentlayer = 3 ;
    }
    else
    {
        if ( bally > 20 )
        {
            limit = 30 ;
            currentlayer = 2 ;
        }
        else
        {
            if ( bally > 10 )
            {
                limit = 20 ;
                currentlayer = 1 ;
            }
            else
            {
                limit = 10 ;
                currentlayer = 0 ;
            }
        }
```

```
        }
}

/* if the ball hits the left boundary, deflect it to the right */
if ( ballx < 1 )
{
    music ( 5 ) ;
    ballx = 1 ;
    dx = -dx ;
}

/* if the ball hits the right boundary, deflect it to the left */
if ( ballx > ( maxx - 24 - 1 ) )
{
    music ( 5 ) ;
    ballx = maxx - 24 - 1 ;
    dx = -dx ;
}

/* if the ball hits the top boundary, deflect it down */
if ( bally < 1 )
{
    music ( 5 ) ;
    bally = 1 ;
    dy = -dy ;
}

/* if the ball is in the area occupied by the bricks */
if ( bally < limit )
{
    /* if there is no brick present exactly at the top of the ball */
    if ( bri[currentlayer][ ( ballx + 10 ) / 32 ] == 1 )
    {
        /* determine if the boundary of the ball touches a brick */
        for ( i = 1 ; i <= 6 ; i++ )
        {
            /* check whether there is a brick to the right of the ball */
```

```
                    if ( bri[currentlayer][ ( ballx + i + 10 ) / 32 ] == 0 )
                    {
                        /* if there is a brick */
                        ballx = ballx + i ;
                        flag = 1 ;
                        break ;
                    }

                    /* check whether there is a brick to the left of the ball */
                    if ( bri[currentlayer][ ( ballx - i + 10 ) / 32 ] == 0 )
                    {
                        ballx = ballx - i ;
                        flag = 1 ;
                        break ;
                    }
                }

                /* if the ball does not touch a brick at the top, left or right */
                if ( !flag )
                {
                    /* check if the ball has moved above the current layer */
                    if ( bally < layer[currentlayer - 1] )
                    {
                        /* if so, change current layer appropriately */
                        currentlayer-- ;
                        limit = layer[currentlayer] ;
                    }

                    /* put the image of the ball at the old coordinates */
                    putimage ( oldx, oldy, p1, OR_PUT ) ;

                    /* erase the image at the old coordinates */
                    putimage ( oldx, oldy, p1, XOR_PUT ) ;

                    /* place the image of the ball at the new coordinates */
                    putimage ( ballx, bally, p1. XOR_PUT ) ;
```

```
                    /* introduce delay */
                    for ( i = 0 ; i <= speed ; i++ )
                        ;

                    /* carry on with moving the ball */
                    continue ;
            }
    }

    /* control comes to this point only if the ball is touching a brick */
    music ( 4 ) ;  /* play music */

    /* erase the brick hit by the ball */
    erasebrick ( ( ballx + 10 ) / 32, currentlayer ) ;

    /* if the brick hit happens to be on the extreme right */
    if ( ( ballx + 10 ) / 32 == 19 )
        line ( maxx, 0, maxx, 50 ) ;  /* redraw right boundary */

    /* if the brick hit happens to be on the extreme left */
    if ( ( ballx + 10 ) / 32 == 0 )
        line ( 0, 0, 0, 50 ) ;  /* redraw left boundary */

    /* if the brick hit happens to be in the topmost layer */
    if ( currentlayer == 0 )
        line ( 0, 0, maxx, 0 ) ;  /* redraw top boundary */

    /* set appropriate array element to 1 to indicate absence of brick */
    bri[currentlayer][ ( ballx + 10 ) / 32 ] = 1 ;

    bally = bally + 1 ;  /* update the y coordinate */
    dy = -dy ;  /* change the direction of the ball */
    score += 5 ;  /* increment score */
    gotoxy ( 16, 25 ) ;
    printf ( "%4d", score ) ;  /* print latest score */

    /* if the first brick is hit during a throw */
```

```
        if ( welldone == NO )
            welldone = YES ;
        else
        {
            /* for the consecutive bricks hit during the same throw */
            outtextxy ( midx, midy, "Well done!" ) ;
            music ( 1 ) ;
        }
    }

    /* clear part of the screen used for displaying Well done message */
    if ( bally > 50 && welldone == YES )
    {
        setviewport ( midx - 32 * 2.5, midy - 32 / 2, midx + 32 * 2.5,
                        midy + 32 / 2, 1 ) ;
        clearviewport( ) ;
        setviewport ( 0, 0, maxx, maxy, 1 ) ;
        welldone = NO ;
    }

    /* if the ball has reached the bottom */
    if ( bally > 180 - 12 )
    {
        welldone = NO ;

        /* if the paddle has missed the ball */
        if ( ballx < paddlex - 20 || ballx > paddlex + 50 )
        {
            /* continue the descent of the ball */
            while ( bally < 177 )
            {
                /* erase the image of the ball at the old coordinates */
                putimage ( oldx, oldy, p1, XOR_PUT ) ;

                /* put the image of the ball at the updated coordinates */
                putimage ( ballx, bally, p1, XOR_PUT ) ;
```

```
/* introduce delay */
for ( i = 0 ; i <= speed ; i++ )
        ;

/* save the current x and y coordinates of the ball */
oldx = ballx ;
oldy = bally ;

/* update ballx and bally to move the ball in
   appropriate direction */
ballx = ballx + dx ;
bally = bally + dy ;
}


chance-- ;  /* decrement the number of chances */
score -= 20 ;  /* decrement 20 points for each ball lost */
gotoxy ( 16, 25 ) ;
printf ( "%4d", score ) ;  /* print latest score */
music ( 2 ) ;

/* erase one out of the available balls */
if ( chance )
      putimage ( 515 + ( chance - 1 ) * 35 - 12 , maxy - 10,
                 p1, XOR_PUT ) ;

/* if the last ball is being played */
if ( chance == 1 )
{
     gotoxy ( 45, 25 ) ;
     printf ( "Your last ball... Be careful!" ) ;
}

/* if all the balls are lost */
if ( !chance )
{
     gotoxy ( 45, 25 ) ;
     printf ( "Press any key...              " ) ;
```

```
                    outtextxy ( midx, midy, "I warned you! Try again" ) ;
                    music ( 3 ) ;

                    closegraph( ) ;
                    restorecrtmode( ) ;
                    exit ( 0 ) ;
                }
            }

        /* if ball is collected on paddle */
        music ( 5 ) ;
        bally = 180 - 12 ;  /* restore the y coordinate of ball */
        dy = -dy ;  /* deflect the ball upwards */
    }

    /* put the image of the ball at the old coordinates */
    putimage ( oldx, oldy, p1, OR_PUT ) ;

    /* erase the image of the ball at the old coordinates */
    putimage ( oldx, oldy, p1, XOR_PUT ) ;

    /* put the image of the ball at the upadted coordinates */
    putimage ( ballx, bally, p1, XOR_PUT ) ;

    /* if all the bricks have been destroyed */
    if ( score == 500 - ( ( 4 - chance ) * 20 ) )
    {
        outtextxy ( midx, midy, "You win !!!" ) ;

        if ( score < 500 )
            outtextxy ( midx, midy + 30, "Try scoring 500" ) ;
        else
            outtextxy ( midx, midy + 30, "You are simply GREAT!" ) ;

        music ( 3 ) ;

        closegraph( ) ;
```

```
        restorecrtmode( ) ;
        exit ( 0 ) ;
}

/* introduce delay */
for ( i = 0 ; i <= speed ; i++ )
        ;

/* if the user has pressed a key to move the paddle */
if ( kbhit( ) )
{
    /* issue interrupt to obtain the ascii and scan codes of key hit */
    ii.h.ah = 0 ;
    int86 ( 22, &ii, &oo ) ;

    /* put the image of the paddle at the old coordinates */
    putimage ( paddlex, paddley, p2, OR_PUT ) ;

    /* erase the image of the paddle at the old coordinates */
    putimage ( paddlex, paddley, p2, XOR_PUT ) ;

    /* if Esc key has been pressed */
    if ( oo.h.ah == 1 )
        exit ( 0 ) ;

    /* right arrow key */
    if ( oo.h.ah == 75 )
        paddlex = paddlex - 20 ;

    /* left arrow key */
    if ( oo.h.ah == 77 )
        paddlex = paddlex + 20 ;

    /* if paddle goes beyond left boundary */
    if ( paddlex < 0 )
        paddlex = 0 ;
```

```
                /* if paddle goes beyond right boundary */
                if ( paddlex > 589 )
                    paddlex = 589 ;

                /* put the image of the paddle at the proper position */
                putimage ( paddlex, paddley, p2, XOR_PUT ) ;
            }
        }
}

/* creates opening screen */
mainscreen( )
{
    /* array showing the positions where a brick is needed to form the
       figure BRICKS */
    int ff[12][40] = {
    1,1,1,1,0,0,0,1,1,1,1,0,0,0,1,1,1,1,0,0,0,1,1,1,0,0,1,0,0,0,0,1,0,0,0,1,1,1,0,
    1,0,0,0,1,0,0,1,0,0,0,1,0,0,0,0,1,0,0,0,0,1,0,0,0,1,0,1,0,0,0,1,0,0,0,1,0,0,0,1,
    1,0,0,0,0,1,0,1,0,0,0,0,1,0,0,0,1,0,0,0,1,0,0,0,0,0,0,1,0,0,1,0,0,0,1,0,0,0,0,0,
    1,0,0,0,0,1,0,1,0,0,0,0,1,0,0,0,1,0,0,0,1,0,0,0,0,0,0,1,0,1,0,0,0,0,1,0,0,0,0,0,
    1,0,0,0,1,0,0,1,0,0,0,1,0,0,0,0,1,0,0,0,1,0,0,0,0,0,0,1,1,0,0,0,0,0,0,1,0,0,0,0,
    1,1,1,1,0,0,0,1,1,1,1,0,0,0,0,1,0,0,0,1,0,0,0,0,0,0,1,1,0,0,0,0,0,0,1,1,1,0,0,
    1,0,0,0,1,0,0,1,0,0,0,1,0,0,0,0,1,0,0,0,1,0,0,0,0,0,0,1,1,0,0,0,0,0,0,0,0,0,1,0,
    1,0,0,0,0,1,0,1,0,0,0,0,1,0,0,0,1,0,0,0,1,0,0,0,0,0,0,1,0,1,0,0,0,0,0,0,0,0,0,1,
    1,0,0,0,0,1,0,1,0,0,0,0,1,0,0,0,1,0,0,0,1,0,0,0,0,0,0,1,0,0,1,0,0,0,0,0,0,0,0,1,
    1,0,0,0,1,0,0,1,0,0,0,0,1,0,0,0,1,0,0,0,0,1,0,0,0,1,0,1,0,0,0,1,0,0,1,0,0,0,0,1,
    1,1,1,1,0,0,0,1,0,0,0,0,1,0,1,1,1,1,1,0,0,0,1,1,1,0,0,1,0,0,0,0,1,0,0,1,1,1,1,0,
    0,0,0,0,0,0,0,0,0,0,0,0,0,0,0,0,0,0,0,0,0,0,0,0,0,0,0,0,0,0,0,0,0,0,0,0,0,0,0,0,
    } ;
    int i, j, lx = 0, ly = 0, ch ;

    /* draw boundary */
    rectangle ( 0, 0, maxx, maxy ) ;

    /* form the word BRICKS */
    for ( i = 0 ; i < 12 ; i++ )
    {
```

```
      for ( j = 0 ; j < 40 ; j++ )
      {
            if ( ff[i][j] )
                  rectangle ( lx, ly, lx + 15, ly + 9 ) ;
            lx = lx + 16 ;
      }
      lx = 0 ;
      ly = ly + 10 ;
}

/* draw pattern at the bottom of the screen */
line ( 0, maxy - 12, maxx, maxy - 12 ) ;
setfillstyle ( XHATCH_FILL, WHITE ) ;
floodfill ( 2, maxy - 2, WHITE ) ;

/* draw the paddle and the ball */
setfillstyle ( SOLID_FILL, WHITE ) ;
rectangle ( midx - 25, maxy - 7 - 12, midx + 25, maxy - 12 ) ;
floodfill ( midx, maxy - 1 - 12, 1 ) ;
circle ( midx, maxy - 13 - 12, 12 ) ;
floodfill ( midx, maxy - 10 - 12, 1 ) ;

music ( 3 ) ;  /* play music */

/* display menu */
while ( 1 )
{
      /* clear the region below the word BRICKS */
      setviewport ( 1, 125 - 12, maxx - 1, maxy - 1, 1 ) ;
      clearviewport( ) ;

      setviewport ( 0, 0, maxx, maxy, 1 ) ;
      outtextxy ( 20, 135, "Select any of the following:" ) ;
      outtextxy ( 20, 155, "Play ( P )" ) ;
      outtextxy ( 20, 165, "Instructions ( I )" ) ;
      outtextxy ( 20, 175, "Exit ( E )" ) ;
```

```
ch = 0 ;

/* continue till the correct choice is made */
while ( ! ( ch == 'E' || ch == 'I' || ch == 'P' ) )
{
    fflush ( stdin ) ;

    /* if a special key is hit, flush the keyboard buffer */
    if ( ( ch = getch( ) ) == 0 )
        getch( ) ;
    else
        ch = toupper ( ch ) ;
}

if ( ch == 'P' )
    break ;

switch ( ch )
{
    case 'I' :
        setviewport ( 1, 125 - 12, maxx - 1, maxy - 1, 1 ) ;
        clearviewport( ) ;

        setviewport ( 0, 0, maxx, maxy, 1 ) ;
        settextstyle ( DEFAULT_FONT, HORIZ_DIR, 1 ) ;
        outtextxy ( 20, 125, "       Instructions       " ) ;
        settextstyle ( DEFAULT_FONT, HORIZ_DIR, 0 ) ;
        outtextxy ( 20, 140, "Use left and right arrow keys to
                        move paddle." ) ;
        outtextxy ( 20, 150, "If you don't collect the ball on the
                        paddle, you lose the ball." ) ;
        outtextxy ( 20, 160, "On loosing a ball you loose 20 points." ) ;
        outtextxy ( 20, 170, "On taking a brick you gain 5 points." ) ;
        outtextxy ( 20, 185, "Press any key..." ) ;
        fflush ( stdin ) ;
        if ( getch( ) == 0 )
            getch( ) ;
```

```
                break ;

            case 'E' :
                closegraph( ) ;
                restorecrtmode( ) ;
                exit ( 0 ) ;
        }
    }

    setviewport ( 1, 125 - 12, maxx - 1, maxy - 1, 1 ) ;
    clearviewport( ) ;

    /* prompt the user for the level desired */
    setviewport ( 0, 0, maxx, maxy, 1 ) ;
    outtextxy ( 20, 135, "Select any of the following levels:" ) ;
    outtextxy ( 20, 155, "Novice ( N )" ) ;
    outtextxy ( 20, 165, "Advanced ( A )" ) ;
    outtextxy ( 20, 175, "Expert ( E )" ) ;

    /* get user's choice */
    fflush ( stdin ) ;
    if ( ( ch = getch( ) ) == 0 )
        getch( ) ;

    clearviewport( ) ;

    /* return the choice made by the user */
    return ( ch ) ;
}

/* draws bricks at the start of the game */
bricks( )
{
    int i, j, lx = 0, ly = 0 ;

    for ( i = 0 ; i < 5 ; i++ )  /* 5 rows */
    {
```

```
        for ( j = 0 ; j < 20 ; j++ )  /* 20 columns */
        {
            /* draw a brick at appropriate coordinates */
            drawbrick ( lx, ly ) ;

            lx = lx + 32 ;
        }

        lx = 0 ;
        ly = ly + 10 ;
    }
}

/* draws a brick at the proper position */
drawbrick ( lx, ly )
int lx, ly ;
{
    rectangle ( lx, ly, lx + 31, ly + 9 ) ;
    rectangle ( lx + 2, ly - 2, lx + 31 - 2, ly + 9 - 2 ) ;
    floodfill ( lx + 1, ly + 1, 2 ) ;
}

/* erases the specified brick */
erasebrick ( b, l )
int b, l ;
{
    /* b - brick number, l - layer */

    setcolor ( BLACK ) ;
    rectangle ( b * 32, l * 10, ( b * 32 ) + 31 , ( l * 10 ) + 9 ) ;
    rectangle ( b * 32 + 1, l * 10, ( b * 32 ) + 31 - 1, ( l * 10 ) + 9 - 1 ) ;
    rectangle ( b * 32 + 2, l * 10, ( b * 32 ) + 31 - 2, ( l * 10 ) + 9 - 2 ) ;
    setcolor ( WHITE ) ;
}

/* plays different types of music */
music ( type )
```

```
int type ;
{
     /* natural frequencies of 7 notes */
     float octave[7] = { 130.81, 146.83, 164.81, 174.61, 196, 220, 246.94 } ;
     int n, i ;

     switch ( type )
     {
         case 1 :
             for ( i = 0 ; i < 7 ; i++ )
             {
                 sound ( octave[i] * 8 ) ;
                 delay ( 30 ) ;
             }
             nosound( ) ;
             break ;

         case 2 :
             for ( i = 0 ; i < 15 ; i++ )
             {
                 n = random ( 7 ) ;
                 sound ( octave[n] * 4 ) ;
                 delay ( 100 ) ;
             }
             nosound( ) ;
             break ;

         case 3 :
             while ( !kbhit( ) )
             {
                 n = random ( 7 ) ;
                 sound ( octave[n] * 4 ) ;
                 delay ( 100 ) ;
             }
             nosound( ) ;

             /* flush the keyboard buffer */
```

```
            if ( getch( ) == 0 )
                getch( ) ;

            break ;

        case 4 :
            for ( i = 4 ; i >= 0 ; i-- )
            {
                sound ( octave[i] * 4 ) ;
                delay ( 15 ) ;
            }
            nosound( ) ;
            break ;

        case 5 :
            sound ( octave[6] * 2 ) ;
            delay ( 50 ) ;
            nosound( ) ;
    }
}
```

User defined functions

bricks( )	Uses function **drawbrick**( ) to draw 5 rows of 20 bricks each.
drawbrick( )	Draws a brick.
erasebrick( )	Draws a brick in the background color, effectively erasing that brick. This function is called whenever the ball strikes a brick.
mainscreen( )	Creates the screen that appears as soon as the program is executed.
music( )	Plays music of different types.

Eater

Here is another popular game you can boast of being able to write - Eater. In this game the Eater has to consume as many titbits scattered all over the maze on the screen as possible, and at the same time, save itself from the bugs - the villains in the story - which try to kill the Eater. The Eater is not as lucky as the cat with nine lives, but lucky enough with the three lives we grant to it. Thus, you have a maximum of three chances in which to clear the screen of all titbits.

The beginning

In this game, the graphics mode is used only for displaying the various starting screens. In the function **startscreen( )**, we call **initgraph( )** to change over to the graphics mode. Now the starting screen, the screen for instructions, and the screen for obtaining the user's choice are created using library functions like **rectangle( )**, **outtextxy( )**, etc. With this over, we revert back to the text mode for the actual game.

The Main Screen

For generating the screen which shows the various paths, titbits, the bugs, and the Eater, we call a function **mainscreen( )**. And what is actually generated by **mainscreen( )** is as shown in Figure 6.2. As we said already, no graphics is involved here. Each titbit is the character corresponding to ascii 250, the bugs are ascii 2, and the Eater itself is ascii 1. So far so good. But what can certainly do with a fuller explanation is the function **monitor( )**, which is what puts life in all our characters.

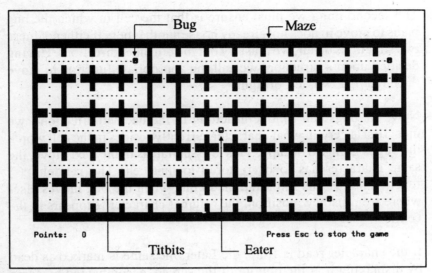

Figure 6.2

Monitoring the Game

Our logic is like this: While no key is hit by the player, the Eater is stationary. Left to their own devices, the bugs move in such a manner that the distance between them and the Eater is reduced. For example, when the Eater is at position (11, 40) on the screen, then a bug present at (20, 50) must move either upward, or to the left, since this is what would take the bug closer to the Eater. This activity is achieved through the function **getkeyhit( )**, which keeps calling the function **bug( )** repeatedly till a key is hit.

In **bug( )**, we first decide in which direction each bug must move in order to reduce its distance from the Eater. Simply ascertaining the direciton is not enough. We have to ensure two more things. Firstly, we check whether there exists a valid path in the direction in which the bug is to move. This is done by checking the contents of array **maze[ ][ ]**. **maze[ ][ ]** has been set up so that it contains a 1 corresponding to the location on the screen where a valid path exists, and a 0 otherwise.

The second thing we must ensure is that the cell in which the bug plans to move in does not already house another bug. If either of these two situations occur, we must try our luck in other directions. Having decided upon a direction, we call the appropriate function to move the bug up, down, left or right.

Now, the bugs can't move headlong in the decided direction - we must first ascertain what character currently resides in the cell which the bug is going to occupy. This is essential, as in the next move, the same character has to be restored to that cell. The **readchar( )** function stores this information, so that when the bug moves elsewhere from its new position, the original character reappears in the cell.

If the character read is 1, i.e. the Eater, the same is marked as dead by displaying it at the bottom of the screen, accompanied by some music. The kill is achieved through the function **killeater( )**. Also, we decrement the variable **chances** to indicate that one life has been used up. If any lives remain, then a fresh Eater is put in the center of the maze, and the game resumes.

When you hit a key

The moment you hit a key, interrupt number 22 is issued, which sets up the variables **ascii** and **scan** with the ascii and scan codes of the key pressed. This information is used in **testkeys( )**. Say you hit the left arrow key. **testkeys( )** checks whether the cell to the left of the Eater is part of a valid path. If there is indeed a path to the left, we read the character there, and if it happens to be a titbit, we increment the score. Now, when the Eater moves out of this cell, we place a space here to indicate that the titbit has been eaten. Had there been a bug present in the cell to the left, it would once again result in loss of a life for the Eater.

That completes the major part of the logic. Let us now look at a few minor issues.

By the way...

The indefinite loop (**while (1)**) in **main**( ) ensures that you can play as many games as you wish, without exiting from the system. However, should you decide to stop any time, all that you have to do is reach the Esc key and the rest is taken care of by **testkeys**( ). **testkeys**( ) has also been made intelligent enough to reject any keys other than the valid keys. Everytime the game is to be played afresh, all the variables are reinitialised through the function **initialise**( ).

The messages that are flashed at the end - whether the Eater devoured all the titbits or got devoured itself - are once again in the graphics mode, and have been managed by the function **endscreen**( ).

Program

```
# include "conio.h"
# include "stdlib.h"
# include "dos.h"
# include "stdio.h"
# include "graphics.h"

# define RIGHT 0
# define LEFT 1
# define UP 2
# define DOWN 3

int maze[25][80], score, row, col, ascii, scan, liveslost, delayfactor ;
int gd = DETECT, gm, midx, midy, maxx, maxy ;
int bugnumber, r[5], c[5], dir[5] ;
unsigned char charbelow[5] ;
char far *vid_mem = ( char far * ) 0xB8000000L ;

main( )
{
    char ans ;

    /* initialise random number generator with a random value */
    randomize( ) ;

    while ( 1 )
    {
        /* initialise variables at the start of each game */
        initialise( ) ;

        /* create opening screen */
        startscreen( ) ;

        /* draw the screen for the game */
```

```
        gamescreen( ) ;

        /* monitor the movement of the bugs and the Eater */
        monitor( ) ;

        /* create ending screen */
        ans = endscreen( ) ;

        /* check whether the user wishes to continue playing */
        if ( ans == 'N' )
            break ;
    }
}

/* creates opening screen */
startscreen( )
{
    char ch ;
    int i ;

    /* initialise the graphics system */
    initgraph ( &gd, &gm, "c:\\tc\\bgi" ) ;

    /* get maximum x and y screen coordinates */
    maxx = getmaxx( ) ;
    maxy = getmaxy( ) ;

    /* calculate the center of the screen */
    midx = maxx / 2 ;
    midy = maxy / 2 ;

    /* draw a double-lined box */
    rectangle ( 0, 0, maxx, maxy ) ;
    rectangle ( 2, 2, maxx - 2, maxy - 2 ) ;

    /* draw two vertical lines */
    line ( 55, 1, 55, maxy - 2 ) ;
```

```
line ( maxx - 55, 1, maxx - 55, maxy - 2 ) ;

/* display the string "EATER", horizontally */
settextjustify ( CENTER_TEXT, CENTER_TEXT ) ;
settextstyle ( DEFAULT_FONT, HORIZ_DIR, 6 ) ;
outtextxy ( midx, midy, "EATER" ) ;

/* display the string "Eater" vertically on both sides */
settextstyle ( DEFAULT_FONT, VERT_DIR, 4 ) ;
outtextxy ( 30, midy, "Eater" ) ;
outtextxy ( maxx - 30, midy, "Eater" ) ;

/* place the Eater character at random on the start screen */
gotoxy ( 10, 7 ) ;
printf ( "%c", 2 ) ;
gotoxy ( 35, 17 ) ;
printf ( "%c", 2 ) ;
gotoxy ( 55, 3 ) ;
printf ( "%c", 2 ) ;
gotoxy ( 65, 23 ) ;
printf ( "%c", 2 ) ;
gotoxy ( 70, 8 ) ;
printf ( "%c", 2 ) ;
gotoxy ( 20, 22 ) ;
printf ( "%c", 2 ) ;
gotoxy ( 15, 12 ) ;
printf ( "%c", 2 ) ;
gotoxy ( 30, 5 ) ;
printf ( "%c", 2 ) ;
gotoxy ( 68, 18 ) ;
printf ( "%c", 2 ) ;

/* play the starting music */
music ( 1 ) ;

/* clear the area enclosed by the double-lined boundary */
setviewport ( 1, 1, maxx - 1, maxy - 1, 1 ) ;
```

```
clearviewport( ) ;

/* draw the screen for displaying instructions */
rectangle ( 0 + 30, 0, maxx - 30, maxy ) ;
line ( 33, 0, 33, maxy ) ;
line ( maxx - 33, 0, maxx - 33, maxy ) ;

for ( i = 15 ; i <= maxy - 15 ; i+= 15 )
{
    ellipse ( 15, i, 0, 360, 6, 3 ) ;
    ellipse ( maxx - 15, i, 0, 360, 6, 3 ) ;
}

settextjustify ( CENTER_TEXT, TOP_TEXT ) ;
settextstyle ( DEFAULT_FONT, HORIZ_DIR, 3 ) ;
outtextxy ( midx, 10, "Instructions" ) ;

/* display instructions */
settextstyle ( DEFAULT_FONT, HORIZ_DIR, 0 ) ;
outtextxy ( midx, 40, "Your goal :- To eat up all the 400 crunchy-munchy" ) ;
outtextxy ( midx, 50, "                titbits scattered throughout the maze." ) ;
outtextxy ( midx, 70, "Your task is not easy!  There are 5 bugs chasing" ) ;
outtextxy ( midx, 80, "the Eater. You will have to watch out for them.   ") ;
outtextxy ( midx, 100, "To help you,  we have bestowed the Eater with 3" ) ;
outtextxy ( midx, 110, "lives.                                           " ) ;
outtextxy ( midx, 130, "You can move around the maze using arrow keys. " ) ;
outtextxy ( midx, 150, "If you are ready to start, press a key.         " ) ;
settextstyle ( DEFAULT_FONT, HORIZ_DIR, 3 ) ;
outtextxy ( midx, 170, "We wish you luck!" ) ;

/* wait for key press */
while ( !kbhit( ) )
    ;

/* flush the keyboard buffer */
if ( getch( ) == 0 )
    getch( ) ;
```

```
/* draw the screen for asking user level */
setviewport ( 0, 0, maxx, maxy, 1 ) ;
clearviewport( ) ;
rectangle ( midx - 200, midy - 60, midx + 200, midy + 60 ) ;

settextstyle ( DEFAULT_FONT, HORIZ_DIR, 2 ) ;
outtextxy ( midx, 60, "Select Speed:" ) ;

settextstyle ( DEFAULT_FONT, HORIZ_DIR, 1 ) ;
outtextxy ( midx, 90, "Slow ( S )    " ) ;
outtextxy ( midx, 105, "Medium ( M )  " ) ;
outtextxy ( midx, 120, "Fast ( F )    " ) ;

/* get user level */
while ( !kbhit( ) )
    ;

/* flush the keyboard buffer */
if ( ( ch = getch( ) ) == 0 )
    getch( ) ;

/* change over to text mode */
closegraph( ) ;
restorecrtmode( ) ;

/* set the value of variable delayfactor according to level selected */
switch ( toupper ( ch ) )
{
    case 'S' :
        delayfactor = 10000 ;
        break ;

    case 'M' :
        delayfactor = 5000 ;
        break ;
```

```
            case 'F' :
                delayfactor = 3000 ;
                break ;

            default :
                delayfactor = 10000 ;
        }
}

/* draws the screen for the game */
gamescreen( )
{
    int i ;

    size ( 32, 0 ) ;  /* hide cursor */

    /* fill the screen with the specified color */
    drawbox ( 0, 0, 24, 79, 39 ) ;

    /* draw horizontal lines of the maze */
    for ( i = 1 ; i <= 21 ; i = i + 4 )
        hline ( 219, 15, i, 1, 79 ) ;

    /* draw vertical lines of the maze */
    for ( i = 1 ; i <= 79 ; i = i + 6 )
        vline ( 219, 15, i, 1, 21 ) ;

    /* draw the rows of titbits */
    hline ( 250, 63, 3, 4, 22 ) ;
    hline ( 250, 63, 3, 28, 57 ) ;
    hline ( 250, 63, 3, 59, 76 ) ;
    hline ( 250, 63, 7, 10, 22 ) ;
    hline ( 250, 63, 7, 34, 76 ) ;
    hline ( 250, 63, 11, 4, 30 ) ;
    hline ( 250, 63, 11, 32, 52 ) ;
    hline ( 250, 63, 11, 64, 64 ) ;
    hline ( 250, 63, 11, 70, 76 ) ;
```

```
hline ( 250, 63, 15, 10, 22 ) ;
hline ( 250, 63, 15, 4, 10 ) ;
hline ( 250, 63, 15, 28, 40 ) ;
hline ( 250, 63, 15, 64, 70 ) ;
hline ( 250, 63, 19, 10, 46 ) ;
hline ( 250, 63, 19, 52, 58 ) ;
hline ( 250, 63, 19, 70, 76 ) ;
hline ( 250, 63, 19, 59, 63 ) ;
hline ( 250, 63, 11, 58, 67 ) ;

/* draw the columns of titbits */
vline ( 250, 63, 4, 4, 19 ) ;
vline ( 250, 63, 10, 4, 6 ) ;
vline ( 250, 63, 10, 16, 18 ) ;
vline ( 250, 63, 22, 4, 6 ) ;
vline ( 250, 63, 22, 12, 14 ) ;
vline ( 250, 63, 22, 4, 10 ) ;
vline ( 250, 63, 28, 4, 10 ) ;
vline ( 250, 63, 28, 16, 18 ) ;
vline ( 250, 63, 40, 8, 14 ) ;
vline ( 250, 63, 46, 12, 18 ) ;
vline ( 250, 63, 52, 12, 18 ) ;
vline ( 250, 63, 58, 8, 14 ) ;
vline ( 250, 63, 58, 16, 18 ) ;
vline ( 250, 63, 64, 8, 19 ) ;
vline ( 250, 63, 70, 8, 10 ) ;
vline ( 250, 63, 70, 16, 18 ) ;
vline ( 250, 63, 76, 4, 6 ) ;
vline ( 250, 63, 76, 12, 18 ) ;
vline ( 250, 63, 34, 4, 16 ) ;
vline ( 250, 63, 34, 18, 19 ) ;
vline ( 250, 63, 46, 4, 6 ) ;
vline ( 250, 63, 58, 4, 6 ) ;
vline ( 250, 63, 16, 9, 17 ) ;

gotoxy ( 51, 24 ) ;
printf ( "Press Esc to stop the game" ) ;
```

```
        gotoxy ( 2, 24 ) ;
        printf ( "Points: %3d", score ) ;

        /* place the five bugs at strategic positions */
        writechar ( 2, 3, 76, 112 ) ;
        writechar ( 2, 3, 22, 112 ) ;
        writechar ( 2, 11, 5, 112 ) ;
        writechar ( 2, 19, 63, 112 ) ;
        writechar ( 2, 19, 46, 112 ) ;

        /* play music */
        music ( 2 ) ;
}

/* draws a box filling the required area */
drawbox ( sr, sc, er, ec, attr )
int sr, sc, er, ec ;
char attr ;
{
        int r, c ;
        char far *v ;

        for ( r = sr ; r <= er ; r++ )
        {
                for ( c = sc ; c <= ec ; c++ )
                {
                        /* calculate address */
                        v = vid_mem + ( r * 160 ) + ( c * 2 ) ;

                        *v = ' ' ;  /* write a space */
                        v++ ;
                        *v = attr ;  /* write attribute */
                }
        }
}

/* writes character and its attribute into VDU memory */
```

```
writechar ( ch, r, c, attr )
char ch ;
int r, c, attr ;
{
    char far *v ;

    /* calculate address */
    v = vid_mem + ( r * 160 ) + c * 2 ;

    *v = ch ;  /* store ascii value */
    v++ ;
    *v = attr ;  /* store attribute */
}

/* draws horizontal line */
hline ( ch, attr, r, c1, c2 )
unsigned char ch ;
int r, c1, c2, attr ;
{
    int c ;

    for ( c = c1 ; c <= c2 ; c++ )
    {
        writechar ( ch, r, c, attr ) ;

        /* if titbit placed at row r and column c, set corresponding element
           of array maze[ ][ ] to 1 */
        if ( ch == 250 )
            maze[r][c] = 1 ;
    }
}

/* draws vertical line */
vline ( ch, attr, c, r1, r2 )
unsigned char ch ;
int c, r1, r2, attr ;
{
```

```
        int r ;

        for ( r = r1 ; r <= r2 ; r++ )
        {
                writechar ( ch, r, c, attr ) ;

                /* if titbit placed at row r and column c, set corresponding element
                   of array maze[ ][ ] to 1 */
                if ( ch == 250 )
                        maze[r][c] = 1 ;
        }
}

/* monitors the movement of the bugs and the Eater */
monitor( )
{
        int key ;
        unsigned char ch ;

        while ( 1 )
        {
                /* place Eater at specified row and column */
                writechar ( 1, row, col, 112 ) ;

                /* move bugs around until a key is hit */
                getkeyhit( ) ;

                /* if all 3 lives of the Eater are lost */
                if ( liveslost == 3 )
                        break ;

                /* place a space in the position currently occupied by the Eater */
                writechar ( ' ', row, col, 63 ) ;

                /* update the position of the Eater according to the key pressed */
                key = testkeys( ) ;
```

```
/* if invalid key pressed */
if ( key == 0 )
{
    /* write back Eater in its original position */
    writechar ( 1, row, col, 112 ) ;
}
else
{
    /* read character at the position which the Eater is to occupy */
    readchar ( row, col, &ch ) ;

    /* if character read is titbit, increment score and sound music */
    if ( ch == 250 )
    {
        score++ ;
        music ( 3 ) ;
    }

    /* if character read is bug, kill the Eater */
    if ( ch == 2 )
        killeater( ) ;

    /* if all three lives of the Eater are lost */
    if ( liveslost == 3 )
        break ;

    /* print the latest score */
    gotoxy ( 2, 24 ) ;
    printf ( "Points: %3d", score ) ;

    /* if all the titbits are eaten up */
    if ( score >= 400 )
    {
        /* erase the last titbit */
        writechar ( ' ', row, col, 63 ) ;

        break ;
```

```
            }
        }
    }
}

/* moves bugs around until a key is hit */
getkeyhit( )
{
    union REGS i, o ;
    int count ;

    /* until the player hits a key, move each bug in turn */
    while ( !kbhit( ) )
    {
        /* introduce delay */
        count = 0 ;
        while ( count < delayfactor )
            count++ ;

        /* move the bug one step in the appropriate direction */
        bug ( &r[bugnumber], &c[bugnumber], &dir[bugnumber],
                &charbelow[bugnumber] ) ;

        /* if all three lives of the Eater are lost */
        if ( liveslost == 3 )
            return ;

        /* go to the next bug */
        bugnumber++ ;

        /* start with the first bug if all five bugs have been moved */
        if ( bugnumber == 5 )
            bugnumber = 0 ;
    }

    /* issue interrupt to read the ascii and scan codes of the key pressed */
    i.h.ah = 0 ;  /* store service number */
```

```
        int86 ( 22, &i, &o ) ;  /* issue interrupt */
        ascii = o.h.al ;
        scan = o.h.ah ;
}

/* reports which key has been hit */
testkeys( )
{
        switch ( scan )
        {
            case 72 :  /* up arrow */

                /* if path is not present in the specified direction */
                if ( maze[row - 1][col] != 1 )
                    return ( 0 ) ;

                /* update row of Eater */
                row-- ;
                break ;

            case 80 :  /* down arrow */

                if ( maze[row + 1][col] != 1 )
                    return ( 0 ) ;

                row++ ;
                break ;

            case 77 :  /* right arrow */

                /* if path is not present in the specified direction */
                if ( maze[row][col + 1] != 1 )
                    return ( 0 ) ;

                /* update column of Eater */
                col++ ;
                break ;
```

```
        case 75 :  /* left arrow */

            if ( maze[row][col - 1] != 1 )
                return ( 0 ) ;

            col-- ;
            break ;

        case 1 :  /* Esc key */

            exit ( 0 ) ;  /* terminate program */

        default :
            return ( 0 ) ;
    }
}

/* reads the character present at row r and column c into ch */
readchar ( r, c, ch )
int r, c ;
unsigned char *ch ;
{
    char far *v ;

    /* calculate address */
    v = vid_mem + ( r * 160 ) + c * 2 ;

    *ch = *v ;
}

/* moves the specified bug in the appropriate direction */
bug ( r, c, dir, ch )
int *r, *c, *dir ;
unsigned char *ch ;
{
    int trials = 1, flag = 0 ;
```

```
char temp ;

/* select a valid direction which takes the bug closer to Eater */
/* in each if statement the 1st condition checks whether the movement in
   that direction would move the bug closer to the Eater, whereas the 2nd
   condition checks if the maze permits a movement in that direction */
if ( abs ( *r - 1 - row ) < abs ( *r - row ) && maze[*r - 1][*c] == 1 )
    *dir = UP ;
else
    if ( abs ( *r + 1 - row ) < abs ( *r - row ) && maze[*r + 1][*c] == 1 )
        *dir = DOWN ;
    else
        if ( abs ( *c + 1 - col ) < abs ( *c - col ) && maze[*r][*c + 1] == 1 )
            *dir = RIGHT ;
        else
            if ( abs( *c - 1 - col ) < abs( *c - col ) && maze[*r][*c - 1] == 1 )
                *dir = LEFT ;

/* check whether the direction chosen contains another bug, if so find an
   alternate direction */
while ( 1 )
{
    switch ( *dir )
    {
        case RIGHT :

                /* if there is a path to the right of bug */
                if ( maze[*r][*c + 1] == 1 )
                {
                    /* read the character to the right of the bug */
                    readchar ( *r, *c + 1, &temp ) ;

                    /* if the character is again a bug find alternate direction */
                    if ( temp == 2 )
                    {
                        /* if path exists to the left of bug */
                        if ( maze[*r][*c - 1] == 1 )
```

```
                        *dir = LEFT ;
                else
                {
                        /* if path exists to the top of bug */
                        if ( maze[*r - 1][*c] == 1 )
                                *dir = UP ;
                        else
                        {
                                /* if path exists below the bug */
                                if ( maze[*r + 1][*c] == 1 )
                                        *dir = DOWN ;
                        }
                }
        }
        else
        {
                /* if there is no bug to the right of the bug being
                   considered, move the bug right */
                movebugright ( r, c, ch ) ;
                flag = 1 ;
        }
    }
    else
    {
        /* since there is no path in the RIGHT direction, try
           another path */
        *dir = random ( 4 ) ;
    }

    break ;

case LEFT :

    /* if there is a path to the left of bug */
    if ( maze[*r][*c - 1] == 1 )
    {
        /* read the character to the left of the bug */
```

```
readchar ( *r, *c - 1, &temp ) ;

/* if the character is again a bug find alternate direction */
if ( temp == 2 )
{
    /* if path exists to the right of bug */
    if ( maze[*r][*c + 1] == 1 )
        *dir = RIGHT ;
    else
    {
        /* if path exists to the top of bug */
        if ( maze[*r - 1][*c] == 1 )
            *dir = UP ;
        else
        {
            /* if path exists below the bug */
            if ( maze[*r + 1][*c] == 1 )
                *dir = DOWN ;
        }
    }
}
else
{
    /* if there is no bug to the left of the bug being
       considered, move the bug left */
    movebugleft ( r, c, ch ) ;
    flag = 1 ;
}
}
else
{
    /* since there is no path in the LEFT direction, try
       another path */
    *dir = random ( 4 ) ;
}

break ;
```

```
case UP :

     if ( maze[*r - 1][*c] == 1 )
     {
          readchar ( *r - 1, *c, &temp ) ;

          if ( temp == 2 )
          {
               if ( maze[*r][*c + 1] == 1 )
                    *dir = RIGHT ;
               else
               {
                    if ( maze[*r][*c - 1] == 1 )
                         *dir = LEFT ;
                    else
                    {
                         if ( maze[*r + 1][*c] == 1 )
                              *dir = DOWN ;
                    }
               }
          }
          else
          {
               movebugup ( r, c, ch ) ;
               flag = 1 ;
          }
     }
     else
          *dir = random ( 4 ) ;

     break ;

case DOWN :

     if ( maze[*r + 1][*c] == 1 )
     {
```

```
                    readchar ( *r + 1, *c, &temp ) ;

                    if ( temp == 2 )
                    {
                        if ( maze[*r][*c + 1] == 1 )
                            *dir = RIGHT ;
                        else
                        {
                            if ( maze[*r][*c - 1] == 1 )
                                *dir = LEFT ;
                            else
                            {
                                if ( maze[*r - 1][*c] == 1 )
                                    *dir = UP ;
                            }
                        }
                    }
                    else
                    {
                        movebugdown ( r, c, ch ) ;
                        flag = 1 ;
                    }
                }
                else
                    *dir = random ( 4 ) ;

                break ;
        }

        /* if the bug has been moved, take control outside the loop */
        if ( flag == 1 )
            break ;

        trials++ ;

        /* if even after 15 trials the correct direction cannot be found, then
           give up */
```

```
            if ( trials > 15 )
                break ;
        }


        /* if the bug collides with the Eater, kill it */
        if ( *r == row && *c == col )
            killeater( ) ;
}

/* moves the bug to the left of its current position */
movebugleft ( row, colm, ch )
int *row, *colm ;
unsigned char *ch ;
{
        /* place back the character originally at the position occupied by the bug */
        writechar ( *ch, *row, *colm, 63 ) ;

        /* update column */
        *colm = *colm - 1 ;

        /* find out the character over which the bug is to be placed */
        readchar ( *row, *colm, ch ) ;

        /* if Eater is present at that position */
        if ( *ch == 1 )
            *ch = ' ' ;  /* associate with the bug a space as the character under it */

        /* place the bug at the updated position */
        writechar ( 2, *row, *colm, 112 ) ;
}


/* moves the bug to the right of its current position */
movebugright ( row, colm, ch )
int *row, *colm ;
unsigned char *ch ;
{
        writechar ( *ch, *row, *colm, 63 ) ;
```

```
        *colm = *colm + 1 ;
        readchar ( *row, *colm, ch ) ;

        if ( *ch == 1 )
            *ch = '' ;

        writechar ( 2, *row, *colm, 112 ) ;
}

/* moves the bug above its current position */
movebugup ( row, col, ch )
int *row, *col ;
unsigned char *ch ;
{
        writechar ( *ch, *row, *col, 63 ) ;
        *row = *row - 1 ;
        readchar ( *row, *col, ch ) ;

        if ( *ch == 1 )
            *ch = '' ;

        writechar ( 2, *row, *col, 112 ) ;
}

/* moves the bug below its current position */
movebugdown ( row, col, ch )
int *row, *col ;
unsigned char *ch ;
{
        writechar ( *ch, *row, *col, 63 ) ;
        *row = *row + 1 ;
        readchar ( *row, *col, ch ) ;

        if ( *ch == 1 )
            *ch = '' ;

        writechar ( 2, *row, *col, 112 ) ;
```

```
}

/* issues interrupt to change the size of the cursor */
size ( ssl, esl )
int ssl, esl ;
{
    union REGS i, o ;

    i.h.ah = 1 ;  /* service number */
    i.h.ch = ssl ;  /* starting scan line */
    i.h.cl = esl ;  /* ending scan line */
    i.h.bh = 0 ;  /* video page */

    int86 ( 16, &i, &o ) ;  /* issue interrupt */
}

/* plays different types of music */
music ( type )
int type ;
{
    /* natural frequencies of 7 notes */
    float octave[7] = { 130.81, 146.83, 164.81, 174.61, 196, 220, 246.94 } ;
    int n, i ;

    switch ( type )
    {
        case 1 :

            /* continue playing music till a key is hit */
            while ( !kbhit( ) )
            {
                n = random ( 7 ) ;
                sound ( octave[n] * 4 ) ;
                delay ( 100 ) ;
            }
            nosound( ) ;
```

```
                    /* flush the keyboard buffer */
                    if ( getch( ) == 0 )
                        getch( ) ;

                    break ;

            case 2 :
                    for ( i = 6 ; i >= 0 ; i-- )
                    {
                        sound ( octave[i] ) ;
                        delay ( 54 ) ;
                    }
                    nosound( ) ;
                    break ;

            case 3 :
                    sound ( octave[6] * 2 ) ;
                    delay ( 50 ) ;
                    nosound( ) ;
    }
}

/* kills the Eater */
killeater( )
{
    int r, c ;

    /* save the values of row and column */
    r = row ;
    c = col ;

    /* write the Eater */
    writechar ( 1, row, col, 112 ) ;

    /* show the dead Eater below the maze, signifying the life lost */
    writechar ( 1, 23, 15 + liveslost * 3, 112 ) ;
```

```
        music ( 2 ) ;

        /* one more life of Eater lost */
        liveslost++ ;

        /* if all three lives of the Eater are lost */
        if ( liveslost == 3 )
            return ;

        /* place the new Eater at the center of the maze */
        row = 11 ;
        col = 40 ;
        writechar ( 1, row, col, 112 ) ;

        /* place the bug which ate the Eater back in its position */
        writechar ( 2, r, c, 112 ) ;
}

/* creates ending screen */
endscreen( )
{
        char ans = 0 ;

        /* initialise the graphics system */
        initgraph ( &gd, &gm, "c:\\tc\\bgi" ) ;

        /* draw a double-lined box */
        rectangle ( 0, 0, maxx, maxy ) ;
        rectangle ( 2, 2, maxx - 2, maxy - 2 ) ;

        /* set the font and alignment of the text to be displayed */
        settextjustify ( CENTER_TEXT, CENTER_TEXT ) ;
        settextstyle ( TRIPLEX_FONT, HORIZ_DIR, 3 ) ;

        /* if all three lives of the Eater are lost */
        if ( liveslost == 3 )
        {
```

```
                outtextxy ( midx, midy - 30, "Bad luck !!" ) ;
                outtextxy ( midx, midy, "Try again" ) ;
        }
        else
        {
                /* if all titbits have been eaten up */
                outtextxy ( midx, midy / 2, "You really are a" ) ;
                settextstyle ( DEFAULT_FONT, HORIZ_DIR, 6 ) ;
                outtextxy ( midx, midy, "GENIUS!!" ) ;
        }

        settextstyle ( TRIPLEX_FONT, HORIZ_DIR, 3 ) ;
        outtextxy ( midx, midy + midy / 2, "Another game (Y/N)..." ) ;

        /* continue till a correct answer is supplied */
        while ( ! ( ans == 'Y' || ans == 'N' ) )
        {
                fflush ( stdin ) ;
                ans = getch( ) ;
                ans = toupper ( ans ) ;
        }

        /* change over to text mode */
        closegraph( ) ;
        restorecrtmode( ) ;

        /* send back choice made */
        return ( ans ) ;
}

/* initialises variables at the start of each game */
initialise( )
{
        int j ;

        /* initialise row and column of Eater */
        row = 11 ;
```

```
    col = 40 ;

    /* initialise starting row and column of bugs */
    r[0] = 3 ; c[0] = 76 ;
    r[1] = 3 ; c[1] = 22 ;
    r[2] = 19 ; c[2] = 46 ;
    r[3] = 11 ; c[3] = 5 ;
    r[4] = 19 ; c[4] = 63 ;
    score = 0 ;
    liveslost = 0 ;

    bugnumber = 0 ;

    /* initialise direction and the character under each bug */
    for ( j = 0 ; j < 5 ; j++ )
    {
        dir[j] = 0 ;
        charbelow[j] = 250 ;
    }
}
```

User defined functions

bug( )	Manages the movement of the bugs. Checks to see if the direction chosen for the bug is valid, i.e whether a path exists in that direction or not, and then calls the appropriate function to move the bug in that direction.
drawbox( )	draws a box filling the required area.
endscreen( )	Displays the ending screen and lets the user decide whether he would like to play the game again.
gamescreen( )	Draws the maze, the titbits and the bugs for the game.
getkeyhit( )	Waits for the user to hit a key. In the mean time, it calls the function **bug**( ) to keep the five bugs moving around the maze in pursuit of the Eater.
hline( )	Draws horizontal line either for the maze or for the titbits.
initialise( )	Initialises all variables at the start of each game.
killeater( )	Kills the Eater.
monitor( )	Monitors the movement of the bugs and the Eater.
movebugdown( )	Moves the bug down after storing in **ch** the character present at the position which the bug is going to occupy.
movebugleft( )	Reads the character immediately below the bug and moves the bug left.
movebugright( )	Reads the character to the right of the bug and then moves the bug to the right.
movebugup( )	Reads the character immediately above the bug and moves the bug up.
music( )	Plays different types of music.
readchar( )	Reads the character present at row **r** and column **c**.
size( )	Changes the size of the cursor.

startscreen( )	Displays the opening screen, followed by the instructions for playing the game. It also decides the speed at which the bugs should move.
testkeys( )	Moves the Eater according to the keys pressed. Arrow keys take the Eater up, down, right or left. Esc key terminates the game. All other keys are ignored.
vline( )	Draws vertical line either for the maze or for the titbits.
writechar( )	Writes a character and its attribute in the VDU memory.

Paratrooper

Let us move on to yet another game you can develop with the ever reliable C. The game comprises of having to shoot down enemy helicopters and the enemy paratroopers that eject from them. In your control is a gun that can be made to fire in any direction within a given angle. You are awarded 20 points for every shot that hits a helicopter and 10 points for hitting a paratrooper, while you lose one point for any shot that doesn't hit either. But that's not all - paratroopers that escape being hit descend to the ground and pose a threat to the gun itself. Less than four paratroopers on any one side are okay, but if four are present, then there is nothing you can do to stop them from blasting the gun. So the only way to avoid the all ending blast is to take care not to allow more than 3 paratroopers to make it to the ground by... Do I detect some restlessness? What you are more interested in knowing is not how to play the game, but what lies within it, right? Well then, lets zoom right in.

The Beginning

By now you can predict what our first action has to be - change over to the graphics mode, as the text mode cannot support any images. This is done using the standard library function **initgraph( )**. Once in the graphics mode, we start with drawing all the images that the game requires - helicopters, paratroopers, parachutes, gunbase, etc. using library functions like **line( )**, **ellipse( )** and **floodfill( )**. To be precise, we draw 2 helicopters - one which moves from left to right and the other from right to left, two paratroopers, two parachutes, one gun base and finally the image of the blast. Since all these images are stored in memory using the function **getimage( )**, we can draw them as many times as we need to throughout the game by using the function **putimage( )**. The gun, however, is drawn repeatedly with different orientations in order to show its motion.

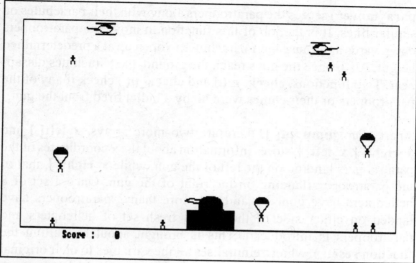

Figure 6.3

The Attack

The enemy attack is set off by two functions, **hmove( )** and **paramove( )**. **hmove( )** controls the movement of helicopters on the screen, moving in opposite directions. The motion is brought about by continuously drawing, erasing and then redrawing the helicopters at successive locations. When two helicopters disappear from the viewport, two more are introduced after a certain delay, one from either end.

From each chopper, during its journey to the other end, four paratroopers drop down. We have provided for 32 different points on the screen from where a set of 8 helicopters can eject the paratroopers. Back in the initialisation stage, we have an array **jump_pt[ ]** which is assigned the x coordinates of these points. The level of the left-bound and right-bound choppers is fixed, and the y coordinates are taken care of in **heli_level[ ]**. The function **hmove( )** calls another function **check_h( )**, which checks whether any of the helicopters was hit.

para_move( ) serves the paratroopers along with their parachutes on similar lines. It is the job of this function to move the paratroopers downwards and cause their parachutes to open up at a predetermined height. Also, once the guys reach the ground, the parachutes dissappear. Two functions, **check_m( )** and **check_p( )** check if any of the paratroopers or their chutes were hit by a bullet fired from the gun.

Apart from **jump_pt[ ]**, there are two more arrays, **x_left[ ]** and **x_right[ ]**. **x_left[ ]**, stores information about the x coordinates of the paratroopers landing on the left of the gun, while **x_right[ ]**, that of the paratroopers landing on the right of the gun. Once a set of 8 helicopters have gone by and not more than 3 paratroopers have landed on either side of the gun, a fresh set of helicopters and paratroopers is introduced. This is brought about by calling the function **reset( )**, which reinitialises all the variables to their original values. Thus, the enemy helicopters are undepletable, and their attack is never ending.

The Counter Attack

For shooting down the enemy, we use the left and right arrow keys to position the gun and the Enter key for firing the bullets. The function **testkeys( )** finds out which of these three valid keys was pressed and then appropriate actions are brought about. The moment a bullet hits either the helicopter, or the paratrooper, **putimage( )** is called which displays an image indicating a successful hit.

The Gun Blast

You tried your best to shoot down as many helicopters and paratroopers as possible. However, the enemy was smarter still and somehow managed to land four paratroopers on one side of the gun? Here's what happens now. The function **sort( )**, busy sorting the x coordinates of the landed enemy, causes the paratrooper nearest to the gun to approach it. The attack from the left side of the gun is manoeuvred by the function **l_attack( )**, and the one from the right, by **r_attack( )**. Finally, the inevitable explosion of the gun is depicted by **gun_blast( )**, accompanied by the sound programmed through **music( )**.

Program

```
/* =============== Checklist of important variables ================ */
/*
pointers:

parachute           points to image of parachute in memory
heli1               points to image of 1st helicopter in memory
heli2               points to image of 2nd helicopter in memory
gunbase             points to image of gunbase in memory
para                points to image of paratrooper in memory
blast               points to image of helicopter blast in memory
clear               points to blank image in memory
blast_man           points to image of paratrooper blast in memory
clear_man           points to blank image in memory

arrays:

heli_x[8]           stores x coordinates of helicopters
heli_level[8]       stores level ( y coordinates ) of helicopters
no_para[8]          stores no. of paratroopers in each helicopter
h_reached[8]        flags to determine whether heli. reached its destination or
                    not
jump_pt[8][4]       stores x coordinates of each paratrooper at point of jump-
                    ing from helicopter; coordinates change as paratroopers
                    descend.
para_y[8][4]        stores y coordinates of each paratrooper in each helicop-
                    ter
para_alive[8][4]    flags to determine whether paratroopers are alive or not
para_in_heli[8][4]  flags to determine whether paratroopers have jumped or
                    not
p_reached[8][4]     flags to determine whether paratroopers reached the
                    ground or not
bullet_present[50]  flags to determine whether bullets are available for firing
                    or not
```

```
x_left[32]          stores x coordinates of paratroopers landed to the left of
                    the gun
x_right[32]         stores x coordinates of paratroopers landed to the right of
                    the gun
bullet_xdir[50]     stores x-direction of bullets ( x = a * cos ( angle ) )
bullet_ydir[50]     stores y-direction of bullets ( y = a * sin ( angle ) )
bullet_x[50]        stores current x coordinates of bullets
bullet_y[50]        stores current y coordinates of bullets

integers:

maxx                maximum x coordinate of the screen
maxy                maximum y coordinate of the screen
score               points earned by the player
finish              flag to determine the end of the game
lmove               flag to control the movement of the gun towards left
rmove               flag to control the movement of the gun towards right
lnum                total paratroopers reached to the left of the gun
rnum                total paratroopers reached to the right of the gun
la                  flag to start gun attack from left
ra                  flag to start attack from right
id_flag             increment/decrement flag for the angle of the gun
angle               angle of the gun
*/
/* ======================================================== */

# include "graphics.h"
# include "conio.h"
# include "stdio.h"
# include "process.h"
# include "alloc.h"
# include "stdlib.h"
# include "math.h"
# include "dos.h"

void *parachute, *heli1, *heli2, *gunbase, *para ;
void *blast, *clear, *blast_man, *clear_man ;
```

```
float x_dir, y_dir, aspect_ratio, bullet_xdir[50], bullet_ydir[50],
        bullet_x[50], bullet_y[50] ;
int maxx, maxy, bullet_present[50], score, x_left[32], x_right[32], finish ;

/* starting x coordinates of helicopters which change as the helicopters
   move */
int heli_x[8] = { 35, 605, 35, 605, 35, 605, 35, 605 } ;

/* level of helicopters, 7 and 21 being their y coordinates */
int heli_level[8] = { 7, 21, 7, 21, 7, 21, 7, 21 } ;

/* number of paratroopers in each helicopter which would reduce as
   paratroopers jump out */
int no_para[8] = { 4, 4, 4, 4, 4, 4, 4, 4 } ;

/* array which determines whether the helicopter has reached its destination
   or not. 0s would become 1s when helicopters reach their destination */
int h_reached[8] = { 0, 0, 0, 0, 0, 0, 0, 0 } ;

/* x coordinates of paratroopers at the point of jumping from helicopters */
int jump_pt[8][4] = {
                        53, 235, 405, 587,
                        600, 574, 66, 40,
                        79, 196, 444, 561,
                        548, 522, 118, 92,
                        105, 209, 431, 535,
                        496, 470, 170, 144,
                        131, 222, 418, 509,
                        483, 457, 183, 157
                    } ;

/* y coordinates of paratroopers at the point of jumping which change as the
   paratroopers descend */
int para_y[8][4] = {
                        16, 16, 16, 16,
                        30, 30, 30, 30,
                        16, 16, 16, 16,
```

```
                        30, 30, 30, 30,
                        16, 16, 16, 16,
                        30, 30, 30, 30,
                        16, 16, 16, 16,
                        30, 30, 30, 30
        } ;

/* status of paratroopers: 1 - alive   0 - hit */
int para_alive[8][4] = {
                        1, 1, 1, 1,
                        1, 1, 1, 1,
                        1, 1, 1. 1,
                        1, 1, 1, 1,
                        1, 1, 1, 1,
                        1, 1, 1, 1,
                        1, 1, 1, 1,
                        1, 1, 1, 1
        } ;

/* position of paratroopers: 1 - still in helicopter  0 - jumped */
int para_in_heli[8][4] = {
                        1, 1, 1, 1,
                        1, 1, 1, 1,
                        1, 1, 1, 1,
                        1, 1, 1, 1,
                        1, 1, 1, 1,
                        1, 1, 1, 1,
                        1, 1, 1, 1,
                        1, 1, 1, 1
        } ;

/* position of paratroopers: 1 - landed  0 - air-borne */
int p_reached[8][4] = {
                        0, 0, 0, 0,
                        0, 0, 0, 0,
                        0, 0, 0, 0,
                        0, 0, 0, 0,
```

```
                          0, 0, 0, 0,
                          0, 0, 0, 0,
                          0, 0, 0, 0,
                          0, 0, 0, 0
              } ;

main( )
{
    int h = 0, i, j, k, delay_counter = 0, t_para_alive, keystroke, lmove = 0,
            rmove = 0, lnum = 0, rnum = 0 ;
    int la = 0, ra = 0, id_flag = -1, angle = 165, reached_left = 0,
            reached_right = 0 ;

    /* initialise graphic system, draw basic images and save them */
    start( ) ;

    /* draw gunbase */
    gbase( ) ;

    /* draw two helicopters */
    putimage ( heli_x[h] - 33, ( heli_level[h] ) - 5, heli1, OR_PUT ) ;
    putimage ( heli_x[h + 1] - 18, ( heli_level[h + 1] ) - 5, heli2, OR_PUT ) ;

    /* draw gun at specific angle */
    gdraw ( angle, 1 ) ;

    while ( !finish )
    {
        /* display score */
        gotoxy ( 10, 25 ) ;
        printf ( "Score : %4d", score ) ;

        /* if a key is pressed */
        if ( kbhit( ) )
        {
            keystroke = testkeys( ) ;  /* collect the key hit */
```

```
/* left arrow pressed, start moving gun to left */
if ( keystroke == 75 )
{
    lmove = 1 ;
    id_flag = 1 ;  /* set up increment/decrement flag */
}


/* right arrow pressed, start moving gun right */
if ( keystroke == 77 )
{
    rmove = 1 ;
    id_flag = -1 ;  /* set up increment/decrement flag */
}

/* Enter key hit, stop gun & fire bullet */
if ( keystroke == 13 )
{
    lmove = 0 ;
    rmove = 0 ;

    /* search the unfired bullet */
    for ( k = 0 ; k < 50 ; k++ )
    {
        /* if bullet has already been fired */
        if ( bullet_present[k] )
            continue ;
        else
        {
            /* set up direction and coordinates of bullet being
               fired */
            bullet_xdir[k] = x_dir ;
            bullet_ydir[k] = y_dir ;
            bullet_x[k] = 320 + 45 * x_dir ;
            bullet_y[k] = 165 - aspect_ratio * 45 * y_dir ;
            bullet_present[k] = 1 ;

            /* decrement score since a bullet has been fired */
```

```
                score-- ;
                break ;
            }
        }
    }

    fflush ( stdin ) ;
}

/* move the fired bullets */
for ( k = 0 ; k < 50 ; k++ )
{
    /* if bullet has not been fired, search for next bullet */
    if ( !bullet_present[k] )
        continue ;

    /* check whether bullet has crossed the boundary */
    if ( bullet_x[k] >= maxx - 2 || bullet_x[k] <= 2 ||
            bullet_y[k] >= maxy - 2 || bullet_y[k] <= 2 )
        bullet_present[k] = 0 ;

    /* draw the fired bullet at new position */
    if ( bullet_present[k] )
        bdraw ( k, 1 ) ;
}

/* if helicopters exist */
if ( h < 7 )
{
    /* if the pair of helicopters have not reached the destination */
    if ( !h_reached[h] || !h_reached[h + 1] )
    {
        sound ( 5320 ) ;

        for ( i = 0 ; i < 4 ; i++ )
        {
            /* if paratrooper is not in helicopter or paratrooper has
```

```
                been hit */
            if ( !para_in_heli[h][i] || !para_alive[h][i] )
                continue ;
        else
        {
                /* if helicopter has reached beyond the jumping
                   point of paratrooper, eject the paratrooper */
                if ( heli_x[h] >= jump_pt[h][i] )
                {
                        jump_pt[h][i] = heli_x[h] ;
                        putimage ( jump_pt[h][i] - 3, para_y[h][i] - 2,
                                        para, XOR_PUT ) ;
                        para_in_heli[h][i] = 0 ;
                }
        }
    }

    /* if helicopter has passed or it has been hit */
    /* whenever a helicopter is hit, the number of paratroopers
       in it is set to 0 */
    if ( heli_x[h] > maxx - 50 || no_para[h] == 0 )
    {
        h_reached[h]++ ;

        /* erase helicopter from last position */
        if ( h_reached[h] == 1 )
                putimage ( heli_x[h] - 33, ( heli_level[h] ) - 5,
                                heli1, XOR_PUT ) ;
    }
    else
        hmove ( h ) ;  /* move the helicopter */


    for ( i = 0 ; i < 4 ; i++ )
    {
        if ( ! ( para_in_heli[h + 1][i] ) ||
                para_alive[h + 1][i] )
```

```
                continue ;
            else
            {
                if ( heli_x[h + 1] <= jump_pt[h + 1][i] )
                {
                    jump_pt[h + 1][i] = heli_x[h + 1] ;
                    putimage ( jump_pt[h + 1][i] - 3,
                            para_y[h + 1][i] - 2, para, XOR_PUT) ;
                    para_in_heli[h + 1][i] = 0 ;
                }
            }
        }

        if ( heli_x[h + 1] < 50 || no_para[h + 1] == 0 )
        {
            h_reached[h + 1]++ ;
            if ( h_reached[h + 1] == 1 )
                putimage ( heli_x[h + 1] - 18, ( heli_level[h + 1] ) - 5,
                        heli2, XOR_PUT ) ;
        }
        else
            hmove( h + 1 ) ;
    }
    else
    {
        delay_counter++ ;  /* increment delay counter */

        /* the delay ensures that the new pair of helicopters do not
           start off immediately */

        /* check whether new pair of helicopters should start off */
        if ( delay_counter == 30 )
        {
            delay_counter = 0 ;

            /* if 4 paratroopers haven't reached on either side of gun */
            if ( !la && !ra )
```

```
                    {
                        h += 2 ;

                        /* if helicopters have not been exhausted, start the
                           next pair */
                        if ( h < 8 )
                        {
                            putimage ( heli_x[h] - 33, ( heli_level[h] ) - 5,
                                      heli1, OR_PUT ) ;
                            putimage ( heli_x[h + 1] - 18, ( heli_level[h + 1] )
                                      - 5, heli2, OR_PUT ) ;
                        }
                    }
                }
            }
        }

        if ( lmove || rmove )
        {
            /* erase the gun */
            gdraw ( angle, 0 ) ;

            angle += ( id_flag * 15 ) ;

            /* if the gun has reached its extreme left position, stop the gun */
            if ( angle >= 165 )
            {
                angle = 165 ;
                lmove = 0 ;
            }

            /* if the gun has reached its extreme right position, stop the gun */
            if ( angle <= 15 )
            {
                angle = 15 ;
                rmove = 0 ;
            }
```

```
        /* draw the gun */
        gdraw ( angle, 1 ) ;
}

/* for each bullet */
for ( k = 0 ; k < 50 ; k++ )
{
        if ( !bullet_present[k] )
            continue ;

        /* erase the bullet */
        bdraw ( k, 0 ) ;

        /* increment the coordinates of the bullet */
        bullet_x[k]+= ( 6 * bullet_xdir[k] ) ;
        bullet_y[k]-= ( 6 * aspect_ratio * bullet_ydir[k] ) ;
}

t_para_alive = 0 ;

/* monitor movement of each paratrooper of each helicopter */
for ( i = 0 ; i < 8 ; i++ )
{
        for ( j = 0 ; j < 4 ; j++ )
        {
            /* go to the next paratrooper if not air-borne */
            if ( !para_alive[i][j] || para_in_heli[i][j] || p_reached[i][j] )
                continue ;

            /* if paratrooper has landed */
            if ( para_y[i][j] > maxy - 18 )
            {
                p_reached[i][j]++ ;

                if ( p_reached[i][j] == 1 )
                {
```

```
                    /* erase paratrooper and parachute */
                    putimage ( jump_pt[i][j] - 12, para_y[i][j] - 16,
                                parachute, XOR_PUT ) ;
                    putimage ( jump_pt[i][j] - 3, para_y[i][j] - 2,
                                para, XOR_PUT ) ;

                    para_y[i][j] = maxy - 17 ;

                    /* draw paratrooper */
                    putimage ( jump_pt[i][j] - 3, para_y[i][j] - 2,
                                para, OR_PUT ) ;

                    /* if paratrooper has landed to the left of gun */
                    if ( jump_pt[i][j] < 300 )
                    {
                        reached_left++ ;

                        /* save x coordinate of paratrooper */
                        x_left[lnum] = jump_pt[i][j] ;
                        lnum++ ;
                    }
                    else
                    {
                        reached_right++ ;
                        x_right[rnum] = jump_pt[i][j] ;
                        rnum++ ;
                    }
                }

            /* if four or more paratroopers have reached left of gun
               and the attack on the gun has not begun from right */
            if ( reached_left >= 4 && !ra )
            {
                /* sort the x coordinates of paratroopers who have
                   reached the left of gun */
                sort ( x_left, reached_left, 0 ) ;
                la = 1 ;
```

```
                    }
                    else
                    {
                        /* if four or more paratroopers have reached right
                           of gun */
                        if ( reached_right >= 4 )
                        {
                            /* sort the x coordinates of paratroopers who
                               have reached the right of gun */
                            sort ( x_right, reached_right, 1 ) ;
                            ra = 1 ;
                        }
                    }
                }
                else
                {
                    t_para_alive++ ;  /* count no. of paratroopers alive */
                    para_move ( i, j ) ;  /* move the paratrooper */
                }
            }
        }

    /* if four men have landed on left, attack from left */
    if ( la )
        l_attack( ) ;

    /* if four men have landed on right, attack from right */
    if ( ra )
        r_attack( ) ;

    /* if all paratroopers have been hit, all helicopters have vanished and
       the attack has not begun from either side of the gun */
    if ( ( !t_para_alive && ( h >= 7 ) && (!la) && (!ra) ) )
    {
        h = 0 ;

        reset( ) ;  /* initialise all the variables and restart the game */
```

```
                /* display two helicopters */
                putimage ( heli_x[h] - 33, ( heli_level[h] ) - 5, heli1, OR_PUT ) ;
                putimage ( heli_x[h + 1] - 18, ( heli_level[h + 1] ) - 5, heli2,
                        OR_PUT ) ;
        }
        nosound( ) ;
}

        /* game finished blast the gun */
        gunblast( ) ;
        music( ) ;
        nosound( ) ;

        /* wait for a keypress */
        if ( kbhit( ) )
                testkeys( ) ;
        gotoxy ( 33, 24 ) ;
        getch( ) ;

        /* shutdown graphic system and restore original VDU mode */
        closegraph( ) ;
        restorecrtmode( ) ;
}

/* initialises graphics system, draws basic images and saves them */
start( )
{
        int gm, gd = DETECT, key = 0, area ;

        initgraph ( &gd, &gm, "c:\\tc\\bgi" ) ;

        /* save maximum values of x and y coordinates */
        maxx = getmaxx( ) ;
        maxy = getmaxy( ) ;

        /* draw outer rectangle and set up working area */
```

```
rectangle ( 0, 0, maxx, maxy - 10 ) ;
setviewport ( 1, 1, maxx - 1, maxy - 11, 1 ) ;

helidraw ( 50, 50, 0 ) ;  /* draw first helicopter */
helidraw ( 150, 50, 1 ) ;  /* draw second helicopter */
pman ( 50, 80 ) ;  /* draw paratrooper */
paradraw ( 50, 80 ) ;  /* draw parachute */
pman ( 150, 80 ) ;  /* draw paratrooper */
paradraw ( 150, 80 ) ;  /* draw parachute */
gbase( ) ;  /* draw gun base */
draw_blast ( 300, 130 ) ;  /* draw the blast image */

/* calculate and allocate RAM required for storing various images */
area = imagesize ( 0, 0, 51, 10 ) ;
heli1 = malloc ( area ) ;
heli2 = malloc ( area ) ;
area = imagesize ( 0, 0, 24, 13 ) ;
parachute = malloc ( area ) ;
area = imagesize ( 0, 0, 6, 7 ) ;
para = malloc ( area ) ;
area = imagesize ( 0, 0, 40, 9 ) ;
gunbase = malloc ( area ) ;
area = imagesize ( 0, 0, 32, 12 ) ;
blast = malloc ( area ) ;
clear = malloc ( area ) ;
area = imagesize ( 0, 0, 14, 10 ) ;
blast_man = malloc ( area ) ;
clear_man = malloc ( area ) ;

/* if memory allocation fails */
if ( heli1 == NULL || heli2 == NULL || parachute == NULL || para == NULL
    || gunbase == NULL || blast == NULL || clear == NULL ||
        blast_man == NULL || clear_man == NULL )
{
    printf( "\nInsufficient memory... Press any key " ) ;
    getch( ) ;
    closegraph( ) ;
```

```
        restorecrtmode( ) ;
        exit( 0 ) ;
}

/* store images in allocated memory */
getimage( 17, 45, 68, 55, heli1 ) ;
getimage( 132, 45, 183, 55, heli2 ) ;
getimage( 38, 64, 62, 77, parachute ) ;
getimage( 47, 78, 53, 85, para ) ;
getimage ( 300, 158, 340, 177, gunbase ) ;
getimage ( 300 - 16, 100 - 6, 300 + 16, 100 + 6, clear ) ;
getimage ( 330 - 7, 100 - 5, 330 + 7, 100 + 5, clear_man ) ;
getimage ( 300 - 16, 130 - 6, 300 + 16, 130 + 6, blast ) ;
getimage ( 330 - 7, 130 - 5, 330 + 7, 130 + 5, blast_man ) ;

/* set font, alignment and character size */
settextstyle ( GOTHIC_FONT, HORIZ_DIR, 4 ) ;
settextjustify ( CENTER_TEXT, CENTER_TEXT ) ;
outtextxy ( 320, 82, "PARATROOPER" ) ;

setviewport ( 0, 0, maxx, maxy, 1 ) ;
settextstyle ( DEFAULT_FONT, HORIZ_DIR, 0 ) ;
settextjustify ( CENTER_TEXT, TOP_TEXT ) ;
outtextxy ( 39 * 8, 24 * 8, "Press I for Instructions or P for play" ) ;

/* continue till either the alphabet I or P is hit */
while ( key != 'p' && key != 'P' && key != 'i' && key != 'I' )
{
        while ( !kbhit( ) ) ;
        key = testkeys( ) ;
}

if ( key == 'i' || key == 'I' )
        message( ) ;  /* display game instructions */

clearviewport( ) ;
```

```
        rectangle ( 0, 0, maxx, maxy - 10 ) ;
        setviewport ( 1, 1, maxx - 1, maxy - 11, 1 ) ;
}


/* draws helicopter at specified coordinates pointing in specified direction */
helidraw ( x, y, d )
int x, y, d ;
{
    int direction, i, j ;

    if ( d )
        direction = -1 ;
    else
        direction = 1 ;

    i = 3 ;
    j = 8 ;

    line ( x - j - 8, y - i - 2, x + j + 8, y - i - 2 ) ;
    line ( x - j + 5, y - i - 1, x + j - 5, y - i - 1 ) ;
    line ( x - j, y - i, x + j, y - i ) ;
    for ( ; i > 0 ; i--, j += 2 )
    {
        putpixel ( x - ( direction * j ), y - i, 1 ) ;
        line ( x + ( direction * j ), y - i, x + ( direction * ( j - 8 ) ), y - i ) ;
    }

    i = 0 ;
    j -= 2 ;

    line ( x - ( direction * j ), y - i, x - ( direction * ( j + 17 ) ), y - i ) ;
    line ( x - ( direction * j ), y - i + 1, x - ( direction * ( j + 7 ) ), y - i + 1 ) ;
    putpixel ( x - ( direction * ( j + 19 ) ), y - i - 1, 1 ) ;

    for ( ; i < 3 ; i++, j -= 2 )
    {
        putpixel ( x - j, y + i, 1 ) ;
```

```
            putpixel ( x + j, y + i, 1 ) ;
        }

        line ( x - j, y + i, x + j, y + i ) ;
        putpixel ( x - j + 3, y + i + 1, 1 ) ;
        putpixel ( x + j - 3, y + i + 1, 1 ) ;
        line ( x - j - 10, y + i + 2, x + j + 10, y + i + 2 ) ;
        putpixel ( x + ( direction * ( j + 12 ) ), y + i + 1, 1 ) ;
}


/* draws paratrooper at specified position */
pman ( x, y )
int x, y ;
{
        rectangle ( x - 1, y - 2, x + 1, y + 2 ) ;
        line ( x, y - 2, x, y + 2 ) ;
        line ( x - 3, y, x + 3, y ) ;
        line ( x - 3, y + 3, x - 3, y + 5 ) ;
        line ( x + 3, y + 3, x + 3, y + 5 ) ;
}


/* draws parachute at specified position */
paradraw ( x, y )
int x, y ;
{
        ellipse ( x, y - 11, 0, 180, 12, 5 ) ;
        line ( x - 12, y - 11, x + 12, y - 11 ) ;
        floodfill ( x, y - 12, 1 ) ;
        line ( x - 12, y - 10, x - 3, y - 3 ) ;
        line ( x + 12, y - 10, x + 3, y - 3 ) ;
}


/* draws gun base */
gbase( )
{
        rectangle ( 280, 171, 360, 189 ) ;
        floodfill ( 282, 173, 1 ) ;
```

```
        line ( 300, 165, 300, 171 ) ;
        line ( 340, 165, 340, 171 ) ;
        ellipse ( 320, 165, 0, 180, 20, 7 ) ;
        floodfill ( 310, 169, 1 ) ;
}

/* draws or erases gun at given angle */
gdraw ( angle, color )
int angle, color ;
{
        int oy = 165, lx = 315, rx = 325, r = 40 ;
        float x1, x2, ly, ry, y1, y2 ;

        setcolor ( color ) ;
        aspect_ratio = 5.0 / 16.0 ;
        x_dir = cos ( 3.14 / 180 * angle ) ;
        y_dir = sin ( 3.14 / 180 * angle ) ;

        x1 = lx + r * x_dir ;
        x2 = rx + r * x_dir ;

        ly = oy - aspect_ratio * 4 * sin ( 3.14 / 180 * ( angle + 90 ) ) ;
        ry = oy - aspect_ratio * 4 * sin ( 3.14 / 180 * ( angle - 90 ) ) ;
        y1 = ly - aspect_ratio * r * y_dir ;
        y2 = ry - aspect_ratio * r * y_dir ;

        line ( lx, ly, x1, y1 ) ;
        line ( rx, ry, x2, y2 ) ;
        line ( x1, y1, x2, y2 ) ;
        line ( lx, ly, rx, ry ) ;
        putimage ( 300, 158, gunbase, OR_PUT ) ;
        setcolor ( WHITE ) ;
}

/* draws or erases bullet */
bdraw ( bno, color )
int bno, color ;
```

```
{
    setcolor ( color ) ;
    putpixel ( bullet_x[bno], bullet_y[bno], color ) ;
    setcolor ( WHITE ) ;
}


/* moves the specified helicopter */
hmove ( hno )
int hno ;
{
    /* if the helicopter which moves from left to right */
    if ( hno % 2 == 0 )
    {
        putimage ( heli_x[hno] - 33, ( heli_level[hno] ) - 5, heli1, XOR_PUT ) ;

        /* if the helicopter is hit by bullet */
        if ( check_h ( hno ) )
        {
            score += 20 ;
            return ;
        }

        heli_x[hno] += 6 ;
        putimage ( heli_x[hno] - 33, ( heli_level[hno] ) - 5, heli1, OR_PUT ) ;
    }
    else
    {
        putimage ( heli_x[hno] - 18, ( heli_level[hno] ) - 5, heli2, XOR_PUT ) ;

        if ( check_h ( hno ) )
        {
            score += 20 ;
            return ;
        }

        heli_x[hno] -= 6 ;
        putimage ( heli_x[hno] - 18, ( heli_level[hno] ) - 5, heli2, OR_PUT ) ;
```

```
    }
}

/* moves the specified paratrooper */
para_move ( h, i )
int h, i ;
{
    if ( para_y[h][i] > 100 )
        putimage ( jump_pt[h][i] - 12, para_y[h][i] - 16, parachute, XOR_PUT ) ;
    putimage ( jump_pt[h][i] - 3, para_y[h][i] - 2, para, XOR_PUT ) ;

    /* if the paratrooper is hit by bullet */
    if ( check_m ( h, i ) )
    {
        score += 10 ;
        return ;
    }

    /* if the parachute is hit by bullet */
    if ( ( ( para_y[h][i] > 100 ) && check_p ( h, i ) )
    {
        score += 10 ;
        return ;
    }

    para_y[h][i] += 2 ;

    /* if paratrooper's y coordinate exceeds 100, draw parachute */
    if ( para_y[h][i] > 100 )
        putimage ( jump_pt[h][i] - 12, para_y[h][i] - 16, parachute, OR_PUT ) ;

    /* draw paratrooper at new position */
    putimage ( jump_pt[h][i] - 3, para_y[h][i] - 2, para, OR_PUT ) ;
}

/* checks whether helicopter is hit by bullet or not */
check_h ( hno )
```

```
int hno ;
{
    int j, k, c1 = 0, c2 = 0, c3 = 0, c4 = 0 ;

    for ( k = 0 ; k < 50 ; k++ )
    {
        if ( !bullet_present[k] )
            continue ;

        /* check if body of helicopter is hit */
        c1 = ( ( bullet_y[k] >= heli_level[hno] - 5 ) &&
               ( bullet_y[k] <= heli_level[hno] + 5 ) ) ;
        c2 = ( ( bullet_x[k] >= heli_x[hno] - 18 ) &&
               ( bullet_x[k] <= heli_x[hno] + 18 ) ) ;

        /* check if tail of helicopter is hit */
        c3 = ( ( bullet_y[k] >= heli_level[hno] ) &&
               ( bullet_y[k] <= heli_level[hno] + 1 ) ) ;
        if ( ( hno % 2 ) )
            c4 = ( ( bullet_x[k] >= heli_x[hno] + 18 ) &&
                   ( bullet_x[k] <= heli_x[hno] + 33 ) ) ;
        else
            c4 = ( ( bullet_x[k] >= heli_x[hno] - 33 ) &&
                   ( bullet_x[k] <= heli_x[hno] - 18 ) ) ;

        if ( ( c1 && c2 ) || ( c3 && c4 ) )
        {
            no_para[hno] = 0 ;
            h_reached[hno] = 1 ;
            for ( j = 0 ; j < 4 ; j++ )
            {
                /* if paratrooper is inside the helicopter that has been hit */
                if ( para_in_heli[hno][j] )
                    para_alive[hno][j] = 0 ;
            }

            /* stop the movement of the bullet that has hit the helicopter */
```

```
                    bullet_present[k] = 0 ;
                    bdraw ( k, 0 ) ;  /* erase that bullet */

                    /* display blast image */
                    putimage ( heli_x[hno], heli_level[hno], blast, OR_PUT ) ;

                    sound ( 250 ) ;
                    delay ( 500 ) ;
                    nosound( ) ;

                    /* clear blast image */
                    putimage ( heli_x[hno], heli_level[hno], clear, COPY_PUT ) ;

                    return ( 1 ) ;  /* report that a blast has occurred */
                }
        }
        return ( 0 ) ;  /* report that a blast hasn't occurred */
}

/* checks whether paratrooper from the specified helicopter is hit by bullet or
   not */
check_m ( hno, pno )
int hno, pno ;
{
        int k, c1 = 0, c2 = 0 ;

        for ( k = 0 ; k < 50 ; k++ )
        {
                if ( !bullet_present[k] )
                        continue ;

                c1 = ( ( bullet_y[k] >= para_y[hno][pno] - 2 ) &&
                        ( bullet_y[k] <= para_y[hno][pno] + 6 ) ) ;
                c2 = ( ( bullet_x[k] >= jump_pt[hno][pno] - 3 ) &&
                        ( bullet_x[k] <= jump_pt[hno][pno] + 3 ) ) ;

                if ( c1 && c2 )
```

```
                {
                        para_alive[hno][pno] = 0 ;

                        /* stop the movement of the bullet that has hit the helicopter */
                        bullet_present[k] = 0 ;
                        bdraw ( k, 0 ) ;  /* erase that bullet */

                        /* display blast image */
                        putimage ( jump_pt[hno][pno], para_y[hno][pno] + 2, blast_man,
                                   OR_PUT ) ;

                        sound ( 500 ) ;
                        delay ( 500 ) ;
                        nosound( ) ;

                        /* erase blast image */
                        putimage ( jump_pt[hno][pno], para_y[hno][pno] + 2, clear_man,
                                   COPY_PUT ) ;

                        return ( 1 ) ;  /* report that a blast has occurred */
                }
        }
        return ( 0 ) ;  /* report that a blast hasn't occurred */
}

/* checks whether the parachute has been hit by the bullet or not */
check_p ( hno, pno )
int hno, pno ;
{
        int k, c1 = 0, c2 = 0 ;

        for ( k = 0 ; k < 50 ; k++ )
        {
                if ( !bullet_present[k] )
                        continue ;

                c1 = ( ( bullet_y[k] >= para_y[hno][pno] - 16 ) &&
```

```
                    ( bullet_y[k] <= para_y[hno][pno] -3 ) ) ;
            c2 = ( ( bullet_x[k] >= jump_pt[hno][pno] - 12 ) &&
                    ( bullet_x[k] <= jump_pt[hno][pno] + 12 ) ) ;

        if ( c1 && c2 )
        {
            para_alive[hno][pno] = 0 ;

            /* stop the movement of the bullet that has hit the helicopter */
            bullet_present[k] = 0 ;
            bdraw ( k, 0 ) ;  /* erase that bullet */

            /* display the blast image */
            putimage ( jump_pt[hno][pno], para_y[hno][pno] - 7, blast_man,
                        OR_PUT ) ;

            sound ( 500 ) ;
            delay ( 500 ) ;
            nosound( ) ;

            /* erase the blast image */
            putimage ( jump_pt[hno][pno]. para_y[hno][pno] - 7, clear_man,
                        COPY_PUT )

            return ( 1 ) ; /* report that a blast has occurred */
        }
    }
    return ( 0 ) ; /* report that a blast hasn't occurred */
}

/* returns the ascii or scan code of the key hit */
testkeys( )
{
    union REGS ii, oo ;

    ii.h.ah = 0 ;
    int86 ( 22, &ii, &oo ) ;
```

```
        /* if ascii code is not 0 */
        if ( oo.h.al )
            return ( oo.h.al ) ;  /* return ascii code */
        else
            return ( oo.h.ah ) ;  /* return scan code */
}

/* sorts the x coordinates of the paratroopers who have landed */
sort ( spx, count, f )
int *spx, count, f ;
{
    int tmp, i, j ;

    /* if paratroopers on left of gun are being considered then sort
       x coordinates in descending order otherwise in ascending order */
    for ( i = 0 ; i < count - 1 ; i++ )
    {
        for ( j = i + 1 ; j < count ; j++ )
        {
            if ( f )
            {
                if ( spx[j] < spx[i] )
                {
                    tmp = spx[j] ;
                    spx[j] = spx[i] ;
                    spx[i] = tmp ;
                }
            }
            else
            {
                if ( spx[j] > spx[i] )
                {
                    tmp = spx[j] ;
                    spx[j] = spx[i] ;
                    spx[i] = tmp ;
                }
```

```
            }
        }
    }
}

/* carries out the attack from right */
r_attack( )
{
    static int i, k, r = 365 ;

    /* move first two paratroopers upto the gun base */
    while( k <= 1 )
    {
        while ( x_right[k] > r )
        {
            /* erase paratrooper from existing position */
            putimage ( x_right[k] - 3, maxy - 17 - 2, para, XOR_PUT ) ;

            x_right[k] -= 2 ;

            /* draw paratrooper at new position */
            putimage ( x_right[k] - 3, maxy - 17 - 2, para, OR_PUT ) ;
            return ;
        }
        k++ ;
        r += 10 ;
    }

    /* if first two paratroopers have reached upto the gun base */
    if ( !i )
    {
        k-- ;
        r -= 10 ;

        /* place one paratrooper on the head of another */
        putimage ( x_right[k] - 3, maxy - 17 - 2, para, XOR_PUT ) ;
        putimage ( x_right[k - 1] - 3, maxy - 17 - 10, para, OR_PUT ) ;
```

```
            i++ ;
            k++ ;
            return ;
        }

    /* move third and fourth paratroopers upto the first one */
    while ( k <= 3 )
    {
        while ( x_right[k] > r )
        {
            putimage ( x_right[k] - 3, maxy - 17 - 2, para, XOR_PUT ) ;
            x_right[k] -= 2 ;
            putimage ( x_right[k] - 3, maxy - 17 - 2, para, OR_PUT ) ;
            return ;
        }

        k++ ;
        r += 10 ;
    }

    /* if three paratroopers have already reached gun base */
    if ( i == 1 )
    {
        k-- ;

        /* place fourth paratrooper on the head of third */
        putimage ( x_right[k] - 3, maxy - 17 - 2, para, XOR_PUT ) ;
        putimage ( x_right[k - 1] - 3, maxy - 17 - 10, para, OR_PUT ) ;
        k++ ;
        i++ ;
        return ;
    }

    /* if fourth paratrooper has climbed on the head of third */
    if ( i == 2 )
    {
```

```
        k-- ;

        /* erase fourth paratrooper who is standing on the head of third */
        putimage ( x_right[k - 1] - 3, maxy - 17 - 10, para, XOR_PUT ) ;

        /* place fourth paratrooper on the head of second */
        putimage ( x_right[k - 3] - 3, maxy - 17 - 20, para, OR_PUT ) ;

        delay ( 400 ) ;

        /* erase fourth paratrooper who is standing on the head of second */
        putimage ( x_right[k - 3] - 3, maxy - 17 - 20, para, XOR_PUT ) ;

        /* let fourth paratrooper climb on the gun */
        putimage ( x_right[k - 3] - 3 - 10, maxy - 17 - 20, para, OR_PUT ) ;

        finish = 1 ;  /* gun is about to be blasted, game over */
        return ;
    }
}

/* carries out the attack from left */
l_attack( )
{
    static int i, k, r = 275 ;

    /* move first two paratroopers upto the gun base */
    while( k <= 1 )
    {
        while ( x_left[k] < r )
        {
            /* erase paratrooper from existing position */
            putimage ( x_left[k] - 3, maxy - 17 - 2, para, XOR_PUT ) ;

            x_left[k] += 2 ;

            /* draw paratrooper at new position */
```

```
            putimage ( x_left[k] - 3, maxy - 17 - 2, para, OR_PUT ) ;
            return ;
        }
        k++ ;
        r -= 10 ;
    }

    /* if first two paratroopers have reached upto the gun base */
    if ( !i )
    {
        k-- ;
        r += 10 ;

        /* place one paratrooper on the head of another */
        putimage ( x_left[k] - 3, maxy - 17 - 2, para, XOR_PUT ) ;
        putimage ( x_left[k - 1] - 3, maxy - 17 - 10, para, OR_PUT ) ;

        i++ ;
        k++ ;
        return ;
    }

    /* move third and fourth paratroopers upto the first one */
    while ( k <= 3 )
    {
        while ( x_left[k] < r )
        {
            putimage ( x_left[k] - 3, maxy - 17 - 2, para, XOR_PUT ) ;
            x_left[k] += 2 ;
            putimage ( x_left[k] - 3, maxy - 17 - 2, para, OR_PUT ) ;
            return ;
        }
        k++ ;
        r -= 10 ;
    }

    /* if three paratroopers have already reached gun base */
```

```
        if ( i == 1 )
        {
            k-- ;
            putimage ( x_left[k] - 3, maxy - 17 - 2, para, XOR_PUT ) ;
            putimage ( x_left[k - 1] - 3, maxy - 17 - 10, para, OR_PUT ) ;
            k++ ;
            i++ ;
            return ;
        }

        /* if fourth paratrooper has climbed on the head of third */
        if ( i == 2 )
        {
            k-- ;

            /* erase fourth paratrooper who is standing on the head of third */
            putimage ( x_left[k - 1] - 3, maxy - 17 - 10, para, XOR_PUT ) ;

            /* place fourth paratrooper on the head of second */
            putimage ( x_left[k - 3] - 3, maxy - 17 - 20, para, OR_PUT ) ;

            delay ( 400 ) ;

            /* erase fourth paratrooper who is standing on the head of second */
            putimage ( x_left[k - 3] - 3, maxy - 17 - 20, para, XOR_PUT ) ;

            /* let fourth paratrooper climb on the gun */
            putimage ( x_left[k - 3] - 3 + 10, maxy - 17 - 20, para, OR_PUT ) ;

            finish = 1 ;  /* gun is about to be blasted, game over */
            return ;
        }
}

/* draws the blast image */
draw_blast ( x, y )
int x, y ;
```

```
{
    line ( x - 16, y - 6, x - 10, y - 2 ) ;
    line ( x - 10, y - 2, x - 16, y ) ;
    line ( x - 16, y, x - 10, y + 2 ) ;
    line ( x - 10, y + 3, x - 16, y + 6 ) ;

    line ( x - 16, y + 6, x - 4, y + 2 ) ;
    line ( x - 4, y + 2, x, y + 6 ) ;
    line ( x, y + 6, x + 4, y + 2 ) ;
    line ( x + 4, y + 2, x + 16, y + 6 ) ;

    line ( x - 16, y - 6, x - 4, y - 2 ) ;
    line ( x - 4, y - 2, x, y - 6 ) ;
    line ( x, y - 6, x + 4, y - 2 ) ;
    line ( x + 4, y - 2, x + 16, y - 6 ) ;

    line ( x + 16, y - 6, x + 10, y - 2 ) ;
    line ( x + 10, y - 2, x + 16, y ) ;
    line ( x + 16, y, x + 10, y + 2 ) ;
    line ( x + 10, y + 2, x + 16, y + 6 ) ;

    x += 30 ;

    line ( x - 7, y - 5, x - 3, y - 2 ) ;
    line ( x - 3, y - 2, x - 7, y ) ;
    line ( x - 7, y, x - 3, y + 2 ) ;
    line ( x - 3, y + 3, x - 7, y + 5 ) ;

    line ( x - 7, y + 5, x - 2, y + 2 ) ;
    line ( x - 2, y + 2, x, y + 5 ) ;
    line ( x, y + 5, x + 2, y + 2 ) ;
    line ( x + 2, y + 2, x + 7, y + 5 ) ;

    line ( x - 7, y - 5, x - 2, y - 2 ) ;
    line ( x - 2, y - 2, x, y - 5 ) ;
    line ( x, y - 5, x + 2, y - 2 ) ;
    line ( x + 2, y - 2, x + 7, y - 5 ) ;
```

```
        line ( x + 7, y - 5, x + 3, y - 2 ) ;
        line ( x + 3, y - 2, x + 7, y ) ;
        line ( x + 7, y, x + 3, y + 2 ) ;
        line ( x + 3, y + 2, x + 7, y + 5 ) ;
}

/* blasts the gun at the end of the game */
gunblast( )
{
        void *a1, *a2, *a3, *a4 ;
        int area, i ;

        area = imagesize ( 0, 0, 10, 2 ) ;
        a1 = malloc ( area ) ;
        a2 = malloc ( area ) ;
        a3 = malloc ( area ) ;
        a4 = malloc ( area ) ;

        getimage ( 310, 173, 320, 175, a1 ) ;
        getimage ( 325, 173, 335, 175, a2 ) ;
        getimage ( 315, 168, 325, 170, a3 ) ;
        getimage ( 330, 165, 340, 167, a4 ) ;

        putimage ( 304, 158, blast, COPY_PUT ) ;

        for ( i = 0 ; i < 40 ; i += 2 )
        {
            putimage ( 310 - i * 3, 177 - i * 2, a1, XOR_PUT ) ;
            putimage ( 325 + i * 3, 177 - i * 2, a2, XOR_PUT ) ;

            putimage ( 310 - i , 177 - i * 2, a1, XOR_PUT ) ;
            putimage ( 325 + i , 177 - i * 2, a2, XOR_PUT ) ;

            putimage ( 310 - i * 4, 177 - i * 2, a1, XOR_PUT ) ;
            putimage ( 325 + i * 4, 177 - i * 2, a2, XOR_PUT ) ;
```

```
                putimage ( 310 - i * 7, 177 - i * 2, a1, XOR_PUT ) ;
                putimage ( 325 + i * 7, 177 - i * 2, a2, XOR_PUT ) ;

                putimage ( 315 - i * 3, 170 - i * 2, a1, XOR_PUT ) ;
                putimage ( 330 + i * 3, 167 - i * 2, a2, XOR_PUT ) ;
            }
        }

/* initialises the variables and restarts the game */
reset( )
{
        int i, j, k ;

        for ( i = 0 ; i < 8 ; i++ )
        {
            if ( i % 2 )
            {
                k = 30 ;
                heli_x[i] = 605 ;
            }
            else
            {
                k = 16 ;
                heli_x[i] = 35 ;
            }
            no_para[i] = 4 ;
            h_reached[i] = 0 ;

            for ( j = 0 ; j < 4 ; j++ )
            {
                para_y[i][j] = k ;
                para_alive[i][j] = 1 ;
                para_in_heli[i][j] = 1 ;
                p_reached[i][j] = 0 ;
            }
        }
}
```

```
/* displays the instructions of the game */
message( )
{
    int sp = 0 ;

    clearviewport( ) ;

    gotoxy ( 31, 2 ) ;
    printf ( "* Your Mission *" ) ;
    gotoxy ( 4, 4 ) ;
    printf ( "Do not allow enemy paratroopers to land on either side of your
             gunbase." ) ;
    gotoxy ( 4, 5 ) ;
    printf ( "If four paratroopers land on one side of your base, they will
             overpower" ) ;
    gotoxy ( 4, 6 ) ;
    printf ( "your defenses and blow up your gun.  " ) ;
    gotoxy ( 4, 8 ) ;
    printf ( "The arrow keys & Enter key control your gun and firing of your
             bullets." ) ;
    gotoxy ( 10, 10 ) ;
    printf ( "<-  Counter clock wise          -> Clock wise " ) ;

    gotoxy ( 4, 12 ) ;
    printf ( "Using Enter key, stop the movement of the gun and fire bullets. " ) ;

    gotoxy ( 15, 15 ) ;
    printf ( "If you hit a HELICOPTER  --  20 points" ) ;
    gotoxy ( 15, 17 ) ;
    printf ( "If you hit a PARATROOPER --  10 points" ) ;
    gotoxy ( 15, 19 ) ;
    printf ( "Each bullet fired costs you 1 point" ) ;
    gotoxy ( 4, 21 ) ;
    printf ( "Press <SPACE> to continue..." ) ;

    /* continue till a space is hit */
```

```
        while ( sp != 32 )
        {
            while ( !kbhit( ) ) ;
            sp = testkeys( ) ;
        }

        clearviewport( ) ;
}

/* plays music at the end of the game */
music( )
{
    int i, j ;

    delay ( 1 ) ;

    for ( j = 0 ; j < 3 ; j++ )
    {
        for ( i = 0 ; i <= 10 ; i++ )
        {
            sound ( 150 + i * 10 ) ;
            delay ( 100 ) ;
        }
        nosound( ) ;
    }
}
```

User Defined Functions

bdraw( )	Draws a bullet at specific location.
check_h( )	Checks whether the bullet has hit the helicopter.
check_m( )	Checks whether the bullet has hit the paratrooper.
check_p( )	Checks whether the bullet has hit the parachute.
draw_blast( )	Draws the blast image which is used when a helicopter or a paratrooper is hit by a bullet.
gbase( )	Draws base of the gun.
gdraw( )	Draws gun at the specified angle.
gunblast( )	Draws the image indicating the blasting of the gun by the paratroopers.
helidraw( )	Draws a helicopter.
hmove( )	Controls the movement of the helicopters.
l_attack( )	Controls the movement of the paratroopers when four of them reach on left side of the gun.
message( )	Displays the instructions for playing the game.
music( )	Plays the music at the end of the game.
paradraw( )	Draws a parachute.
para_move( )	Controls the movement of the paratroopers.
pman( )	Draws a paratrooper.
reset( )	Initialises all the variables required for the game if the set of 8 helicopters and 32 paratroopers could not blast the gun.
r_attack( )	Controls the movement of the paratroopers when four of them reach on right side of the gun.
sort( )	Sorts the x coordinates of the landed paratroopers such that the nearest paratrooper approaches the gun first. On left side of the gun the sorting is in descending order whereas, on right side it is in ascending order.
start( )	Initialises graphics system, draws various images like helicopters, paratroopers, gun, etc. and saves those images in memory.

testkeys( )   Checks the key pressed and returns either the ascii
                     code or the scan code.

7

Assorted Utilities

This chapter contains utilities which couldn't be included in any of the earlier chapters but are still good enough to justify a full chapter devoted to themselves. Utilities which let you view the boot sector and the partition table, edit any sector on the disk, change internal DOS commands, diskcopy a disk and more. All the seven programs developed here are independent and unrelated, so you can start with any one of them. And I am sure at the end you will appreciate how apparently difficult things are handled with amazing ease by C. Let's begin with the first program.

Tie your Bootstraps

By far the most widely used storage medium are the floppy disks. They come in various sizes and capacities but they all work basically in the same way: Information is magnetically encoded on their surface in patterns. Although the type of storage device is important, it is the way the stored information is laid out and managed that concerns C programmers most. Every floppy disk is divided into four separate areas. These are: (a) Boot sector (b) File Allocation Table (c) Directory (d) Data space. Let us now explore the boot sector.

Sector 1 on side 0, track 0 of a floppy disk is known as boot sector. The Boot sector on the floppy disk contains two things, namely, Boot parameters and the Disk bootstrap program. Boot parameters contain vital information about how the disk has been formatted. The list of boot parameters is given below.

Description	Length	Typical Values
Jump instruction	3 bytes	EB 34 90
System ID	8 bytes	IBM 3.0
No. of bytes per sector	2 bytes	512
No. of sectors per cluster	1 byte	2
No. of sectors in reserved area	2 bytes	1
No. of copies of FAT	1 byte	2
No. of root directory entries	2 bytes	112
Total number of sectors	2 bytes	720
Media descriptor	1 byte	FD
No. of sectors per FAT	2 bytes	2
No. of sectors per track	2 bytes	9
No. of sides	2 bytes	2
No. of hidden sectors	2 bytes	0

Figure 7.1

How do we access this information from the floppy disk? You may not be able to imagine to begin with. But the Turbo C compiler is a fatherly old chap. It understands the pressures that a C programmer has to contend with and hence provides a standard library function called **absread( )** which lets you access any sector on the floppy disk. So tie your bootstraps and try this program. Be forewarned that this program would work correctly only if the boot sector has not been virused.

```
# include "dos.h"
# include "stdio.h"
```

```
main( )
{
    struct boot
    {
        unsigned char jump[3] ;
        char system_id[8] ;
        int bytes_per_sec ;
        unsigned char sec_per_clus ;
        int res_sec ;
        unsigned char fat_copies ;
        int root_dir_entry ;
        unsigned int no_sects ;
        unsigned char format_id ;
        int sec_per_fat ;
        int sec_per_trk ;
        int no_sides ;
        int no_sp_res_sect ;
        char rest_code[482] ;
    } ;

    struct boot b ;
    int drive, i ;

    clrscr( ) ;

    printf ( "Enter drive no. 0 = A, 1 = B, 2 = C, ..." ) ;
    scanf ( "%d", &drive ) ;

    absread ( drive, 1, 0, &b ) ;

    printf ( "\n\nJump instruction" ) ;
    for ( i = 0 ; i < 3 ; i++ )
        printf ( " %X", b.jump[i] ) ;

    printf ( "\nSystem ID %s\n", b.system_id ) ;
    printf ( "Bytes per sector %d\n", b.bytes_per_sec ) ;
```

```
    printf ( "Sectors per cluster %d\n", b.sec_per_clus ) ;
    printf ( "Reserved sectors %d\n", b.res_sec ) ;
    printf ( "FAT copies %d\n", b.fat_copies ) ;
    printf ( "Root directory entries %d\n", b.root_dir_entry ) ;
    printf ( "No. of sectors on disk %u\n", b.no_sects ) ;
    printf ( "Format ID %X\n", b.format_id ) ;
    printf ( "Sectors per FAT %d\n", b.sec_per_fat ) ;
    printf ( "Sectors per track %d\n", b.sec_per_trk ) ;
    printf ( "No of sides %d\n", b.no_sides ) ;
    printf ( "No of reserved sectors %d\n", b.no_sp_res_sect ) ;
}
```

The best way to master any concept is to experiment with it. So let
your mind roam free with **absread( )** and then turn to the next piece.

Exploring the Partition Table

Boot sector is alright, but the murky depths of Partition Table (PT)
don't look terribly inviting to most people. It is viewed as sinister and
full of technical details that most people do not want to test their
strengths with. But if we examine the PT with a thick lens it is straight
and simple. Moreover, since you have been using hard disks since
you were knee-high in Computers, it's all the more meaningful to get
to know the details of the PT. After all it is the driving force behind
the hard disk.

The PT exists only on the hard disk. This is because today we have
hard disks which range in capacity from 20 MB to 300 MB. So huge
is this capacity that it would be foolish to use the entire hard disk only
for DOS. Hence it is divided into several logical parts called partitions. One partition may contain DOS whereas the other might
contain Xenix and so on. The hard disk is partitioned using DOS's
FDISK command. While partitioning the hard disk, FDISK stores the
details like where one partition ends and the next begins, which is the
bootable partition etc. in the first physical sector (side 0, track 0,

sector 1). It also stores a program called the 'Master Boot Program' in the PT. Thus a PT consists of the data part and the code part. The following figure shows how the PT is logically divided.

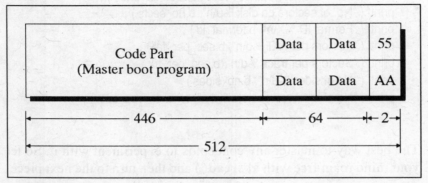

Figure 7.2

The data part begins at 447th byte. The last two bytes in the PT are always 0x55, 0xAA. The data part is 64 bytes long and is further divided into four parts of 16 bytes each. Each 16 byte chunk consists of information about a partition on the hard disk. Hence there can be a maximum of four partitions on the hard disk. The break-up of the 16 bytes is given below.

Byte	Meaning
0	Boot indicator. Contains 0x80 for the active partition, 0 for all others. Only one partition can be active at a time.
1	Side where the partition begins.
2	The low 6 bits are the sector where the partition begins. The high 2 bits are the 2 high bits of the track where the partition begins.

Figure 7.3

Byte	Meaning
3	Low 8 bits of the track where the partition begins
4	Partition type indicator. The following values may exist. 0 - Unused partition 1 - DOS with 12-bit FAT 2 - Xenix partition 4 - DOS with 16-bit FAT 5 - Extended partition 6 - Huge partition
5	Side where the partition ends.
6	Low 6 bits are the sector where the partition ends. The high 2 bits are the high 2 bits of ending track number.
7	Low 8 bits of the track number where the partition ends.
8-11	Number of sectors preceding the partition.
12-15	Number of sectors in the partition.

Figure 7.3 (Continued)

Once these details have been imbibed it is fairly simple to write a program to explore the PT on your hard disk. Let us now put this theory into a program.

```c
# include "bios.h"

struct partition
{
    unsigned char bootable ;
    unsigned char start_side ;
    unsigned int start_sec_cyl ;
    unsigned char parttype ;
    unsigned char end_side ;
    unsigned int end_sec_cyl ;
    unsigned long part_beg ;
```

```c
    unsigned long plen ;
} ;

struct part
{
    unsigned char master_boot[446] ;
    struct partition pt[4] ;
    int lasttwo ;
} ;

struct part p ;

main( )
{
    unsigned int s_sec, s_trk, e_sec, e_trk, i, t1, t2 ;
    char type[20], boot[5] ;

    biosdisk ( 2, 0x80, 0, 0, 1, 1, &p ) ;
    printf("\nPart.  Boot  Starting location    Ending  Location   Relative \
            Number of");
    printf("\nType       Side Cylinder Sector  Side Cylinder Sector  Sectors\
            Sectors\n" );

    for ( i = 0 ; i <= 3 ; i++ )
    {
        if ( p.pt[i].bootable == 0x80 )
            strcpy ( boot, "Yes" ) ;
        else
            strcpy ( boot, "No" ) ;

        switch ( p.pt[i].parttype )
        {
            case 0 :
                strcpy ( type, "Unused" ) ;
                break ;

            case 1 :
```

```
                     strcpy ( type, "12-Bit" ) ;
                     break ;

            case 2 :
                     strcpy ( type, "Xenix" ) ;
                     break ;

            case 4 :
                     strcpy ( type, "16-Bit" ) ;
                     break ;

            case 5 :
                     strcpy ( type, "Extended" ) ;
                     break ;

            case 6 :
                     strcpy ( type, "Huge" ) ;
                     break ;

            default :
                     strcpy ( type, "Unknown" ) ;
                     break ;
       }

       s_sec = ( p.pt[i].start_sec_cyl & 0x3f ) ;
       t1 = ( p.pt[i].start_sec_cyl & 0xff00 ) >> 8 ;
       t2 = ( p.pt[i].start_sec_cyl & 0x00c0 ) << 2 ;
       s_trk = t1 | t2 ;

       e_sec = ( p.pt[i].end_sec_cyl & 0x3f ) ;
       t1 = ( p.pt[i].end_sec_cyl & 0xff00 ) >> 8 ;
       t2 = ( p.pt[i].end_sec_cyl & 0x00c0 ) << 2 ;
       e_trk = t1 | t2 ;

       printf ( "\n%6s   %3s", type, boot ) ;
       printf ( "%4d %6d %8d", p.pt[i].start_side, s_trk,s_sec ) ;
       printf ( "%7d %6u %8u", p.pt[i].end_side, e_trk, e_sec ) ;
```

```
        printf ( "%8lu %10lu" , p.pt[i].part_beg,  p.pt[i].plen ) ;
    }
}
```

Refer Figure 8.3 while reading the above code. It would help you to understand the program better. To amalgamate the disparate bodies in the data part of the PT, what we need is a structure. So first we create a structure **struct partition**, 16 bytes long. But as we know the PT contains 4 such data blocks, alongwith 446 bytes of code and 0x55, 0xAA at the end. To combine these we need another structure - hence the definition **struct part**. Having created the space to store the contents of PT, we make a call to **biosdisk( )** to read the contents of side 0, track 0, sector 1. Once the contents are read, we enter into a **for** loop within which we separate out the information about each partition and display it on the screen.

Examine the program carefully and hold it to the light of all that you have imbibed so far and appreciate how nasty looking concepts can be easily mastered using C.

PC Tools be not Proud!

When I ran PC Tools for the first time, it left me wondering from where do software developers acquire so much of technical knowledge and develop such best-selling software packages. More so when the technical details are not documented in books.

One thing that I found most impressive in PC Tools was the option View/Edit a sector. This option reads a sector from the floppy disk and produces a hex and ascii dump of the sector on the screen. Here is a program which does just this.

```
# include "conio.h"
# include "dos.h"
```

```
main( )
{
    int num, r, c, i = 0, s = 0 ;
    unsigned char buffer[512] ;

    absread ( 0, 1, 0, buffer ) ;

    for ( num = 1 ; num <= 2 ; num++ )
    {
        clrscr( ) ;

        gotoxy ( 0, 0 ) ;
        printf ( "\nRelative sector displayed is %06d\n", s ) ;
        gotoxy ( 0, 2 ) ;
        printf ( "\nOffset -----------------" ) ;
        gotoxy ( 32, 2 ) ;
        printf ( "Hex codes -----------------Ascii values" ) ;

        for ( r = 6 ; r <= 21 ; r++ )
        {
            gotoxy ( 2, r ) ;
            printf ( "%04d(%04X)", i, i ) ;
            gotoxy ( 14, r ) ;

            /* printing Hex codes */
            for ( c = 0 ; c <= 15 ; c++ )
            {
                printf ( "%02X ", buffer[i] ) ;
                i++ ;
            }

            i = i - 16 ;
            gotoxy ( 64, r ) ;

            /* printing Ascii codes */
            for ( c = 0 ; c <= 15 ; c++ )
            {
```

```
                    buffer[i] ;

                    if ( buffer[i] < 32 )
                        printf ( " " ) ;
                    else
                        printf ( "%c", buffer[i] ) ;

                    i++ ;
                }
            }

        if ( num == 1 )
        {
            gotoxy ( 1, 24 ) ;
            printf ( "Press any key to continue..." ) ;
            getch() ;
        }
    }

    getch() ;
}
```

The entire program revolves around **absread( )**, which reads the
absolute disk sectors. In **absread (0, 1, 0, buffer)**, the first 0 stands
for drive number (Drive A = 0, B = 1) and the second 0 stands for
sector number to be read. Side 0, Track 0, Sector 1 is treated as logical
sector number 0. The contents of a sector once read are stored in the
array **buffer** and then displayed byte by byte on the screen in hex and
ascii format. Since all 512 bytes in a sector cannot be displayed at a
time, they are displayed in 2 parts of 256 bytes each. The conversion
specification **%X** is used to print hex codes whereas **%c** is used for
printing ascii codes. Control characters having ascii value less than
32 are printed as blanks.

So, the next time you see PC Tools or Norton Utilities don't be too surprised. Such programs are only as great as their writers claim!

Freedom at last!

Viewing items is one thing. Being able to make changes in what one sees is a totally different cup of tea. Ever dreamt of editing a floppy sector by sector? Overwriting existing contents with gibberish, or gibberish with meaningful, or of wiping out a few files or changing the attributes of a few? Try the following program. It not only displays the desired sector from the desired drive, but also allows you to edit it. Freedom at its best!

```
# include "conio.h"
# include "dos.h"
# include "bios.h"

# define Esc   0x11B
# define Right 0x4D00
# define F1    0x3B00
# define F2    0x3C00

unsigned char buffer[512], temp[512] ;
int lsect, maxc, i, x, y, indicator ;

main( )
{
    int drive ;

    clrscr( ) ;
    printf ( "\nSelect drive ( 0=A, 1=B, 2=C, etc. ) " ) ;
    scanf ( "%d", &drive ) ;
    printf ( "\nEnter logical sector you wish to edit ? " ) ;
    scanf ( "%d", &lsect ) ;
```

```
    absread ( drive, 1, lsect, buffer ) ;
    display( ) ;
    edit( ) ;
}

display( )
{
    int r, c, i = 0 ;
    unsigned char ch ;

    clrscr( ) ;
    printf ( "Relative sector displayed is %06d", lsect ) ;
    printf ( "\n -------------------- Hex codes " ) ;
    printf ( "--------------------  Ascii values" ) ;
    for( r = 3 ; r <= 24 ; r++ )
    {
        for( c = 2 ; c <= 55 ; c += 2 )
        {
            ch = buffer[i] ;
            gotoxy ( c, r ) ;
            printf ( "%02X", ch ) ;
            gotoxy ( 57 + ( i % 24 ), r ) ;

            if ( ch == 7 || ch == 8 || ch == 13 || ch == 10 )
                printf ( " " ) ;
            else
                printf ( "%c", ch ) ;

            i++ ;

            if ( i % 4 == 0 )
                c++ ;

            if ( i == 512 )
            {
                maxc = c ;
                break ;
```

```
                }
            }
        }

        printf ( "\nF1-Restore ; F2-Save Changes ; Esc - Exit" ) ;
}

edit( )
{
    int ch, ch1, j ;

    x = 2 ;
    y = 3 ;
    indicator = 1 ;
    i = 0 ;

    for ( j = 0 ; j <= 511 ; j++ )
        temp[j] = buffer[j] ;

    while ( 1 )
    {
        gotoxy ( x, y ) ;
        ch = bioskey ( 0 ) ;
        ch1 = toupper ( ch ) ;

        if ( ch1 >= '0' && ch1 <= '9' || ch1 >= 'A' && ch1 <= 'F' )
        {
            ch1 = ch1 - 48 ;

            if ( ch1 > 9 )
                ch1 = ch1 - 7 ;

            if ( indicator == 1 )
            {
                ch1 = ch1 << 4 ;
                temp[i] = temp[i] & 0x0f ;
            }
```

```
            else
                temp[i] = temp[i] &  0xf0 ;

            temp[i] = temp[i] | ch1 ;
            putch ( toupper ( ch ) ) ;
            gotoxy ( ( 57 + ( i % 24 ) ), y ) ;
            printf ( "%c", temp[i] ) ;
            update( ) ;
        }
        else
        {
            switch ( ch )
            {
                case Right :
                    update( ) ;
                    break ;

                case F1 :
                    display( ) ;
                    return ;

                case F2 :
                    for ( j = 0 ; j <= 511 ; j++ )
                    buffer[j] = temp[j] ;
                    abswrite ( 0, 1, lsect, temp ) ;
                    display( ) ;
                    return ;

                case Esc :
                    return ;
            }
        }
    }
}

update( )
{
```

```
x++ ;
indicator = !( indicator ) ;

if ( x >= 55 )
{
    x = 2 ;
    y++ ;
}

if ( y == 24 && x == maxc )
{
    y = 3 ;
    i = 0 ;
    x = 2 ;
}

if ( indicator == 1 )
{
    i++ ;
    if ( ( x != 2 ) && ( i % 4 == 0 ) )
        x++ ;
}
}
```

The program opens with **#include**s and **#define**s. The macros ESC, RIGHT, F1 and F2 are defined with their scan codes. The function **absread( )** reads the specified logical sector from the specified drive into the array **buffer[ ]**. The contents of the buffer are displayed in hex and in ascii. For control characters like 7, 8, 10 and 13 a space is displayed. Columns 2 to 55 are used for printing hex codes, whereas columns 57 onwards are used for printing ascii values. The variable **maxc** is used to keep track of the column in which the last character from the buffer is printed.

Having displayed the contents of a sector, let us now shift our focus to the **edit( )** function, which is the mind and heart of this program. To begin with, the contents of **buffer[ ]** are copied into another array

temp[ ]. Then the cursor is placed on the first character, and using **bioskey( )** a key is received from the keyboard. If the key hit is a valid hex digit, then the digit is collected in **ch1**. Each character in the buffer when printed in hex is displayed as a 2 character sequence. For example, a 9 is displayed as 09 whereas a 10 is displayed as 0A. The variable **indicator** is used to keep track of whether the cursor is placed on the 1st or the 2nd character. Depending on which character is modified, the array **temp[ ]** is appropriately updated (using bitwise operators), and then displayed on the screen. The function **update( )** keeps track of current cursor position and modifies it as per the key hit from the keyboard. On hitting F1 the original contents of the sector are restored, whereas F2 updates the sector contents.

So that's another program which lays bare the concepts which appear awe-inspiring at first glance. That's the spirit of C.

Diskcopied!!

Maintaining secrets is the order of the day! In this world of closely guarded secrets, neither Microsoft nor PC Tools nor Norton tell you how they copy a source disk to a target disk. I wonder why they hold it so close to the chest when really speaking it's no big deal... as I am sure you would agree after going through the following program. Before running the program, make sure that your source disk is free of a boot sector virus. This is because the program uses the boot parameters to perform some calculations.

```
# include "bios.h"
# include "dos.h"
# include "alloc.h"
# include "conio.h"

main( )
{
    struct boot
```

```
    {
        char x[19] ;
        int tot_sec ;
        char y[3] ;
        int sptrk ;
        int no_of_sides ;
        char rest[484] ;
    } b ;

    int source, target, head, trk, sec, i, flg, col, cyl ;
    void far *d[80] ;

    clrscr( ) ;
    printf ( "Enter source drive ( 0 = A, 1 = B )" ) ;
    scanf ( "%d", &source ) ;
    printf ( "Enter target drive ( 0 = A, 1 = B )" ) ;
    scanf ( "%d", &target ) ;
    puts ( "Enter source disk & press any key..." ) ;
    getch( ) ;

    absread ( source, 1, 0, &b ) ;
    cyl = b.tot_sec / ( b.sptrk * b.no_of_sides ) ;
    gotoxy ( 20, 10 ) ;
    printf ( "                1           2           3" ) ;
    gotoxy ( 20, 11 ) ;
    printf ( "Track   012345678901234567890123456789012345 6789" ) ;
    gotoxy ( 20, 12 ) ;
    printf ( "side 0" ) ;
    gotoxy ( 20, 13 ) ;
    printf ( "side 1" ) ;

    head = trk = i = 0 ;
    sec = 1 ;
    col = 28 ;

    while ( trk < cyl )
    {
```

```
d[i] = malloc ( b.sptrk * 512 ) ;

if ( d[i] == NULL )
{
    printf ( "Memory allocation error" ) ;
    exit ( 1 ) ;
}

gotoxy ( col, 12 + head ) ;
printf ( "R" ) ;
flg = biosdisk ( 2, source, head, trk, sec, b.sptrk, d[i] ) ;

if ( flg != 0 )
{
    gotoxy ( col, 12 + head ) ;
    printf ( "E" ) ;
}

i++ ;
head = !head ;
if ( head == 0 )
{
    trk++ ;
    col++ ;
}
}

puts ( "\nInsert target disk & press any key..." ) ;
getch( ) ;
head = trk = i = 0 ;
sec = 1 ;
col = 28 ;

while ( trk < cyl )
{
    gotoxy ( col, 12 + head ) ;
    printf ( "W" ) ;
```

```
flg = biosdisk ( 3, target, head, trk, sec, b.sptrk, d[i] ) ;
gotoxy ( col, 12 + head ) ;
flg != 0 ? printf ( "E" ) : printf ( "." ) ;
i++ ;
head = !head ;

if ( head == 0 )
{
        trk++ ;
        col++ ;
}
        }
}
```

The first few lines are fairly simple. We just collect the source and target drive numbers and then use **absread( )** to figure out how many total cylinders are there on the floppy. Then comes the crucial part: the **while** loop. In this we first allocate memory equivalent to the size of one track, and if successful, store the base address of the allocated memory in an array **d[ ]**. Next comes the **biosdisk( )**, which reads the contents of a track and stores them in the allocated memory. This is repeated for all the tracks on the disk. The other **while** loop does just the reverse. It writes what has been read into allocated memory onto the target disk, cylinder by cylinder. Before compiling the program, select 'Compact Model' from the 'Options' menu item of Turbo C.

This program works for a 360 KB disk. How about making a small modification and making it work for a 1.2 MB disk?

COMMAND.COM I am your Master

Which is the best way of ensuring that nobody is able to see the contents of your hard disk? Or better still, which is the best way of ensuring that nobody else can format your hard disk? How can we fool the user with malicious intentions who attempts to look at your disk contents by using the DIR command or format your disk by saying FORMAT C:? It's very simple. All you have to do is fool 'command.com'.

Out of the three DOS files, IO.SYS, MSDOS.SYS and COMMAND.COM, it is COMMAND.COM which contains the information about DOS internal commands like DIR, COPY, TYPE etc. If you explore COMMAND.COM, after a few hundred bytes you will find the DOS error messages, followed by a list of DOS internal commands. And this is where we intend to modify COMMAND.COM. We would change the name of the internal command and save the changes to the disk. For example, we can change DIR to YPK, or TYPE to ICIT and so on. Here is a program which will show you how.

```c
# include "stdio.h"
FILE *fp ;
main( )
{
    char original[9], new[9] ;

    fp = fopen ( "c:\\command.com", "rb+" ) ;
    if ( fp == NULL )
    {
        puts ( "Error opening file" ) ;
        exit ( 1 ) ;
    }

    printf ( "\nWhich command do you wish to change ? " ) ;
    scanf ( "%s", original ) ;
    printf ( "\nTo what ? " ) ;
    scanf ( "%s", new ) ;

    if ( strlen ( original ) != strlen ( new ) )
    {
        printf ( "Enter an alternative command name of the same length" ) ;
        exit ( 2 ) ;
```

```
        }

        strupr ( original ) ;
        strupr ( new ) ;
        findcommand ( original, new ) ;
        fclose ( fp ) ;
}

findcommand ( char *s1, char *s2 )
{
        int k = 0, ind = 0, length, ch, flag = 0 ;
        long int i = 0 ;

        length = strlen ( s1 ) ;
        while ( ( ch = getc ( fp ) ) != EOF )
        {
                if ( ind == k  && ch == s1[k] )
                {
                        ind++ ;
                        k++ ;
                }
                else
                {
                        ind = 0 ;
                        k = 0 ;
                }

                i++ ;

                if ( ind == length )
                {
                        flag = 1 ;
                        fseek ( fp, ( i - length ), SEEK_SET ) ;
                        fputs ( s2, fp ) ;
                        ind = 0 ;
                        k = 0 ;
                }
```

```
        }
    if ( flag != 1 )
    {
        printf ( "No such DOS command" ) ;
        exit ( 1 ) ;
    }
}
```

The program first opens COMMAND.COM in read/write mode, and then receives the name of the DOS command to change and the new command name. The **findcommand**( ) function finds the place where the command is present in COMMAND.COM and changes it to the new name. Remember two things. Firstly, run this program only after quitting out of Turbo C. Secondly, boot the computer again after you run this program, so that the modified COMMAND.COM is loaded from the disk. And now if a hacker visits your system and tries to execute a command like DIR or TYPE, he would keep getting the message 'Bad command or file name'.

That's yet another fascinating facet of C for you.

Delete as you wish

Next to FORMAT, which DOS command sends a chill down the programmer's spine? Possibly the DEL command. Agreed its a powerful command, but how many programmers have thought about the limitations of this command? How does one delete all files created on 15/10/92? Certainly, the DEL command cuts no ice if one says DEL 15/10/92, because all that it understands is a filename(s) or at the most some wildcard characters as in DEL A*.C. But then how many of us create all files on 15/10/92 beginning with the letter 'A'? So what do we do? Don't despair. You can get around the limitations of the DEL command. The following program does this by accepting any field (be it size, date, time or the routine filename) in the directory entry of the file and then deleting the matching file(s).

```c
# include "stdio.h"
# include "dir.h"
# include "string.h"

int counter = 0 ;
char field[25] = "1-01-80", path[80] = "a:*.bak", fileinfo[80], drive[15] = "" ;
struct ffblk file ;

main ( int argc, char *argv[ ] )
{
    if ( argc != 3 )
    {
        puts ( "Correct usage Mydel <matching field> <path>" ) ;
        exit ( 1 ) ;
    }

    strcpy ( field, argv[1] ) ;
    strcpy ( path,  argv[2] ) ;

    if ( argv[2][1] == ':' )
    {
        strncpy ( drive, argv[2], 2 ) ;
        drive[2] = '\0' ;
    }

    process_files( ) ;
}

process_files( )
{
    int flag ;

    flag = findfirst ( path, &file, 0 ) ;
    if ( flag == -1 )
```

```
        {
            printf ( "File not found" ) ;
            exit ( 1 ) ;
        }

        stuff_file_info( ) ;

        if ( strstr ( fileinfo, field ) != NULL )
            deletefile( ) ;

        while ( ( flag = findnext ( &file ) ) != -1 )
        {
            stuff_file_info( ) ;
            if ( strstr ( fileinfo, field ) != NULL )
                deletefile( ) ;
        }

        printf ( "\nTotal number of files deleted: %d\n", counter ) ;
    }

    deletefile( )
    {
        if ( drive )
        {
            strcat ( drive, file.ff_name ) ;
            if ( unlink ( drive ) == -1 )
                printf ( "%s could not be deleted\n", file.ff_name ) ;
            else
                counter++ ;
        }
        else
        {
            if ( unlink ( file.ff_name ) == -1 )
                printf ( "%s could not be deleted\n", file.ff_name ) ;
            else
                counter++ ;
        }
```

```
}

stuff_file_info( )
{
    unsigned int yr, mth, day, hr, min ;

    yr =  80 + ( file.ff_fdate >> 9 ) ;
    mth =  ( file.ff_fdate << 7 ) >>  12 ;
    day =  ( file.ff_fdate << 11 ) >> 11 ;
    hr = file.ff_ftime >> 11 ;
    min = ( file.ff_ftime << 5 ) >> 10 ;
    sprintf ( fileinfo, "%13s\t%10ld\t%02u-%02u-%02u\t%02u:%02u\n",
            file.ff_name, file.ff_fsize, day, mth, yr, hr, min ) ;
}
```

What the program does is very simple. It uses **findfirst( )** and **findnext( )** functions to get the files matching the pattern as specified in <path>. Once the file is obtained, the date and time are broken up into day-month-year and hour-minute, and then stuffed into the array **fileinfo[ ]** using the **sprintf( )** function. This dissembly and assembly is done through the function **stuff_file_info( )**. The **strstr( )** function compares the contents of **fileinfo[ ]** with the matching field supplied through the keyboard. If a match is met, then the file is deleted using **delfile( )**, otherwise the next matching file is searched, and the above process repeated. This goes on till **findnext( )** fails. A sample execution of the program would be:

A> Mydel 12-09-92 *.C

This would delete all C files created on 12-09-92.

Tailpiece

C is fast. It performs. It has power, portability and punch. What more can one ask for? Through a few short programs given above we have just tried to catch the essence of this power. There can be many more utilities which can tap this power further. But then a journey which starts has to end somewhere. And we thought it fit to let you explore the boundless horizons of this wonderful language. Do that and then marvel at the treasures that C places at your doorsteps. To ignore them or to pick them up with both hands is of course your choice.

8

Indentor

```c
#include "stdio.h"
#include "dos.h"
main( ){int i,row=7; char far *scr=(char far *)0xB8000000L;
clrscr( );for(i=0;i<=3999;i+=2) *(scr+i)='A';
clearwindow(5,30,21,50);drawbox(6,31,22,51);
for(i=0;i<=255;i++){gotoxy(38,row);
printf("%d   %c",i,i);row++;if(row==20){gotoxy(33,21);
printf("Press any key...");fflush(stdin);getch( );
clearwindow(6,31,20,49);row=7;}}getch( );}


drawbox(sr,sc,er,ec)int sr,sc,er,ec;{int row,col;
for(row=sr;row<=er;row++){gotoxy(sc,row);
printf("%c",186);gotoxy(ec,row);printf("%c",186);}
for(col=sc;col<=ec;col++){gotoxy(col,sr);
printf("%c",205);gotoxy(col,er);printf("%c",205);}
gotoxy(sc,sr);printf("%c",201);gotoxy(ec,sr);
printf("%c",187);gotoxy(sc,er);printf("%c",200);
gotoxy(ec,er);printf("%c",188);}


clearwindow(sr,sc,er,ec)int sr,sc,er,ec;{
union REGS ii,oo;ii.h.ah=6;ii.h.al=0;ii.h.bh=7;
ii.h.ch=sr;ii.h.cl=sc;ii.h.dh=er;ii.h.dl=ec;
int86(16,&ii,&oo);}
```

What in the name of Donald Duck is this program doing? Compile and execute it, and it prints out the ascii table without faltering for a second. The only reason why we find it difficult to understand is that it has not been properly laid out. Proper indentation does for a program what good manners do for a dinner table. Of course, it isn't that one can't survive without proper indentation or good table manners. But I'm sure you'll agree that we can hardly deny the importance of either. A hopelessly askew, but totally error free program, like the one above, will run just as smoothly as it would if it were meticulously indented to the last '}'. This is because the C compiler cares two hoots about what it encounters between two words, be it any number of spaces, tabs or lines. Nor does it bother about whether the **if**s and the **else**s or the **do**s and the **while**s have been properly aligned. The trouble starts when such a program is read by someone else, or, for that matter, even when it is reread by the programmer himself! Even though many a programmer doesn't tend to exercise a lot of care while writing a program, one and all would prefer a properly laid out one when it comes to reading or under-standing a program. Further, debugging a lengthy and complicated unindented or a poorly indented program would almost prove to be a Herculean task! In Indentor, we have used C to 'think' and decide what a well-written program should look like.

The Rules

Due to the lenient attitude adopted by the C compiler, different people have come to follow different rules of indentation as may suit them, and which may differ from person to person. We too would follow certain guidelines for writing a program, which serve as ground rules for the Indentor. These rules are mentioned below:

(a)   The most elementary rule has to do with blocks of **if, else, for, while** and **do-while**. The opening brace (when present) should lie immediately below these keywords, and statements within the block should start from the next line, indented one tab to the right. Thus, the domain of each block can be discerned at a glance when such statements occur nested within each other.

(b)   A blank line should be left before and after every control structure like **if, while, for, do-while** or **switch** to improve the readability of the program. An exception to this rule is the case when there is only one statement in the **if, for** or **while**.

A blank line should be left after every **case** of a **switch** and after every block of statements enclosed within a pair of braces.

(c)   A blank line should also be left before every function definition and after the variable declarations in the function.

(d)   Two consecutive lines should never be blank.

(e)   Spaces play as big a role as blank lines in making a program readable. Towards this end, a space must be left on either side of operators like **+, -, *, /, %, <, >, =, !, &&, ||, ?, :,** etc. However, care should be exercised not to give a space within operators like **++, --, -=, +=, ->,** etc.

(f)   There should be no space before a comma, but a space should be incorporated after it and before the semicolon present at the end of each statement.

(g)   In **switch**, all the **case**s should begin from the same column, indented one tab in, and the statements belonging to each **case** should be further indented one tab to the right.

(h)   While defining functions, the function name, the variable declarations and the opening brace, should all start from the first column, one below the other. The statements comprising the function should be tabbed once.

(i)   While declaring structures, unions and multi-dimensional arrays, the component statements should begin one line below the opening brace and indented by one tab from the opening brace.

(j)   Comments should start on the same column as the statement that comes after them. Even in multiple line comments the level of indentation should be same as the statement below the comment.

If a comment happens to occur in the same line as the statement, then it should be placed two spaces after the end of the statement.

The Logic

With practice, these norms can be easily mastered and one starts getting the feel of how the layout of the program should be. But believe me, putting the whole logic across to the computer is an altogether different story! With all the super-intelligence of the computer, it still lacks common sense, which plays a leading role in matters like these. While our faculties allow us to judge by sight what needs to come where, the same is done on the computer by reading, counting, comparing, checking, verifying, and then finally deciding what should be written where. It was a hard decision for me to take whether to give you the logic readymade on a platter, or to let you work it out yourselves. After a lot of thinking I decided on the latter. So don your starched thinking caps and go ahead. As a guide I am providing you the EXE file of the logic I developed. However, we would like it more should you work out the logic independently.

Appendix A

Standard Library Functions

Given here is a list of all the standard library functions that have been used in the various programs in this book, along with the purpose they are used for. This should not be looked upon as a complete description of the functions, for which you are referred to the Turbo C manual.

Function	Description
abs( )	Returns the absolute value of an integer.
absread( )	Reads absolute disk sectors.
abswrite( )	Writes absolute disk sectors.
arc( )	Draws a circular arc.
asin( )	Calculates the arc sine.
atof( )	Converts a string to a floating point number.
bar3d( )	Draws a 3-D bar.
biosdisk( )	ROM BIOS disk services.
bioskey( )	Keyboard interface, using BIOS services directly.
ceil( )	Rounds up to a value representing the smallest integer that is greater than or equal to the argument.
chdir( )	Changes current directory.
circle( )	Draws a circle of the given radius at (x, y).
clearviewport( )	Clears the current viewport.
close( )	Closes a file.
closegraph( )	Shuts down the graphics system.
clrscr( )	Clears contents of window in text mode.
coreleft( )	Returns the amount of RAM available for application programs.
cos( )	Calculates the cosine of the angle specified in radians.
delay( )	Suspends execution for an interval.

difftime( )	Computes the difference between the two times.
ellipse( )	Draws an ellipse.
exit( )	Terminates execution of a program.
fclose( )	Closes file which has been opened earlier.
fflush( )	Flushes the specified stream.
fgetc( )	Gets a character from the specified stream.
fgets( )	Gets a string from the specified stream.
findfirst( )	Searches disk directory for the specified entry.
findnext( )	Continues **findfirst**( ) search.
floodfill( )	Flood-fills a bounded region.
fnsplit( )	Splits a file's path into four components - drive, directory, name, extension.
fopen( )	Opens a file in specified mode.
fprintf( )	Writes formatted output to the specified stream.
fputs( )	Outputs a string to a file.
fread( )	Reads data from a stream.
free( )	Frees allocated block of memory.
fscanf( )	Scans and formats input from the specified stream.
fseek( )	Repositions a file pointer on the specified stream.
fwrite( )	Writes data to a stream.
gcvt( )	Converts floating point number to a string.
getc( )	Gets character from a file.
getch( )	Gets character from keyboard, does not echo it to screen.
getcwd( )	Gets current working directory.
getdisk( )	Gets current drive number.
getimage( )	Saves the bit image of the specified region of the screen into memory.
getlinesettings( )	Gets the current line styles, pattern, and thickness.
getmaxx( )	Returns maximum x-coordinate of screen.
getmaxy( )	Returns maximum y-coordinate of screen.
getpixel( )	Gets the color of a specified pixel.
gets( )	Gets a string from keyboard.

getvect( )	Gets the address of a ROM BIOS/DOS routine from Interrupt Vector Table.
gotoxy( )	Positions cursor at specified position on screen.
graphresult( )	Returns an error code for the last unsuccessful graphics operation.
imagesize( )	Returns the number of bytes required to store a bit image.
initgraph( )	Initialises the graphics system.
int86( )	Issues software interrupt for calling ROM BIOS routine.
intdos( )	Issues software interrupt for calling DOS routine.
isalnum( )	Tests whether a character is an alphabet or a number.
isascii( )	Tests whether a character is an ascii (0 to 127) character.
iscntrl( )	Tests whether a character is a control character.
itoa( )	Converts an integer to a string.
kbhit( )	Checks for currently available keystroke.
line( )	Draws a line between two specified points.
lineto( )	Draws a line from the current position to (x, y).
ltoa( )	Converts a **long** to a string.
malloc( )	Allocates a block of memory in RAM.
memmove( )	Copies a block of specified number of bytes.
memset( )	Sets a given block of memory to specified byte.
moveto( )	Moves the current position (CP) to (x, y).
nosound( )	Turns the speaker off.
open( )	Opens a file for reading or writing.
outtext( )	Displays a string in the viewport.
outtextxy( )	Displays a string at a specified location on the screen.

peek( )	Returns the word at memory location specified by segment:offset.
pieslice( )	Draws and fills a pieslice.
pow( )	Calculates x to the power of y.
printf( )	Writes formatted output to the screen.
putc( )	Outputs a character to a file.
putchar( )	Outputs character on stdout.
putimage( )	Outputs a bit image on the screen.
putpixel( )	Draws a pixel at a specified point on the screen.
puts( )	Outputs a string on the screen.
random( )	Generates a random number.
randomize( )	Initialises random number generator with a random value.
read( )	Reads a chunk of bytes from a file.
rectangle( )	Draws a rectangle.
registerfarbgidriver( )	Registers a linked in graphics driver code with the graphics system.
registerfarbgifont( )	Registers linked in font code.
restorecrtmode( )	Restores the screen mode to its pre-initgraph setting.
rewind( )	Repositions a file pointer to the beginning of a stream.
scanf( )	Receives input from keyboard.
sector( )	Draws and fills an elliptical pie slice.
setcolor( )	Sets the current drawing color.
setfillstyle( )	Sets the fill pattern and color.
setlinestyle( )	Sets the current line width and style.
settextjustify( )	Sets text justification for graphics function.
settextstyle( )	Sets the current text characteristics for graphics output.
setvect( )	Sets the address of a routine in Interrupt Vector Table.
setviewport( )	Sets the current viewport for graphics output.

sin( )	Calculates the sine of the angle specified in radians.
sound( )	Turns the speaker on at a specified frequency.
sprintf( )	Writes formatted output to a string.
strcat( )	Appends one string to another.
strcmp( )	Compares one string with another.
strcpy( )	Copies one string into another.
strlen( )	Calculates the length of a string.
strncmp( )	Compares a portion of one string to a portion of another.
strncpy( )	Copies a given number of bytes from one string into another.
strnset( )	Sets a specified number of characters in a string to a given character.
strstr( )	Scans a string for the occurrence of a given sub-string.
strupr ( )	Converts lowercase letters in a string to upper case.
system( )	Issues a DOS command.
textmode( )	Puts screen in textmode.
time( )	Gets time of day.
toupper( )	Converts character to uppercase.
write( )	Writes a chunk of bytes to a file.

Appendix B

The BGIOBJ Utility

In chapters 3 through 6 we have used the **initgraph( )** function to initialise the graphics system. We have used **initgraph( )** in the following form:

```
initgraph ( &gd, &gm, "c:\\tc\\bgi" ) ;
```

initgraph( ) initialises the graphics system by loading a graphics driver from disk and putting the system into graphics mode. We can tell **initgraph( )** to use a particular graphics driver and mode, or to autodetect the attached video adapter at run time and pick the corresponding driver. If asked to autodetect (by setting **gd = DETECT**), it calls another function **detectgraph( )** to select a graphics driver and mode. By using DETECT, the graphics mode (the variable **gm**) is set by **initgraph( )** to the highest resolution available for the detected driver. The third argument to **initgraph( )** represents the path where the graphics driver files (*.BGI) and character font files (*.CHR) would be looked for. Usually these files are in C:\TC\BGI directory. If they are in current directory then the third argument should simply be NULL.

In all programs in chapters 3 to 6 these driver and font files are loaded from disk at execution time and hence are not part of the EXE files. It means if you create an EXE file for say MYCAD.C and run it on a computer which doesn't have the driver and font files your program would not work. How do we get around this limitation? By linking the driver and font files into your program, making them a part of the EXE file. For this we need to use the utility BGIOBJ.EXE. This converts the driver or font files to linkable object files. You have to execute BGIOBJ.EXE at DOS prompt in the following syntax:

```
C>BGIOBJ /F CGA
C>BGIOBJ /F SANS
C>BGIOBJ /F LITT
```

```
C>BGIOBJ /F GOTH
C>BGIOBJ /F TRIP
```

Since several files (driver and font) are to be linked while creating the EXE file, all of them may not fit in a 64K segment. To overcome this we have used the /F option, which directs BGIOBJ.EXE to use segments other than the default segment. Once this conversion to OBJ files is over you must add the object filenames to the project list. This is done by creating a file MYCAD.PRJ with the following contents:

```
mycad
c:\tc\bgi\cgaf.obj
c:\tc\bgi\sansf.obj
c:\tc\bgi\littf.obj
c:\tc\bgi\gothf.obj
c:\tc\bgi\tripf.obj
```

With the project file ready, now we need to modify MYCAD.C to register all the drivers and fonts we want linked in. This is done by calling the functions **registerfarbgidriver( )** and **register-farbgifont( )**. These functions inform the graphics system of the presence of these files, and ensures that they will be linked in when the executable file is created by the linker. The usage of these functions is shown below.

```
/* MYCAD.C */
/* all preprocessor directives */
main( )
{
    int gd = DETECT, gm ;

    registerfarbgidriver ( CGA_driver_far ) ;
    registerfarbgifont ( sansserif_font_far ) ;
    registerfarbgifont ( small_font_far ) ;
    registerfarbgifont ( gothic_font_far ) ;
    registerfarbgifont ( triplex_font_far ) ;
```

```
    initgraph ( &gd, &gm, NULL ) ;

    /* rest of the program */
}
```

The parameter passed to **registerfarbgidriver( )** depends on the driver file. Since we ran this program on a CGA adapter, in our case the parameter is **CGA_driver_far**. These functions tell **initgraph( )** not to load the BGI/CHR files since they are a part of the EXE file. Note two things carefully. Firstly, these functions should precede a call to **initgraph( )**. Secondly, the path to the driver and font files should now be NULL.

Now we have converted the BGI/CHR files to their respective OBJ files. We have also created the project file MYCAD.PRJ and we have appropriately modified the MYCAD.C file to register the driver and the fonts. Now all that remains to be done is to load the MYCAD.C file and choose the 'Project' option from Turbo C's Integrated Development Environment. At the 'Project name' prompt type the name MYCAD.PRJ and then compile the program. Observe that the resulting EXE file is much bigger in size, but now this EXE file can run even on computers which do not have the BGI/CHR files. But then don't we say "to gain something one has to pay a price".

Index